# The Rise and Fall of the East Asian Growth System, 1951–2000

This book examines a recurring pattern of rapid economic growth in East Asia from 1951 to the present and explores how far a single East Asian Growth model can be said to exist. Assessing the various theories put forward to explain the phenomenon and supported by the most comprehensive data, the book finds that methods of institutional enhancement were at the core of the growth. This institutional enhancement affected state structure and functions, economic policy, corporate arrangements, social structure and relations, individual behavior, and domestic and international interaction. Each of these elements was a critical aspect of the growth system that defined and propelled the rapid growth.

**Xiaoming Huang** is a senior lecturer in East Asian politics at Victoria University of Wellington, New Zealand. His research interests focus on the patterns of political and social change in different institutional settings, and frameworks for their meaningful description and explanation to people across critical boundaries – national, cultural, or otherwise.

# RoutledgeCurzon studies in the growth economies of Asia

HC
460.5
H83
2005
Web

# The Rise and Fall of the East Asian Growth System, 1951–2000

Institutional competitiveness and rapid economic growth

**Xiaoming Huang**

RoutledgeCurzon
Taylor & Francis Group
LONDON AND NEW YORK

First published 2005
by RoutledgeCurzon
2 Park Square, Milton Park, Abingdon, Oxon OX14 4RN

Simultaneously published in the USA and Canada
by RoutledgeCurzon
270 Madison Ave, New York, NY 10016

*RoutledgeCurzon is an imprint of the Taylor & Francis Group*

© 2005 Xiaoming Huang

Typeset in Times by
Florence Production Ltd, Stoodleigh, Devon
Printed and bound in Great Britain by
Antony Rowe Ltd, Chippenham, Wiltshire

Transferred to digital printing 2005

All rights reserved. No part of this book may be reprinted
or reproduced or utilized in any form or by any electronic,
mechanical, or other means, now known or hereafter
invented, including photocopying and recording, or in
any information storage or retrieval system, without
permission in writing from the publishers.

*British Library Cataloguing in Publication Data*
A catalogue record for this book is available
from the British Library

*Library of Congress Cataloging in Publication Data*
A catalog record for this book has been requested

ISBN 0–415–35212–6

To all the men and women
in China, Japan, Korea, Singapore, and Taiwan
for their hard work, determination, and wise decisions

# Contents

# Figures

# Tables

# Abbreviations

| | |
|---|---|
| ACUs | Asian Currency Units |
| ADM | Asian Dollar Market |
| ADU | Asian Dollar Unit |
| APEC | Asian Pacific Economic Cooperation |
| ASEAN | Association of Southeast Asian Nations |
| BOK | Bank of Korea |
| BPI | Bribe Payers Index |
| BSBL | Basic Small Business Law |
| CAEDS | Costal Area Economic Development Strategy |
| CBL | Central Bank Law |
| CCP | Chinese Communist Party |
| CDF | Cluster Development Fund |
| CEP | Council on Economic Planning |
| CEPD | Council for Economic Planning and Development |
| CETRA | China External Trade Development Council |
| CFETS | China Foreign Exchange Trading System |
| CIEC | Council on International Economic Cooperation |
| CIECD | Council on International Economic Cooperation and Development |
| CIPMP | Computer Industry Promotion Master Plan |
| CIRR | Composite ICRG Risk Rating |
| CLA | Council on Labor Affairs |
| CNAW | China's National Association of Women |
| CNDP | Comprehensive National Development Plan |
| CNFI | Chinese National Federation of Industries |
| CPEO | Committee to Promote Enterprise Overseas |
| CPF | Central Provident Fund |
| CPI | Corruption Perceptions Index |
| CPTE | Council of Professional and Technical Education |
| CRA | Corporate Restructuring Agreement |
| CRCC | Corporate Restructuring Coordinating Committee |
| CRS | Contract Responsibility System |
| CSC | Committee on Singapore's Competitiveness |

| | |
|---|---|
| CSP | Comprehensive Stabilization Plan |
| CYL | China's Communist Youth League |
| CUSA | Council on US Aid |
| DBS | Development Board of Singapore |
| DBUs | Domestic Banking Units |
| DPP | Democratic Progressive Party |
| DRC | Development Research Centre |
| DSDP | Economic and Social Development Plan |
| EA | Employment Act |
| EAEs | East Asian economies |
| EAP | Economically Active Population |
| EC | Economic Council |
| EDB | Economic Development Board |
| EEIA | Economic Expansion Incentives Act |
| EFSG | Economic and Financial Special Group |
| EFW | Economic Freedom of the World |
| EIPSML | Electronics Industry Promotion Special Measures Law |
| ELG | exports-led growth |
| ELSFF | Emergency Law for Stabilizing Financial Functions |
| EPA | Economic Planning Agency |
| EPB | Economic Planning Board |
| EPC | Economic Planning Council/Export Promotion Center |
| EPS | Employers Pension System |
| EPZ | Economic Processing Zone |
| ERPL | Enterprise Rationalization Promotion Law |
| ESB | Economic Stabilization Board |
| ESDP | Economic and Social Development Plan |
| FCC | Foreign Capital Council |
| FCL | Foreign Capital Law |
| FEN | Foreign Exchange Notes |
| FFER | Free Floating Exchange Rate |
| FKI | Federation of Korean Industries |
| FKTU | Federation of Korean Trade Unions |
| FSA | Financial Supervisory Agency |
| FSRP | Financial Sector Reform Plan |
| FTA | Fair Trade Act |
| FTL | Foreign Trade Law |
| FWC | Financial Work Commission |
| FYEDP | Five Year Economic Development Plan |
| GATT | General Agreement on Tariffs and Trade |
| GCI | Global Competitiveness Index |
| GCKTU | General Council of Korean Trade Unions |
| GDP | Gross Domestic Product |
| GDPC | GDP per capita |
| GFCF | Gross Fixed Capital Formation |

| | |
|---|---|
| GPFDIC | Guidelines for the Promotion of Foreign Direct Investment in China |
| HCIDP | Heavy and Chemical Industry Development Plan |
| HDB | Housing Development Board |
| HDI | Human Development Index |
| HRS | Household Responsibility System |
| IBH | International Business Hub |
| ICEA | international comparisons of education attainment |
| ICPL | Industrial Cities Promotion Law |
| IDA | Industrial Development Act |
| IDB | Industrial Development Bureau |
| IDC | Industrial Development Commission |
| IDP | Income Double Plan |
| IDS | Industrial Development Scheme |
| IFS | International Financial Statistics |
| IICRS | Institutional Investors Credit Rating |
| IIDP | Information Industry Development Plan |
| ILO | International Labor Organization |
| IMS | International Monetary Fund |
| IP21 | Industrial Land Plan 21 |
| ISC | Industrial Structural Council |
| ISRC | Insurance Supervision and Regulation Commission |
| ISI | import substitution industrialization |
| JACE | Japan Association of Corporate Executives |
| JCCI | Japan Chamber of Commerce and Industry |
| JDB | Japan Development Bank |
| JIEB | Japan Import-Export Bank |
| KCCI | Korea Chamber of Commerce & Industry |
| KCIA | Korea Central Intelligence Agency |
| KDB | Korea Development Bank |
| KEACO | Korea Assets Management Corporation |
| KFEB | Korea Foreign Exchange Bank |
| KFI | Federation of Korean Industries |
| KFTU | Federation of Korean Trade Unions |
| KMT | Kuomintang |
| KOST | Korea, Singapore, and Taiwan |
| KTPC | Korean Trade Promotion Corporation |
| LDA | Land Development Act |
| LDP | Liberal Democracy Party |
| LGEA | Leading Group for Economic Affairs |
| LIUP | Local Industry Upgrading Program |
| LSL | Labour Standards Law |
| LTA | Land-to-Tiller Act |
| MAS | Monetary Authority of Singapore |
| MEA | Ministry of Economic Affairs |

| | |
|---|---|
| MFER | Managed Floating Exchange Rate |
| MITI | Ministry of International Trade and Industry |
| MNCs | multinational corporations |
| MOFET | Ministry of Foreign Economy and Trade |
| MSD | medium-sized district |
| MTEDP | Medium-term Economic Development Plan |
| MWE | monthly wage earnings |
| NAIC | National Association of Industrial and Commerce |
| NBER | National Bureau of Economic Research |
| NCC | National Council of Commerce |
| NIP | New Industrial Policy |
| NITP | National Information Technology Plan |
| NLDP | National Land Development Plan |
| NPB | National Productivity Board |
| NPS | National Pension System |
| NRGPs | non-rapid growth periods |
| NSTB | National Science and Technology Board |
| NSTP | National Science and Technology Plan |
| NTP | National Technology Plan |
| NTUC | National Trade Union Congress/ National Trade Union Corporation |
| NWC | National Wage Council |
| ODA | Official Development Agency |
| OEDC | Organization of Economic Cooperation and Development |
| OHQ | Overseas HQ |
| OWTI | Older Workers Training Initiative |
| PA | People's Association |
| PAP | People's Action Party |
| PBC | People's Bank of China |
| PBEC | Pacific Basic Economic Cooperation |
| PCFR | Presidential Commission for Financial Reform |
| PCIRR | Presidential Commission on Industrial Relations Reform |
| PCP | Productivity Code of Practices |
| PCSD | Physical Capital Stock Data |
| PLEP | Promising Local Enterprise Program |
| PMEPC | President's Monthly Export Promotion Conference |
| POSBank | Post Office Savings Bank |
| PPP | purchasing power parity |
| RDF | Research & Development Fund |
| RGP | rapid growth period |
| SAD | Statue for Agriculture Development |
| SATU | Singapore Association of Trade Unions |
| SCDP | State Commission on Development and Planning |
| SCNR | Supreme Council for National Reconstruction |
| SDB | State Development Bank |

| SDF | Skills Development Fund |
|---|---|
| SEC | State Economic Commission/Supreme Export Council/ Security and Exchange Commission |
| SEOC | Stock Exchange Oversight Committee |
| SETC | State Economic and Trade Commission |
| SEZ | Special Economic Zone |
| SFCTC | Shanghai Foreign Currency Trade Center |
| SIFC | Small Industry Finance Scheme |
| SIMEX | Singapore International Monetary Exchange |
| SIPB | Singapore Industrial Promotion Board |
| SIRP | Steel Industry Rationalization Plan |
| SITAS | Small Industry Technical Assistance Scheme |
| SME | Small Medium Enterprises Master Plan |
| SMTI | Ministry of Trade and Industry |
| SNTV | single-nontransferable vote |
| SPP | Special Procurement Program |
| SPSB | Singapore Productivity and Standards Board |
| SSE | Singapore Stock Exchange Market |
| STDB | Singapore Trade and Development Board |
| STPB | Singapore Tourism Promotion Board |
| TDB | Trade Development Board |
| TFP | Total Factor Productivity |
| TMESDI | Temporary Measures for the Establishment of Specially Designated Industries |
| TPCS | Total Physical Capital Stock |
| TSE | Taiwan Stock Exchange |
| UER | unitary exchange rate |
| WCI | World Competitiveness Index |
| WDI | World Development Indicators |
| WDR | World Development Report |
| WEF | World Economic Forum |
| WIPO | World Intellectual Property Organization |
| WRDS | Western Region Development Strategy |
| WTO | World Trade Organization |
| WTS | Workers Training Plan |

# Preface

There are not many other events in recent history like the rapid economic growth in East Asia that have received so much attention from academics, policy makers, opinion shapers, and the public in general, and created so many scholarly and public policy debates for so long. While the scale of that historical happening is indisputable, what makes the problem of East Asian Growth so enduringly interesting to us is the fact that it has challenged many of the conventional theories in development studies, international political economy, and growth economics, as well as widely held assumptions and predictions in the 1950s and 1960s about Asia's prospects of industrialization, development, and modernization. Also, the views and debates over East Asian Growth have been forced to adjust again and again over time as the whole pattern continued to evolve.

The Asian financial crisis of 1997–8, in my view, symbolized the ending of that historical process in which rapid economic growth was generated and sustained in a unique institutional setting, or growth system. The ending was reflected not only in key historical indicators of economic growth in East Asian countries, but, more importantly, in the declining effectiveness of the growth system itself, which I call "institutional aging."

Given the above, a comprehensive look at the overall growth experiences at this historical juncture appeared to be desirable and perhaps more useful and feasible than before. While this book will certainly not end the debates on the model of East Asian Growth, it can, I hope, lift them to a higher level – and that, I suppose, is what the social sciences are all about, if we understand Thomas S. Kuhn (1970) and Imre Lakatos (1978) well.

I wish to thank many people from whom I have intellectually benefited from over the years on this project and beyond. Space here, though, will not allow me to list all of them individually. On the other hand, mapping the network behind one's work runs the risk of the work being unnecessarily categorized into a narrow camp of theories and approaches. However, I do want to record my sincere gratitude to many others who have provided practical support, without which the book would have been impossible: Hazel Bennett, International Labor Organization; Lauren Deslandes, OASIS Official; Joshua S. Goldstein, American University; Roopnarine

Mahabir, International Monetary Fund; William Easterly and the Development Data Group, World Bank, Zhou Manli and Sheng Yang of Peking University, Beijing; Seiji Endo, Satoko Uno, Toshiaki Ooi, Naoko Muroi, and Eiko Akanegakubo of Seikei University, Tokyo; Chung Yong-jae, Jung Sung chul, Younghee Choi, and Sulin Shim of the Academy of Korean Studies, Seoul; Sue O'Donnell, Jenny Neale, Kim Willcox, Sue Baker, Janey Bedggood, Phillipa Mulligan, and Jenny Lilley at my home university, and many of those working at various international and national authorities, who kindly made statistical data available and accessible. I also want to acknowledge the financial support in two research grants for this project from the Faculty of Humanities and Social Sciences, Victoria University: FHSS Research Grant AR99144 in 1999 and AR01108 in 2001. Finally, I wish to thank my research assistant, Andrew Seymour, for the work he has done on this book.

I dedicate this book to all the men and women in China, Japan, Korea, Singapore, and Taiwan. It is their hard work, sacrifices, devotion, and smart decisions over the decades that have ultimately made economic growth possible.

Finally, this book would perhaps not have existed in its present form without the unwavering support of my wife, Dr Kyong-ju Kim. At some low points during this project, she insisted and convinced me that the project was a valuable work and deserved to be carried on. In the end, the news that this book was to be published came on the same day that our first baby, Del, arrived.

Xiaoming Huang
Unjung-dong, Bundang, Seoul
Broadmeadows, Wellington

# Introduction

This book investigates a recurring pattern of roughly 30-year periods of rapid economic growth in each of the East Asian Five: Japan, Korea, Taiwan, Singapore, and China[1] in the 50 years from 1951 to 2000, and explores what underlay this recurring pattern. The pattern this study wants to establish and the form of growth it is designed to ascertain have significant implications for many of the ongoing debates and long-held controversies over modern economic development in East Asia. Later in Chapter 1, I will examine in some detail these debates and controversies and explain why this research is necessary as well as useful for a better understanding of the form of East Asian Growth.

Before that, we need to deal briefly with two "problem-defining" questions. First, why do we need a better understanding? Second, what do the terms, "pattern of growth" and "form of growth," entail? On the first question, a better understanding is necessitated by at least three factors. The first one has to do with the wide-ranging debates and controversies concerning the facts of East Asian Growth, and their assessment and interpretation. Almost each and every aspect of East Asian Growth could be a point of debate or controversy.

The second factor has to do with viewing East Asian Growth in a large context of world historical experiences of modern economic growth. Where mainstream theories of economics and development proclaim models of industrialization, modernization, and economic growth for developing countries, the East Asian experiences have brought to the field rich evidence and counter-evidence that need to be recognized, reconciled, and incorporated in our understanding of the nature of modern economic growth. As we shall see later, the existing studies on East Asian Growth have not been very successful in this regard.

The third factor has to do with the present anxieties over the future directions of the East Asian economies, intensified by what is called "the lost decade" of Japan, the Asian financial crisis in 1997 and 1998, and the rights and wrongs of the Chinese economic reforms and expansion. We all have different kinds of theories about East Asian Growth, but we still seem unable to understand these phenomena in a coherent fashion.

On the second "problem-defining" question, I am of the view that, at least in terms of East Asian Growth, it is difficult, if not impossible, to isolate one or a set of factors as the cause of the rapid growth. Even if one manages to come up with the factor(s), as attempted in those various theories to be discussed shortly, it would be hard to establish a measurable, testable, and verifiable relationship of the causal factor(s) to the growth.

In a profound sense, economic growth is the effect of all individual activities affecting the economy, such as those of exporting, manufacturing, investing, banking, street corner shop retailing, etc., which I call *growth activity*. What matter, I would argue, are the incentives and constraints, or, more broadly, institutions, as used by Douglas North (1990), as well as the cultural conditions, social structure, and historical (internal and external) environment – aspects of the growth system[2] – that sustain these institutions. It is these arrangements and conditions that determine the directions and content of the growth activity. If these institutions can be "transformed" – directed by a growth agenda in terms of the overall purposes and benchmarking targets, industrial structure, priority in resource allocation, etc. – to the extent that the growth system can support, or accommodate and/or adapt to, then the fundamental question about economic growth shall not be so much about the "causes" of economic growth, but rather the methods or mechanisms of it. Consequently, a more effective way of investigating economic growth can focus on the growth system itself: how it comes to exist, evolves, operates, and, most importantly, relates to growth activity and its movement. And this is how this study is framed.

This research framing is significant at two different levels. At a more fundamental level, it reflects a view about the nature of social phenomena and what is a sensible, meaningful way of understanding them, given all the technical and epistemological limitations we have. The reductionist approach, to which many models and theories of growth belong, believes that we can and should break the research subject into pieces, identify them as variables, and ascertain their relations. More so in economics and development studies, it is believed that this ascertainment can and should be numerically measurable.

On the other hand, the holistic approach, of which this study finds itself to be part, treats the research subject as a system. As such, elements in the system can be *themselves* only within the system in relation to one another. They are mutually affected and defined. Here one cannot simply isolate, for example, growth rate and the role of government, and measure *their* relationship. The government detached from the system may not be the same government the findings wish to claim.

Moreover, the fact that the system is more than just the sum of its components, and that the extra system-level data are often elusive to our observation and analytical breakdown, distinguishes holistic studies from reductionist studies. The holistic approach leaves room for the system to demonstrate itself by an exposure of how the system forms itself, evolves over time, organizes internally and externally, and responds to stimulations; and what drives these movements and defines the internal and external relationships in a particular system.

As far as this research is concerned, such a framing underlies its theoretical thinking. If the growth system revolves around effective institutions and the mechanisms of induction of growth activity, growth participants ought to be related to one another through these effective and relevant institutions. The role of these participants in growth generation can therefore be assessed by their capacity and actual efforts to interact with and influence the institutions and thus shape growth activity from their own position. This study's focus on the rise and fall of the growth system in a framework of participant–institution interaction reflects such a theoretical interest. Furthermore, the function of the institutions and their change and adaptation takes time to manifest, thus a reasonable length of time period is required for a full examination of how the institutions, conditions and structures, and participants interact with one another to effect growth outcomes. The historical treatment of East Asian Growth in this study allows an exposure of its institutional dynamism over time.

The notion of the pattern of growth therefore refers to the historical and dynamic process where growth activity is directed to yield an accumulated change in the total value as well as the content of final goods and services within an economy. The form of growth refers to those methods and mechanisms that have effectively generated and directed the growth activity. The growth system finally refers to the institutional setting that has evolved over the rapid growth period in which these methods and mechanisms became relevant and effective. These three concepts are the defining elements of the framework for this study in which the growth experiences of the East Asian Five are investigated and generalized. They are also the primary concepts around which this book is organized.

More specifically, the book will start, in Chapter 1, with an investigation of the accumulated change that took place in the 50 years from 1951 to 2000, to ascertain whether there is a recurring pattern of rapid growth in each of the East Asian Five and the general characteristics of the rapid industrialization and growth, against the benchmarks of the "industrially advanced" economies for the same period. This initial aspect of the research – what I call the "reality check" – is important because of the persistent ambiguity about the facts of East Asian Growth and the dissatisfying contentiousness in existing theories in recognizing and explaining the rapid industrialization and economic growth. In fact, these two issues are related to each other and together they have made the field unnecessarily weak for such a strong phenomenon: without empirically sound facts, many of the theoretical explanations and debates about East Asian Growth have been founded on a fragile empirical basis; and with the theories and debates becoming increasingly self-indulged in narrowly framed political and moral arguments, less interest has developed in getting the facts right for theoretical purposes in the first place.

Chapter 1 therefore will be led, before the empirical investigation, by a critical review of the leading theories on East Asian Growth. While this review is designed to relate this study to the broad scholarship on the subject, much of the evidence from the findings on the general character-istics will show the limits to the explanatory power of the existing theories and how new knowledge can be gained not simply by rearranging or re-selecting "independent variables," but, rather, by adopting an alternative perspective and framework.

The investigation on the pattern and characteristics of East Asian Growth is necessary not only to serve as a reality check on the claims by contending theories, and thus as a way of making the case for this study, but is also expected to lay the foundation for this study's main investigation of the form of growth and to develop such a new perspective and framework. A recurrence of a similar growth pattern in a series of countries across a long historical period could point to a possibility of a similar set of growth activities, institutions, cultural conditions, social structure, and historical environment, and a similar set of methods and mechanisms that define the interaction between growth activity, institutions, and conditions. If this study can prove that the "purely economic" factors, such as capital, market, labor, and productivity, at the beginning of their respective rapid growth period were also similarly inadequate or insufficient, as they were in most developing countries in their earlier times, then those non-economic aspects of the growth system could be essential for economic success and definitive for the unique growth form.

Once this is established, the main body of the book is devoted to exam-ining and explaining the process, mechanisms, and institutional setting that led to the growth outcomes. Chapter 2 will examine a common set of initial conditions facing the EAEs at the beginning of their rapid growth periods; how these conditions set the imperatives for the EAEs; and how they responded to these conditions against a range of other possible scenarios and options at the time. Chapter 3 then discusses the emergent growth methods in response to the initial conditions, in a broad sense of a theory of economic growth. In particular, it focuses upon the necessity of inter-national competitiveness and the dynamic nature of comparative advantage, and the institutional requirements to meet the challenge of sustaining inter-national competitiveness. At the core of the institutional requirements was the need to reorganize the nation's production, distribution, and exchange for acquiring and sustaining international competitiveness.

As the national reorganization involved significant institutional building and manipulation, the effective working of which required the support of a unique set of social and cultural conditions, Chapter 4 will investigate the nature of the cultural and social conditions in the East Asian Five, and how they fared with the requirements of the determined response.

Chapter 5 looks at the national reorganization, i.e. the crafting of the growth system itself: the principal structure and critical elements of the growth system; where each of the critical elements came from and how they related to one another; what unique functions each element fulfilled, and, more importantly, how, in the building of the growth system, various productional and social forces were either incorporated or subdued, and aspects of the cultural and social conditions were either preserved or transformed.

With the economic, cultural, and social conditions, the principal institutional framework, and their historical sequence established, Chapter 6 will look at the two key operational mechanisms of East Asian Growth that defined the rise and fall of the growth system: growth cycles and institutional aging. The chapter will discuss how growth cycles were driven by product cycles and the efforts of the EAEs to manage the cycles and prolong rapid growth, and how growth cycles shaped the dynamic pattern of movements of growth activity in the EAEs. Institutional aging is seen as critical in determining the fate of East Asian Growth, as international competitiveness relies primarily upon the effectiveness of institutional arrangements and manipulations. The chapter will end with a discussion of various scenarios concerning the ending of the rapid growth and the associated growth form in the EAEs.

# 1 Making sense of the 50-year growth

## Theories and evidence

Remarkable economic growth and social development in East Asia has been a phenomenon for decades. Similarly, the debates inspired by these social and economic transformations – regarding what was done, how it was done, and the permissibility and replicability (or otherwise) of the transformations – have become commonplace in the social sciences (Amsden 1994; Bienefeld 1989; Evans 1998; Cline 1982). Along with much-celebrated challenges to mainstream theories and models in political science, development studies, economics, and international relations (Ruttan 1998; Evans and Stephens 1988; Barrel and Whyte 1982; Hicks and Redding 1982), myths and misunderstandings have also been prevalent (Wade 1992; Friedman 1988; Bradford 1986; Lim 1983). It would be prudent therefore to start our depiction of the pattern and general characteristics of East Asian Growth with a brief survey of what has already been said in debates about East Asian Growth. The purposes of this review are threefold. First, to assess the state of the field and thus lay out the scholarly context in which this study is undertaken; second, to identify and clarify those theoretical claims and prepare them for empirical test in the subsequent section; third, to demonstrate the contentiousness among existing theories, driven by their reductionist pursuit of singular independent variables, and why a new theoretical thinking on East Asian Growth is necessary. In doing so, it helps to make the case for this study.

## Theories and debates

Major works on the subject can be summarized in six theories or issues of debate. This critical review will succinctly identify and examine the principal arguments of each theory. Space and the purposes of the review will not allow a comprehensive collection and detailed recount of all the theories and their variations, which readers can access easily from existing studies.[1]

### *Developmental state theory*

Ever since Chalmers Johnson's ground-breaking work in the late 1970s and early 1980s on Japan's Ministry of International Trade and Industry

(MITI) (Johnson 1982), the developmental state theory has become a leading contender in explaining rapid economic growth in East Asia (White 1988; Amsden 1989; Wade 1990; Moon and Prasad 1994; Chan *et al.* 1998; Woo-Cumings 1999).

However, as with many other popular theories, the developmental state theory has been debated and interpreted, so much so that only one or two catchphrases ("interventionist state," or "industrial policy") are still remembered and their alleged link with rapid economic growth is still heavily contested. So, to understand this critical theory, one needs to know what Johnson essentially says and what his "admirers" and "challengers" have left with us.

Meredith Woo-Cumings goes to great lengths to interpret Johnson's original work not as "an analytical account in search of causal arrows" (1999: 2), but rather as an effort to investigate how the modern economic rationale envisaged in Weber's theory of the modern state can be achieved in a non-Western cultural environment, through means other than market or state ownership and management. Thus, it is more about "the history of economic growth and the context in which such growth occurred."

While the theoretical and historical underpinnings of the work are often missed in debates and discussions surrounding it, and thus Woo-Cumings' effort should be applauded, a reading of Johnson's work still gives the reader a dominant impression of a causal link, though not on the basis of a well-developed analytical framework: it is essentially a historical account of how the MITI worked from 1925 to 1975, and, through the MITI, how the Japanese developmental state worked. Second, it offers a model, or the "Japanese model" in Johnson's own words, the "essential features" of which, much smaller in scale than what Woo-Cumings summarizes,[2] include a small, but powerful, elite bureaucracy staffed by the best managerial talent available in the system; a political system in which the bureaucracy is given sufficient power to take initiatives and operate effectively; the perfection of market-conforming methods by the state in the economy; and a pilot organization like MITI to lead and coordinate the process of policy formulation and implementation (Johnson 1982: 305–24).

Third, on the basis of the historical observation, the study makes a central claim that the Japanese developmental state, in the context of the world's contending political economic systems of the time, can do a better job than the Soviet-style "fully bureaucratized command economy" or the Anglo-Saxon market economy, as – in Johnson's words – it manages "to find ways to intrude politically determined priorities into their market systems without catching a bad case of the 'English disease' or being frustrated by the American-type legal sprawl" (Johnson 1982: viii).

The original notion of the developmental state focuses narrowly, which is certainly justifiable, on the role, effectiveness, and efficiency of state agencies in national growth activity. The notion of "developmental" defines the vision and purpose of the state, and its relationships with various participants, primarily with industrial elites, in the growth process. The state's "developmental" vision is transformed – through industrial policy and various other functions of the state – into prioritizing mechanisms in the economy, which often endures limited allocable resources. It is this "developmental purpose and function" that distinguishes this type of state from others, especially from the one perceived by many mainstream theorists that does not normally claim responsibility for promoting the nation's economic activities.

At the same time, it is the effectiveness of the developmental state that matters the most. Such effectiveness is the result of the clear and consistent priority the state accords to high-speed growth; the solutions sought by the state to the fundamental problem of "the relationship between the state bureaucracy and privately owned business" through "self-control, state-control and cooperation"; and the "developmental, strategic quality of economic policy," which "is reflected within the government in the high position of the so-called economic bureaucrats." The elite bureaucracy "makes most major decisions, drafts virtually all legislation, controls the national budget, and is the source of all major policy innovations in the system" (Johnson 1982: 17–18). While the working of the developmental state involves various large factors envisaged in Woo-Cumings' broad interpretation of Johnson's argument, Johnson's original work did not cover that much. This is perhaps one of the reasons why Johnson's original thesis has been challenged.

From this original work, there have been at least three major lines of further study which have together contributed to the emergence of the developmental state "research program" (Lakatos 1970). Those following the first line endorsed the notion of the developmental state and worked hard to prove the power of the model beyond Japan, both in theory and in empirical evidence. On the theoretical front, the word "Japanese" is often omitted from Johnson's original term. A general theory of the developmental state has been attempted by many. In his "economic theory of the developmental state," for example, Ha-Joon Chang sees the developmental state as one that "can create and regulate the economic and political relationships that can support sustained industrialization," and that

> takes the goals of long-term growth and structural change seriously, "politically" manages the economy to ease the conflicts inevitable during the process of such change (but with a firm eye on the long-term goals), and engages in institutional adaptation and innovation to achieve those goals.
>
> (Chang 1999: 183)

Chang declares that "the idea that state can be developmental was at the heart of the writing of early development economists, such as Gunnar Myrdal, Paul Baran, P. N. Rosenstein-Rodan, and Simon Kuznets" (1999: 192).

To substantiate empirically the developmental state theory beyond Japan, a great number of works have emerged. Notable among those successfully doing so are Alice Amsden (1989) and Robert Wade (1990). Their works find working examples of the developmental state in Korea and Taiwan respectively. Echoing the view of Alexander Gerschenkron in the 1960s that economically "backward" countries require a unique role of the state for growth and catching up (Gerschenkron 1962), Amsden demonstrates how this has been the case with South Korea. Wade's study follows a style similar to Johnson's 1982 work, but in a more substantive way, and investigates how an MITI equivalent evolved and worked in Taiwan's industrialization drive.

In the second group of researchers are those who agree with Johnson that the developmental state played a critical role in rapid economic growth in East Asia, but are uneasy with his over-, or single-factored, emphasis on the role of the state, and ignorance of the institutional, social, and historical context in which the developmental state worked (Moon and Prasad 1994; Chan *et al.* 1998; Evans 1995). They wanted to put the state in a larger context. Here the state is seen as "embedded" in networks, society, political processes, and relations with social forces, particularly the business, the military, etc. This institutional context not only defines what the state is and what it can be. It is these aspects that made the state work, and thus made rapid growth possible. The developmental state theory only sees the surface of the growth experiences, and misses out what really made growth possible behind the up-front state. Moreover, as the institutional context is culturally and historically specific, there is a limit on how a successful growth story can go beyond its original context and be used as a broadly applicable development model.

To these challenges, there have been efforts in the debates, best represented in Woo-Cumings' recent collection (1999), to (re)interpret Johnson's original work, so much so that it is seen as a comprehensive account of Japan's, and perhaps East Asia's, rapid economic growth: its history, institutional context, ideology, society, government operations, political system, international environment, etc. This version of Johnson's work makes the critics in the second group seem to have not only misinterpreted the work (the social, institutional, historical context is well addressed in the work), but also missed the whole point (the work is not about causal relations).

Then, there is a third group of researchers who dismiss the whole case that Japan was, or is, a developmental state as defined by Johnson, and who thus argue that the successful economic growth had to do with something else. There is a whole range of theories in this group. Some see the Japanese state as a "societal state" (Okimoto and Rohlen 1988, 1989), or a "political market" (Ramseyer and Rosenbluth 1993), where a resolute, determined, unitary, capable, and national interest-minded developmental state does not exist. In its place are active voters, or interest groups. Others see that the private sector instead of the government has a more decisive role (Calder 1993).

There are even those who think that Johnson might have been right for that period of time, but that things have changed, and that the "paradigm has shifted" after 20–30 years of rapid growth (Pempel 1999; Calder 1993). T. J. Pempel, for example, argues in his recent study that, if one defines the Japanese developmental state, or what he calls "the regime" in the 1960s, as a web of a highly concentrated political and economic institutions with a policy of "embedded mercantilism" and a socio-economic coalition resting on agriculture and business, the regime in the 1980s and 1990s was already different. There have been significant changes in the public policy profile, the conservative-dominated political and economic institutions, and the support base of the socio-economic coalition.

The challenges against the notion of Japan as a developmental state point to a clear gap in Johnson's 1982 work between its Weberian conception of the Japanese state and the reality in Japan where the state and society are so closely intertwined with each other that a clear depiction of the state as a unitary actor would have to be achieved at a cost. While one can argue that it was Johnson's intention to reflect the cultural and social conditions under which the Japanese state worked, his very Weberian treatment of the Japanese state seems to have prevented him from doing so.

## *Exports-as-engine theory*

Just as the developmental state theory has caused great debate, so too a debate has arisen regarding the role of exports in East Asian Growth. In what might be called the *alternative engines debate*, concerning whether East Asian Growth is generated primarily by production at home, or by demands from international markets, the exports-as-engine theory argues that East Asian Growth has been driven primarily by exports (Chow and Kellman 1993; Evans and Alizadeh 1984; Mathews and Ravenhill 1994; Chu, Wan-wen 1989; Haggard and Chien-kuo Pang 1994; Keeing 1988; Leudde-Neurath 1988).

At the core of the exports-as-engine theory is a chain reaction which links world market demands to exports expansion in the EAEs, and ultimately to their economic growth. Such demands led to a particular growth strategy that focused upon competitive export products. This growth strategy further necessitated the restructuring of national industries, forced the government to engage in a growth drive, and forced the redeployment of capital, labor, and materials, and the construction of various corporatist arrangements. Exports are not seen to be the source of the economic growth, but rather are a crystallizing part of the growth process, driven – in the main – by external forces. Beyond the rapid export expansion, one should see the importance of international market demands, and the domestic efforts to meet such demands.

The exports-as-engine theory has been best explained by a study conducted by Peter C. Y. Chow and Mitchell H. Kellman (1993). Examining

25 years of export performance in Hong Kong, Korea, Singapore, and Taiwan (from the 1960s to 1990s), their study finds that the "export drive of the NICs contributes the major feature and causal factor explaining why the NICs succeeded in breaking their particular vicious cycles of poverty in such a short time." There is a causal relationship "between the growth of exports and their concurrent and subsequent economic growth" (Chow and Kellman 1993: 7).

Asserting the important role of export expansion in East Asian Growth, the Chow–Kellman study focuses upon the sources of export growth, with the premise that, if it can be established that export growth in the four EAEs was, primarily, a response to external factors, then a theory of the causal sequence – from world demands to EAE export expansion, and then to their economic growth – would have a solid foundation. The study establishes the *responsiveness* of the EAE export growth on several key indicators. First, with respect to the composition of their exports, "although the four EAEs differed significantly from each other at any given time, they all share a clear dynamic tendency to emulate Japan." Second, with regard to the compositional shifts of their exports, there is a clear linear "maturation" process over the period in which the four EAEs followed successive shifts in their export composition. Third, with regard to the structure of their exports, there is a clear homogeneous export response by the four EAEs to the demands of the USA. Fourth, the four EAEs "shared an unusually similar and uniform experience in the manner in which their respective patterns of export specialization and diversification changed over the period." With the empirical basis established, the study claims that it was demands from the international market that generated the export growth of the EAEs and ultimately their domestic production.

The theory has done a good job in linking EAE export growth with global market demands. But, as with many other theories discussed here where a necessary historical context is often missing in favor of a more parsimonious single-factor explanation, the study is not in a position to explain why the EAEs chose to, and were able to, respond to international market demands rather than, for example, to their domestic market demands in the first place. It may well be, as will be shown in this study, that it was the combined conditions of the early phase of the rapid growth period – domestic and international – in terms of capital, purchasing power, and market opportunities, that shaped the pattern of industrial production of the EAEs. Thus, what mattered was not only the existence of international market demand, but also how well the factors of production fared in both domestic and international markets. The "initial conditions" were more complex than simply international market demands.

### Enterprise system theory

Beyond the developmental state and external market demands, there is a great interest in the role of the enterprise system in East Asian Growth

(Hamilton and Biggart 1988; Aoki and Dore 1994; Fields 1995; Fruin 1992; Cutts 1992; Gerlach 1992; Tai 1989; Imai 1986; Kim 1987; Lincoln *et al.* 1992; Steers *et al.* 1989; Unger and Chan 1995). "Enterprise system" here refers to the way corporations are organized and managed. In the EAEs, the theory finds a more collaborative relationship between management and labor, team spirit, great support for research and development, encouragement and reward for innovations and inventions, quality control mechanisms, life-long employment systems, family-level trust among members of the enterprise, work ethics, or humane human resource management. Together they contributed to, in Fruin's words, "an institutional environment of interdependence" (Fruin 1992: 16): interdependence between management and labor, among employees themselves, between the social welfare of employees and the enterprise's long-term competitiveness, etc. A key contribution of the "competitive strategies and cooperative structure" (Fruin 1992: 16) to economic growth, according to the enterprise system theory, is to help suppress competitive and confrontational elements often found in Western enterprises, and thus reduce organizational costs.

More importantly, according to the theory, such an institutional environment of interdependence is extended to relations *among* enterprises, where a widespread practice of intra-enterprise rules and procedures is found among otherwise independent enterprises, through interlocking shareholdings, market entry alliances, cooperation in product development, and corporate financing. These groupings or networks, from Japan's *kereitsu* to Korea's *chaebol*, and from Taiwan's *guanxi qiye* (related enterprises) to China's *qiye jituan* (corporate groups), have turned enterprises of open competition into a giant association of production, market, and financial partners, with a controlled level of inter-enterprise integration. Such associations have softened the possibly destructive competition among associated partners, reduced repetitive investments and marketing, and evened out the business risks and unique costs associated with the function of business cycles. It gave the EAEs an edge to be competitive in international markets (Fields 1995: 238).

The rise of the enterprise system theory can be seen as a recognition of the role that the unique enterprise systems have played in East Asian Growth, as well as a response to the call in mainstream studies for culture-sensitive models of successful economic organization. On the latter aspect, the enterprise system theory echoes the main theme in the original study by Oliver E. Williamson in 1985 that the form of economic organization, firms in particular, is determined by the transaction costs involved in the firm's operations (Williamson 1985; Biggart 1997; Biggart *et al.* 1997). Entrepreneurs can organize their economic activities in an institutional framework that is most efficient in relation to the transaction costs. In Williamson's words, they can organize their economic activities to take place either in a market, or in a managed "hierarchy" (a firm or group of firms). They can "integrate" with a group of firms vertically or horizon-tally. This intra-firm hierarchy, or inter-firm integration, is very close to the East Asian enterprise systems described above. If one delves more deeply, underlying these studies, as Biggart points out, is perhaps Max Weber's classical concept of social action-oriented economic organization, where a particular enterprise system is an institutional reflection of the pattern of interaction between entrepreneurs and their economic environment. In this large theoretical context, the enterprise systems in East Asia came close to being understood, justified, and accepted as a legitimate form of economic organization.

However, on the first aspect in recognition of the role of enterprise systems in East Asian Growth, the enterprise system theory has never prevailed in mainstream growth economics. In fact, many in academia and the public media believe that East Asian enterprise systems are still a myth in their internal organization and management, and that inter-firm association and integration are primary causes of corrupt business community and government–business relations, and constitute the fundamental fault in the overall growth system.

For those who do recognize East Asian enterprise systems as a positive part of the growth experience, opinions vary on the reasons for the rise of such systems, and this, as in many other cases, made it difficult for people to take the theory seriously. In her original article, which is later included to introduce a collection of papers on the economic organization of "East Asian capitalism," Nicole W. Biggart lists and details four major approaches to explaining economic organization in East Asia (Biggart 1997). The market approach explains industrial organization as a response to economic conditions, such as transaction costs, "an industry's structure of opportunity and constraint" (1997: 10). The political economy approach, essentially a structural analysis, focuses on different political structures, or regime types, such as socialist states, mercantilist states, corporatist states, and fascist states, which "necessarily maintain different social institutions to support their different characteristic economies" (1997: 6).

The cultural approach "reverses the market theory's hypothesized causal relation, viewing the economic system as a product of the social order: society produces economy. . . . Economic institutions emerge from, are possible only because of, society" (1997: 17). Finally, the institutionalist approach views organizations as "socially constructed – a product of actors' subjective realities, rather than as objective, material artifacts" (1997: 21). An enterprise system, according to this approach, is an institutionalized pattern of social relations through which members of the enterprise are connected with each other and to the economy for shared purposes by the prevailing organizational logic. Under this approach, enterprise organizations would be different among the EAEs, but very similar within each EAE.

*Cultural theory*

As the EAEs have all, to some extent, been influenced by Chinese traditional culture, or, more specifically, the Confucian tradition, there is a natural interest in pursuing the link between their similar experiences of rapid economic growth and the cultural conditions (Berger 1991; Clegg and Redding 1990; Gardels 1995; Harrison 1992; Hofheinz and Calder 1982; Kahn 1979; Lam and Clark 1994; Morishima 1987; Redding 1993; Tai 1989; Tu 1991b). The cultural theory proceeds along two different lines of argument. First, it is the affective qualities of the people, unique in a Confucian society, that provided the necessary cultural setting for the growth push. These qualities are sometimes called "Asian values" (Han 1999).

In a challenge to the popular notion of Confucianism claimed in the Weberian thesis, Tai argues that people of Confucian faith are as "duty bound" and hardworking as those of Christian faith. The Confucian world has its own "transformative" dynamism, but also "puts a premium" on emotional human bonds, the family and the group, and social harmony (Tai 1989: 11–19). Confucianism is thus a better alternative to the rational capitalist model. Following a different line of argument but arriving at a similar conclusion, S. Gordon Redding and others try to convince us about the "cash value" of Confucianism (Bond and Hofstede 1990: 383; Redding 1993). By making a positive connection between Confucianism and capitalist economic growth, they see Confucianism and, indeed, Chinese capitalism just as a working variation of modern capitalism.

Either way, Confucianism so defined is more conducive to modern economic growth, as it allows – if not promotes – social harmony and human-centered activity, a constructive working attitude in the work place, entrepreneurism in the market, prudence in expenditure and savings, and a focus on education (and thus reinvestment in human resources). Consequently, both the EAEs and their individual enterprises are in a more competitive position and have far greater capacity than their international competitors.

Confucianism is also seen as a type of authority structure in a society, where the general orientation of people's attitudes toward authority is unique (Hamilton 1984; Hamilton and Biggart 1988; Pye 1985; Redding 1993). The Confucian model of "paternalistic authority," argued Lucian W. Pye in his study on the varieties of Confucian authority in Asia, "stressed the banding together of ruler and subject, with each clearly needing the other. As father figures the leaders needed to picture themselves as looking after their children" (Pye 1985: 89). In such an authority structure, "power was supposed to flow inexorably from the morally superior. . . . The social and political order was perceived as arranged hierarchies . . . the formal government [is treated] as the sole legitimate basis for power . . ." (Pye 1985: 86).

Pye does not go further to apply this model to the rapid economic growth in the EAEs, but Hamilton and Redding do. Building on the pioneering work of Hamilton, and examining the "institutional legacy of China" and "society at large," Redding argues that the prevalent paternalism, personalism, and vertical order, among other things, formed the distinct style of Chinese capitalism and contributed to the success of East Asia in general and Chinese business organization in particular.

Moving along the same lines, there is a general interpretation of the Confucian tradition that is often used to explain the authoritarian political environment said often to be found in close association with East Asian Growth; the mutually dependent relations between government and business, state and society, management and labor; why such authority structure could have operated for a prolonged period; and, further, the whole "authoritarianism-growth nexus" (Johnson 1987; Clague *et al.* 1997; Dick 1974; Haggard 1997; Marsh 1979; Zweig 1999). The underlying assumption is that, in this type of political environment, distributional conflicts are low and it is much easier to make growth-related decisions and carry them out effectively.

### Looters' game theory

It can often seem expedient to link East Asian Growth with corruption, lack of legal, civil, and business standards, and failure to respect human, social, and environmental values. The general charge is that East Asian Growth has been achieved at tremendous cost, and that these deficiencies in modern standards and values have effected "incomplete modernization" in the EAEs which will in the long term render sustainable development impossible (Clifford 1994; Hutchcroft 1991; Lingle 1998; Bello and Rosenfeld 1992).

There is a persistent charge, for example, that East Asian Growth has been achieved at the expense of precious human, social, and environmental values (Bello and Rosenfeld 1992; Lele and Tettey 1996). Often, labor and working conditions have been deliberately kept low. In many of the EAEs, the gap between the few who have benefited most and the large portion of those who have benefited least has been large. In particular, the environment has always been accorded a low priority in the EAEs.

Added to this line of charges are criticisms on East Asian Growth by Marxists. Paul Burkett and Martin Hart-Landsberg, for example, argue that East Asian Growth is nothing but the working of the "self-destructive" capitalist development, and call for a sustainable and workers' community-centered development. This alternative development "can and must move beyond the simple dichotomy of free markets versus state activism, by critically engaging with popular struggles in and against particular regimes of capital accumulation" (Burkett and Hart-Landsberg 2000: viii).

Corruption is also seen as a fundamental problem in East Asian Growth. Rent-seeking activities force the government to take economically unsound spending decisions, reduce the productivity of capital spending (and therefore the rate of returns), and eventually retard long term economic growth (Mauro 1995; Tanzi and Davoodi). In Mark L. Clifford's depiction of Korea's growth experience (1994), corruption is not just a cultural phenomenon. It is an integral part of East Asian Growth, and defines the nature of the economy and sets the limits of its growth. Rather than a coordinated national drive and individual sacrifice for the collective good, as claimed by other theories, growth in Korea is seen as a process in which everyone, from the president to union activists, from army generals to *chaebol* executives, from government bureaucrats to demonstrating students, and from stock market speculators to Buddhist monks, aims to maximize their personal gains. Businessmen "rose on the strength of not only their skill but their political connections. They were political entrepreneurs"; government officials

> extract corporate donations for their projects, whether in the form of cash or employees . . . , lent the *chaebol* money at cheap rates, jailed and blacklisted workers who tried to organize unions, allowed the companies to earn oligopolistic profits in the domestic market and helped them beg, buy and steal needed technology from abroad.
>
> (Clifford 1994: 6–7)

It was under these conditions, Clifford claims, that 30 years of fast growth of a "high-cost low-efficiency economy" (1994: 5) was achieved. It is the nationwide, relentless, and immoral pursuit of personal gains, by all that drove the growth machine, with all its costs and consequences. The growth was the brutal function of a corrupt but militaristic machine.

Along the same lines, one can certainly make a case that the relentless and immoral pursuit of personal gains and the corrupt but militaristic growth machine were also the driving forces behind the growth of many other EACs (for example, Bello and Rosenfeld 1992). The underlying but often unspoken assumption is that the people, cultures, social structures, or political systems in the EACs are more conducive to these growth diseases. Greedy people, an incompatible culture, a lawless society, and ill-willed politicians do not just plague the growth machine; they become an essential part of it.

East Asian Growth, as viewed in the looters' game theory, is, if you will, the result of a marketplace aggressively looted by everyone. In the end, the driving force behind growth is not a "national purpose," but rather the looters' expectation of ensured flows of growth outputs into their bank accounts. The strong and interventionist state is merely the embodiment of the "looting alliance," which uses state machineries to institutionalize their random and opportunistic looting actions. The growth strategy is necessary only because it produces profit margins, and is able to adjust to the changing economic conditions, in order to ensure that these profit margins are maintained.

Moreover, growth of this nature tends to lack long-term planning, co-ordination, discipline, and respect for both human values and modern standards. Whether political donations in Japan, state–business collaboration in Korea and Taiwan, environmental depletion in China, or labor control in Singapore, as long as it leads to profits, there is no worry about either methods or consequences. The theory claims that, as the looting process will constantly erode both the capital and resource bases of growth, sustained growth is unattainable in the EAEs.

### Economic nationalism theory

Last but not least, it is argued that East Asian Growth has been achieved at the expense of a sound and fair world economic system as well as the interests of domestic private entrepreneurs. Though not in a coherent theory, loose charges of this nature often lead people to link East Asian Growth to economic nationalism, and to hypothesize that East Asian Growth has been possible because of their nationalistic economic policies: from trade protectionism to state ownership and nationalization. Economic nationalism sees the national economy as the primary unit of world economic activity, and believes that national interests should prevail in the management of economic activities over sectoral and societal interests within the country as well as those of international and global economic forces. Since the principal function of the EAEs matches these descriptions perfectly, East Asian Growth is naturally seen as a manifestation of economic nationalism.

Economic nationalism is not new, but what it entails has evolved over time. As Peter J. Burnell noted:

> there does not exist one single definition of economic nationalism. Conventional usages, not originated in a priori reasoning or abstract thought but strongly influenced by the ways in which people have perceived and reacted to specific practical event . . . undergo alternation as fashions in economic thinking change.
>
> (Burnell 1986: 16)

There have been roughly three sets of such "specific events" and corresponding economic thinking under the general banner of economic nationalism: European economic nationalism in the late nineteenth century and early twentieth century; that of the new states in the early post-World War II period; and the one often associated with East Asian economies. As with the term of nationalism itself, economic nationalism has turned from being a positive concept to a negative one over time.

European economic nationalism originated in the era of mercantilist economic policies of the seventeenth and eighteenth centuries as a response to the challenge of the emergent world economic system of colonialism, imperialism, and industrial powers, and the need to protect the national economy. As Roger W. Weiss noted, "nineteenth-century European nationalism and nation-building were in large part a response to the industrial preeminence of Great Britain" (1967: 32). This protectionist underpinning of early European economic nationalism is clearly reflected in the thinking of Friedrich List (1841), whose theory of the national system of political economy makes a case for a "fairer," more rational, world system of national economies against the chaos, uncertainty, and unfairness embedded in the world structure dominated by imperialist powers (List 1841).

This pressure to protect the national economy became intensified in the turbulent years after the World War I, when industrial and imperialist competition reached an unprecedented level of intensity and the world economic system went from post-war severe fluctuations to collapse in the inter-war years. As Frank H. Golay observes:

> references to economic nationalism appeared in the years following World War I when the international economy was subjected to stresses arising out of the economic and political dislocation inherited from the war. Governments seeking to escape from the external constraint on their freedom to make decisions sought to insulate their economies from external forces in order to exercise greater autonomy in stimulating internal economic expansion. By the mid-30s, the term had come into widespread use to describe the power-oriented systems of fascist Italy and Nazi Germany.
>
> (Golay 1969: 1)

Economic nationalism of the new states came to catch people's attention in the 1950s and 1960s when a large number of former colonies gained independence and started nation-building in these newly established states. In contrast to early European economic nationalism aimed primarily at external economic forces, economic nationalism in the 1950s and 1960s in the new states was driven by their nationalist ideology, anxiety to catch up economically, and need for domestic mobilization. "The concept has been broadened to connote the planned integration of diverse policies to pursue social goals" (Golay 1969: 3). As Gunnar Myrdal noted, "a system of economic nationalism is necessary to insulate economies not only from uncertainties, but from cumulative causal relations" inherent in specialization and trade in a world of economic inequality and which are insurmountable obstacles to "national integration" (1957, cited in Golay 1969: 4).

There seems to be a theory behind this version of economic nationalism. Harry Johnson in his 1968 study suggests that economic nationalism in these new states involves an "exchange by the community of real private consumption for collective consumption of a public good, national ownership and control of the economic system" (1968: 2). Thus, there are two possible roles for economic nationalism in the establishment of a new state:

one is that nationalism is a necessary basis for effecting the social transformation required to establish a modern state capable of the take-off into self sustaining growth. ... The other possibility is that collective consumption of the public good of nationalism is the only way in which a new nation can hope to raise its real income, given adverse initial economic and social circumstances. Nationalism would thus serve as a substitute for the modernization process.

(Johnson 1968: 2)

Government policy driven by this version of economic nationalism often pursues import-substituting industrialization as a way of eventually eliminating dependence on foreign capital; rejection of international capital and subduing of domestic capital through nationalization; total control of the economy by the government; and economic independence, self-reliance, and autarky.

Often, economic nationalism in the 1950s and 1960s was a major concern for international capital and often attributed to the eventual failure of these economies largely in Africa and Latin America. Michael Heilperin's remarks in 1960 were representative of such thinking: "economic nationalism is an unmitigated evil associated with growing collectivism and the baneful influence of Keynes which is leading the world to irrationally sacrifice the bounties of economic liberalism (isolation, insulation, autarky)" (1960: 20).

Finally, economic nationalism is cited by some commentators, often in a casual fashion, as one of the unfair tricks played by East Asian countries to their growth advantage – often in the distortion of the world economic system and the suppression of domestic private interests. What constitutes this economic nationalism and how it links to their rapid economic growth, however, is not always clear – not least because there have been surprisingly few substantive studies on economic nationalism in East Asia, except some that focus on trade protectionism as a form of economic nationalism (Brander and Spencer 1985; Evans and Alizadeh 1984; Jung and Marshall 1985; Yoffie 1981). The difficulty perhaps lies in the fact that economic nationalism, particularly the European version, has been a policy the advanced economies followed in the past when the time was appropriate, and there is little base for charges against other countries doing the same; and that many believe that economic nationalism, particularly its new states version, has been the cause of the economic failure in other parts of the world, and it is difficult to reconcile this with the case of East Asia.

Whatever the reasons, the charge of economic nationalism against East Asian countries remains an elusive one, and this elusion has created confusion among watchers of East Asian Growth. To start with, economic nationalism in East Asian Growth is not simply trade protectionism. Trade control is only a small part of the growth system that has evolved to meet the challenge of late industrialization. Simply trade protection alone, however, would not bring sustained growth over a long period of time. As will become apparent in this study, it is the dual market (domestic and international) and the whole growth system found in these EAEs that allowed trade control to play a growth-supportive role. Differently from the early European experience (and perhaps that of the early post-war new state as well), trade control in East Asia did not serve to insulate the economies, but to provide a necessary form of management over cross-border flows of products and capital. It is a set of mechanisms not just against external vulnerability for these latecomers in the established world economic system, but also for structuring and coordinating domestic production and consumption to achieve competitive effects at the national level. Both are necessary and important for an economy aimed solely at international competitiveness.

Economic nationalism in East Asian Growth is not the new states version of economic nationalism either. There were various forms of state owner-ship and central planning in the EAEs, but these came to function within the overwhelming framework sustained by grass-roots private economic activities. Nationalism in this context perhaps connotes best a sense of direction and discipline orchestrated by the state at the national level for private economic activities. The notion of economic nationalism with regard to EAEs therefore should not conceal the fact that the root sources of East Asian Growth are these private economic activities.

### How these theories relate to each other

For the convenience of the theoretical critique here, I have treated these major theories separately. In reality, they are interconnected and often over-lapped, and form a complex and yet dynamic "research paradigm." There are several reasons for the overlapping and interconnectedness. The first is of course what the elephant's shape story suggests: East Asian Growth is too complex a phenomenon for a single-factor explanation that can see only one aspect of it. Moreover, a different theory may see the same picture from only a slightly different perspective, and inevitably its claims would overlap with those of other theories.

The developmental state theory, for example, is considered to be the primary explanation for East Asian Growth. It claims that this different type of state does certain kinds of things that would lead to a better growth performance. The economic nationalism theory, on the other hand, focuses on one of the key things the state actually does to make the economy perform well in the world economic system. To explain why and how the state does it, however, the theory would have to go back to the type of state: its sense of mission, growth vision, economic philosophy, ability to organize and implement, etc.

The cultural theory, for another example, is interested in how people's attitudes, value systems, social relations, and behavioral patterns relate to economic performance. As these are not a direct growth input, their positive link to economic performance would have to be established through some variables identified in other theories as prominent in East Asian Growth: the enterprise system or the developmental state, through which the cultural conditions can be positively linked to economic performance.

The second reason is perhaps the evolutionary process of the research paradigm, in which theories respond, challenge, and go beyond earlier ones – a process that makes these theories overlapped and interconnected. In retrospect, East Asian Growth started to catch the attention of the mass media and academics in the 1960s and 1970s because of its aggressive export expansion. Comments and arguments regarding exports from Japan first, then the other EAEs, reflected the initial reactions of the world to East Asian Growth. As rapid growth continued and people had opportunities to look into how the things worked in these countries, the assertive, aggressive, dominant, and sophisticated state machinery often impressed people most. Starting from the 1980s, there was a series of major efforts to investigate how the state, i.e. the government machinery, in the EAEs functioned to direct, organize, coordinate, and discipline nationwide growth activities. The developmental state theory emerged with much stronger explanatory power than the exports-as-engine theory. Exports are an important part of the growth, but it is the state that promotes exports and it is this type of state that is capable of redirecting growth activities to focus on exports with its industrial policy and long-term industrial planning.

It is not just the state that impressed those watching Asia growth. Confucian values are also identified as a common denominator for these EAEs in the early search for explanations. The efforts to operationalize the cultural variable led the cultural theory to move in two specific directions: to connect with the developmental state theory, where the cultural conditions provide the necessary macro environment for the type of state to function; or to connect with the enterprise system theory, where the cultural conditions serve as a micro setting in support and sustenance of the economic organization. Between the original developmental state theory and the cultural theory, there has emerged a sizeable body of literature in the 1990s on the state's embeddedness, networks, state–society relations, government–business relations, interest groups, etc. to enrich the original state-as-actor theory and make an operational link between the cultural theory and growth performance.

Along with those seeing a positive link between the above factors and growth performance are those who adventure to explore how the developmental state, cultural conditions, enterprise systems, and/or export concentration led to things other than growth that were deplorable and harmful for the society and to the world economic system. The looters' game theory focuses on how the form of growth and its supporting mechanisms are harmful to modern values, civility, the environment, and society's ability for sustained development. The charge embedded in the economic nationalism theory, on the other hand, calls people's attention to the unfairness of the nationalistic economic policies and practices and what harm they could do to the world economic system, and ultimately to East Asian Growth itself, as it depends so much on the world economic system.

## Reality check

With these various theories about East Asian Growth and their claims on the causal factors briefly identified, we will now do two things. First, we will check the empirical basis of these claims and determine to what extent they are supported. In some cases where an empirical investigation is not practical, further theoretical critique will be offered. Second, we will discuss problems in these theories and explain why they failed to provide a convincing account of East Asian Growth. As will be seen shortly, the reality check involves measurement of a wide range of indicators of East Asian Growth, and will thus inevitably result in an overall description of the pattern of East Asian Growth.

### *East Asian Growth*

The ascertainment of the pattern of East Asian Growth is carried out at two levels: first, it is placed in benchmark comparison with the industrially advanced countries, represented by the original members of the Organization of Economic Cooperation and Development (OECD) in 1961;[3] second, the EAEs are placed in comparison with each other in searching for shared qualities as well as variations in their individual growth patterns.

The OECD benchmarking is used for three reasons. First, the OECD was established in 1961, as a club of "industrialized countries," and has since been recognized as comprising the industrialized, or "core," developed countries of the world.[4] A key element of the growth-at-any-cost mentality prevalent in the EACs has been their determination to catch up with the more advanced industrialized countries in the shortest possible time. Much of their growth efforts for the 50 years under scrutiny were geared up for rapid industrialization and catch-up modernization. It is historically sensible that the assessment of East Asian Growth be benchmarked against the industrially advanced economies. It allows in our assessment and discussion here for a reflection on the underlying thinking among the East Asians in their historical pursuit of rapid economic growth.

Second, this study is partially driven by a popular view that East Asian Growth is somehow an "abnormal" growth exercise, deviating from the standards and norms of a truly capitalist economy, in terms of the role of government and market, domestic economic freedom, external economic freedom, labor conditions, transparency, corporate ethics, etc. Taking the

OECDEs as a benchmark in comparison will allow us to see how "abnormal" East Asian Growth was and how much it deviated from the standards of the market economy.

The OECD benchmarking also runs against an almost paradigmatic trend in the field to compare East Asia with Latin America (for example, Haggard 1990; Gereffi and Wyman 1990; Birdsall and Jasperson 1997; Felix 1989). While such a comparison makes a great sense in terms of comparability on the "how" question, it does not provide for a real assessment of the overall qualities of the growth in the first place. The OECD benchmarking allows for an effective assessment of the industrial level and the quality of growth of the EAEs, and further for a judgment as to whether the East Asian Five have obtained an industrial level comparable to that of the industrialized countries, and whether East Asian Growth has had a positive relationship with the broad development of the economy, and of society as a whole. It is designed to produce empirical evidence with regard to the various claims about East Asian Growth, and, in doing so, provide a collective assessment of East Asian Growth in scale, speed, and duration as well as individual assessment of the characteristics of each EAC's growth experience. The resultant pattern of growth will thus not only be used for an empirical check on the competing theoretical claims, but also serve as the empirical foundation for the investigation of the form of growth.

Three sets of indicators have been designed to measure the rapid economic growth of the EAEs as a whole, each responding to one of the major concerns regarding East Asian Growth: industrial level indicators, as East Asian Growth is perceived by most as a process of industrialization; growth indicators, measuring economic growth; and development indicators, measuring the quality of growth in a broader sense of development. The growth indicators will be further examined to identify the individual characteristics of the growth pattern of each EAE.

The data, and their comparative analysis, will cover the 50-year period from 1951 to 2000, with the assumption that East Asian Growth is a postwar phenomenon. World War II put the EAEs and the OECDEs at a similar level of resources, capacity, and market opportunities, regardless of their pre-war levels. Moreover, 50 years is a reasonably long period to allow a growth pattern to manifest itself in a quantitatively measurable fashion. Time series analysis for such a long period was not possible in the past because of the limited availability of high-quality, standardized data comparable across the economies and over the substantial period.

To avoid the problems of selective and even random data support and the problem in consistence and integrity of the data used – problems often found in early studies on the subject (World Bank 1993; Chowdhury and Islam 1993; Islam and Chowdhury 1997, for example) – the data used and presented in this study are the most up-to-date, comprehensive, and authoritative possible at this time. To ensure an authoritative quality, I have in principle used data available from major international organizations:

primarily the International Monetary Fund (IMF), the World Bank, and the United Nations. In addition, Penn World Tables (6.1)[5] have been used for many indicators where necessary and appropriate. Where data are missing, particularly in the case of Taiwan, national statistics have been utilized.

### *Growth qualities of the EAEs as a whole*

INDUSTRIAL LEVEL

The industrial levels of the EAEs and the economies of the OECD members (OECDEs) are measured and compared in two sets of data: industrial value added in total gross domestic product (GDP) and industrial employment within total employment; and between two points in time: 1960, when the OECD was established, and 2000.[6]

On the assumption that there is a threshold that can be used to separate *industrialized* countries from *industrializing* ones, Chowdhury and Islam (1993: 4) have suggested a minimum of 20 percent of the industrial value added in total GDP and industrial employment within total employment. As Figures 1.1 and 1.2 show, in 1960, the EAEs had an average of 13.8 percent in industrial employment and 26.6 percent in industrial output, while the OECDEs had 36.9 percent and 38.3 percent respectively. By 2000, the EAEs surpassed the OECDEs in industrial employment with 22.9 percent over 17.4 percent, and in industrial output with 33.9 percent over 22.3 percent. The EAEs are more "advanced" in industrial levels.

Regarding the individual EAEs, in 1960 only Japan (28 percent) was above the threshold in industrial employment. However, in 2000 they had all moved up above the threshold with Japan moving slightly below (19.5 percent). In industrial output, Korea and Singapore were below the threshold in 1960, but in 2000 they had risen above the threshold, to the same level as the other EAEs, with China at the highest (43 percent).

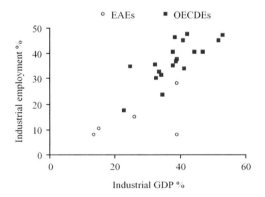

*Figure 1.1* EAEs and OECDEs: industrial level (1960).

*Sources*: OCED-2001; EAEs: national statistics.

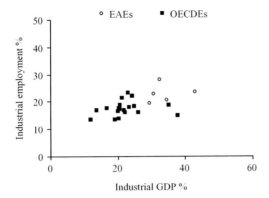

*Figure 1.2* EAEs and OECDEs: industrial level (2000).

*Sources*: OECD-2003; EASs: national statistics.

The facts are clear: over the 40 years between 1960 and 2000, the EAEs reached a level of industrialization substantially higher than that of the OECDEs. A higher industrial level, however, is not necessarily the same as a higher level of development, if development can be progressively measured. Indeed, studies have demonstrated that a *de-industrialization* process occurs once an economy reaches the threshold of US$5,000 GNP per capita (Chow and Kellman 1993: 156; Chowdhury and Islam 1993: 8–9), because "post-industrial" economic activities grow mainly in the service sector. However, a relatively low industrial level is not necessarily an indicator of a post-industrial economy either. Many OECDEs are in fact dominated by the agricultural sector. That said, it is clear that the EAEs have gone well beyond the level of "newly industrializing." Overall, the EAEs have been industrialized.

GROWTH

With the EAEs' industrial level established, let us look at their half-century journey to where they are now. Here, the 50-year economic growth experiences of the EAEs are of interest. Two key indicators are used: annual change of GDP and GDP per capita annual change, both in constant prices. As Figure 1.3 illustrates, the average GDP annual growth rate of the EAEs over the period from 1951 to 2000 was 7.85 percent, while that of the OECDEs was 3.68 percent. The EAEs' average GDP annual growth rate, therefore, has been more than twice that of the OECDEs. Among all 24 countries compared, the top five (which have recorded more than a 5 percent average growth rate over the 50-year period) are all EAEs, with Taiwan at 8.39 percent; Singapore, 8.39 percent; China, 7.93 percent; Korea, 7.28 percent; and Japan, 7.23 percent.

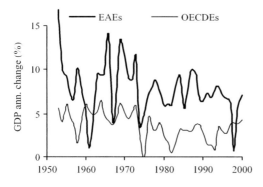

*Figure 1.3* EAEs and OECDEs: GDP annual change (1952–2000).
*Source*: Appendix B1.

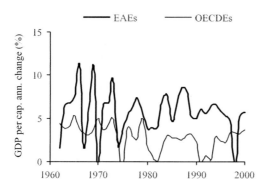

*Figure 1.4* EAEs and OECDEs – GDP per capita annual change (1962–2000).
*Source*: Appendix B2.

The same pattern is found regarding per capita GDP annual growth from 1962 to 2000 (as shown in Figure 1.4), for which credible and consistent data are available, with the average per capita GDP annual growth rate of the EAEs being 5.65 percent, and that of the OECDEs, 2.82 percent. Again, the EAEs' rate is more than twice that of the OECDEs. The top five, whose growth rates are above 4 percent, are all EAEs, with Taiwan at 6.68 percent; Singapore, 5.78 percent; Korea; 6.11 percent; China, 5.44 percent; and Japan, 4.27 percent.

DEVELOPMENT

Now let us look at how growth has been related to the broader problem of social, human, and environmental development in the EAEs. Indeed, a common charge made is that the growth has, in fact, failed to effect such development. Such a charge, however, has not come in the form of systematic academic enquiry, but rather has often surfaced randomly in public speeches and in media coverage. Thus, it is necessary for our reality check to explore this aspect.

Going beyond the conventional views of development – those that focus on the individual's potential entitlement – this study measures development in three aspects in 2000: individual advancement, social distribution, and global competitiveness. I use GDP per capita at current international prices and the GINI Index, both from the World Bank's Development Indicators Dataset, as general indicators for individual and social development. Both sets of data are tested against the *Human Development Index* (HDI), as a broad indicator of human development. A historical comparison of HDI and GDP per capita shows the general trend of change on these two indicators. For national development, I test the *Global Competitiveness Index* (GCI), from World Economic Forum (WEF), against data of GDP world weight in purchasing power parity (PPP), from the IMF. While the GDP world weight indicates a country's relative position in the world economy, the GCI can be seen as a measure of a country's ability for potential growth, as it "looks at the set of institutions and economic policies supportive of high rates of economic growth in the medium to long term (over the coming five to eight years)" (WEF 2002).

Concerning individual development (Figure 1.5), the average real GDP per capita of the EACs ($18,642 in 2000, in international dollars) is significantly lower than that of the OECDEs ($26,464). Further, the EAEs are

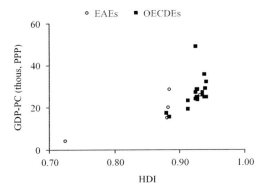

*Figure 1.5* EAEs and OECDEs: individual development (2000).
*Source*: PWT6.1; UNDP-HDI (2003).

all, with the exception of Japan, ranked low in HDI. The EAE average is 0.857 and the OECDEs' is 0.925. These two indicators, when taken together as shown in Figure 1.5, locate the EAEs within the lower left area, while the OECDEs are placed within the upper right area.

With regard to social development (Figure 1.6), the picture is mixed. The income gaps within Singapore (42.5) and China (40.3) are among the highest according to the GINI index for individual countries), with the USA sandwiched between (40.8). Japan is placed very low on the list, with Korea and Taiwan in the middle. The EAE average (34.24), however, is still higher than the OECDEs' (32.09). It is safe to say that the EAEs – overall – have a slightly higher concentration of income distribution at the top. In correlation with HDI, the variation among the EAEs is greater than that among the OECDEs.

If this data is examined historically, however, it becomes clear that the EAEs tend to be much faster in improving on these development indica-tors. Figure 1.7 shows, for example, that the gap in HDI between the EAEs and the OECDEs in 1975 was 0.147. In 2000, it had been reduced to 0.068. In a similar trend, the EAEs have increased their average GDP per capita level 60 times, from $310 in 1951 (in current international dollars) to $18,642 in 2000. For the same period, that of the OECDEs incresed 21 times ($1,271 in 1951 to $26,464 in 2000).

For the indicators of national development, the GCI (2002) of the WEF is used against the world weight of GDP in current international prices. Four of the five EAEs are among the 11 economies whose GDP weight in the world's total is more than 1 percent: China, 11.52 percent; Japan, 7.52 percent; Korea, 1.70 percent; and Taiwan, 1.04 percent. On the global competitiveness ranking, Taiwan (5.50), Singapore (5.42) are among the top, with Japan (5.08) in the middle, and Korea (4.89) and China (4.37) at a low rank. The EAEs' average is 5.05, higher than that of the OECDEs

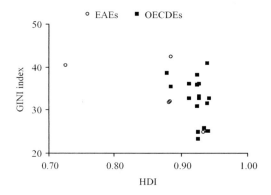

*Figure 1.6* EAEs and OECDEs: social development (2000).

*Source*: UNDP-HDI (2003).

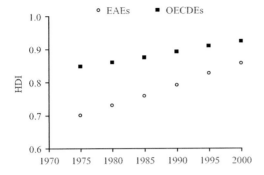

*Figure 1.7* EAEs and OECDEs: change in HDI (1970–2000).
*Source*: UNDP-HDI (2003).

(5.03). Cross-examining (Figure 1.8) shows that the EAEs are leading the OECDEs on these indicators.

The development data suggest that, while the EAEs lead in global competitiveness, they are clearly behind the OECDEs on individual advancement and, to a lesser extent, on social distribution. While there are a number of theories explaining the existing gaps, the progressive growth of the EAEs along different timeframes – and thus the effects of growth cycles – should help further our understanding of the issue at hand. A 1 percentage point increase in GDP growth rate in a highly developed economy is very different from the same increase in a developing economy. In fact, treating the EAEs as a group may conceal real and important variations in their growth performances, due to different levels

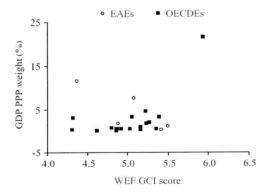

*Figure 1.8* EAEs and OECDEs: national development (2000).
*Sources*: IMF-WEO (2003); WEF-GCR (2003).

of economic development at a particular point in time. Earlier studies either ignore or discard these discrepancies in defense of the validity of their shared qualities. Or, they reject the idea of a collective pattern of East Asian Growth on the basis of these discrepancies. This study sees these discrepancies as the effects of the growth form operating in various national and historical settings. However, we need first to establish how growth indicators manifested in each of the EAEs over the 50 years from 1951, to see if there is a more informative pattern to their growth experiences beyond the EAEs-as-a-group aggregates and averages.

### Growth patterns of the individual EAEs

Let us now look at the characteristics of the growth indicators of each EAE over the 50-year research period covered in this study. The next five graphs will summarize each EAE's pattern of annual change in GDP over the 50 years. In each of the graphs, the main data line reflects the annual changes in the EAE's GDP (in local currency at constant prices) moving in five-year averages. Data in local currency, and in constant prices, gives a more realistic measure of the activity. A five-year moving average is necessary to deflect isolated, short-term disruptions. The gray data line in the background shows the same data for the USA. A gray x-bar is placed at a 7.85 percent (the EAEs average growth rate for the 50-year period) data point. As the data will show, this is a critical threshold that separates the rapid growth period of an EAE, where the form of growth was intensively pursued, from other periods. The dotted gray box highlights the period with annual growth rate above the 50-year average – the period referred to here as the rapid growth period.[7]

In the Chinese case (Figure 1.9), much of the period before 1978 – when the Chinese started to embark on their reform and restructuring program

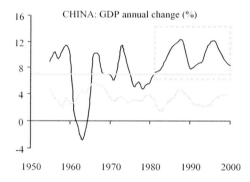

*Figure 1.9* China: annual real GDP change in five-year moving average (1953–2000).

*Source*: Appendix A1, China: 1.3.

and experienced a fundamentally new course of growth and development – is dominated by drastic fluctuations in growth performance. From 1982, the growth rate started to rise above 8 percent, and has since stayed above this level. For the non-rapid growth period from 1953 to 1978, the average growth rate is 6.6 percent, while, for the rapid growth period from 1982 to 2000, the average is 9.98 percent. The average for the whole period from 1953 to 2000 is 7.93 percent.

For Japan (Figure 1.10), the threshold was crossed in the opposite direction in the early 1970s, which presumably was the effect of the oil shock in 1973. From then on, Japan's GDP growth rate has never come back again to rise above 8 percent. Japan's average growth rate over its rapid growth period from 1952 to 1973 is 11.93 percent, while that of the non-rapid growth period from 1974 onward to 2000 is 3.20 percent. The average over the 50 years is 7.23 percent.

In Korea's case (Figure 1.11), except for the late 1970s and early 1980s, when the Kwangju Massacre threw the national economy into chaos, Korea's rapid growth period spanned from the 1963 – when a new development program was put in place after Park Chung Hee staged a military coup and turned Korea into the Third Republic – to 1992, when the growth rate started to drop below the threshold. The average growth rate for Korea's 30-year rapid growth period is 8.52 percent, and that for the non-rapid growth periods – from 1954 to 1962 and from 1992 to 2000 – is 5.11 percent, with the 50-year average being 7.28 percent.

The same pattern holds for Taiwan (Figure 1.12), whose growth rate moved above the threshold in 1962 – after the almost decade-long period of primary import substitution in the 1950s. For a 30-year period since then, its growth rate is averaged at 9.17 percent, all above the threshold except for some disruptions in the late 1970s and early 1980s – apparently the effects of Nixon's rapprochement with Beijing from the early 1970s.

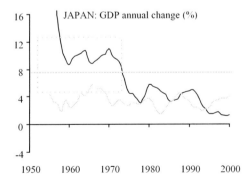

*Figure 1.10* Japan: annual real GDP change in five-year moving average (1951–2000).

*Source*: Appendix A2, Japan: 1.3.

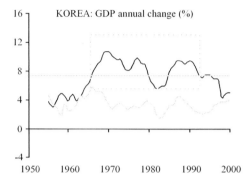

*Figure 1.11*  Korea: annual real GDP change in five-year moving average
(1954–2000).

*Source*: Appendix A3, Korea: 1.3.

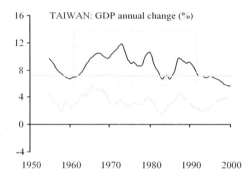

*Figure 1.12*  Taiwan: annual real GDP change in five-year moving average
(1953–2000).

*Source*: Appendix A5, Taiwan: 1.3.

For the non-rapid growth periods of the 1950s and the 1990s, the average
growth rate is still a comfortable 7.16 percent. The 50-year average is 8.39
percent. Even though showing a similar growth pattern, Taiwan's performance has been slightly better than Korea's, and the contrast between its
rapid and non-rapid growth period was not as clear as in the other EAEs.

Finally, Singapore's formative years in the early 1960s were chaotic,
caused by trouble with the Malay Union and trade difficulties with
Indonesia. The growth rate (Figure 1.13) started to move above the
threshold in 1968 after the break-up of the Union and the inauguration of
the Republic of Singapore in 1965. It had been able to maintain a 30-year
rapid growth at an average 8.88 percent, even with the dampening
effects of the government's management of wages and the exchange rate

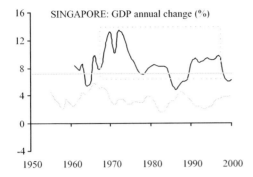

*Figure 1.13* Singapore: annual real GDP change in five-year moving average (1960–2000).

*Source*: Appendix A4, Singapore: 1.3.

manifested themselves in the mid-1980s. The 1997–8 Asian financial crisis has ended the rapid growth period for Singapore.

As a background benchmark, the US growth rate for the 50 years moves steadily at around 4 percent. To be more specific, the average growth rate is 3.48 percent. Further, there is no particular period that matches a rapid growth period similar to those of the EAEs.

There will be further discussions regarding the characteristics of the EAEs' rapid growth periods in Chapter 7, but for now it is sufficient to observe from the above data that, first, each EAE had a particular period that exhibits a substantially higher growth rate, generally above 8 percent. Second, each rapid growth period was preceded by a few years of domestic and international political difficulties and economic devastation, as well as major institutional and policy changes. Third, the rapid growth periods ran for, roughly, about 30 years. Regarding China, its rapid growth period is still running, after 20 years of high-speed growth. Japan's rapid growth period lasted about 20 years for the period researched. Fourth, and perhaps more importantly, even though their rapid growth periods spanned different timeframes (which further reflects the different conditions and growth responses), the overall growth pattern is similar, and key characteristics of the growth pattern as discussed above are shared.

### Evidence and critique

With the growth qualities and general patterns established, let us turn now to look specifically at the empirical basis, or in some cases – where empirical evidence is not applicable – the logical qualities, of the six leading theories about East Asian Growth, and see how each of them stands up against empirical and analytical challenges – again, in the broader context of a benchmark comparison with the OECDEs.

*How much is the state involved?*

The developmental state, by definition, implies large government size presumably because of the large number of functions and activities it has to carry; less market domination of the economic structure because of the state dominance; and less freedom in areas such as financial markets because of the state's guidance and restrictions. With the availability of a coherent set of data on these indicators from the database, *Economic Freedom of the World 2002* (EFW data),[8] the analysis below should lead to a measure of domestic economic freedom, which typically is lacking in a developmental state.

On the level of freedom in terms of government size, the EFW data (Area I, Size of Government: Consumption, Transfers, and Subsidies) gives a measure in terms of "general government consumption spending as a percentage of total consumption," and government "transfers and subsidies as a percentage of GDP," "government enterprises and investment as a percentage of GDP," and "total marginal tax rate." Data concerning this indicator shows that governments in the EAEs had much less spending, fewer subsidies and transfers, fewer state enterprises and less investment, and less taxation than their counterparts in the OECDEs, contrary to popular perceptions. The collective EAE index on the level of freedom in government size has always been above that of the OECDEs throughout the period, with the period average at 5.98, over that of the OECDEs' 4.71. In 2000, the EAEs' index is 6.08, while the OECDEs' is 5.01. As far as individual EAEs are concerned, they occupy different positions in the overall rankings. In 2000 for example, Singapore is at the top (8.08), China is fifth from the bottom (3.84), with Korea (7.11), Taiwan (6.04), and Japan (5.35) in the upper middle.

A second indicator is the level of freedom with respect to regulation on credit, labor, and business. This indicator measures the level of freedom based on how much the credit market is controlled in terms of bank ownership, competition, credit extension, and interest rate controls; how much the labor market is regulated in terms of minimum wages, employment practices, collective bargaining and unemployment benefits; and the extent business is regulated in terms of price controls, administrative restrictions on new business, time with government bureaucracy, starting a new business, and irregular payments. The higher on the index, the less the economy is regulated and controlled. The evidence suggests that the EAEs are consistently less liberal (5.32 over the period), thus with more economic regulation, than the OECDEs (5.92), though only slightly. The OECDEs lead the index in 2000 with 6.90 over the EAEs' 6.16. As on the first indicator, the positions of the EAEs vary.

Put together, the average of the two indices constitutes what I call the domestic economic freedom index. As Figure 1.14 shows, the internal economic freedom rating of the EAEs (5.48 over the period) has been

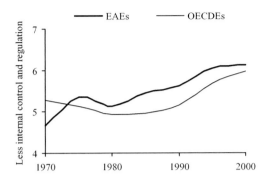

*Figure 1.14* EAEs and OECDEs: domestic economic freedom (1970–2000).

*Source*: Gwartney and Lawson (2002).

constantly higher than the OECDEs (5.30) for much of the 30-year period. However, breaking the data down into individual economies indicates that the EAEs' positions – whether in 2000, or on average over the whole period – are spread across the board on the internal freedom ranking (Singapore, for example, is at the top at 7.01, while China is at the bottom at 3.74).

The overall picture that emerges from the data suggests that a developmental state that is heavily involved in, and carefully manages and controls, national economic activities is not limited to the EAEs. In some cases, the EAEs have been more free than the OECDEs, and, in others, less free. Moreover, even among the EAEs themselves, the picture is far from clearcut. From this evidence, one cannot conclude that states in the EAEs are all active and interventionist, nor can one argue that the EAEs are more so than the OECDEs. Also, the variations among the EAEs may suggest that some things were dictated by the different timeframes of their rapid growth periods. This will be seen more clearly on other indicators below.

### How much has it to do with exports?

The export-as-engine theory claims that East Asian Growth was propelled mainly by exports, that there was a greater concentration of exports in the EAEs, and that much of the global flows of products are from Asia. Let us look at each of these claims.

First, how much is really made in "Asia"? This is, perhaps, not too difficult to answer. Examining their share of the world total in 2000 shows that the EAEs' exports (18.65 percent) are about one-third of the OECDEs' (53.34 percent), while their GDP world weight total in international dollars (22.0 percent) is half that of the OECDEs (44.2 percent). The total volume

of EAE exports is, therefore, relatively low in comparison with that of the
OECDEs. The weighing factor of exports in relation to GDP is much lower
than that of the OECDEs.

Moreover, the EAEs reached their 18.65 percent share in 2000 from
4.82 percent in 1951, while the OECDEs' changed from 50.22 percent in
1951 to 53.34 percent in 2000. As shown, the EAEs' share has been steadily
increasing while the OECDEs' has not changed greatly. The same trend
is also confirmed by the rates of growth in total exports for the EAEs and
the OECDEs. The average annual rate of growth in exports from 1951 to
2000 is 15.46 percent for the EAEs and 10.28 percent for the OECDEs,
with that of the world being 9.78 percent.

Second, a more interesting question concerns the relationship of exports
to GDP growth. Often, references to the exports–growth relationship in
the EAEs leave an impression that these economies have a high share of
exports in their total GDP, and it is this fact that makes these economies
substantially different from other ones. The data (Figure 1.15) shows that
there are higher exports–GDP ratios in the EAEs than those in the OECDEs.
For the period from 1960 to 2000, the EAEs' average ratio has risen from
39.85 percent in 1960 to 52.69 percent in 2000, and the period average is
40.57 percent. For the same period, the OECDEs' share changed from
21.71 percent to 33.79 percent, with the period average at 23.77 percent,
just over half of the EAE average. The higher ratio of the EAEs, however,
may have to do with the unusually high ratio of one particular EAE, i.e.
Singapore. The period average ratio for Singapore is 125.99 percent. If the
EAE ratio is calculated with Singapore excluded (EAE-NS, shown in
the dotted data line in Figure 1.15), which allows comparison for a longer
period from 1951 to 2000, the EAEs' average would have risen from 10.71
percent in 1951 to 29.56 percent in 2000, with the period average being
16.97 percent. For the same period, the OECDEs' ratio has risen from

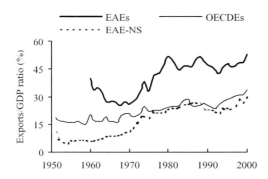

*Figure 1.15* EAEs and OECDEs: exports/GDP ratio (1951–2000).

*Source*: Appendix B6.

18.82 percent in 1951 to 33.79 percent in 2000, with the period average being 22.48 percent. Thus the EAEs ratio without Singapore would have been much less than the OECDEs'.

Third, examining the correlation between changes in the export growth rate and GDP can also test the exports–growth relationship. Figure 1.16 shows how the average GDP growth rate correlates with the exports growth rate, for both the EAEs and the OECDEs. The OECDEs show low correlations (concentrating in the lower left-hand corner), while the EAEs are on the high side.

There are other aspects to the exports–growth complex in East Asian Growth, such as the size of the economy or the level of overall economic development. But, from what has been discussed so far, several conclusions can be made. First, there has been a rapid growth of exports among the EAEs. Second, there is no clear evidence that exports are important only to the EAEs. In many cases, exports have had a substantially larger role in the OECDEs. Third, the image of exports domination in the EAEs may have more to do with the particular characteristics of individual EAEs, than with the collective characteristics of the EAEs as a whole.

### Why the enterprise systems?

The enterprise system theory does indeed highlight one of the key aspects of the growth arrangements in the EAEs. It touches upon a core issue that motivates this study: institutional manipulations as a way of enhancing competitiveness.

While details on how the unique organizational forms, both within and among enterprises, were translated into growth inputs need further analytical clarification, studies along the lines of this theory often focus on describing the organizational forms rather than explaining why they

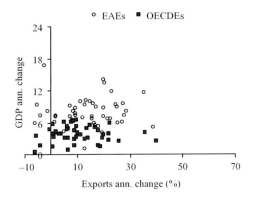

*Figure 1.16* EAEs and OECDEs: exports/GDP correlation (1951–2000).

*Sources*: Appendix B1, B4.

were preferred in the first place, and thus what exact role they played in East Asian Growth is not altogether clear.

In terms of why they were the preferred forms of growth arrangement, the cultural and social settings, along with the historical growth conditions, are often missing in the accounts of these forms of the organization of production and distribution. Without the setting and conditions explained, these organizational forms tend to become a cultural myth. We do not know what conditions those unique organizational forms responded to and what problems they were intended to solve. Thus, we have learnt little from this theory that can be applied to other growth settings: whether these types of organizational forms would be possible, or even necessary.

A good explanation of the cultural and social settings for these organizational forms shall lead to a better understanding of the role they played in East Asian Growth, and thus the fundamental nature of East Asian Growth itself. Instead of treating the rise of these organizational forms as a cultural myth, I argue that these organizational forms were shaped by the initial and subsequent growth conditions that offered only a narrow range of options in the growth drive, and by the cultural and social conditions that allowed different sets of incentives and cost calculations for these options. They were part of the growth system where competitiveness enhancement would have to come mainly, if not solely, from the internal reorganization of production and distribution. From here, one might be in a position to isolate some indicators and see how the organizational forms translated into growth performance. Unfortunately, the organizational forms in many of the studies on enterprise systems are mostly isolated rather than linked phenomena. Without their link to the initial growth conditions and the cultural and social settings in which they operated, it would be difficult to explain their ultimate link to growth performance.

## *What has Confucianism to do with East Asian Growth?*

Confucianism, rightly or wrongly perceived as the cultural foundation of the Asian societies, has become a convenient analytical construct for scholarship on East Asian Growth. The notion that the Confucian tradition provided unique cultural support for East Asian Growth is an effort in the right direction in solving the growth puzzle. There are, however, two issues at a deeper level that seem to have limited the explanatory power of the cultural theory.

The first has to do with the classic Weberian thesis that tries to link Confucianism to the lack of development of modern capitalism in China (Weber 1930, 1951). The German sociologist contrasted Confucianism with Protestantism and argued that Confucianism – apparently devoid of the Protestant ethics of valuing hard work, risk-taking, and asceticism – was responsible for the failure of modern capitalism to emerge in the East. Weber's conception of Confucianism appears to be different from the

Confucianism understood in the cultural theory discussed earlier. More-over, Confucianism in this cultural theory becomes a constructive factor for economic growth, presumably capitalist in nature. Something must be wrong with our conceptions of Confucianism.

There have been efforts to take a second look at Confucianism and its adaptations in recent times, so that some reconciliation can be reached with the Weberian thesis (Elvin 1984; Sun 1986; Tu 1991b; Yu 1985; de Bary 1981; Mettzger 1977). The notion of Neo-Confucianism was developed to recast the link between Confucianism and modern capitalist development in East Asia. The Confucian societies of Singapore, Hong Kong, and Taiwan, for example according to Tu (Tu 1991a), no longer resemble the society found in mainland China, not to mention the China that existed when Confucius had his ideas recorded. The people in the EACs are modernized, if not Westernized, more entrepreneurial and innovative, and less constrained by conformist values (Berger 1991; Hirschmeier 1964; Redding 1988, 1993).

This leads to the second problem with the Confucianism–growth thesis. Even under the general category of a Confucian society, these EACs can be quite different in terms of their specific characteristics (Pye 1985; Rozman 1991; Morishima 1982; Tu 1996; Redding 1993). The Japanese, for example, are seen as better team-workers than the Chinese, and thus Japan should have performed much better than China in encouraging growth, development, and modernization. The Koreans, for another example, are seen to be more aggressive and willing to take risks than the Japanese and, therefore, Korea's growth has been much faster and more ambitious. Moreover, China's political structure is considered to be more centralized than that of Japan. Indeed, if one follows what Fukuyama depicts in his social trust categorization, the EACs can fall into two signifi-cantly different cultural camps: the Chinese-speaking areas on one side, and the oceanic Japan and Korea on the other (Fukuyama 1995).

The key question here is whether these differences are mainly the result of variations within the Confucian tradition, or whether they suggest a wider range of institution-cultural dynamics in these EACs. And, together with the first issue, what is Confucianism in the first place? The cultural theory has never been able to address these questions convincingly, and thus there always seems that something is missing in their explanations of the relationship between the varied Confucian traditions found in the EACs and their growth experiences. As a way of answering these questions, this study will show, in Chapters 4 and 5, what, in my view, Confucianism is, and how it fits into the overall picture of East Asian Growth.

Beyond these theoretical difficulties, the problem with the cultural theory also lies in the empirical evidence in relation to the overall nature of the cultural conditions and how they relate to economic performance. On the overall nature of the cultural conditions, there is one specific piece of evidence often cited for the Confucianism–growth thesis, and in fact for the notion that the cultural conditions in the EAEs are favorable for economic growth. That is the unique "cultural habit" of the people in the EAEs to save, resulting in higher saving rates in the EAEs that are believed to have helped solve the problem of financing East Asian Growth. This is something on this "non-quantitative" cultural problem that we can technically check. Indeed, with the newly available data from PWT6.1, we are in a position to offer an authoritative examination. We use the data on current savings to test the basic premise of the claim: the EAEs have higher saving rates. As Figure 1.17 shows, OECDEs seem to have maintained a steady level of savings at around 25 percent of GDP. In contrast, the EAEs' collective level of savings as a share of GDP has changed dramatically, starting at about 10 percent in the 1950s, and moving to close the gap with the OECDEs at around the mid-1970s. It surpassed the OECDEs and has maintained a level substantively higher than that of the OECDEs since then. It is safe to say that the EAEs had much lower saving levels during their rapid growth period. Only as a result of the rapid growth did their savings start to catch up.

As far as the nature of the link between Confucian traditions and economic performance is concerned, there seems to be conflicting evidence. As Sung-Joo Han puts it:

> There are values which can be described as particularly Asian. Whether these values play a positive or negative role seems to depend on a particular country's stage of development, as well as how specific values within the basket of so-called Asian values are selected and combined.
>
> (1999: 8)

Contributors to his collection provide evidence that this link shows up quite differently in the EAEs, with Singapore and Japan seeming to be

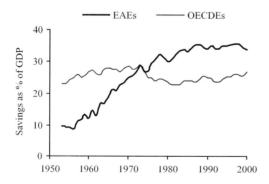

*Figure 1.17*  EAEs and OECDEs: current savings as percentage of GDP
           (1951–2000).

*Source*: Appendix B3.

more successful in ensuring a positive link, while Korea and China are less so (Han 1999).

*What is "Asian" about the Asian disease?*

The looters' theory points to many aspects of what might be called the "Asian disease" – corruption, lack of legal, civil, and business standards, and failure to respect human, social, and environmental values – that are worth investigating, both in terms of the facts themselves, and how these facts relate to East Asian Growth. What seems to be appropriate here, therefore, is to provide an assessment of the level of corruption, lack of legal, civil, and business standards, and disrespect for human, social, and environmental values in the EAEs, with those of the OECDEs as a benchmark. Unless this picture is made reasonably clear, much of this debate will lack a necessary factual basis.

To measure the level of corruption, the Corruption Perceptions Index (CPI) and Bribe Payers Index (BPI) – both from Transparency International – are utilized. They are not perfect indicators, especially considering the fact that the CPI is based primarily on the *perceptions* of those surveyed, while the BPI is drawn from surveys of *business executives* doing business with Asia. However, they are the best available and are widely used by academics.

The BPI (1999) confirms that the EACs have a higher perceived level of bribery (4.16 on a 0–10 scale with 10 as the least corrupt) than that of the OECDEs (6.67). The same pattern is also found with the CPI (5.62 vs. 7.81 in 2000). The CPI shows that, in addition to a considerable gap between the EAEs (5.70) and the OECDEs (7.59) over the period from 1980 to 2000, the level of corruption in the EAEs has increased from 6.23 in 1980 to 5.58 in 2000, while the OCEDEs recorded a slight improvement – from 7.62 in 1980 to 7.81 in 2000 – over the period.

Lack of legal, civil, and business standards is another aspect of East Asian Growth that is often discussed. To assess the problem, two sets of data are examined. One is the institutional risk indices from the World Bank *World Development Report* (WDR) *1999/2000*, comprising the 1999 Composite ICRG Risk Rating (CIRR) and the Institutional Investors Credit Rating (IICR). Another is the Legal Institution Index, concerning judicial independence, impartial courts, protection of intellectual property, military interference in legal and political processes, and integrity of the legal system, from the EFW 2002 data, part of which was used earlier with regard to domestic economic freedom.

The CIRR index is an assessment of the political, financial, and economic risks of individual countries, with the risk index on a scale of 0–100 (100 indicating the lowest level of risk). The IICR index is based on information from leading international banks and indicates the probability of default (100 being the lowest level of risk). In both counts, the EAEs have a higher average level of risk (80.2 over the OECDEs' 83.3) and default probability (69.4 over 84.1). While the risk gap is not wide (3.1), the probability gap is considerably large at 15.3. On the Legal Institution Index, the 30-year-data presents a slightly more complicated picture (Figure 1.18). While the EAEs' overall level of integrity, effectiveness, and independence of legal institutions was about the same as the OECDEs during the 1970s, the gap with the OECDEs seems to have widened from the early 1980s.

To check the environmental conditions associated with East Asian Growth, I use Adjusted Net Saving (formerly Genuine Saving) data developed by the World Bank in its Environment Economics and Indicators study. Adjusted Saving, according to the study, is "the true saving rate in a country after taking into account investments in human capital, depletion of natural resources and damage caused by pollution," and is a good indicator of the effects of environmental conservation. Adjusted Net Saving as a percentage of GDP is used here as a measure of the relative inclination of the EAEs and the OECDEs to favor resource-sensitive growth.

Figure 1.19 shows that the average figures for EAEs (26.96 percent in 2000 and 20.84 percent on average over the period from 1970–2000) are considerably higher than those for the OECDEs (12.98 percent and 11.94 percent respectively). The level of the EAEs steadily rose from 13.53 percent in 1970 to 26.96 percent in 2000, while the OECDEs had not changed much. In some years it even worsened. Over the period, the accumulative year on year change is 10.84 percentage points for the EAEs, and 2.84 for the OECDEs.

The overall picture gleaned from these three datasets is mixed. The EAEs, as a whole, do have higher levels of corruption, risk, and default probability. On value prioritization, however, particularly in terms of a growth–environment tradeoff, the EAEs as a whole have a more positive record in

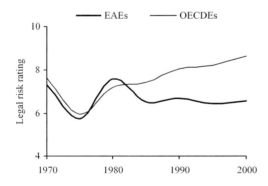

*Figure 1.18* EAEs and OECDEs: level of legal risk (1970–2000).

*Source*: Gwartney and Lawson (2002).

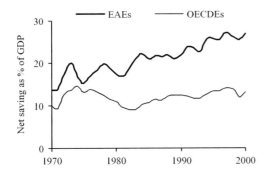

*Figure 1.19* EAEs and OECDEs: adjusted net savings as percentage of GDP (1970–2000).

*Source*: Appendix B7.

the preservation of, and investment in, resources, in contrast to the general perception. Such complexity becomes even clearer if one looks at the EAEs individually. In all three datasets, the EAEs' values are widely distributed. In the corruption rankings, for example, Singapore is among the cleanest of both the EAEs and OECDEs, while China and Korea are among the least clean, with Japan and Taiwan in the middle. A similarly wide-ranging distribution is also found in the risk rankings, with Singapore and Japan faring well in legal integrity over the period, while Korea and China trail.

Overall, one can conclude that there is some evidence that supports certain aspects of the "Asian disease." But, with substantial variation concerning these indicators among the individual EAEs, this data is not sufficient to make the case that there is a "disease" shared by these EAEs – and much less evidence that the disease is an integral part of economic growth in the EAEs.

### How much are domestic and international markets separated?

The economic nationalism theory argues that East Asian Growth has been built primarily upon separation of domestic and international markets, and control and protectionist management of cross-border transactions and flows. To empirically verify this popular claim, this study looks at and compares the EAEs and the OECDEs in their levels of freedom in exchange with foreigners, again using the EFW data (Gwartney and Lawson 2000). Under this indicator, the EFW data measures taxes on international trade, regulatory trade barriers, actual size of trade sector compared to the expected size, gaps between official exchange rates and black market rates, and international capital market controls. It thus gives a basic indication of how much the national economy is separated from the world economic

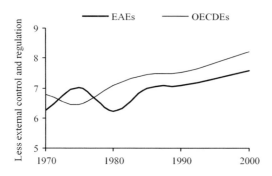

*Figure 1.20*   EAEs and OECDEs: less external control and regulation
(1970–2000).

*Source*: Gwartney and Lawson (2002).

system. Here again, ranging from 0 to 10, the higher the index number, the lower the external control and regulation, and thus the fewer barriers between the domestic and international market.

Figure 1.20 shows that the EAEs had more external control and regulation from the early 1980s onwards, while changes in the 1970s were dramatic for them. Over the 30-year period, the EAEs' average level is 6.92 over that of the OECDEs at 7.33. In 2000, the EAEs' is 8.74 while that of the OECDEs is 9.18. Among the EAEs themselves, the same pattern is also found as in the earlier cases considered: the EAEs do not share the same level of external control and regulation at one particular point of time. In 2000, for example, China has the highest barriers at 6.69, while Singapore has the lowest barriers at 9.32.

## Putting the pieces together

What can we learn from the discussions so far? On general growth patterns and qualities, we have established that there is a rapid and prolonged period of economic growth in the EAEs, at a much higher rate than in the OECDEs. At the end of the 1990s, the EAEs had much higher levels of industrialization than the OECDEs and comparable levels of individual, social, and national development.

Second, each EAE has a rapid growth period that generally lasted for about 30 years. The EAEs' average growth rate during their rapid growth periods is 9.48 percent, while that for their non-rapid growth periods is 5.58 percent. The collective growth rate for the whole 50-year period was 7.85 percent. As a point of reference, the average growth rate for the USA from 1951 to 2000 was 3.48 percent.

Our reality check has also found that there are different timeframes in which each EAE's rapid growth period occurred. Consequently, while they shared the overall pattern of 30-year rapid growth and similar levels on their key growth indicators, such as levels of industrialization, GDP annual growth rates, levels of GDP per capita, levels of export concentration, levels of protectionism, levels of institutional risk, etc., throughout their respective rapid growth periods, the EAEs differed from one another on these indicators at any given time point.

As far as the theoretical claims discussed earlier are concerned, some are confirmed, to various degrees, but many are found to be not unique to the EAEs. Quite a number of them are proven to be false. There is conflicting evidence on many others. For some, it is a matter of empirical accuracy. For others, it is a matter of the facts themselves. But, for many of them, it is the interpretation of the facts within a coherent theoretical framework that matters.

In other words, the problems with existing accounts go beyond the empirical evidence. Each of the theories is a single-factor explanation that treats the factor as an "independent variable." It tries to answer the question of whether this factor has an effect on East Asian Growth, and, if you are lucky, to what extent the effect might be. The historical and institutional setting in which the factor became relevant, desirable, or effective on growth is, in most cases, missing; the sequence in the path of growth activity is left unaccounted for; and the overall dynamic growth experiences are reduced in mechanical equations to one or a list of "causal" factors.

As such, even though each theory does individually say something significant about East Asian Growth, they have failed either individually or collectively to form a coherent account – one that can stand a reality check, make sense of all the elements identified with East Asian Growth, and explain the variations in growth performance among the EAEs.

What is missing, perhaps, is a better conceptualization of economic growth in general, and East Asian Growth in particular. Economic growth, in its narrow sense, is an aggregate effect of human economic activities: exports, imports, savings and investment, public and private consumption, etc. The properties of growth, i.e. its speed, scale, structure, duration, timing, etc., are thus directly related to the collective patterns of human behavior: why in some economies, for example, is there a concentration on exporting businesses rather than importing businesses? Why, for some periods of time, is an economy dominated by labor-intensive manufacturing? Why, in some countries, do those people who have been "laid off" prefer to live on government benefits rather than to explore business opportunities on their own?

Needless to say, there are various forces shaping human behavior: "material and cosmological beliefs" (Lal 1999), cultural traditions (Pye 1985), local and personal conditions, utility calculations, sequences of events (path dependence), effective institutions, etc. Among them, institutions are most crucial. For a given period of time, most other factors are "fixed" in their relation to a consequent pattern of behavior. Oil-rich countries are most likely to concentrate on oil-exporting activities. Protestantism leads to modern capitalism, in Max Weber's view. Individuals' rational calculations lead to the collective action problem, according to Mancur Olson (1965). There is not much one could do if these factors, in a given collective setting, do not lead to desirable behaviors. The unique qualities of institutions, however, are different. They can be intentionally "built," "restructured," or "fine-tuned" for the purpose of achieving, or sustaining, a desirable behavioral pattern – for example, moving people from importing to exporting activities. Institutions can be utilized to achieve a desirable behavior or a system to counter the effects of the other fixed factors.

The institutions referred to here are sets of rules and procedures intended to achieve or sustain a particular type of behavior among the members in a given collective setting (for more discussion, see North 1990; Clague 1997; Jepperson 1991). These could include tax law, electoral systems, import–export regulations, a government's industrial policy, labor law, and property relations, as well as community regulations, standards of conduct, corporatist arrangements, and multi-party agreements. If economic growth is an effect of human economic activities, and thus determined by the effective qualities of these activities, then the institutions that are able to manipulate these qualities in terms of their directions and content are crucial to economic growth.

The chapters that follow are an attempt to examine the role of institutions in growth generation, not so much as the cause of East Asian Growth, but rather as an ever-evolving set of incentives and constraints that induced the kind of growth activity which ultimately effected East Asian Growth; and to investigate the rise and fall of the growth system through a series of questions. What were the initial conditions in the EAEs in their pre-takeoff years? How did these conditions severely limit EAEs' options in growth generation? (Chapter 2) Why did international competitiveness become crucial for EAEs' survival and subsequent growth, given the initial conditions? How did the EAEs' success in their response to the initial conditions lead to the emergence of a set of growth methods and mechanisms? What further institutional change was demanded to strengthen their effectiveness and perpetuate their functions? (Chapter 3)

How did the prevalent social and cultural conditions fare with the challenge of institutional change? What elements were supportive of the new institutional constructs and what elements were detrimental and thus needed to adapt or transform to satisfy the institutional requirements? (Chapter 4) How did the national growth system evolve in response to the challenge of institutional change and the surrounding social and cultural conditions? What institutional changes took place at various levels of society and in various areas of production, distribution, and consumption to perpetuate the growth mechanisms? (Chapter 5)

How did the institutions and growth conditions interact at the operational level? Why did the institutional arrangements gradually lose their effectiveness? What impact did this institutional aging have on the further evolution of the form of East Asian Growth? (Chapter 6)

Let us now turn to these questions.

# 2 Initial conditions
## Growth imperatives and alternative scenarios

East Asian Growth in the second half of the twentieth century began as a desperate quest for survival and catch-up. In a sense, the initial conditions provided a mind-set that transformed the anger, fear, and despair present in the countries concerned, to determination, solidarity for growth, and willingness to sacrifice and compromise. More importantly, however, these initial conditions limited the options for the EAEs in growth generation and motivated them into a form of growth that derived its power for rapid and prolonged expansion from institutional manipulation and national reorganization for international competitiveness.

As discussed earlier, Japan's rapid growth period started in the early 1950s and ended in the early 1970s. Both the rapid growth periods of Korea and Taiwan started in the early 1960s and ended in early 1990s. Singapore's rapid growth period ran from the mid-1960s to mid-1990s. China's rapid growth period started in the late 1970s and is continuing. The initial conditions concerned here, thus, are those present in these EAEs in the years leading to their respective rapid growth periods, and in the early years of these periods.

At one level, the initial conditions are well discussed in various existing studies on the EAEs individually or collectively. The EAEs were generally located in a severe environment, where national security was placed under serious threat, economies were collapsing, and their futures as legitimate nations and viable economies were exceedingly doubtful. People were desperate and willing to work for anything. Labor conditions and wages were not an issue. The government was determined to try anything that would work. Things couldn't get worse. These conditions effected a feeling of anxiety, a sense of urgency for rapid economic recovery and catch-up, a mood of pragmatism and opportunism for quick results, and a high level of consensus among all parties involved – the government, the business community, and the general public – to do their part, while expecting the commitment and devotion of others.

There was, however, more to the initial conditions. As will be shown in the following sections, it was the nature of growth factors at the core of these conditions, aided by the domestic and international events and developments at the time, that not only led to the early responses of the EAEs, but also – more profoundly – helped shape the form of growth over time. Building upon the early responses, and to sustain the emergent growth pattern, the EAEs focused primarily on national reorganization of their production and distribution to gain international competitiveness for their products. These growth factors thus served as constraining and redirecting conditions for the structure, process, and methods of growth to emerge in the EAEs.

## Growth factors and imperatives

Economic growth, at least in capitalist markets, is made possible ultimately by the input of capital, labor, and land in their broad sense in economics, and competitive output for effective consumption. Hence, natural resources, capital provision, employment, productivity, and markets are essential for economic growth. The EAEs are no exception. What we are interested in here is the unique nature of these factors and their combination at the start of the EAEs' rapid growth periods and how they tripped a sequence of growth activity by the EAEs that gradually built into a pattern of growth. The land factor is also important. But, in the case of the EAEs, all of them except China had limited raw resources, which added to the pressure for them to seek growth factors from external markets – a key characteristic of East Asian Growth that we are to establish below with other growth factors. Other than this, the land factor will not feature in our case of how the initial conditions helped shape East Asian Growth.

More specifically, capital provision, employment, market demand, and labor productivity are empirically examined to test a series of propositions, the confirmation of which would form a basis for the link between the initial conditions and the form of growth that has subsequently emerged: that the levels of capital provision in the formative years of the EAEs' rapid growth periods were low, and that such low levels would have motivated the EAEs to rely on foreign capital for initial growth financing; that effective markets were mostly located outside the economies; that these two factors, together with others, would have effected an industrial structure that concentrated on hard currency-earning exports; that such export-led growth would have required the international competitiveness of the economy; and that, with the EAEs' labor productivity substantially low in comparison with the economies where their primary markets were located, the EAEs had to rely mainly on the domestic reorganization of their production and distribution to gain such competitiveness, besides utilizing their cheap labor forces.

To map out these factors at the time of the initial stage of the rapid growth periods, I utilize several datasets, including, primarily: PWT6.1; the World Bank's *Physical Capital Stock Data* by Vikram Nehru and Ashok Dhareshwar (WB-PCSD);[1] IMF's *International Financial Statistics*

(IMF-IFS) on various variables; *Economically Active Population* data from the International Labor Organization (ILO 1997) regarding employment conditions (ILO-EAP); and data from the National Bureau of Economic Research by Robert J. Barro and Jong-Wha Lee (1993), concerning international comparisons of education attainment.

Because of the complementary nature of these datasets – and some overlap between them – the same (or similar) variables that are relevant for our discussion have been regrouped into our four growth factors: capital, labor, market, and productivity. The data is presented in such a way that the initial state of the growth factors of the EAEs is assessed against their overall historical pattern for the period, along with that of the OECDEs. Further, the EAEs will also be placed in sub-groups – China (CHN), Japan (JPN), and Korea, Singapore, and Taiwan (KOST) – to reflect variations among them due, mainly, to the timing of their rapid growth periods, as discussed earlier. In the latter case, the USA will be used as a point of reference.

### *Capital provision*

First, let us look at several aspects of capital provision. We examine volumes of both real capital investment and physical capital stock[2] as percentages of GDP. For real capital investment, data from PWT6.1, *Real Investment as Percentage of GDP,* in current international dollars, is used. This provides an internationally comparable measure of how much capital investment occurred in countries from 1951 to 2000. First, I compare the EAEs and the OECDEs. As Figure 2.1 shows, from 1951 to 1970 the average GDP share for the EAEs was well below that of the OECDEs. The EAEs surpassed the OECDEs' level in the early 1970s, and

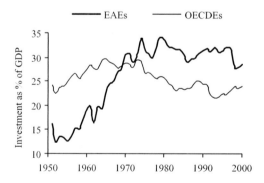

*Figure 2.1* EAEs and OECDEs: real investment as percentage of GDP (1951–2000).

*Source*: Appendix B8.

have maintained that position since. In 1951, the EAEs' real investment share in GDP was 16.14 percent, while that of the OECDEs was 24.12 percent. Over the period, the OECDEs remained roughly at the same level, at 23.91 percent in 2000, while the EAEs' share rose to a peak in 1979 at 34.21 percent. It is clear that the EAEs' overall level of capital investment was much lower than that of the OECDEs in 1951, and throughout the early years of their growth. If one takes into consideration the real size of their GDP then,[3] the actual amount of capital available among the EAEs would be even lower.

Among the EAEs themselves, the picture is clear. The real investment share of GDP for the USA moved around the 20 percent level. While Japan started at the same level as the USA, KOST and China all started at around 10 percent and remained at the low levels in their early years. If 25 percent is a benchmark level – as suggested by the average level of the OECDEs – then conditions within the remaining EAEs were even worse. KOST remained at a level of around 10 percent throughout the 1950s, and only after this did it rapidly pick up (this supports the argument that KOST's rapid growth period started only after the early 1960s). The same case can be made concerning China. It has basically followed a pattern similar to those of the other EAEs, only in different timeframes: low in the 1960s, and then – slowly – moving up.

The pattern becomes even clearer with regard to total physical capital stock, for which the data from WB-PCSD are used. This study looks at the human capital and physical capital stocks as sources of growth from 1950 to 1990 in 1987 constant prices. In the same form of comparison, the gap between the EAEs and the OECDEs in the total physical capital stock (TPCS) share of GDP is equally clear (Figure 2.2). Particularly in 1951, the level of TPCS in the OECDEs (2.13 percent) was about three

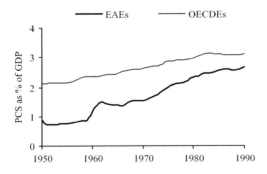

*Figure 2.2* EAEs and OECDEs: total physical capital stock as percentage of GDP (1951–90).

*Source*: Appendix B9.

times that of the EAEs (0.71 percent). This gap became even bigger over the 1950s and 1960s. Only from 1970 did the EAEs start to catch up.

The data examined in the three sub-groups provide further evidence that a serious lack of capital provision within the EAEs existed in the years leading to their rapid growth periods. In 1951, Japan's TPCS was 0.93 percent, about one-third that of the USA (2.59 percent), while KOST had only 0.49 percent, just half of Japan's. KOST reached Japan's 1951 level in 1964 (0.93 percent), a further piece of evidence pointing to the different timings in rapid growth period takeoff. China was unique in the 1960s, when it had a very high level of TPCS throughout. After 1970, it dropped below the level of Japan and the USA. By the early 1980s – when China started its East Asian Growth – its level was the lowest of all compared.

Overall, the data on capital provision confirm, provisions at the start of the EAEs' rapid growth periods, it was substantially low. Only at a later stage did the EAEs surpass the OECDEs in capital provision. Such low levels made it imperative for the EAEs to rely on foreign capital for their initial growth push.

### Employment conditions

The labor factor is measured here in terms of employment pressure. We will look at labor productivity later. The argument is that the EAEs had far greater employment pressures in the years leading to their rapid growth periods. Such pressures provided the initial push for the opportunistic pursuit of industrial expansion and ad hoc forms of production organization in the EAEs. In particular, the global distribution of employment pressure during this period pushed EAE economic activities to concentrate on exports. The data on employment pressure is from the International Labor Organization's six-volume *Economically Active Population 1950–2010* (ILO 1997). The ratio of the total economically active population to the total population, therefore, provides data on both employment and unemployment.

In a comparison of the crude activity rates of the EAEs and the OECDEs (based on raw data on 1950, 1960, 1970, 1980, 1990, and 2000), the two groups do not differ greatly in terms of the overall pattern for the years considered. Among the EAEs themselves, the picture is more complicated. Japan started with the same activity rate (43.8 percent) as that of the USA (42.7 percent). After 20 years of the rapid growth period in the 1950s and 1960s, where Japan recorded a higher activity rate than the USA, it started to drop from the early 1970s. China has recorded a markedly high rate from the very beginning (57.1 percent), while KOST recorded the lowest. The data do not tell us much of interest.

There are two aspects to the problem. The first has to do with the notion of an *economically active population*. Defined in the United Nations systems of national accounts and balances, the "economically active population" comprises "all persons of either sex who furnish the supply of labor for the production of economic goods and services" (ILO 1997, V: x). This broad definition allows those working in such areas as agriculture, or "self-employers" who are considered to be employed – but are not necessarily employed in the real sense, in terms of wages, production, productivity, employment benefits, and, most importantly, in terms of employment pressure – to be taken into account. They are hidden forms of unemployment, and can be unleashed at any time. This was particularly true in the case of the EAEs.

To deal with the problem, I take a further look at the data, considering the sectoral distribution existing in 1950. Because of the unique sectoral structure of Singapore (with little activity in agriculture), it is removed from KOST for this examination. Figure 2.3 shows that much of the "economically active population" of the EAEs was concentrated in the agricultural sector. While the large size of the economically active population in agriculture may indicate the stronger ability of the traditional EAE economic system to absorb unemployment, this quasi-employment hid the reality of *relative unemployment* lurking in the background of subsequent economic growth, which – essentially – was related to the expansion of the industrial sector, as the Lewis–Fei–Ranis model has advised (Lewis 1954; Fei and Ranis 1961). Moreover, such quasi-employment did tend not to be accompanied by the purchasing power normally associated with modern industrial employment, which is necessary for growth. In other words, it limited the capacity of local markets.

In addition to the problem of a concentration in agriculture, there is a second problem that the data deal with – the *relative* size of the economically active population (and, thus, that of the economically inactive population), i.e. a percentage of the total population, rather than actual unemployment pressure in terms of the *absolute* size of the population.

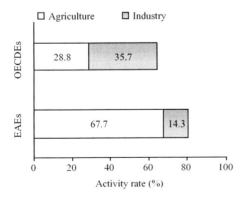

*Figure 2.3* EAEs and OECDEs: economic activity rate by sector (1950).
*Source*: ILO-EAP.

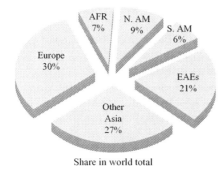

Share in world total

*Figure 2.4* Global distribution of unemployment (1950).
*Source*: ILO-EAP.

I deal with this by introducing a measure of the global distribution of the unemployed population in 1950, based on the ILO data.[4] As Figure 2.4 demonstrates, world unemployment pressure was mainly concentrated in Europe and Asia in 1950. The five EAEs housed almost 21 percent of the world total unemployed labor force, while North America had only 9 percent, Africa 7 percent, and South America 6 percent; an important consideration given the fact that the EAEs' GDP share in the world total – in current international prices in 1960 – was only 10.17 percent.[5] This large pool of unemployed labor is significant, as the rising demands for foreign capital-driven manufacturing would be met well by the abundant low-cost labor supply.

### Market demands

It is logical to expect from the discussions above that weak purchasing power would lead to the lack of consumption demands, and thus very weak domestic markets. We will test this in this section. Levels of total domestic consumption per capita measure the market factor. A further argument is that low levels of consumption in the EAEs motivated them to seek to complete the cycle of production–recapitalization in international markets. This not only solved the problem of finding initial outlets for their unproportionally large scale of production; the consequent profits also provided additional sources of financing, which was often a major problem in encouraging sustainable growth in industrializing economies. To present this larger picture, I will, therefore, not only explore domestic consumption within the EAEs, but also the comparison with that of the OECDEs, and, further, the global distribution of domestic consumption in the early post-war years.

The base data used to measure domestic consumption per capita is from the PWT6.1 dataset. Based on real consumption as share of GDP (cc) and real GDP per capita (CGDP) – both in current international dollars – a new indicator, real consumption per capita in current international dollars, is constructed.[6] As Figure 2.5 demonstrates, in 1951 the OECDEs' average level of real consumption per capita (1,322) was 7.91 times higher than that of the EAEs (167). The individual EAEs' levels – with Japan's being highest, at 330 – were, similarly, much lower than that of the USA (1,484). As another indicator of the staggered takeoffs of the EAEs' rapid growth periods, KOST levels in the early 1960s were similar to Japan's in the 1950s – and China's in the late 1970s – at around 300 in current international dollars. The low level of real consumption in the EAEs suggests a generally low level, both of effective purchasing power and effective market size, in relation to their populations.

Having established that the domestic market was limited in the EAEs, it is important to determine whether, at the same time, markets outside the EAEs – particularly those that would later become key destinations for EAE exports – were significantly larger. This is done via an examination of the world distribution of total real consumption.[7] As shown in Figure 2.6, the two main regions of concentration in real consumption and, therefore, market demand, were North America (N. AM, 35.735 percent of the world total) and Europe (EUR, 32.0 percent), while the EAEs had only 9.68 percent, and the other Asian countries (OAS), 12.7 percent. South America (S. AM) and Africa (AFR) had even less (5.72 percent and 4.12 percent respectively). As a point of historical comparison, this pattern has been sustained through the 1990s, with only the consumption of the EAEs rising. In 1992, the real consumption of the EAEs rose to 16.7 percent of the world total, while North America's dropped to 27.6 percent. The share

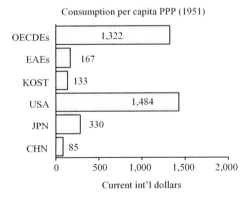

*Figure 2.5* EAEs and OECDEs: real consumption per capita (1951).

*Source*: PWT6.1.

Consumption as % of world total PPP (1951)

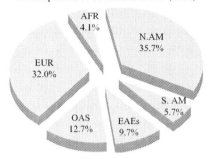

*Figure 2.6* World distribution of real consumption (1950).

*Source*: PWT6.1.

of the other regions remained the same as 40 years earlier. Compared to 1950, North America had lost 7 percent to the EAEs.

The market data shows that global market demands came primarily from North America and Europe, the two main export destinations for the EAEs later on. This, combined with the fact that they were also the main sources of growth financing in the EAEs, would have a decisive structuring effect on the EAEs.

## *Labor productivity*

Finally, let us take a look at labor productivity. The underlying interest here is that a low level of labor productivity would generally mean a low level of competitiveness for the products. As international competitiveness was necessary for the EAEs, other ways of gaining competitiveness must have been effective for them to have achieved the rapid and prolonged export-led growth.

I use the dataset, real GDP per worker at constant international dollars, again from the PWT6.1 (GDPW). The data show that the labor productivity of the EAEs has been constantly and substantially lower than that of the USA, the primary destination of their exports. In 1951, when Japan prepared to take off, its GDPW ($4,492) was only about 17.1 percent of that of the USA ($26,194) and 29.8 percent of that of the OECDEs on average ($15,086). Such a large gap in labor productivity is not easy to close up quickly with improvement in technological efficiency. In fact, this gap has largely maintained itself over much of the last 50 years.

The above finding is further reinforced by a look at the data on investment in labor quality in a key aspect: years of schooling. The dataset from Robert J. Barro and Jong-Wha Lee's study (Barro and Lee 1993) provides an internationally comparable measure of education attainment, which is widely considered to be the best available indicator of "human capital stock."[8] The data on the earliest year, 1960, indicates that the level of education in the EAEs was much lower (3.86) than that of the OECDEs (6.11). It is safe to assume that this gap would be even greater in 1950. This evidence calls into doubt the notion that the EAEs invested more heavily in education than the OECDEs, and therefore had a better endowment of human capital, which presumably led to their rapid economic growth.

In fact, one could argue that the rise of educational levels among the EAEs, over the years, was more a consequence – than a cause – of their economic growth. A look at the variations among the EAEs shows clearly that all of the EAEs have been well below the USA in terms of years of schooling. KOST's level has continually risen since 1960, while China's remained flat until the early 1980s – again, evidence of the differing times of growth takeoff.

Now, what do all these discussions on capital provision, employment conditions, market demands, and labor productivity lead us to? First, the lack of capital provision eliminated the possibility of raising productivity through increasing the stock of capital goods. At the same time, it invited the influx of capital from international sources, which have structured the consequent production toward hard currency-earning industries.

Second, the insufficient employment, particularly in the salary-paying manufacturing sector, allowed employers the abundant availability of labor supply, and thus less incentive to invest for labor efficiency. It also contributed to the lower purchasing power of the general public, and thus the weakness of the domestic market. Our investigation of the global market structure, in terms of the distribution of consumption, confirmed that much of world consumption in the early decades was concentrated in North America and Europe. This, in connection with the structure of capital provision, furthered the necessity to search for international markets for their takeoff economies.

Consequently, international competitiveness became essential for the EAEs to survive and to grow at the rates and scales they have achieved. The competitiveness of an economy, as envisaged in the theory of Total Factor Productivity (TFP), is driven largely by its productivity. But, as has been shown, labor productivity among the EAEs was substantially and constantly low internationally. Thus, there must have been two alternative scenarios for the EAEs: either their subsequent rapid growth would not have been possible as the imperatives for international competitiveness were not satisfied by their low productivity; or some *other ways* of enhancing their competitiveness must have developed in respect to the fact that international competitiveness has been at the core of the EAEs.

## Alternative scenarios

Before we move on to systematically examine these "other ways" that have developed over the decades in the EAEs, let us first look at some of the options that the EAEs might have taken, other than what has actually emerged in the EAEs during their rapid growth periods. These options were indeed a reality in many other countries facing similar growth conditions, and even in many EAEs at some points prior to taking on East Asian Growth. This brief examination should allow us to put into historical context the early responses of the EAEs to their initial conditions, and understand the various growth-driving institutions that have subsequently developed.

### *Import substitution*

Import substitution seems to be almost a natural option for many countries seeking industrialization and rapid growth under initial conditions similar to those experienced by the EAEs (Haggard 1990; Felix 1989; Schive 1990). Stephan Haggard paints a clear picture of how import substitution became – and, for many, remains – a critical phase of economic development. The general idea of import substitution is that the government would implement a coherent set of policies to reduce imports of targeted products, and improve the capacity of national manufacturers to produce the same products domestically. As a response to the initial conditions, a national economy with import substitution would have focused on building a complete system of production and consumption on its own, rather than working on the possibility of combining the capacity to produce at home with market potentials abroad; it would try to solve the capital shortage problem by suppressing consumption at home, rather than generating new capital from abroad.

For the EAEs, import substitution was not a potential option they avoided, but rather one that was experimented with before moving on to their rapid growth. The import substitution phase in Taiwan and Korea, for example, occurred between the end of World War II and the early 1960s – a period that preceded their rapid growth periods (Haggard 1990: 25).

With regard to Japan, a quick look at the import statistics of Japan in the 1950s clearly reveals a pattern of import substitution. Figure 2.7 shows that the share of manufactured products in total imports in the early 1950s declined from 12.41 percent in 1949 to 7.44 percent in 1951, and stayed at about 10 percent until 1955. After 1955, it jumped back rapidly – to above 20 percent in 1957. A broader picture is provided by research conducted by Ryoshin Minami (1986). He calculates the share from 1874 to 1978, and shows that the 1950s was the lowest (Table 2.1).

Before China reoriented its economic program (in the late 1970s) it had a socialist economy, where import substitution was an essential component. Even after the new program was implemented, a brief period of "import substitution" can be observed (Figure 2.8). The share dropped from 65.5 percent in 1980 to 60.2 percent in 1982, and recovered soon after, moving to 80 percent (and above) for the next 10 years. China's larger

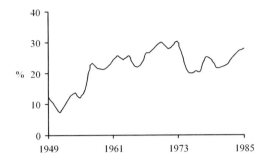

*Figure 2.7* Japan: share of manufactured products in total imports (1949–85).
*Source*: JPN-JSY.

*Table 2.1* Japan: share of manufactured products
in total imports (1874–1978)

| Period | Percentage |
| --- | --- |
| 1874–80 | 92.0 |
| 1881–90 | 83.9 |
| 1891–1900 | 64.2 |
| 1901–10 | 55.0 |
| 1911–20 | 47.3 |
| 1921–30 | 44.1 |
| 1931–9 | 40.8 |
| 1951–60 | 19.9 |
| 1961–70 | 29.5 |
| 1971–8 | 25.5 |

*Source*: Minami (1986: 231).

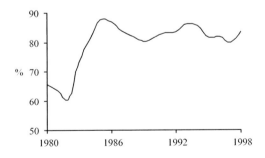

*Figure 2.8* China: share of manufactured products in total imports (1980–98).
*Source*: CHN-CSYB (1999).

domestic supply of raw materials, and its early stage of industrialization, left it with a much higher share of manufactured products in total imports than Japan, but the overall pattern of import substitution (before export-led growth began) is similarly clear.

There are different views on why the EAEs took on import substitution, and both views can shed some light on why they soon moved on to export-led growth. For Haggard, import substitution in Taiwan and Korea, and, perhaps by the same logic, in Japan and China as well, was a response to "external constraints," such as – in the case of KOST – political partition, a loss of major markets, and persistent balance-of-payments problems (Haggard 1990: 51–125). Import substitution, thus, was used to balance "trade at lower rather than higher levels of exports" (Haggard 1990: 98).

The experiences of the EAEs provide evidence to support Haggard's argument, as all of them practiced import substitution more as a "short-term firefight strategy" to address "immediate concerns" (Felix 1989: 1467). The import substitution period, for most of them, was very brief; evidence of the impact of external constraints was strong; and the fact that they moved swiftly out of the practice indicates the temporary and expedient nature of their import substitution experience.

David Felix's study (Felix 1989) reflects a different view on import substitution, particularly its relation to development strategy. For him, import substitution is

> a development strategy by which a technologically backward economy tries to accelerate industrial investment primarily for the home market through heavy reliance on government manipulation of market prices, barriers to entry and access to imports and finance. The intent is to induce investment by improving profit-risk tradeoffs.
>
> (Felix 1989: 1455)

Felix's interpretation differs from that of Haggard on at least two points. First, the forces that led to import substitution in many countries were primarily internal rather than external. Second, import substitution is more of a coherent attempt at industrialization (thus "import substitution industrialization," or ISI), rather than simply an ad hoc response to momentary macro-economic conditions. Import substitution thus tended to occur at an early stage of industrialization.

There is also evidence to support Felix's interpretation. All the EAEs were at the early stage of their industrialization when import substitution occurred. Japan's situation was somehow different. But, with a completely destroyed economy and infrastructure, and a determination to survive and recover, Japan can be seen as an instance of "late" industrialization. As the data above show, sudden drops in manufacturing imports in the EAEs during their import substitution reflected efforts on the part of the government to impose high tariffs upon imported consumer products, in an attempt to make them uncompetitive in the domestic market. On the other hand, the import of raw and semi-manufactured materials was encouraged, to stimulate domestic industrial manufacturing.

The theory that import substitution in the EAEs was a coherent attempt at late industrialization would find some difficulty in explaining the EAEs' swift moving out of import substitution to export-driven growth. There were no obvious signs of the failure of import substitution on growth, except perhaps in China, which would have motivated them to give it up. For the three years from 1950 to 1952, Japan's GDP grew at around 23 percent. Likewise, Korea and Taiwan experienced an average growth rate of 3.82 percent and 6.71 percent respectively for the five years from 1956 to 1960, an import substitution period leading to their rapid growth periods. If it had not failed at what it was intended for as a coherent growth strategy, why was it abandoned? As discussions on the shaping of the individual EAE's responses in the following section will show, external opportunities and demand did have an effect on the shift, but the responses may not be as rationally coherent as many believe. Indeed, while they all responded to a similar set of external conditions, the interplay of the dominant internal forces, particularly the political ones, rather than a coherent rational strategy, may have profoundly shaped the emergent responses (Haggard 1990; Cheng 1990, 1998).

### *Dependent development*

A second possible scenario is what is often referred to as *dependent development* – a phenomenon that was widely observed in Latin America and Africa (Biersteker 1978; Cardoso and Faletto 1979; Evans 1978; Frank 1967) in the 1960s and 1970s, and perhaps beyond. Dependence, according to Peter Evans, is "a situation in which the rate and direction of accumulation are externally conditioned" (1978: 27). Dependent development, therefore, is a theory about the conditions, possibility, and consequences of economic growth under these conditions. While different dependency theories differ on these points (Palma 1978), they all agree that the success or failure of an economy in a dependent country is determined, primarily, by the larger system of economic forces, and the intentions and capacities of those that dominate the system.

In "normal" dependent development, the state is seen as both irrelevant and insignificant, and there tend to be efforts from both sides of the border to make sure this remains the case (Biersteker 1980, 1987). It is the close collaboration between international and local capital that defines the direction and structure of the local economy. As an alternative response to the initial conditions, dependent development would have been a scenario where local capital would have faced fewer constraints in seeking preferential arrangements with international capital and positioning themselves as their local agents.

For many of the EAEs, the prevailing mode of economic operation before World War II (that is, before their brief period of import substitution right after the war) can be considered to be a type of dependent development, where external capital dominated. This was particularly true for KOST. The economies of Korea, Taiwan, and Singapore were a direct part of the economies of their respective ruling colonial powers: Britain and Japan. To some extent, this was also true of Japan and China. In the case of Japan, the Occupation era fundamentally reoriented Japan's economy and tied it firmly to that of the USA, at least before Japan started to take on a more self-assertive economic policy in the 1950s. On the other hand, the first half of the twentieth century saw China almost "dismembered" and placed into the hands of multinational capital. Even in the early post-war years, the Chinese economy was very much dominated by the Soviet Union and operated as part of the socialist world system, before China retreated into extreme economic isolation in the 1960s and 1970s.

This argument could be pushed further. There is an element of dependent development obvious in East Asian Growth after the EAEs' import substitution attempts. Export-led growth relied heavily upon international capital and markets, and upon the functioning of existing international regimes of trade and finance.

But the differences between dependent development and East Asian Growth that emerged in the EAEs are profound. In the EAEs, there is a clear and powerful intermediate layer between international and local capital: the state itself, which dominated local capital, and was able to operate on behalf of local capital in the international economic system. If capital accumulation is found in both forms, it has been driven in East Asian Growth largely by "local" capital, led by the state, in their outgoing search for export expansion elsewhere, much more so than the result of their domestic markets serving as destinations for foreign products. The question is not so much whether there was dependence in the EAEs, but, rather, whether they themselves gained from such dependence, and what mechanisms made it possible.

There are a number of reasons why the EAEs failed to take the path of dependent development. There was a tradition of strong states in the EACs. The state had a wide range of interests encouraging its involvement in directing national economic activity, and, further, possessed the institutional capacities to define the relationship between local and international capital. Moreover, local capital in the EACs, as shown in our discussions of the initial conditions, was generally very weak – hampering its ability to act on its own. The business community very much relied upon the state for survival and recovery in the early years. Much of the foreign capital that came to the EAEs in the early years was official aid, of which the government naturally became the local agent. Finally, events and circumstances in the early years led to a greater international demand for local production, rather than international demand for access to local markets.

### Socialist economy

A third possible scenario was the socialist economy. In the late 1940s and early 1950s almost half of the countries in Europe and Asia aligned themselves with the socialist camp and practiced socialism as a development model, with many others contemplating such a move with great enthusiasm. Unlike the two options discussed above, the socialist model was – first and foremost – part of a grand project of social engineering and institutional reconstruction. Many of the countries that pursued the socialist option (including China, from the 1950s to 1970s), acted according to ideological principle as much as policy necessity.

As a response to the initial conditions, the socialist economy would have focused on building a stand-alone economic system of its own, with no trade with the outside world and no internal market. It would consider the initial conditions as the effects of the long-standing and unfair relations between local and international capital. Therefore, cutting off these relations would be seen as a natural solution. Furthermore, the initial conditions within the country could also be seen as the result of the function of the capitalist market and private ownership. Therefore, eliminating the market and private ownership would be a plausible solution, in the socialist's eyes, to the problems imbedded in the initial conditions. In particular, the socialist model would attempt to solve problems such as lack of capital by taking advantage of the restructured relations between the industrial and agricultural sector.

With a closed national unit, and without the instruments of macro-economic policy that were usually available in a market economy, the form of growth – indeed the form of response to the initial conditions – centered on working against, rather than for, "equilibrium," and on the fight against a "shortage" of resources and products, rather than for their economical use (Kornai 1971, 1980). Socialist economists may have agreed with other economists on the necessity of growth, but they had their own take on the purposes of, and mechanisms for, that growth. At best, these purposes and mechanisms were economically unclear, as the system did not operate upon the bases of profits. Without profits as the driving force, capital accumulation became an ambiguous concept in theory. In reality, it became a process of a mainly political and administrative nature.

This was indeed what China had long experienced before it moved to East Asian Growth. The reasons for China's shift from the socialist model were therefore quite straightforward: the failure of the socialist economy to satisfy the basic economic needs of the people. But, for the other EAEs, it is not so clear. One could argue that many of the elements found in the socialist model were shared in East Asian Growth. The EAEs had a quite substantial portion of the national economy owned or controlled by the state. There was a significant level of central planning administrated by the government for the national economy. There was a significant level of monopoly or control over growth resources. But the East Asian Growth that the EAEs have taken on is qualitatively different from the socialist model. The market and private ownership rest at the core of East Asian Growth, as a primary force for production efficiency and, ultimately, profits.

Besides the fact that their emergent model was fundamentally different, circumstances in the 1950s and 1960s, in each of the EAEs, also positioned them against the very idea of a socialist economy. South Korea had North Korea as its arch-enemy. Taiwan had mainland China. Singapore had communist activities at home and communist China perceived as a threat from abroad. Japan, firmly in the grip of the USA, saw both the Soviet Union and China as the primary security and ideological threat. Even though they had elements in their economies that resembled those in the socialist model, the EAEs were the strongest voices against what they considered their socialist enemies, and the values and economic systems associated with them. The socialist economy was never an option for the EACs.

## Shaping of the responses in the EAEs

There is a widely circulated and, I argue, often false view, that East Asian Growth was the result of the strategic visions of key policy makers combined with careful, comprehensive long-term planning in the EAEs.[9] There are two problems with this popular perception. At the theoretical level, this view assumes the importance of human vision and planning in shaping the direction of economic growth. Those who rely upon this theory to explain failures in economic growth, or to rally support for a new growth agenda, must focus upon the social, cultural, and intellectual qualities of individual policy makers. It is obvious, however, that, if economic growth were only a matter of vision and planning, socialism would probably enjoy a more impressive historical legacy today.

Further, at the empirical level, evidence is not strong enough to support such a theory. We will see, in the discussion that follows, that – instead of beginning with a clear vision and well-planned programs – the EAEs were, generally, muddling through, and taking desperate steps in response to the severe domestic and international conditions of the time. These steps not only solved the immediate problems faced by the EAEs, but also gradually evolved into a set of preferred policy options, and a pattern of growth activity, which required subsequent industrial policy and long-term planning for their sustenance.

### *Japan in the late 1940s and early 1950s*

Let us first look at Japan, to see how ad hoc responses to the immediate problems were transformed into the building blocks of the pattern of growth over the decades that followed. I will concentrate upon three key defining cases: intra-*keiretsu* capitalization, industrial reliance upon oil imports, and export-led growth.

First, how did intra-*keiretsu* capitalization become a primary form of industrial financing? Due to the direct economic controls of the wartime state, the shortage of capital in the early post-war years, and the dominant role of the state in organizing and promoting the national economy, one would, naturally, be led to believe that the government would be the primary financier of rapid growth. In reality, however, the sequence of events led to a markedly different scenario. A shortage of funds prompted the government to develop a series of policies that promoted capital accumulation. As the government itself could not be the primary source of funds, it encouraged industrial enterprises to solve the financing problem themselves, which – over the long term – paved the way for the rise of giant corporate groups, with a financing function built into their cores. These corporate groups, the *keiretsu*, consequently became one of the key operators in Japanese economic growth.

The Japanese economy (in the late 1940s) was a combination of quasi-inflation, low-income underemployment, an oversupply of labor, and government deficit (Nakamura 1981: 21–35). In particular, there was a severe shortage of funds in both government and the private sector (Kosai and Kaminski 1986: 44). This was, perhaps, the combined effect of the ever-present fear of large-sum reparations,[10] the cancellation of indemnity payments to private enterprises, and a prohibition on issuing long-term government bonds in the Financial Act of 1947 (Nakamura 1981: 38). In addition, there was uncertainty regarding the prospect of Japan receiving US aid. In fact, in 1948, the US Congress passed the aid bill, reinforcing suspicions in Tokyo.

On the other hand, in response to the problem of low-income underemployment, serious shortages of energy and food, and inflation, the Emergency Financial Measures Act was passed in 1946, as an attempt to curb inflation. After a brief period of working within the Tanzan vision[11], the Dodge Plan finally placed the government's fiscal policy on a solid, conservative grounding in 1948. It transformed government deficits into surpluses, suspended new loans from the Reconstruction Bank, and reduced and abolished subsidies. The government tightened credit supply, strictly enforced tax collection, and reduced lending (Nakamura 1981: 37–9).

The combined effect of these trends resulted in a tightened supply of funds available from the government, and necessitated that much of the capital formation required for post-war recovery be organized by the private sector itself. As Figure 2.9 shows, the pattern of the share of government and private capital formation in the post-war years differed substantially from the pre-war years. The average ratio of government vs. private sources in total capital formation in the first half of the century was 0.62. In the second half – from 1955 to 1980 – it dropped to 0.38. In 1955, private capital formation was 72.3 percent and government capital formation was

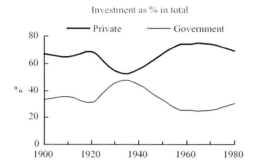

*Figure 2.9* Japan: private and government fixed capital formation (1900–80).
*Source*: Minami (1986: 169).

27.7 percent; while, in 1938, the private was 54 percent, and the government, 46 percent. The private sector must have found a new way of financing themselves. Due to the dissolution of the *zaibatsu* (i.e. family-centered industrial conglomerates before World War II), the lack of funds, and uncertainty surrounding the continued flow of capital from the USA, the bank-centered *keiretsu* emerged as an important and effective form of capital formation. The semi-corporate link between financial institutions and industrial firms at the core of the *keiretsu* was encouraged by the government through its *Tight Money Neutralizing Measure*, as a form of urgent response to the severe financial difficulties faced by firms, worsened by deflationary monetary policy (Nakamura 1981: 39).

The second element of Japan's emergent growth pattern involves the government's use of industrial policy to effect an industrial structure – in this particular case, to engineer a shift in the energy industry from relying on domestically produced coal to using imported oil. Coal used to be the primary energy source for Japan's industrial production. Nakamura observes that, at the end of World War II, Japan's coal production had fallen to 21 million tons, slightly less than 40 percent of what it had been during the war. Considering the amount used by the railroads and the Occupation forces, "hardly any remained for industrial use" (Nakamura 1981: 33). The *priority production system* was established to revive industrial production through "the lever of crude oil." The idea was to use specially authorized oil imports in the steel industry, hopefully reviving the steel industry, which would provide further investment for the coal industry. At the same time, labor problems in coalmines – and hydro-electric power plants – forced industrialists to experiment with crude oil-based energy, forcing an expansion of the fleet of oceangoing ships (Kosai and Kaminski 1986: 84). The response to the high coal price, and falling coal production, in the early 1950s forced the shift in energy sources, and set a precedent for promoting an industrial shift of this kind through government policies. Industrial growth and expansion based on imported oil has become a distinctive feature of Japan's post-war growth, while government industrial policy promoting a particular industrial agenda has become a defining element of its growth methods.

Finally, we must consider the rise of export concentration as a core element of Japan's post-war rapid growth. While export-led growth has been widely recognized among the EAEs, there is a need to explain the circumstances for the beginnings of the drive to export, particularly in the case of Japan, as the originator of the phenomenon. These circumstances, which tend to be viewed as trivial as they did not feature in the subsequent unfolding of the pattern of export promotion through government policies, were the initial push to the chain reaction leading to the shaping of the pattern of export concentration. The Korean War, in relation to Japan's export-led growth pattern, is such a case in point. In 1950, the Korean War started, and, in 1952, world exports increased around 30 percent – but Japan's exports jumped more than 60 percent.

What is important is not just the initial push for exports, but how momentum was sustained and transformed – primarily through the government's response – into a dominant feature of Japan's post-war growth. Nakamura (1981) explains the impact of the Korean War upon the Japanese economy and its post-war growth pattern. First, there was the market factor. At a time when domestic purchasing power was severely weakened, and productive capacities underutilized, the war in Korea gave the Japanese economy much-needed capital input and market demand. Second, there was the chain reaction among growth factors. The Korean War also caused the appreciation of the US dollar that, in turn, raised the unit price of exports from Japan. Japan's exports, according to Nakamura, "jumped in response to the rise in international prices, and along with them production, employment, and business profits all rose rapidly as the economy surged forward into a boom" (1981: 41). Third, there was the vast amount of foreign exchange income from the expenditures of US military personnel. The balance-of-payments problem, which would occur with the increased import of raw materials associated with an increase in the export of manufactured products, was offset by this extra foreign currency income. The combination of export growth and a higher ceiling on the balance of payments not only helped the expansion of trade, but also made possible the overall growth of the economy (1981: 41–8).

With the drastic rise in exports between 1950 and 1952, Japan could not maintain them at the same level in the years that followed. In 1952 its exports dropped by 6.1 percent. From high export growth in the early 1950s, how to keep exports rolling became a government priority. From 1951 onwards, a series of efforts by the government to promote production in export-oriented industries was put in action. These included the establishment of the Japan Development Bank to "supply the key industries with low-interest funds for plant and equipment"; the establishment of the Japan Export-Import Bank to "promote exports with financing to export firms"; a progressive corporate tax system with "particular emphasis on special tax measures for the promotion of plant and equipment investment and exports"; reform of the foreign exchange allocation system; and the passing of the Foreign Capital Law and the Foreign Exchange Administration Order to restrict unwanted imports, but encourage imports of foreign technology on a large scale. All these, according to Nakamura, became the "the prototype for Japan's post-war industrial policies" (Nakamura 1981: 43).

The cases discussed above suggest that there was a chain of events that led to a series of reactions, by government and corporations alike, that snowballed into a pattern of growth and a set of growth methods in the post-war Japanese economy. Whether concerning imported oil dependency, exports concentration, corporate structure, or proactive government practices, one can see the seeds of these developments in the late 1940s and early 1950s. Some of these developments, such as export subsidies, were just a matter of the restoration of practices interrupted by the war; others, such as the *keiretsu*, were reformed arrangements necessitated by new conditions, such as the US Occupation; and still others, for example export-led growth, were largely new developments. It was the transformative power of these early post-war conditions (both inside and outside Japan) which motivated the government, corporations, and individuals to respond in a particular way, and which – in turn – worked to reinforce these structures and conditions.

### Korea, Singapore, and Taiwan in the 1950s and early 1960s

There were unique factors present in Korea, Singapore, and Taiwan (KOST), related mainly to their reconstruction as separate political entities and growth units, and the civil conflicts and political tensions associated with this. These factors were significant enough to cause variations in the working of East Asian Growth in these "second wave" EAEs. Most significant – in terms of the response to the initial conditions – was the fact that East Asian Growth did not take place until the early 1960s in Korea and Taiwan, and the mid-1960s in Singapore.

While the political factor complicated the timings of KOST's takeoff, the rapid growth that subsequently developed in KOST followed a pattern similar to that set by Japan earlier, which saw the use of innovative government policies to reshape the organization of production and distribution, and re-rationalize industrial restructuring, to solve the problems associated with the unique distribution of growth factors in the initial conditions. Here, we will look at some unique factors that helped to shape the initial responses of KOST and their subsequent forms of rapid growth.

The first factor is *the political setting and the onset of East Asian Growth.* Unlike Japan, Korea, Singapore, and Taiwan had no earlier opportunity to respond to the initial conditions and move quickly to economic recovery and takeoff. In Taiwan, the civil war between the Nationalists and the Communists occupied much of the latter part of the 1940s. The initial resurgence in GDP growth after the Nationalists moved to the island in 1949 suggests both that the Nationalists brought substantial economic activity to the island, and that the sudden increase in population (and public and private expenditure) prompted an increase in production in the early 1950s. Therefore, much of the high rate of growth in the 1950s was due to this relocation adjustment. Moreover, this growth was very much along the lines of import substitution, as discussed earlier. Toward the end of 1950s, this growth regime could no longer be sustained, and the rate of growth began to fall, to around 5 percent. The need for a change of direction then became apparent.

At the same time, military tensions across the Taiwan Strait persisted throughout the 1950s, climaxing in the Jinmen and Mazhu crisis in 1958. Intensive preparations by the Nationalists for military recovery of the main-land occupied much of the government's agenda. It was only after the 1958 offshore clashes that the attitude of the USA became clear: Chiang's government in Taipei would not be able to count on US military support in its ambitions to recover the mainland. Taipei then started to focus its attention upon the economy, contemplating the possibility that its "temporary stay" on the island might have to be permanent.

The environment for Korea was even harder. As in China, the ending of World War II ushered in civil conflict between the communists and the republicans over the control of the government. The war ended with the major powers ready to divide the peninsula into North and South. But the civil war never ended. The Korean War (from 1951 to 1953) not only made a national focus upon economic recovery impossible, but also the devastation inflicted upon the Korean people – and the productive infrastructure – meant that Korea took much longer to recover.

The process of the emergence of Singapore as a separate political entity and growth unit was no less dramatic than that experienced in Korea and Taiwan. Like its northern counterparts, Singapore had long been a colonial possession. Toward the end of its relation with colonial Britain, however, the Singaporean position became ambiguous. It obtained self-governance in relation to the Crown. At the same time, Singapore tried to fashion a long-term relationship with Malaya. Singapore's historical role as an entrepôt for the greater Malay hinterland, and its staple economy, put great pressure upon Singapore to remain within the greater Malay economy. However, political differences and ethnic problems made its integration into the Malay Union difficult. After several years within the Union, in 1965 Singapore was finally forced to survive on its own. Consequently, it was only in the mid-1960s that Singapore was able to pursue an economic agenda for itself. Moreover, this new political and economic reality forced Singapore to redirect its economy, and take unusual measures to promote a separate economic basis for the new republic.

The second factor is *the rise of an economic decision-making structure.* The problem of political/national security in these three cases created a sense of solidarity among fellow countrymen. In Korea and Taiwan, continuing security threats reinforced the wartime system of management aimed at economic recovery and further growth. In Singapore, labor unrest, communist rebellions, and problems with Malaysia and Indonesia, and later with Great Britain withdrawing its military presence in Singapore, added to the immediate economic hardship.

In all cases, maintenance of a political order – dictated by the Cold War realities – became a shared priority for the ruling political party and US-led international interests. In Taiwan, suppressive actions by the government, particularly against local indigenous elites, as well as the re-establishment of the military–party–state apparatus on the island, removed any chance for political opposition to emerge. The government suspended the constitution and introduced the notorious Temporary Provisions that severely curtailed civil liberties. In Korea, following the apparent inability of a corrupt government to maintain political order and produce stable economic growth, a military coup was launched in 1961; soon Korean society was placed firmly under the control of an authoritarian regime. Similar trends were also observed with regard to Singapore. Targeted mainly against political oppositions (particularly those of Chinese communist background), an aggressive state – dominated by the ruling People's Action Party – was established, with a wide range of institutional tools (including the Internal Security Act) to ensure the survival of the political order.

Under the authoritarian regime, there was also the rise of a powerful core economic decision-making structure in the government. As soon as Park Chung Hee took power in 1961, he established the Economic Planning Board, reporting directly to him and charged with responsibility for all major aspects of economic planning and operations. Similarly, there was the Economic Development Board in Singapore, and the Council for Economic Planning and Development (under different names over the years) in Taiwan. These economic decision-making bodies were vested with a wide range of powers and proved to be the core planners, coordinators, and decision makers of national growth activity.

The third factor concerns *growth financing.* The conflicts – and lingering political tensions – in which Korea, Singapore, and Taiwan found themselves in the 1950s and early 1960s, prevented these countries from taking on economic recovery and growth in a serious manner, and, further, created a general environment which encouraged a wartime style of organization and management by their governments – one that also demanded sacrifice and submission from their populations. More importantly, it had a great impact upon the way recovery – and subsequent rapid economic growth – took place. A key element of that impact was the critical role of foreign capital, particularly in the early years, in the form of foreign aid from the USA. American military and economic aid was a primary source of growth financing for Korea and Taiwan. In the case of Taiwan, as shown in Table 2.2, US economic and military aid amounted to US$3,447 million for the period from 1949 to 1962. Around the same period, from 1951 to 1962, Taiwan's total fixed capital formation was US$2,061 million; total government current expenditure, US$2,598 million; and total government development expenditure, US$555.4 million. Considering that key enterprises were at this time either owned or controlled by the government, and investment by government enterprises accounted for 54 percent of the total fixed investment in 1955–60 (Ho 1978: 235), there is reason to believe that US aid formed a substantial part of the capital formation, through government current and development expenditure.

In the case of Korea, data from the IMF shows that, from 1953 to 1962, average annual government financing from foreign aid was US$849 million, and, for the same period, government expenditure was US$1,049 million, while gross fixed capital formation was US$777 million. As Figure 2.10 indicates, financing from foreign aid increased dramatically in the second half of the 1950s, providing a substantial portion of government expenditure and gross fixed capital formation. Ungson *et al.* estimated that 70 percent of all reconstruction projects from 1954 to 1959 were financed by other countries, notably the USA (1997: 47).

The critical role that foreign capital – in these two cases, US aid – played in government finance, and ultimately in the inflows of capital to the economy, had considerable impact upon the economic and military survival of the two countries in the 1950s, and, more importantly, upon the way subsequent economic growth was achieved. It provided the initial "jump-start" capital that is often most lacking in a developing economy. It helped

*Table 2.2* Taiwan: US aid and growth financing (1949–62)

|  | *1949–52* | *1953–7* | *1958–62* | *1949–62* |
|---|---|---|---|---|
| TEA | 467.8 | 529.5 | 502.3 | 1,499.6 |
| TMA | 48.0 | 1,178.9 | 720.4 | 1,947.3 |
| Total | 515.8 | 1,708.4 | 1,222.7 | 3,446.9 |
| *Year* | *1951–2* | *1953–7* | *1958–62* | *1951–62* |
| TFCF | 189.0 | 651.0 | 1,221.0 | 2,061.0 |
| GCE | 297.0 | 860.0 | 1,440.0 | 2,598.0 |
| GDE | 38.0 | 184.9 | 332.5 | 555.4 |

*Notes*: TEA: total economic aid; TMA: total military aid TFCF: total fixed cap. formation; GCE: gov. current expenditure; GDE: gov. development expenditure (all in US$ millions).

*Source*: Ho (1978: 110, 287–8).

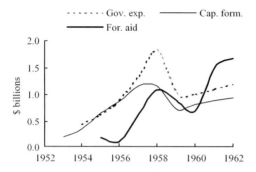

*Figure 2.10* Korea: foreign aid and growth financing (1953–62).
*Source*: IMF-IFS (1979: 265).

to forge a close relationship between government and the business community. The government had at its disposal an unusual tool to bring private industrial activities into line. Further, the private sector developed a tendency to depend upon government for industrial support and direction. The reliance of corporate financing on foreign capital, through government control and manipulation, had a great impact upon industrial structure and corporate culture, particularly in the case of Korea.

The capital situation in Singapore in the 1960s differed from Korea and Taiwan, and helped shape a different kind of model of growth financing, with the domination of foreign direct investment as a key feature. There was no foreign aid, as seen in Korea and Taiwan. Instead, in 1968, Britain decided to reduce its military presence in Southeast Asia and, at the same time, because of its balance of payments problem, imposed (in 1964) a 15 percent "special import charge" on all manufactured goods (Youngson 1982: 25). This reduced the level of military payments that Singapore received from London, and forced Singapore to spend much-needed resources on defense. It also increased the cost of Singapore's export to its traditional markets in Europe.

However, capital formation in new pioneer firms in Singapore actually "jumped" in the 1960s, according to Lim Chong Yah and Ow Chwee Huay, due not so much to contributions from local capital, but from foreign capital – from $8.6 million in 1962 to $84.4 million in 1966, and then to $252.8 million in mid-1969. The share of foreign capital shows an increase between 1966 and 1969 – from 31 percent to 43 percent. And from 1962 to 1969, net private long-term capital inflow in Singapore's balance of payments increased from $24 million to $145 million (Lim and Ow 1971: 22). There were various reasons for the increase of foreign direct investment in Singapore. As Lim and Ow (1971) have noted, it had much to do with the strategic location of Singapore, and the decision by many global manufacturers – particularly those in the petroleum industry – to shift to local manufacturing in Singapore, to reduce the increasingly high costs of transportation and real, or feared, protectionist measures. However, once foreign capital inflows appeared, they became a positive mechanism in solving the shortage of funds – and the balance of payments problems – faced by Singapore in its formative years.

The fourth factor concerns *exports concentration*. The fact that Taiwan and Korea could not begin focused on growth until roughly a decade later than Japan created a set of unique conditions for these countries that shaped their growth structure and direction. Japan was the primary destination for Taiwanese exports until the late 1960s (Figure 2.11). Taiwan's exports to Japan in the early post-war period stood at around 30 percent of its total. This figure rose sharply in the late 1950s and early 1960s, apparently driven by the early export surge – and subsequent growth boom – experienced in Japan.

The fact that both Taiwan and Korea's exports concentrated upon Japan in the early years of their growth cycles suggests several things. First, in what was later called the "flying geese" phenomenon,[12] or "progressive vacating" (Chowdhury and Islam 1993), the spillover effects of growth among the EAEs was clear. Taiwan and Korea provided early-phase products and materials to support Japan's rapidly growing industrial production and exports. A natural division of labor was formed. The incorporation of Taiwan and Korea into this cross-border production process was made necessary – as well as possible – by, first, their shared colonial connection to Japan; second, the nature of Japan's economy, in terms of size and potential; third, their geographical proximity to Japan; and, fourth, perhaps most significantly, the importance of Japan's established market access and networks, which helped Taiwan and Korea break into markets in North America and Europe. The volume of their exports to North America

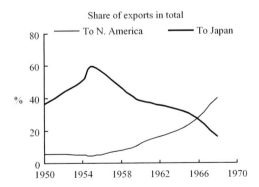

*Figure 2.11* Taiwan: exports destinations (1950–68).
*Source*: Ho (1978: 392).

surpassed those to Japan in the late 1960s, clearly confirming the manner in which a peripheral economy enters into an established economic system. This same entry facilitation was found to exist, later, between Hong Kong/Taiwan, and China in the 1980s.

Such targeted export-led growth also had a lasting impact upon the nature of the economies that took form over the years. While there is evidence of efforts, by the governments in question, in the encouragement of strategic planning and export promotion, one may certainly argue that this planning and industrial policy was part of the growth momentum built upon the unique set of conditions experienced, and of the success of their initial responses.

The conditions in Singapore meant that the need for a new, outward-looking economy was more pressing. A key to the survival of Singapore, as a viable economy, was to locate substitute markets to replace those over which it no longer held advantage, due to changing economic relations with Malaysia, Indonesia, and Great Britain. This "market problem" was initially offset by gaining access to new regional markets associated with the wars in Korea and Vietnam.

Market substitution and diversification was not a long-term solution to Singapore's fundamental economic problem. A more "Singaporean approach," for economic survival and sustainable growth, was to transform Singapore into some form of international operational hub, different to the traditional entrepôt or staple economy Singapore had earlier operated (Huff 1994), and also different to the export-driven economy found in its fellow EAEs in Northeast Asia. Singapore had been an entrepôt economy, where the transactional benefits from their entrepôt role had been sufficient to support a population of their size. After the problems with Malaysia and Indonesia in the 1960s, Singapore found itself in the position of an economy based primarily upon re-exports which had suddenly lost its – necessary – hinterland basis. It needed to develop a manufacturing basis of its own, in order to achieve stable economic growth. Budget difficulties and capital shortage in the mid-1960s motivated the government to focus upon attracting foreign capital as a way of solving the growth problem. Gradually, with the increase of foreign direct investment – and the use of Singapore as an operational hub for regional production and distribution by multinational corporations – Singapore's *transitory* economy began to take shape. This transitory economy still maintained certain elements of the old entrepôt economy. However, the direction of trade differed fundamentally from the earlier model. The focus turned, increasingly, toward overseas inflows and outflows. Further, unlike the other EAEs, Singapore had much smaller indigenous industrial and manufacturing bases. As such, many of the exports and imports were, in fact, logical parts of the transitory production and distribution carried out by the multinational corporations themselves. It required far less effort, on the part of the Singapore government, to "promote" exports – a practice seen as critical in the other EAEs.

### China in the late 1970s and early 1980s

Among the EAEs, the Chinese case is unique – not so much in terms of the form of growth that was eventually adopted but, rather, with regard to the time frame in which it finally came to terms with such a form of growth. Despite this, the Chinese experience provides additional evidence for the argument that East Asian Growth has been the product of the painstaking readjustment of the EAEs in response to the initial conditions encountered, in the search for survival. The series of actions – and reactions – in the early years of their growth experience gradually grew into a pattern of growth activity that provided the logic for subsequent actions, plans, policies, visions, habits, and attitudes, for government, corporations, and individuals alike.

China did not start its East Asian Growth experience until 30 years after Japan's post-war takeoff. The growth rate trend, in the years surrounding the start of East Asian Growth in the late 1970s and early 1980s shows a picture similar to that of KOST in the late 1950s and early 1960s, and of Japan in the late 1940s and early 1950s: the years leading up to East Asian Growth saw a rate of around 5 percent, while in the years of East Asian Growth, it moved to above 8 percent.

The conditions facing China in the late 1970s, however, were not greatly different – and were perhaps worse – than those experienced in the other EAEs in the takeoff years. Among other things, these conditions constituted what can be called "pre-East Asian Growth syndrome," in which China responded in a similar way to the other EAEs earlier. Underlying this syndrome was typical of the development predicament, where a lack of capital suppressed production. Weak production limited income growth. Low income led to weak purchasing power. The shrinking market, in turn, further reduced demand for production.

Similar to the external stimuli facing Japan, Korea, and Taiwan in the 1950s and 1960s, an international element also contributed to the conditions facing China in the late 1970s. This element not only shaped China's export-led growth, as it had with the other EAEs earlier, but also further strengthened the regional dynamism of East Asian Growth. When China finally came out of its political turmoil in the late 1970s, it found that its economy was near collapse, and that surrounding it were the earlier EAEs – Japan, Korea, Singapore, and Taiwan – all with considerably high rates of growth, levels of productivity, and living conditions, and with an availability of abundant capital and products, that looked toward the awakening hinterland giant. The data based on PWT6.1 shows that the gap was significant between China and the other EAEs in 1980, in the overall level of economic development in general and productivity in particular. China's GDP per capita in international dollars was $617 in 1980, while Japan and Singapore were in the range of $6,000–9,000, Taiwan and Korea were at $2,000–4,000, with the USA at $12,170. As for labor productivity, China's GDP per worker in international dollars was 1,946 in 1980, while Japan and Singapore were in the range of $24,000–26,000, Taiwan and Korea were at $12,000–15,000, with the USA at $44,217. For China, these earlier EAEs were not only a source of capital, products, technology, and market access, but also a model of growth management and promotion.

Aspects of the emergent form of growth in China as a response to these initial conditions in the late 1970s resembled closely those found in its predecessors in East Asian Growth. Like them, and perhaps more so because of China's statist tradition, the government continued to see itself as the chief organizer of the national economy, though serving a somewhat different purpose considering the more complicated policy environment. A similar range of policy instruments – such as government subsidies, disciplinary powers, monopoly of growth resources, and a powerful economic policy decision-making core structure – were very much part of the existing system they wanted to move away from, except that they were more aggressive, coercive, and arbitrary than those of its fellow EAEs.

In terms of growth financing, the luring of foreign capital was a key aspect of the government's response to the problem of a lack of growth capital. Unlike its East Asian Growth predecessors in the early years, China's foreign capital came in the form of loans from both international financial institutions and direct private investment in the early years of rapid growth, and then became dominated by direct private investment (Figure 2.12).

Foreign capital played a vital role in the jump-starting of China's rapid growth. As shown in Figure 2.13 (data on 1983 is for the period from 1979 to 1983), foreign capital as a percentage in government total expenditure rose quickly from 4.2 percent in the early years of the rapid growth

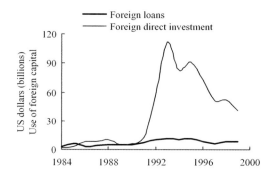

*Figure 2.12* China: composition of foreign capital (1984–99).
*Source*: CHN-CSYB (2000).

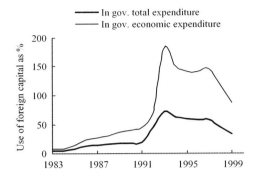

*Figure 2.13* China: actual use of foreign capital as percentage in government
financing (1983–99).

*Source*: CHN-CSYB (2000).

period to 29 percent in 1992, and reached 72.3 percent, the highest level, in 1993. More specifically, foreign capital as a percentage of the government's spending on economic affairs rose from 7.3 percent in the early years, to 183 percent in 1993. For an economy where capital formation was traditionally provided by the government, and the government's heavy involvement in economic activities required extra resources, an influx of foreign capital at such a scale was critical.

With regard to export concentration, that the initial and subsequent rapid growth has ridden on the rapid expansion of exports was undisputable in the case of China. Growth in total exports was almost flat until the end of the 1970s, when China started to take steps in moving toward East Asian Growth. For 30 years, from 1950 to 1978, exports grew from US$0.6 billion to 10 billion. For the next ten years, from 1979 to 1988, it changed from 13.6 billion to 47.5 billion. As an indication of the importance of exports for its new growth model, exports as a percentage of total GDP had been resting at about 4 percent for the 30 years from 1951 to 1980. It then rapidly climbed to 10 percent in ten years from 1980, and to 20 percent for another ten years.

Despite the government's initial reluctance in appreciating the value of East Asian Growth – particularly the fact that it had been successful in Taiwan, South Korea, and Hong Kong – the pattern of growth activity that emerged in China over the past 20 years has reflected the intricacies of East Asian Growth more than that of any other EAEs. Into the 1990s, with various external challenges and internal difficulties facing many of the EAEs, China stood out as a major economy that still squarely practiced those golden rules of East Asian Growth.

## Summary and discussion

The initial conditions faced by the EAEs, both at home and abroad, around the time of the takeoff of their rapid growth periods saw the severe lack of capital needed for the jump-start, and sustainable growth, of the economy and the influx of foreign capital in various forms; the lack of purchasing power in the domestic market, but high demand from international markets for domestic products; and international non-competitiveness of the national economy on all the factors of production except labor costs, but the willingness on the part of the government, business community, and the general public to do whatever it would take to survive and catch up economically.

There were several possible scenarios in which the EAEs might have responded to these initial conditions in a way different from what they actually did. I have argued that, for each of the EAEs, a set of reasons existed as to why they didn't take the other options, or, more precisely, why their responses didn't follow the other paths. There was a sense of muddling through or expediency for the parties involved in the initial efforts. But the fact that the EAEs' responses resembled each other regarding essential aspects of the form of their growth, and that there was a similar pattern of growth over the decades, one after another, forces us to take a deeper look at the underlying logic of their responses, and what impact it has had on subsequent growth activities and on the shaping of the growth form itself.

The key to understanding the underlying logic of their responses is to see how these responses solved the critical problems embedded in the initial conditions in terms of capital, labor, market, and productivity, and how they consequently generated a positive growth process in which these factors were able to complement each other. At the core of the initial conditions was the availability of growth capital, a competitive labor supply, and potential market demands on different sides of the national borders. To allow these factors to achieve their natural combination would likely lead to a dependency development solution. To keep these factors separate would likely lead to a socialist solution. What the EAEs did was to incorporate these factors into their growth system with proactive management of cross-border transactions and the restructuring of domestic production, distribution, and exchange, so that over time each of these factors became a positive input in their growth cycles.

Foreign capital is the first factor found to be strong among all the EAEs. Use of foreign capital was necessary for the EAEs to fill the gap in growth financing, and jump-started the growth process. But the second factor – export concentration – is equally, if not more, important, as it provided the mechanism for earning hard currency that offset the foreign capital influx and satisfied the continual need for growth financing in the long run. More importantly for East Asian Growth, exports connected market and production separated by national boundaries into a single growth process, and thus created market outlets for products and allowed capital accumulation. Thus, the EAEs' responses solved the problems of capital shortage, labor oversupply, and underdevelopment of domestic markets, by taking advantage of growth factors, both inside and outside the national system.

Taking advantage of growth factors across national borders, however, required a significant reorganization of production, distribution, and exchange within the country. I have argued that East Asian Growth was uniquely driven by the need for international competitiveness because of the separation of production and markets. It was this reorganization – centered on enhancing international competitiveness – that dealt with the problem of relatively low productivity in the EAEs, and provided a unique basis for sustained competitiveness and growth.

# 3 Striving for sustainable international competitiveness

The initial conditions and responses discussed above marked the beginning of the EAEs' growth experiences. The growth form that emerged from these early responses bore the effects of the growth imperatives. Subsequently, mechanisms of institutional enhancement, e.g. the core economic decision-making structure, the dual market, corporate grouping, labor subordination, new entrepreneurship, etc., were developed, reinforced, or preferred as part of the national campaign to sustain and enhance the emergent growth form. To understand the internal logic that exists among these mechanisms, and how they related functionally to the overall growth pattern driven by the growth imperatives, we must further explore both the fundamental nature of these growth imperatives and why they called for institutionally enhanced competitiveness as the primary source of growth.

## The problem of international competitiveness

There are two critical "coordination mechanisms" (Naughton 1996: 8) at the core of the emergent growth form: *international competitiveness* and *comparative advantage*. Let us deal with international competitiveness first. External demands for products (export concentration) and external sources of growth financing (reliance on foreign capital) can lead national economies in different directions. Foreign capital and export concentration in the pre-World War II colonial economies, for example, fostered a narrow and vertical economic relation with the "parent" country. A colonial economy, however prosperous in a historical context, is structured to be supplementary to the parent country's economy. Growth driven by external demands and capital does not necessarily yield growth in wealth for the colony, as the capital operating, and products produced, in the colonial economy are, more or less, owned by the parent country. What is missing in the colonial economic system is a clear and enforceable line between the colony and the parent country, in terms of the right to property and profit. The competitiveness of the colonial economy, because of its low costs in labor and materials, is not *international*, but rather *domestic*, in that the colonial economy is only a part – or an extension – of the parent economy.

The initial conditions faced by the EAEs determined, however, that their competitiveness has to be international because their products are capitalized in international markets that are not part of their economies. Moreover, the competitiveness is that of the products of the economy as a whole, more so than the products of each individual corporation. As explained earlier, the initial conditions – among other things – necessitated the expansion of exports in international markets, which in turn led to pressures for the reorganization of production, exchange, and distribution at home, and, further, for significant social change and cultural adaptation in support of international competitiveness. Because of the initial distribution of the growth factors in the EAEs, the main directions of the flow of capital and products, and the limited means available for the improvement of competitiveness, the forming of the unit of competition at the national level became not only necessary but also possible. The promotion of international competitiveness, thus, is more than a project of technological efficiency. It becomes "a social process" (Bienefeld 1980: 28). It requires adjustment in a wide range of relations that have effects on the costs of production, exchange, and distribution, and ultimately on the competitiveness of national products: relations within individual corporations and among them – those in the business community and those between the state and the business community, and those of an economic nature and those of a social, political, and cultural nature.

Why was international competitiveness able to be achieved in the EAEs, and how did their efforts for competitiveness differ from those in non-EAEs? To answer these questions, we, perhaps, need to borrow another concept from Bienefeld 's theory of national development within the international context. Bienefeld argues that there is a deeply contradictory element in the competitive economy, which "makes the maximization of consumption its raison d'être, while at the same time transforming it into a cost in production, which the logic of the system forces each producer to minimize" (1980: 28). In a conventional market economy, this contradiction is solved (and, therefore, a level of competitiveness is achieved), through an improvement in efficiency as a result of the better use of resources, organization, and technology.

In the EAEs, as found in early discussions of the initial conditions, this contradiction was worked out in a significantly different way. While Bienefeld is more interested in the role of the separation of domestic and international markets, and thus the development of domestic market, the EAEs' market separation was aimed more at their expansion in international markets. Indeed, the very working of East Asian Growth eliminated this contradiction from the economy. The principle of international competitiveness could be successful, ideally, in the kind of conditions that faced the EAEs in their formative years. The fact that markets were mainly located outside the country (a situation prevalent in the EAEs' initial conditions) meant that the economy did not require domestic consumption, and, therefore, no significantly higher costs were passed on to production. In other words, the maximization of consumption and low production costs could happen at the same time *for*, rather than *within*, the economy. Without the normal tensions between consumption maximization and production costs, sustained growth became possible.

The consequences, however, were, first, often the underdevelopment of consumption within an EAE (at least in its early stages); and, second, a separation of the domestic market and the international market, with the control and management of transactions between the two. These aspects – along with rapid growth – have been part of East Asian Growth. "In this sense," Bienefeld suggests, "the competitive system comes close to incorporating that apparent 'absurdity' of mercantilist thought which saw the prosperity of the nation achieved through the poverty of its inhabitants" (Bienefeld 1980: 28); and a significant organization of the national economy with strong central management, coordination, and long-term planning.

The principle of international competitiveness explains the unique foundation of the competitiveness of the EAEs, and provides a critical link between the initial conditions and their subsequent growth form. It gives insight as to why the EAEs – with severely limited access to resources, and limited abilities in capital mobilization and technological differentiation – have excelled in staying competitive in international markets.

However, there are further limits to competitiveness concerning individual products. One can only stay competitive on the basis of particular products for a particular period of time, and in a particular market. How did the EAEs manage to stay competitive over such a long period and with generations of products? The discussion in the second "coordination mechanism" will explain that.

## The problem of comparative advantage

Growth driven by external demands and capital can also be found in *dependent* economies in the post-World War II era – in the sense of the word as used by Fernando H. Cardoso (Cardoso and Faletto 1979). A dependent economy shares much of what was embedded in the colonial economy, in that the division of property and profits is still not effective – much less enforceable – even with the achievement of state sovereignty by these, mostly former colonial, countries. What is new, in a dependent economy, is that the local economy has a far broader range of interactions with international capital. Even though they are still related to multinational capital (at low levels of production and supply), they do have more leverage than the colonial economy in defining their economic relations with international capital.

However, in the dependent economy, a great deal of economic activity undertaken focuses upon gaining profit via an *absolute advantage.* Absolute advantage allows an economy or a corporation to become competitive over certain particular products because of its relatively lower costs of labor, capital, and/or land, in their broad sense as defined in Total Factor Productivity. Competitiveness based on absolute advantage, however, cannot provide a solid foundation for sustainable economic growth, unless some unique condition is present (such as the exclusive possession of huge petroleum reserves). The function of the market economy will force up the cost of labor, capital, and/or land over time, and other competitors with the same cost levels would have an equal opportunity to share, and eventually reduce, the profit margins on the same products.

*Comparative advantage*, upon which East Asian Growth triumphed, is different. It enables an economy or a corporation to be competitive in particular products because of the growth planning and execution on the basis of the *opportunity costs* of alternative products and markets. To pursue comparative advantage, one has to constantly research, identify, and promote new *strategic products*, ones that are to become the core basis for the future competitiveness of the economy, when the economy appears to lose its competitiveness in existing products. The idea of strategic planning and promotion on the basis of opportunity cost is that, if you do not plan, invest in, and promote new strategic products well in advance (which itself incurs considerable costs), the inevitable result, in which you will no longer be competitive when the current competitiveness diminishes, and the subsequent end to economic growth, would be much more costly.

As comparative advantage is concerned primarily with the long-term prospects of the competitiveness of an economy and preservation of economic advantage must involve public goods, the dependent economy lacks proper entities, at both the national and corporate levels, to be concerned with such long-term prospects and able to provide such public goods. Like the dependent economy, the EAEs started their rapid growth period based on their absolute advantage – mainly their low-cost labor and land. What distinguished them from other late-developing economies is that the challenge to seek new strategic products for their continual competitiveness soon became paramount, because of the rise in labor and land costs within the country and competition from their fellow EAEs.

Japan in the 1960s, for example, was able to continue to produce labor-intensive products "cheaper" than the USA, but, at the same time, it was far more costly for it to enter into competition with the USA in the emergent semi-conductor industry. The principle of absolute advantage would urge that Japan continue to focus solely on labor-intensive products until the marginal profit runs out. What Japan did, pursuant to the principle of comparative advantage, was quite different. What mattered, instead, was the range of opportunities open to Japan, and the varied opportunity costs associated with them. Anticipating the loss of competitiveness in labor-intensive industries, due to a tight labor market and rising wages, Japan was encouraged to move into the auto-manufacturing industry, the semi-conductor industry, and the chemical and heavy machinery industries. Here, the initial costs in research and development, jump-start investment, and market entry with new strategic products ensured the continual competitiveness of Japan's economy after its "good days" of labor-intensive manufacturing in the 1950s and 1960s.

This was also true with Korea's efforts to build its petrochemical and shipbuilding industries in the 1970s and Taiwan's campaign to develop its semi-conductor industry in the 1980s, well before China embarked on competing with them on cheaper-labor products in the 1980s. Singapore has been constantly moving itself as well – from an entrepôt economy, to a service economy, and to a global hub economy. Indeed, these shifts have become regular exercises for the EAEs, toward the end of their intensive expansion and growth based on a generation of products.

What is more critical for East Asian Growth, however, is that the institutional setting in the EAEs that took shape over the years, in response to the growth imperatives, enabled them to meet the challenge of securing and promoting new strategic products. Identification and promotion of new strategic products has to start well ahead of the anticipated diminishing of the competitiveness of existing products, and is often a costly process that requires long-term research, learning, planning, policy implementation, monitoring, concerted efforts and compliance among growth participants, and a considerable level of resources to invest with no immediate profit returns. It is very much the kind of public good that a pure competitive market setting will not be able to provide, and it is the reason for the growth-supportive institutional setting that emerged in the EAEs.

With the logic of international competitiveness and comparative advantage explained, particularly in the context of East Asian Growth, the next question is: what, specifically, needed to be done, and, in fact, has been done, in the EAEs to ensure their comparative advantage and international competitiveness? And, further, what institutional conditions were required for the striving for sustainable international competitiveness to be effective? This is the subject of the following two sections.

## Striving for sustainable international competitiveness

Driven by the initial conditions, and thus the growth imperatives, the efforts in competitiveness enhancement in the EAEs were, essentially, to achieve three main aims: to forge a national unit of competition aimed primarily at international markets; to enhance the collective competitiveness of the national unit; and to ensure the sustainability of such competitiveness over a longer period. These efforts included selective control of access and rents; the internalization of transaction costs; the marginalization of distributional costs; and the centralization of growth planning, coordination, and management.

*Access controls*

Access controls are primary mechanisms by which the state in the EAEs plays its role in promoting the national growth unit, and the competitiveness of the unit. Access controls thus have two functions. Externally, they facilitate the separation of the national economy from the international economic system, and thus promote a key condition necessary for the growth form to work. Internally (within the national growth unit), they are mechanisms for competitiveness enhancement, through the optimization of the industrial structure, the re-prioritizing of resource allocation, and the reduction of excessive competition within the national unit.

Externally, there are controls both on international capital's access to domestic markets, and on the access of national industries to international capital and markets. Controls over incoming international capital and products are often in the form of import tariffs; quotas and other procedural and technical barriers; and restrictions on foreign business within the country. Controls over domestic growth activities involve restrictions on international financial transactions; restrictions on access to foreign material, credit, and capital; and export quotas. In the EAEs, trade and investment and financial liberalization all gradually took place only toward the end of their rapid growth periods. Over time, those controls created privileges for national growth activities and helped form a "zone" of shared business interests with the national borders as its boundaries.

Access controls don't have to result from deliberate government policy. They may just be a subtle part of corporate and social relations. One typical sample of this is Japan's retail industry. In his study on Japanese distribution markets and market access, Motoshige Itoh finds that the Japanese distribution system was traditionally "dominated by small and medium size firms and that many goods go through long tunnels of wholesalers before they reach consumers." Under this structure, there is a close relationship between manufacturers and wholesalers through various ensuring mechanisms such as the supply of sales staff to stores, various forms of rebate system, retail price maintenance, etc. (Itoh 2001: 140). This system effectively became an entry barrier to outsiders, particularly to international capital, and a major trade issue between Japan and the USA in the 1980s.

Internally, there are two categories of access controls. First, there exist controls designed to redirect growth activities toward desired industries and sectors. They came in the forms of varied interest rates, credit provision or limitation, tax manipulation, government purchases, licenses, quotas, and fees, etc., all aimed at causing an optimal distribution of growth interests and activities across different industries and sectors. This set of controls, or, more precisely, preferential treatments with both restrictions and promotions, is significant when international competitiveness and comparative advantage are at stake. The higher level of certainty these controls provided, in terms of the forward directions of the industrial structure, helped reduce the risks and costs associated with investment in a market economy. Moreover, it helped rationalize the industrial structure and, with its resultant optimization, helped promote a national unit with a coherent and consistent industrial basis.

Second, there exist controls to promote exports. Again, they include both restrictions and promotions as well. Export subsidies, insurance, credit, import tariffs, quotas, and other restrictions are all part of this category. Export promotion, however, is not just a matter of picking up winners. It provides a profound rationale for East Asian Growth, where the separation of production and consumption is critical. As found earlier, there is a displacement of market and production potentials in the EAEs. The promotion of exports is meant to separate consumption from production, and thus ensure that consumption which materialized elsewhere would not drain the investment capital necessary for continual growth, and that international market potentials and domestic production capacities are fully incorporated into the growth process.

Unlike the classical colonial economy, where there also tended to be a separation of production and consumption, a strong and engaging state acted as the primary enforcer of this separation in the EAEs. The EAEs' separation was also in contrast to the dependent economy, where production and consumption were separated, not necessarily by the state, but as the consequence of the ownership and management of production by multinational corporations. Furthermore, the separation of consumption in the EAEs was not achieved through internal suppression, as would be the case in the socialist economy, but by its removal from the national system. Concentration on exports to international markets, and the construction of a nationally controlled dual market structure (domestic vs. international) through these control mechanisms, were a central part of the separation. Access controls not only restrict the access of international capital to domestic market, but also marginalize the role of the link between growth and domestic consumption, eliminate the necessity of consumption maximization, and thus reduce the costs that such maximization would pass on to production.

### Internalization of transaction costs

The second major area of competitiveness enhancement focuses upon corporate arrangements, within which costs associated with normal business transactions can be internalized. Internalization, in this context, means that, as a result of institutional restructuring, transactions that were once conducted among interdependent corporations (with additional transaction costs) would be treated as *intra-corporate* transactions, which often carry no (or, at least, cheaper) added transaction costs.

Generally, transaction costs are those "other than the money price that are incurred in trading goods or services" (Johnson 2000). In theory, transaction costs are those other than production costs (such as those involving contract enforcement and business information acquisition), and are not, therefore, supposed to be part of the measurement of productivity and competitiveness in their genuine sense. In reality, however, transaction costs are a necessary investment that can significantly affect the trading value of a good. Because of the increasing complexity of modern industrial and business activities, and, therefore, the higher costs involved in economic transactions, they are simply treated as part of the cost of a product.

With regard to the EAEs, transaction costs were extremely high. Paul M. Johnson lists three categories of transaction costs – information costs, bargaining costs, and enforcement costs – and points out that:

> elementary versions of economic theorizing often make the simplifying assumption that information and other transaction costs are zero (and, indeed, in a generally law-abiding society with a stable money system, cheap transportation and cheap communications, they are often pretty negligible).
>
> (Johnson 2000)

In the EAEs, all these transaction costs were extremely high domestically – due to the institutional and cultural environment in which business found itself, and internationally – because of the additional costs associated with exports to foreign markets, and costs related to fluctuations in exchange rates, tariffs, credit, insurance, and facility costs, etc. Effective ways have to be found to reduce (or share) these costs, for the trading of goods and services to take place "economically."

Information costs, for example, are certainly not non-existent. They concern the circumstances for market entry, the forms of growth organization, and the business culture prevalent in the EAEs. If a Japanese auto-part manufacturer wants to market its products in the USA, for example, there would be tremendous information costs incurred if the manufacturer decided to operate on its own, rather than if it chose to be part of an established business, where such information would be readily available with no (or, at least, lower) costs. The same is true for a Chinese businessman in terms of the different transaction costs involved in establishing a business in the US market on his own, rather than going through, for example, a Hong Kong partner.

Moreover, in all the EAEs, export business was tightly regulated by the government in the early phase of growth, from licenses to quotas, and from information on the direction of the government's strategic plans to changes in world market demands. Costs would be incurred in gambling with the government's moves. While it is, ultimately, a bargaining process between trading partners, it was a process largely shaped by the government. These were the kinds of costs deemed "negligible" in a pure market economy.

Finally, there is the matter of whether business culture makes a difference to information costs. In terms of policing and enforcement costs, for example, quite a lot of business in the EAEs tended to be conducted outside the system of legal contracts. In fact, the earlier the growth period, the less effective the enforcement of contractual arrangements by the public authority appears to be. The problem may have something to do with the government's ability – and even willingness – to police business activity with its legal authority, and perhaps with the general quality of existing legal and economic institutions. Consequently, business tends to be arranged – and business disputes settled – through customary routines and conventions, either as alternative arrangements, where results, for better or worse, are considered to be much more certain; or as remedying methods, where formal contractual processes have failed. While this may reduce transaction costs in one sense, it may also pose the more serious problem of business risk. A Chinese business, for example, may be quite successful in securing contracts to sell its goods, and may manage to deliver these goods. But, in the end, it may end up being unable to receive payments for the delivered products.

Two methods have often been employed by the EAEs in the reduction of costs of this nature. First, unique relationships have been nurtured between individual businesses and individuals in government. While the building of such relations brings its own price, the working of these relations (through the selective channeling of information, and individually tiered preference management), eventually results in a reduction of the costs faced by business. Relations of this kind differ from those shaped by the strategic targeting and preferential schemes developed by government with regard to the business community as a whole. They are not part of formal government plans, and are not even a legitimate part of the formal system, but often operate in a "gray area" of government–business relations.

Second, more "institutionalized" forms of collaboration have developed among the individual firms themselves. These arrangements have taken different forms in the individual EAEs, whether the *kereitsu*, the *chaebol*, or *guanxi qiye*. These corporate arrangements go beyond the normal boundaries of business organization in a market economy, and are aimed (among other things) at reducing transaction costs and mitigating business risk. Being part of a giant corporate network not only makes access to information, facilities, rents, capital, and markets both easier and cheaper, but also makes the survival of individual firms in the face of business and product circles, and industrial competition, far smoother, due to the mutual support of member firms.

Hirotaka Yamauchi in a study on Japan's aviation industry, details how the international competitiveness of Japanese airlines was strengthened through government campaigns in the early 1950s and 1960s. In 1953 the new private small airline JAL was reorganized under the government's auspices to "strengthen JAL's international competitiveness" (Yamauchi 2000: 196). Later two small companies were merged by the government into one big airline, ANA. This government orchestrated reorganization, as in other cases of corporate grouping and integration, and effected the reduction of transaction costs and domestic competition.

### Marginalization of distributional demands

Distributional demands, in the sense that Jack Knight (1998) uses it, concern the allocation of resources and growth revenue by the state, or corporate management, and a dilemma often faced by many developing economies. It is only fair and natural for growth participants, be they labor workers, managers, professionals, public servants, or various social interests, to demand growth benefits. But distributional demands have to be satisfied with potential growth resources and will eventually come down as part of production costs. For the EAEs, suppressing and marginalizing these demands was pursued as a principal mechanism of cost reduction, and thus of competitiveness enhancement.

There are a few general categories embodying these distributional demands: wages, compensations for industrial restructuring, public services, employment security, pension, medical care, housing, education, etc. But distributional demands arose in the EAEs with a focus, mainly, on wages, at least in the early stage of their rapid growth periods. Because of the importance of labor costs for the EAEs in their striving for international competitiveness, it should be quite revealing to determine how the EAEs managed to confine labor costs.

Cheap labor has been cited, almost universally, as a major factor in the competitiveness of the EAEs. It seems to be an established fact that the EAEs began their post-war growth with relatively cheap labor costs. However, cheap labor is not a permanent quality in conditions for economic growth. Labor costs will rise as a combined effect of several factors. The first factor is that of labor demand. Labor costs rise with the rising demand for labor. Even though the EAEs initially had relatively low labor costs, these costs rose rapidly with the expansion of the economy, which grew out of proportion given the size of their labor pools. The second factor is that demands for higher salaries and better working conditions (such as holiday provisions, limited working hours, minimum wages, etc.) are often associated with an advance in economic and social development. A third factor is that the successive phases of growth in the EAEs were based upon different "comparative advantages," which require labor of differing levels of skill and knowledge. A final factor concerns the fact that, with the EAEs increasingly becoming part of the global economic system, there is also the impact of the system-wide dynamism of cost equilibration. Driven by national or regional differences, global forces will move in directions to take advantage of the cost gaps, and these gaps will eventually be closed. This will certainly push up labor costs where they were previously relatively low.

All of these factors had a great impact upon the EAEs. Because of the nature of the initial conditions and their consequent responses, the effects of rising labor costs on the EAEs were severe. There was not much the EAEs could do with regard to many of the factors that worked to force labor costs up. However, the efforts of the EAEs to control labor costs appear to have focused upon the first two areas, i.e. labor supply and employment compensation. The problem of shortages in labor supply compelled the EAEs (with perhaps the exception of China) to upgrade and restructure their industries. Economic activities shifted to industries and services that were less labor intensive, and therefore required less labor supply overall.

Moreover, while mainstream economic activities *vacated* traditional industries, it was not just a matter of abandoning these traditional industries. From an investor's point of view, these traditional industries could still be profitable if the increased costs of the supply of labor, and perhaps of raw materials, could be neutralized. This neutralization has been achieved with the relocation of these industries from the more advanced EAEs to those less advanced. This happened in the 1960s and 1970s from Japan to Korea, Singapore, and Taiwan, and in 1980s and 1990s from Taiwan, Korea, and Singapore to China. The regional dynamism among the EAEs, driven by this "progressive vacating" (Chowdhury and Islam 1993), not only provided a solution to the labor problem (and therefore a basis for sustained competitiveness), but also linked EAEs, at different stages of growth, into a mutually beneficial process.

In the second area, where labor costs rose due to rises in both wages and non-production costs, the methods of cost control and suppression in the EAEs – especially in their early phases of growth – have inspired much of the debate surrounding the growth model itself (Chowdhury and Islam 1993; Deyo 1989; Bello and Rosenfeld 1992). In applying what can be called the principle of *minimum production necessity*, the EAEs started with – and tried to maintain – a very low minimum provision of working conditions and compensation. This principle requires that labor costs be kept to the lowest possible level, so that productive efficiency and growth competitiveness are not compromised.

To be sure, this principle operates in any profit-driven economy to some extent. But what the minimum is, or should be, is an economic, social, political and, more often than not, legal issue, and the EAEs took a narrow view on this. The EAEs began their growth with low wages and the lowest possible working conditions. Many of the EAEs started to have state regulations on pensions, medical care, and insurance only in the latter stages of their rapid growth periods. As the factors that push up labor costs came into play, the EAEs faced a critical challenge in keeping wage levels stable. There were various reasons why the EAEs were able to keep labor costs low. Some concern intentional efforts on the part of management and government. Others were simply the side effects of the prevailing corporate practices. Life-long employment, and corporate culture in general, for example, incorporated workers into the corporate structure, and provided them with a sense of job security, and the certainty of long-term wage and welfare benefits. These can be seen as alternative forms of tension reduction in industrial relations.

On the other hand, the legal, political, and social setting made genuine organized union activity difficult to conduct effectively. When labor disputes went beyond the ability of management to control, the state often stood behind management. In the 1960s, when labor disputes emerged as a real issue in Japan, serious industrial relations bills were passed to curtail the unrest. The same drama was repeated in Korea, up until the early 1990s. In Singapore, China, and Taiwan, such unrest was firmly under government control during their rapid growth periods.

### Centralization of planning, coordination, and promotion

Central planning, coordination, and promotion are other crucial mechanisms for the working of East Asian Growth, particularly in reducing competitive costs among growth participants and thus helping to improve the overall competitiveness of the national growth unit, and in reducing costs associated with adjustment to shifts in comparative advantage and thus helping to sustain competitiveness over generations of products.

In each of the EAEs, for example, there are various kinds of short-term (for the year), medium-term (five-year, for example), and long-term (ten-year) general economic plans. Japan started with its first five-year plan from 1955, its first seven-year *Comprehensive National Development Plan* in 1962, and its first three-year *Economic and Social Development Plan* in 1967. China had its comprehensive planning system long before it embarked on East Asian Growth, but has maintained the system into the present, with the intertwining of five-year medium-term and ten-year long-term plans. Korea started its five-year planning right after Park took power in 1962, while Taiwan had its first four-year plan dating back to 1952. These plans often set targets for macro-economic factors such as growth rates, tax revenues, monetary supply, government budget, and growth in various sectors; identify major problems affecting the economy over the period and how to solve these problems; and outline the general directions of industrial development and government priorities, and the resources and efforts required in their facilitation.

These plans came about mainly through the government's surveying, monitoring, and policy planning systems, with inputs from formal consultations with business associations, and informal undertakings from various interested parties at large. Once they are accepted by the legislative body, the operational side of the plans will develop in the form of specific laws, government policy directives, regulations, and guidelines that have a disciplinary effect on the activities of growth participants.

In addition to plans at regular intervals, and of a comprehensive nature, there are also more focused campaigns in the form of central policy planning and implementation for solving particular problems or dealing with particular situations. Under the Technology Development Promotion Act in 1972, for example, an aggressive industrial restructuring took place in the 1970s to move Korea from an economy of labor-intensive industries to one of auto-manufacturing, chemical, and shipbuilding industries. Likewise, in Taiwan major campaigns to upgrade industries led to the development of ten major infrastructure projects in the early 1970s, and 14 others in the 1980s. In Singapore, reorientation to highly skilled high-value-added industries in the 1970s and cluster development in the 1990s were examples of these campaigns. These campaigns are particularly important for the sustained international competitiveness of the EAEs in the changeover to new strategic products. They often involved the government's support, with capital, land, credit, insurance, tax holidays, and exports and imports facilitation, in development of and research into new strategic products and industries, in investment and production, and in market promotion.

There are also mechanisms for monitoring and discipline for the central planners, decision makers, and bureaucratic operators to utilize with regard to the various growth participants, as well as representation of growth participants and rationalization of central plans in the core economic decision-making body. In addition to, and often in spite of, formal institutions for public policy debates, these mechanisms operated more effectively through informal, and even personal, relations and encounters.

In a non-EAE, planning, coordination, and promotion can be found at the level of individual corporations. As Mancur Olson shows, the optimization of individual corporations may not necessarily lead to that of the corporations as a whole (Olson 1965). In the EAEs there is the centralization of these activities in the hands of the state. Such centralization helps share the costs of planning and reorientation by individual corporations; reduce the costs incurred by unnecessary competition that might otherwise be natural among corporations; smooth adjustment in response to periodical shifts in comparative advantage; and thus make sustained international competitiveness possible.

## Institutional requirements

The efforts to control access, internalize transaction costs, marginalize distributive costs, and centralize planning, coordination, and promotion, however, may not have succeeded – in terms of leading to growth effects and achieving sustained international competitiveness – without proper institutional support. Indeed, some of them may not even be seen as desirable in certain social and cultural settings. As discussed earlier, institutions have rules and procedures meant to direct human activities and affect human behavior in a given collective setting. The efforts for sustained international competitiveness can be seen, essentially, as employing rules and procedures to direct growth activities and change the behavioral patterns of growth participants. It is, therefore, necessary for us to take a look at the institutional conditions the effective working of these efforts has demanded, or led to, before we move on to investigate how these conditions were satisfied in the EAEs.

The first is the necessity to have a chief planner, coordinator, organizer, or enforcer, as well as a promoter for nationwide growth activity. As the national unit of growth is essential for international competitiveness, an entity to represent the interests, and rationalize and organize the growth activities, of the national unit is only natural. Such an entity should have an effective leverage over growth participants; be able to provide public goods for the national unit where market mechanisms and private interests dominate; be able to rationalize growth activities within the economy as a whole and over the long term; and be able to represent and promote the interests of the national unit in the world economic system. Such an entity carries the final accountability for growth performance, and a role as the ultimate bearer of the burdens – be they financial costs, resource pressures or institutional tensions – generated from the growth process.

Second, there needs to be a basis upon which nationwide growth activities can be incorporated into a coherent unit of competitiveness. It requires compromising or conciliatory relations between government and business, between management and labor, between business and society at large, and among corporations themselves. It celebrates whatever forms of the relations that would help suppress, internalize, and/or marginalize growth-impacting costs. It also requires a growth system that is conducive to central management in resources and revenue allocation, tax, interest rates, wages, exchange rates, monetary supply, financial transactions, imports and exports consumption, investment, industrial structure, capital provision, market access, etc.

Third, the efforts for sustained international competitiveness require the "spirit of capitalism" on the part of growth participants, particularly at the individual level. As a capitalist economy, however managed they may be, the fate of individual businesses in the EAEs is ultimately the business of the individuals themselves. It is imperative, therefore, that individuals have full control of their business or their work, and take full responsibility for whatever they undertake. The efforts also compel them to take a whole new set of attitudes and values in planning personal careers, solving moral and ethic dilemmas, managing businesses, and dealing with social relations.

Finally, the formation of a national growth unit, and the promotion of its competitiveness, requires the separation of such a unit from the natural flows of global capital, products, and personnel, so that rationalization within the national unit can be operative. It may be true that the international system of finance and trade greatly supported such separation in the early years of East Asian Growth. However, over time it has increasingly been a challenge for the EAEs to maintain and reinforce such boundaries. Increasingly, they rely upon the internal coherence of their economic and political systems to hold the national unit together. For some, this coherence is embedded in their long tradition of centralized state and centripetal society. For others, their coherence derived largely from their contemporary efforts in fashioning the dual market.

## Summary and discussion

In this chapter we have discussed the two key aspects of the underlying logic of East Asian Growth: international competitiveness and comparative advantage. To be internationally competitive has been imperative for the EAEs, because of the initial distribution of their growth factors and the historical circumstances that led to their heavy reliance upon exports and foreign capital. Identifying and promoting comparative advantage, and ensuring swift and effective industrial restructuring and upgrading in response to shifts in comparative advantage, have been key mechanisms by which the EAEs were able to secure their continued competitiveness in international markets over decades, and across generations of products and industrial advances.

To secure sustained international competitiveness, a range of measures were undertaken in the EAEs over the years of their rapid growth periods, both by the state as well as other growth participants: from access controls to cost internalization, cost marginalization, and the centralization of planning, coordination, and promotion. These measures helped to bring about a coherent national unit of economic growth; rationalized the deployment of various growth resources and inputs; and ultimately strengthened the competitiveness of the national unit.

The pursuit of sustained international competitiveness, however, required proper institutional support. Fundamentally, East Asian Growth was a "social process" (Bienefeld 1980: 28) in which the structure and organization of the national economy were turned into a giant corporation. The function of this giant corporation not only twisted the workings of the market itself, but also placed great pressure on the social and cultural setting under which the social process took place. The key question we need to pursue next then is whether the social and culture settings would support the institutional understanding and how. Chapter 4 will show that the answer may not be as straightforward as many enthusiasts as well as critics of East Asian culture would think. Some aspects of the social and cultural settings were supportive of the growth imperatives and consequent institutional requirements; others were not. Still others were either supportive or non-supportive, dependent upon the subtle, interactive, and institutional manipulation on them. In Chapter 5, we will see how these social and cultural conditions were tackled within the formation of the growth system to meet the challenge of East Asian Growth. But, first, let us turn to an in-depth look at the social and cultural settings in the EAEs, and how they related to the growth imperatives and their institutional requirements.

# 4 Cultural and social setting

## Culture and society in East Asian Growth

The striving for sustained international competitiveness requires the support of institutional arrangements possessing certain qualities. However, institutions must develop and function within a given social and cultural setting. Contrary to certain popular views as discussed earlier, which suggest that the culture and societies of the EACs are either perfectly supportive of East Asian Growth or are in the main a hindrance to the development of a modern capitalist economy (of which East Asian Growth is arguably an instance), there are certain elements present within the social and cultural settings of the EACs that became the foundations for new growth-promoting institutions, and there are others that had to be overcome if these new institutional arrangements were to be effective. The precise nature of the impact of the cultural and social conditions on East Asian Growth, therefore, has to do with the specifics of the new growth-promoting arrangements, and the methods that the growth imperatives demanded.

Under the cultural and social conditions encountered within the EACs, for example, some of the new arrangements and methods in East Asian Growth, which may be considered unconventional or unethical in other growth settings, were taken to be both natural and practical. The formation of corporate groups is such an example. In an ideal neoclassical setting, the primary unit of production and transactions, and therefore of efficiency, would be the individual firm. In corporate grouping in the EACs, the boundaries between individual corporations can be blurred, and individual group members were able to take advantage of cost- and risk-sharing among group members, while remaining separate corporations. For those operating according to neoclassical principles, this form of business practice was unethical, and would result in unfair competition. But in a social and cultural setting where informal relations are preferred over formal, particularly legal, relations in business operations, this informal grouping was widely accepted and practiced.

The same can be said about the larger problem of the role of the state in the working of the national economy. A neoclassical environment operates on the assumption of the existence of *free* competition among economic actors, for the optimal function of the market. The state is generally not considered to be a legitimate economic actor. For those operating within the neoclassical environment, therefore, various forms of state involvement in economic activities (be they subsidies, preferential loans, the manipulation of financial markets, mediation in industrial relations, or even owning the business itself) are seen as unethical. While neo-liberals do see the utility of state activism in enhancing competitiveness, it would be difficult – if not impossible – for them to develop state activism of this scale under their prevailing social and cultural conditions. But, in a social and cultural setting where there are deep and historically significant traditions of centralized state control, bureaucratic management of the national economy, and a centripetal society, a strong and engaging state active in the national economy is very much a natural expectation of growth participants.

The subtleness of the role of the cultural and society can also be observed in the cultural qualities of the people in the EACs and how they related to their growth experiences. It is, perhaps, over-simplistic to argue that Asian people work hard, love family, tolerate hardship, are submissive to authority, and are therefore good for state-led growth. One needs to understand that there are cultural qualities of the people in these societies that are not necessarily positive for the function of a modern market economy in general, and that of East Asian Growth in particular.

I have argued that the effective working of the new growth-promoting institutions required a set of social and cultural qualities that not only made the chosen set of options possible – or even desirable – in the first place, but also, once these options were put in place, helped reduce the tensions generated by these options, and provide a greater capacity for society to bear the burdens – and absorb the consequences – of the options implemented.

In this chapter we will discuss key aspects of the "traditional" social and cultural settings in the EACs prevalent during the formative years of their East Asian Growth, against the institutional requirements generated from the growth imperatives. The discussion will focus on two areas: the general patterns of individual behavior and interpersonal relations, and the properties of social structure in terms of the role of the family unit, importance of the model of family relations; and mutual dependence of the state and society. Individual behavior patterns are critical for the modern capitalist economy, while social structure can be either a constraint, a facilitator, or a mixture of both on such economic activity. It will become evident from this discussion that some of these aspects could be readily incorporated into the new institutional arrangements, but others would need to be significantly transformed if the institutional arrangements were to work effectively in the capitalist economy. How these conditions are either incorporated or transformed will be the subject of the next chapter.

## The pattern of individual behavior

The discussion here of the cultural qualities of the individual in the EACs is led by the assumptions that East Asian Growth requires the spirit of capitalism, i.e. rational individualism (for the market side of the growth), and, at the same time, the norm of collective compliance (for the governing side of the growth); that the EACs had been predominantly influenced by the Chinese cultural tradition centered upon Confucianism (thus, were Confucian societies); and that individuals of Confucianist convictions are ambivalent with regard to these two seemingly contradictory requirements on the individual.

### *The Chinaman*

Before discussing whether and how individuals in Confucian societies could satisfy these two requirements, we must first look briefly at the origins of Confucianism. What was the original problem to which Confucianism rose in response? What is the nature of Confucianism as a perceived solution to this original problem? What are the consequences of this solution on individual behavior? Answers to these questions should help us understand the cultural developments in the EACs, and the nature of the cultural conditions in these Confucian societies, in relation to their post-war economic growth.

Extensive studies concerned with the rise of Confucianism in China, and its adaptation and modification in the rest of East Asia, have been undertaken (Pye 1985; Tai 1989; Yu 1985; Rozman 1991; de Bary 1988; Tu 1991a). The argument to be made here, however, is that it was the original cultural traits of *the Chinese*, elements of which can still be seen in Chinese communities today, that gave rise to Confucianism as a moral remedy. Bo Yang, a well-received writer from Taiwan, for example, tries to identify certain "genetic" cultural traits of the Chinese – what he refers to as the "deep-rooted bad habits" of the "Ugly Chinaman," as the critical cause of the problems long associated with Chinese society: poverty, illiteracy, and bloody internal fights. Chinamen, according to Bo, are "crass, arrogant, noisy, uncivilized, uncooperative, boastful, dirty, unforgiving . . . "passive, braggarts, exaggerators, liars, slanderers, and dishonest" (Bo 1992: 30–1). According to Bo, these deep-rooted bad habits are what he calls a *filtering virus* that has made the Chinese sick.

It would, perhaps, be an overstatement to say that Chinese people before Confucius were all as "ugly" as Bo describes. We do not have enough evidence to determine this. What we do know is that Confucius' life was dominated by a constant tension within himself, between, on the one hand, the noble traditions he inherited from his family and found well-preserved in his native state, Lu, in the early Zhou period (1027–771 BC), and, on the other hand, the increasing decay of court governance and civic life –

corrupt government, collapsed morals, and fighting states – in the late Zhou period (770–221), when he lived. Moreover, according to Wu-chi Liu (1955), there was, increasingly, an influx of the landless class into towns, to become part of the aristocracy working for the feudal court, or to become service men working for themselves between different trades, and between farmers and the government. For these newcomers, noble standards were less important, and perhaps irrelevant. A consequence of this expansion of court and town activities was the increasing complexity in the sustaining of the noble order over the feudal court. In Confucius' view, newly appointed court bureaucrats and traders needed to be properly educated and taught to behave in an accepted manner, follow proper rules, respect existing relations, and ultimately become a "perfect gentleman" as the system required.

Over the thousand years following his death, his teachings were collected, promoted, and established, not so much as the basis for a moral order within government, or for the ruling classes themselves, but as moral guidelines for society as a whole. More importantly, Confucianism was adopted and transformed into a state ideology for the purpose of helping maintain political and economic order. This moral order, often combined with state coercion and societal pressures, proved indispensable for a system comprising a feudal economy, a centralized state, and a top-down style of social management. Having been firmly established in China as a state ideology and *the* way of life, Confucianism also spread to neighboring Korea and Japan. Except for Japan, which started to "de-Confucianize" from the Meiji Restoration, well before its post-war rapid growth period, Confucianism had been dominant in the EACs prior to their post-World War II economic takeoff.

Confucianism, seen in this historical context, rose to impose a model of life for the individual, i.e. a model of the Confucian Man: self-cultivating, following the rules, respecting and preserving social relations, going through education, working for the government, and doing good things for the country. At the level of the individual, Confucianism, with the support of the system of government and society that it engendered, placed great pressures upon the individual to conform to centrally prescribed norms and values. However, as a moral solution, the system is not able to reconcile what is good for public interests and what is good for private interests. Under such a system, self-interest would either be marginalized or would proceed regardless of moral principles. Collective conformity and private distrust thus coexist within the system. Over time, the Confucian model of moral conformity increasingly requires a level of suppression of private interests, mainly through state coercion and social discipline.

The implications of the complex effects of Confucianism are twofold. First, collective compliance, and thus concerted actions by individuals and their associations, are much easier than would be expected otherwise. For a growth process where the concerted efforts of growth participants are a key to its success, this aspect served as a beneficial factor. East Asian Growth has taken advantage of this cultural condition and incorporated it into the growth efforts.

Second, collective compliance on a moral basis sustained through state coercion and societal pressures is often achieved at the expense of private interests. This, in turn, leads to the blurring of the boundaries between public and private, to great distrust in the notions of private property and interests (and of the rights and obligations associated with them), and to the lack of incentives or moral confidence for individuals to pursue private interests, as required by the modern market economy. This has been a critical problem for East Asian Growth. While the blurred boundaries may have helped provide a basis for some of the unconventional methods of competitiveness enhancement (such as corporate grouping or growth alliance), the whole problem of the subordination of private interests in the Confucian moral order had been confronted in different ways in the EACs, well before their post-war rapid growth periods, and certainly has since experienced an institutional solution of some sort during their rapid growth periods, as will be shown in the next chapter.

### *Social capital and informal relations*

While Confucian society generally anticipates collective compliance, not all compliance is secured with "moral coercion." There are other bases upon which people cooperate. Trust among concerned parties, for example, is one such basis. The problem of trust has recently become part of a large debate regarding social capital (Coleman 1988; Fukuyama 1995; Kim 1998; Putnam 1993; Pye 1999; World Bank 2001). While there is a broad acceptance of the claim that high levels of trust, confidence, and predictability of path-dependent actions exist among family members in the EACs, these qualities do not necessarily have to do with family. As well as family relations, higher levels of trust can be found among groups of people with shared ethnic identity, religious faith, dwelling closeness, a similar situation for action, satisfactory experience of past encounters, or some combination of them – what Clifford Geertz might call "primordial bonds" (Geertz 1973). Social capital thus is the propensity of members of a group, or a population, to trust each other and cooperate in collective action that would make unnecessary the costs in building or developing such a level of trust that might be incurred otherwise in relations without these bonds.

Viewed from this perspective, there is perhaps more to the problem of social capital in the EACs than Lucian Pye and Francis Fukuyama have argued in their works (Pye 1985, 1999; Fukuyama 1995). In the pre-rapid growth period EACs,[1] like other traditional societies where modern institutions such as those concerning law and the market were yet to rise to their primacy, people were more likely to engage – feeling secure, certain, and confident – with others who could identify with them on some assuring bases. Due to the role of family in the EACs, family connections tended to be one primary basis. Coming from the same home town or same region was another. Likewise, the fact of graduating from the same university, and – if abroad – coming from the same country, are seen as such bases. Levels of social capital, therefore, were always relative in terms of the boundary of the circle of people among whom the bases for the level of social capital could be identified. At the national level however, high levels of social capital in certain groups may not necessarily lead to the same high levels of social capital at the national level. One would expect this to be compensated for by the functioning of either traditional social structures or modern institutions, or a combination of both.

Consequently, for East Asian Growth, as many businesses were family controlled and managed, and thus "social capital" was relatively higher in that regard, competitiveness was generally gained at this level. However, as East Asian Growth has been a concerted nationwide campaign, cooperation had to be effected through the adaptation of existing social structures and the construction of modern institutions. To incorporate both into East Asian Growth would require both significant social transformation and efforts in building new institutions.

The point regarding the existence of tensions between "primordial bonds" and modern institutions leads us to a further observation of the cultural and social settings in the pre-rapid growth period EACs. Modern institutions (those governing the electoral process, the banking system, dispute settlement, corporate accounting, etc.) were not strong, not effective, nor even fully established in the EACs, particularly in the early years of their rapid growth periods. Informal relations played a considerable role in ensuring security and certainty in collective action, and were more widely used as effective platforms for interest representation, pursuit, and reconciliation. Lucian Pye advances a valuable understanding of the importance of informal relations in various Asian countries, in relation to formal structure and institutions (1985: 283–319). Informal relations, according to him, are those yet to be "institutionalized." Perhaps a better way of defining them is to see informal relations as those exclusively between or among concerned parties on a shared basis of social capital. Some of the informal relations, such as those based upon family ties, local connections, past encounters etc., may never be institutionalized, because they exist primarily on an idiosyncratic basis, and their benefits and obligations are normally not transferable.

Informal relations were widely pursued – and deemed to be effective – in the EACs, particularly during the early years of their rapid growth periods. Relational thinking placed a premium on informal relations. Moreover, in addition to the lack of many modern institutions, those already established – such as the banking system, legal system, accounting system, and corporate management system – were not necessarily efficient and effective, but often proved to be poorly designed, incompatible with local conditions, and subject to heavy interference by dominant political and social forces. This reinforced the power of these informal relations. Even given the growing presence of modern institutions, informal relations were still preferred as being convenient, time-efficient, and cost-effective. Instead of going to court to settle business disputes, for example, they were more likely to be settled through family mediation or mutual friend involvement. Instead of relying on the formal bidding process for a construction project, interested parties may seek influence over the process through personal relations.

As for East Asian Growth, informal relations supplemented – or substituted for – formal institutions, and encouraged growth activity to operate in a gray area between these formal institutions and informal relations. This allowed a sense of control on the part of growth participants over the transaction costs associated with the function of formal institutions, and provided a social basis for the various growth methods that were not permissible under strict formal institutions. At the same time, the persistent power of informal relations further eroded the effectiveness of modern institutions and led to huge costs for investment in informal relations, and, further, to corruption and unconventional business practices in accounting, corporate organization, and government relations. As will be seen in the following chapter, the EACs have been relatively "liberal" in allowing these informal relations to play an important part in the growth campaign – even in Japan, where modern institutions had developed long before its post-war growth.

## Social structure

The social structure in the EACs is critically important for East Asian Growth, and is closely tied to the notion of family in Asian societies – often cited as an important part of the cultural and social conditions facilitating East Asian Growth (Hamilton and Gao 1990; Okochi and Yasuoka 1984). It is claimed that growth in the EAEs has been made possible by the strong family values that exist among people: appreciation of family ties, mutual support among family members, loyalty to the family, etc. The assertion that East Asian Growth has uniquely benefited from the appreciation of family implies that the family is not significantly important in non-Asian countries. This is obviously not the case. It is possible to identify people in many non-Asian countries who are not less family oriented than Asian people. The Italians are one good example. Even in the USA, which many consider to be a place where the family has difficulty functioning normally, there are a great number of people who are well supported and respected by – and command loyalty and attachment from – family members, who support their lives and careers.

At issue, perhaps, is not whether Asian people are more family oriented than non-Asian people. Rather, what matters is the role of "family values" beyond the family – the extent to which family norms and rules are respected and practiced in the greater context of human association and organization. Of interest is not just the level of importance people attach to their family per se, but – more importantly – the way in which people organize themselves for various purposes, following the model of the family in terms of structure, processes, and procedures. What is particularly significant about the family in the EACs is that family norms and rules penetrate society and government far deeper and wider than anywhere else. For East Asian Growth – where concerted collective action is essential for its international competitiveness – growth activities facilitated by family principles could help reduce uncertainty in the market, provide a level of trust among growth participants, and reduce transaction costs.

In this section, therefore, we should undertake an examination of the family model predominant in the pre-rapid growth period EACs. Then we will show how this family model manifests itself – beyond the family – in business management, in the development of wide-ranging social relations, in competing with formal institutions as effective methods and procedures of interest representation and pursuit, and in the management of society and government as a whole. One thing is clear: unless modern institutions firmly establish themselves, the structures and methods of traditional society (such as those embedded in the family model) will continue to play an important role in the functioning of society. We shall explore the tension this has brought upon East Asian Growth and, in next chapter, how the EACs coped with this tension in their institutional building for rapid growth.

### The family model

With all the variations in family structure, it is the parent–child relationship that underlies the organization of the family, and that defines the distribution of authority and obligations within the family and the role of each family member. Generally, one may argue that the parent–child relationship is framed in a different way in the EACs than it is in the countries of Western civilization.[2] An EAC family, for example, would see a much larger differentiation of status and roles between parents and children, and, to a great extent, between wife and husband. In a Western family, such status and role differentiation is limited. One could argue that this difference may be related to the fact that the Christian tradition in the West relates each individual equally to God. Also, modern institutions – based upon constitutionalism and citizenship – ensure equal rights and obligations for each individual.

Related to this differentiation in status and roles is a pattern of dependence, between the various parties, on these differentiated relationships. Often, this dependence is mutual. Not only do family members depend upon the family head – often the father – for support and protection, but the family head also depends upon the individualized relationships with family members to perform his functions.[3] Prevalent within the EAC family is a unique set of expectations between members of the family. Parents work hard and sacrifice for the children, with hopes that eventually the children will take care of them when they get older. In the life-long process of forging and fortifying relationships of this nature, the parents – usually the father – see it as their obligation to exercise decision-making and disciplinary powers for their children. As such, this relationship of mutual dependence centers upon the family head. Consequently, there is always a strong father figure present in the family relations of the EACs. This father figure operates as the center of decision-making, operation, and organization for the family, and commands the assumed authority and expected obligations found in this relationship of mutual dependence.

Beyond these commonalities, there are subtle but important variations among the EACs themselves, regarding family structure, processes, and procedures. Lucian Pye, for example, finds that, in the Chinese family, the "model father" appears "larger than life," a "can't-fail" type of hero figure, who has full responsibility for the well-being and unity of the family, and "can expect total deference and no explicit criticism." The Japanese family is at the other extreme, where the father is less heroic, "can adopt a more reticent posture, allowing others to make the first moves, indeed soliciting views rather than determining them" (Pye 1985: 66–7). On Pye's scale of the family model, Korea, Taiwan, and Singapore are located between the Chinese and the Japanese, with Korea closer to the Japanese model, and Taiwan and Singapore closer to the Chinese model. I myself think, however, that the Koreans are also closer to the Chinese, at least in terms of the father figure in family relations.

The system of inheritance is another example. The Japanese family "operated under a rigid system of primogeniture which favored the eldest son." In the Chinese family, "the inheritance was more equally divided among all the sons." Here, birth order "determined the roles and obligations of family members," and younger sons are "subordinate to the eldest." In Japan, the power of birth order is reduced by the freedom of the younger sons to break away from their subordinate status and strike out on their own – if successful, becoming the founder of a new family line (Pye 1985: 68–9).

This basic family model has several implications regarding its practice in a wider social setting. First, this model nurtures a strong sense of order and management, which can be easily utilized in the running of business or the managing of society. Second, there is the predominance of relational thinking in human decision-making and behavior. Presumption of special relationships, based upon the individual's roles and status in a given setting, allows the individual to develop a higher level of trust and mutual understanding to supplement, if not substitute for, formal institutions. Finally, this family model forges relations among members of the family such that each family member is a *different* but *coherent* part of the family, and his or her interests and capacity are incomplete without those of the other family members. On that basis, family members are more inclined, and more likely, to act for the family as a whole. It is also relatively easier for such a family to operate with the family as the basic unit, utilizing the combined capacities of its members.

The reason the family model has been seen as the preferred form of human organization in the EACs has much to do with lingering traditional social legacies in these EACs. Social methods and mechanisms, once established and widely exercised in society, tend to become integral parts of social institutions, and are resistant to removal. Furthermore, most EACs – particularly in the early stage of their rapid growth periods – were slow in constructing effective modern institutions. The family model – with the physical comfort, emotional security, material welfare, trust, and effectiveness in reaching and carrying out group-wide decisions – became a natural option in organizing and managing a wide range of human activities.

### Business by family

One aspect of the utilization of the family model in non-family circumstances is related to the fact that much of the economic activity of the society is centered around the family in the EACs. One thing that often puzzles observers of East Asian Growth is that, in many EACs, there has been no substantial provision of social welfare and social security benefits, particularly in the early years of their rapid growth periods (White *et al.* 1998). How can people survive the fluctuations of a competitive market economy if the state does not provide for, and protect, those unable to compete? How can these societies sustain such a high level of population density and labor-abundance?

The answer may involve the notion of the family as an economic unit. The concept here concerns not so much the fact that the family can operate as an effective unit of economic activity (see for example Blau *et al.* 1998), but, rather, the idea that family members could fulfill certain socioeconomic functions for each other. These functions, in a society of more modern institutions, are often carried out by, or have been expected from, the state.

If one walks the streets of the EACs, one is likely to find that the streets are crowded with self-employed family members working in their shops. East Asian Growth has taken advantage of this tradition of mutual support, or intertwinement, between family and business. It allows government to channel unemployment and other social welfare burdens to individual families. The economic family functions as a labor pool – one that absorbs labor surplus at times of economic downturn, and provides required labor when the market is upbeat. Such an economic model is often not subject to the regulations of industrial relations, where they exist.

This intertwinement is also manifested in the management of larger-scale modern corporations, but serves somewhat different purposes (Fields 1995; Fukuyama 1995; Pye 1985; Redding 1988). There are two aspects to this manifestation. First, corporations are managed as families in terms of decision-making and the relations that exist among members of those corporations, which I will discuss further as part of the investigation of the family as an organizational model in a centripetal society. Second, corporations are controlled and/or managed by family members. Many major corporations in the EAEs started as family operations, and grew with substantial holdings and management by generations of the family. This tradition was interrupted in Japan following World War II, but is still very much alive, for example, in Taiwan. Family control and connections provide an organizational basis for greater efficiency and effectiveness of the corporation, and for corporate groupings, from which East Asian Growth has greatly benefited. They also, however – in combination with the primogeniture system and narrow trust boundaries – limit the expansion of the corporation in size and scale. While this tends to lead to small and medium-sized enterprises, it also encourages the formation of informal corporate groups for the sake of greater efficiency and competitiveness.

## Centripetal society

More important than the connection between family and business, perhaps, is the replication of the family structure, procedures, and methods in the organization of society at large. When it is charged that Singapore is a paternalistic state, what essentially is being said is that the state of Singapore is run as a family, with the head of state as the father figure, and with the methods of family affairs – such as in decision-making, the distribution of authority, the responsibilities and obligations among family members, etc. – applied in state affairs.

The overall effect of the replication of the family model in the organization of society is the development of a *centripetal society* in the EACs. Such a centripetal society is often built upon an assertive, engaging, and proactive state that commands the loyalty, as well as submission, of the general population; a greater level of what Pye calls *mutual dependence* (Pye 1985) between the state and society; a tradition of elite governance by government bureaucrats and representatives of dominant social forces; and a sense of sovereignty and self-sustainability.

The first element of the centripetal society is best conceptualized in the notion of the "paternalistic state." As the term suggests, a paternalistic state concerns, first, a father figure who manages state affairs, much like a father manages family matters. This father figure, in reality, can be either a very effective, charismatic, and nationalistic political leader – Lee Kuan Yew of Singapore, Chiang Ching-kuo of Taiwan, Park Chung Hee of Korea, and

Deng Xiaoping of China all fall into this category; or an assertive, engaging and pro-active government with a powerful economic decision-making bureaucratic core.

What is more important than what this father figure symbolizes is the manner in which government operates. In this respect, it is not so much the style and philosophy of the fatherly figure that is of concern, but rather the methods of family management utilized in the management of state affairs. Japan did not have an imposing father figure as in Singapore, but the substance of the paternalistic state, operating in accordance with many of the principles of the family model, is more or less similar. The government tends to think their authority and powers exist simply because of the fact that they are the government, just like the father would think his authority and obligations exist and need to be obeyed because he is the father.

The centripetal society is not simply dominated by the state. As in the family, there were deep-rooted mutual dependence and expectations between the state and society in the pre-rapid growth period EACs. The people expect the state to provide or promote security, prosperity, order, and national pride, and, to a great extent, for the head of the state and those working in the government to lead as a moral example and as a symbol of life values for the whole society. At the same time, the government expects the people to cooperate and sacrifice for the interests of the whole society, to be supportive in times of difficulty, and to be respectful for the sake of the effective functioning of government.

The society depends on the state because the system is constructed such that the state exclusively controls resources; variations in government policy would have direct and significant impact upon the individual; there is not much that "ordinary people" can do to effectively influence government policy; and the government expects to stay in power indefinitely. The state also depends upon society because, as the old Chinese saying suggests: "a river can carry a boat, but can also sink the boat." If the members of society are not seen as part of the "family structure," the paternalistic state will not work. The loyalty to, and at times the natural trust in the government by, members of society become the political capital that the government could make claims on and utilize.

The centripetal nature of society in the EACs is further reinforced by the dominance of elites in these societies, and their role in helping pull society together centripetally. These elites fall into two categories: those who work in the government and those who are the representatives of various societal sectors. Bureaucratic elites in the first category represent a career model that constantly brings the best and brightest people in to work for the government. They help shape social values, and the belief that the best of us work in the government and the government is run by the best people. For the young and brightest, their ambitions are to rise into the government, rather than falling into opposition against the government. Moreover, the expertise, credibility, and loyalty of the bureaucratic elites are barely questioned or challenged by society. They have enjoyed rather a free hand in running government services and programs. This, as will be shown in next chapter, provides both a historical and a structural basis for a strong and effective bureaucratic decision-making core in the overall growth apparatus in the EACs. Finally, it is their daily work at all government levels – from central government to those in the provinces, counties, and villages – that brings the interests of the government and those of society into a mixture that often favors the government.

In the second category, social elites also played a role in bridging the divide between government and society. Influential families, industrial leaders, military elites, and intellectuals were often at the core of the social elites. Because of the perception of the government as the primary and permanent center of power and resources, these elites worked hard to develop relations with the government, and invest in key personnel in the government. As these were key opinion shapers and interest movers in society, the government relied on them to promote its programs and policies and reach out to their respective constituencies. This was the social basis for the growth alliance.

Finally, the centripetal society was sustained by the tradition of the centralized state in the EACs. The centralized state, different from a federal state model, is a system of government where the functions extend all the way down to the basic level – village and community – but are all controlled and managed by the central government. Local governments are only the agents of the central government, rather than a form of governance by local communities. China's long history has seen the domination of the centralized state model, since the First Qin Dynasty (221–207 BC). Communist rule before Deng's reforms pushed the centralized state model to its extreme.

Japan had been a "feudalistic" country, both before and after the introduction of the Chinese centralized state system, which occurred intensively during the Tang Dynasty (618–907). Several hundred years of civil wars and rule by regional warlords led to the disintegration of central government. In a way, the Meiji Restoration was to restore the power of the central government. With the building of modern state machinery and early industrialization, the centralized state model was largely restored in the name of the Emperor. Some of the supporting elements of the centralized model, such as the military, industrial families, and the emperor himself, were destroyed or damaged during the American Occupation after World War II. But the historic experience of the centralized state was rich, and the social bases for the centralized state model were quickly rebuilt as soon as the Americans allowed it.

In the case of Korea, Taiwan, and Singapore, the influence of the Chinese model on their authority structure was much deeper. Even with the complications of colonial government, one can comfortably argue that the inspiration for the centralized state was very much built into their societies. The next chapter will show how this inspiration was materialized prior to the takeoff of their rapid growth periods.

The tradition of the centralized state provided a much-needed administrative basis for the national unit of growth and competition. East Asian Growth requires concerted collective action among growth participants, and the internalization of growth activities by various participants and at different levels – requirements that the centralized state model can relatively easily satisfy. The centralized state model also provided the structural basis for the separation of the domestic market from the international one, as was pursued in the EAEs. Because of the clear systemic boundaries, and their institutional support, the centralized state model made the dual market option natural. Perhaps that can explain why, in those countries that took the path of dependency development, the dual market failed to become part of their growth efforts.

It is clear from our discussion that the traditional social structure in the pre-rapid growth period EACs was, to a great extent, influenced by the dominant family model. The role of the family in society provides alternative solutions to problems, for which either modern institutions do not exist, or cannot operate effectively or efficiently. More importantly, the utilization of the family model in society served to facilitate the reorganization of production necessary for East Asian Growth, and encouraged the growth of the various versions of "Nation Inc." in the EACs. China may be different from Japan, and Korea from Singapore, but at the critical level of social organization they have much in common. The incorporation of social as well as economic forces into the growth process contributed to the formation of the nation as a competitor in international markets, and satisfied an important condition for international competitiveness.

As will be shown in the next chapter, the centripetal society allowed many of the critical methods of growth promotion to be possible in East Asian Growth. The interplay of forces in this centripetal society tends to produce a centrally located platform that, in turn, serves as an infrastructure for a nationally managed growth process. Various forces nurtured this centripetal social quality, whether they derived from the incentives or coercion of the government, from the inclusionary and exclusionary nature of elite power, or from the dependency and confirmative nature of the civic culture. The centripetal society was a principal part of the "social capital" necessary for the socially engineered growth in the EACs. It provided a general setting for a growth alliance to be forged among major growth participants. It allowed the state to play a considerable, and aggressive, role in growth promotion and management. It had the capacity to facilitate effective collective action and concerted growth activity.

## Summary and discussion

The efforts for international competitiveness in the EACs focused upon the reorganization of production and distribution within the EAEs, and thus their effectiveness was significantly affected by the social and cultural setting in which these efforts took place. There is generally the question of the compatibility of the setting with the growth attempts and, further, its responsiveness to institutional manipulation for international competitiveness. There is a tendency, however, in examining and debating East Asian Growth, to see the pre-rapid growth period setting as either favorable for, or prohibitive of, growth, without looking closely at the setting itself, and its variations in these EACs.

This problem obviously concerns, initially, the often ambiguous notion of growth itself. East Asian Growth is an instance of the modern capitalist economy, which requires, among other things, rational individualism as the basis for individual behavior and activity. At the same time, East Asian Growth is also a unique instance of rapid growth centered upon international competitiveness, through concerted efforts on the part of growth participants within the EAE and institutional enhancement and manipulation in forging the national unit of competition. It is this contradictory nature of East Asian Growth that determined the complicated relationship between East Asian Growth and the social and cultural conditions in the pre-rapid growth period EACs.

We have found in this chapter that there were elements in the settings of the EACs that were favorable for East Asian Growth, while others were not. There were others still that were simply conditions that the growth participants had to deal with, and their relation to East Asian Growth was unclear at the beginning. The end of colonial rule in Korea, Taiwan, and Singapore, for example, can be seen as an example of the category of neutral conditions. It was simply a condition that forced the post-colonial states to seek new markets, new sources of capital, and, in fact, ultimately helped shape their export-led growth pattern.

As another example, trust – as a unique social and cultural trait – was necessary in East Asian Growth, where institutions were often poorly developed, or where institutions with high costs were often less desired. However, it became increasingly irrelevant – or even prohibitive – where a mature system of legal codes and administrative regulations were in place to perform the same function of providing certainty in growth activities, as trust might otherwise be counted upon to do.

The tradition of the centripetal society and Confucian values, on the other hand, can be seen as conditions favorable for providing social support for concerted growth efforts at the national level, but unfavorable for generating entrepreneurial growth activity or for allowing the development of the modern capitalist economic system centered upon private property rights, and their supporting legal, political, and financial institutions.

While a more sophisticated examination of the social and cultural conditions in the EACs may be useful for an accurate depiction of the variations among the EAEs in their pre-rapid growth period cultural and social setting, one may see from the discussion above that there was something largely shared by the EACs in terms of the general pattern of individual behavior and the overall social structure. This "something" provided a similar cultural and social setting under which their rapid growth took place.

Moreover, given the nature of the setting, substantial growth efforts by private investors, government, corporations, social groups, and individuals can be seen as focusing upon incorporating these social and cultural conditions into the growth campaign – whether to take advantage of, and reinforce, favorable conditions; constrain and modify unfavorable ones; or turn neutral conditions into something positive. The formation of the national unit of growth and competition, and the reorganization of production, distribution, and exchange within the unit, may not have been so effective without the support of the cultural and social conditions. But many aspects of these conditions have, themselves, been significantly transformed in the process of the development of the national growth unit and the methods of enhancement in its international competitiveness. A closer examination of this incorporation and transformation is part of the subject for the next chapter.

# 5   Crafting the national growth system

In previous chapters, we have examined the initial conditions prevalent at the time of the takeoff of the rapid growth periods, and the response of the EAEs that they generated. The unique distribution of growth factors, and the historical circumstances at the time, led the EAEs to concentrate upon exports with successive generations of strategic products. We have also investigated the nature of the coherent set of growth methods employed by the EAEs that promoted this type of growth, and their institutional implications. The EAEs' rapid and prolonged growth was essentially driven by their striving for international competitiveness and comparative advantage, which demanded a reorganization of production, exchange and distribution, and the forging of a national unit of growth and competition. We have also looked at the cultural and social conditions of the EACs. While many aspects of these conditions were supportive of the new institutional arrangements emerging from the reorientation and "Nation Inc." building, and were easily incorporated into them, many others were the very conditions that the new institutional arrangements were designed to modify or transform so that the cultural and social setting overall would be more conducive to desirable growth activities and efforts.

This chapter will examine the reorientation and the formation of the national system of growth and competition to meet the challenge of acquiring and sustaining international competitiveness. The emphasis here is twofold: first, what the key components of the national system are; and, second, how they came to be part of the growth system. The growth efforts in the EAEs were more than just profit-seeking activities by individual businesses. They were part of a coherent national campaign for international competitiveness. Such a campaign not only led to the incorporation of various productive and social forces to form the growth system, but also functioned to justify the emergent growth arrangements and methods.

Moreover, the formation of the growth system was made possible by a series of institutional innovations and manipulations in the EAEs. The institutional innovations and manipulations were, in essence, efforts by those involved – not just government, but also corporations, interest groups, individual participants, etc. – to take advantage of, or reshape, these cultural

and social conditions for the formation, and working, of the new arrangements that would increase efficiency, and reduce the costs of production,
distribution, and management, and enhance competitiveness of the national
economy itself, as the primary unit of competition.

Before moving on to key aspects of the growth system, and the process
of their taking shape under the growth imperatives and existing social and
cultural conditions, we will first take a look at the phenomenon of economic
growth as a national campaign, found across the EAEs, as a principal way
of promoting and justifying the growth system.

## Economic growth as a national campaign

The notion of economic growth as a national campaign revolves around
two issues: first, the necessity of nationally organized and concerted growth
activities, and, second, the power of growth goals or mandates that would
justify the arrangements and methods in the organization of growth activities. In earlier discussions, I have explained why growth activities in the
EAEs were to be organized at the national level, and how their growth
arrangements were to be justified in general. However, the factors identified in earlier discussions, i.e. the initial conditions, the drive for international competitiveness, the cultural and social conditions, etc., are part
of the greater dynamics effective upon the rise of the growth system: one
relating to the larger issue of institutional dynamics in modern society,
and another to the historical dynamics in the EACs.

### *The role of new institutional arrangements*

At a more fundamental level, the emergence of the growth system in the
EACs can be seen as an instance of institutional manipulation for desirable growth activities and their coherence. Under what conditions, for
example, would individual businesses move to export? Under what conditions would corporations invest to upgrade to new products? Under what
conditions would people appreciate that "becoming rich is glorious"? Under
what conditions can rent-seeking activities be reduced?

There are always reasons, known or unknown, behind the existing
patterns of behavior. Individual businesses, for example, do not normally
want to export, due to the associated higher costs of market entry, the risks
and uncertainties involved in the international business environment, and
thus extra transaction costs in insurance, tariffs, and dispute settlement.
Laws, regulations, rules, and policies that affect the extra costs form an
institutional framework that shapes the pattern of business behavior. Once
the nature of the institutional framework is understood, new institutions
can be designed to effect change in the pattern. The government, or banks,
for example, can provide insurance, credit, subsidies, and market information, etc., so that exports can become an industry with assured high-profit

returns. Thus, East Asian Growth can be seen as an effect of the systematic, coherent, and focused growth activities generated by a new set of transformative institutional arrangements. The striving for international competitiveness was just such a process, where institutional innovations and manipulations redefined relations among growth participants, and changed their calculations regarding growth activity.

While the state was not the only force that shaped the growth-promoting institutions, it was the state in the EACs that became the primary shaper of the effective institutional framework, because of its monopoly over both resources and the policy-making process. Moreover, because of their interaction in the development of new institutional arrangements, the relations between the state and other growth participants were unusually close. The existing cultural and social conditions provided significant support for the top-down and closely intertwined growth collaboration at the national level, led by the state.

### Growth as a historical mandate

Even with the institutional dynamics built in, questions remain in terms of the growth "mandate" and "vision" that often served as an important justification for East Asian Growth. Why was growth both necessary and paramount (over competing political, development, and social interests)? Why did labor forces have to make sacrifices for the sake of the national good? Why was the national economy more important than specific sectors in the economy on the one hand, and the global economy on the other?

Pondering over these questions, one would probably find a very high level of anxiety among both elites and the general public in the EACs at the time of their takeoffs, concerning the prospects of their rapid industrialization and modernization, as well as a similarly high level of willingness to do whatever it would take to make that happen. This – what I call the "growth mentality" – grew out of the long, painful, and often shameful experience of these EACs in modern history, where they found themselves at the periphery of the world economic and political system, and at the mercy of European-dominated global dynamics. This sense of being at the periphery of the world system of wealth and power was much stronger in Korea and China than in Japan, with mixed feelings among the other post-colonial states.

A central theme in the mainstream view in China – regarding its relation to the world system – has been (and still is) that China would have "returned" to the core of the system long ago, had its efforts not been interrupted or sabotaged by the Western powers, in their relentless expansion and intrusion within East Asia in recent history. This was the foundation for the sense of historical mission among Chinese elites, and the general public, in their pursuit of a rapid upward movement in the international system since the 1950s – first, following the Soviet model in the 1950s, then in the name of Four Modernizations in the 1970s, and, finally, when they came to terms with the form of East Asian Growth in the 1980s via Deng's opening and reform programs. The overwhelming organizing concept behind these efforts has been one of "catching up with the powers" and "restoring past glories." Post-Mao growth was ideologically framed in Deng's proposition that "lagging behind is to be punished" (*luohou jiuyao aida*) and "development is the only solution" (*fazhan shi ying daoli*), against the background of the disastrous failures of Mao's socialist experiment and the frustrations of the Chinese – particularly their elites – for almost a century, regarding China's inability to rise above its chaotic internal infightings and regain its past glory. Such reasoning articulated a sense of urgency for rapid growth, and the necessity both for whatever growth methods were imaginable, and for the populace to tolerate the hardship, dislocation, and preferential treatments the growth process brought upon them.

In Japan's case, the sense of its modernization being interrupted – or even sabotaged – by the Western powers carried, perhaps, more substance than the view promoted by the Chinese. Japan had already reached a level comparable to the West with regard to industrial capacity, economic wealth, military power, and modern institutionalization in the early twentieth century – manifested clearly in its victory over China and Russia in Northeast Asia at the turn of the twentieth century, and its rapid expansion in the Asia-Pacific region in the first half of the twentieth century. The end of World War II put Japan back to the starting point – back to the periphery, so to speak.

Defeat in World War II – and the subsequent imposing structure of the Cold War – forced Japan to adopt a very narrow, growth-focused, line of thinking. The Yoshida Doctrine[1] clearly reflected the mood of the populace of the time, in focusing national energy and resources on economic recovery and development. However, at a deeper level the sentiments of post-war Japan were still very much part of the century-long ambition to "enrich the country and strengthen the army," although – under the new domestic and international circumstances of the time – much energy was concentrated on stretching themselves to survive, and grow economically, rather than militarily overcoming external challengers. The overall national environment, dictated by the realistic pessimism derived from military defeat and Yoshida's pragmatic vision, laid the foundations for the prioritizing of various interests and the preferential allocation of resources. Moreover, given such an environment, members of society were more susceptible to the labor conditions, and corporations were more responsive to government directives.

For South Korea, Taiwan, and Singapore, feelings at the periphery were different from those experienced by Japan or China. Generally, it was more a sense of being lost, with the colonial connection gone, and being faced with the need to survive on their own. The determination for rapid economic growth – at any price – had been driven by a sense of "growth-or-death" necessity. After the armed conflicts of the late 1940s and early 1950s in Taiwan and Korea, a new front – economic recovery and growth – opened up, and rapid growth became a prime mandate for governments in "growth-or-death" competition with their communist rivals. Indeed, the very survival and legitimacy of the ruling regimes in Taipei and Seoul depended upon the extent to which they could surpass the other side economically.

In Singapore, conditions of a similar level of "national urgency" also materialized, although not necessary in the form – or as the result – of armed conflict. The split from the Malay Union left Singapore in a position where it had no substantial economic basis for the survival of the economy, and the survival of the state of Singapore itself seemed to be contingent upon the viability of Singapore as a "stand-alone" economy.

There was one more factor adding to the growth-or-death mentality in Singapore, Taiwan, and South Korea. All three gained independence before their rapid growth periods. There was a sense of opportunity, as well as responsibility, among the elites of the first post-independence generation, to push for rapid industrialization and modernization, and to produce significant improvement in living conditions for the citizens of the new independent country. There was a deep-rooted, but freshly regenerated, expectation in society for the young, energetic, and ambitious government to meet the challenges of rapid economic recovery in the short term, and industrialization and modernization in the long term. There was, thus, from the government's point of view, an assumed mandate from the populace for rapid economic growth and development.

The mentality that drove East Asian Growth was reinforced by the fact that policy makers and business and social elites alike in the EACs were united behind one side of a debate that had long troubled the EACs throughout their modern history. This debate was concerned with the value of *modernization* and *industrialization*. While industrialization and modernization have increasingly faced criticism of late, they were almost universally accepted in the EACs as a higher stage in human history worth pursuing long before embarking upon their post-World War II growth. In both China and Japan, the debate about industrialization and modernization occurred in the late nineteenth century, when European powers poured into that part of the world and caused a lasting impact among the Chinese and Japanese, creating both confusion and frustration concerning the appropriate models of government, society, and development. The Japanese solved their problem intellectually, culturally, and politically, mainly through the Meiji Restoration. The Chinese solved their problem intellectually in the late nineteenth century, in the name of "Western learning for China" (*yang wei zhong yong*), culturally in the early twentieth century, via the New Cultural Movement (*xin wenhua yundong*) but not politically until Deng Xiaoping took over power in Beijing in the late 1970s, with his modernization program.

The resolution of the historical dilemma in favor of industrialization and modernization helped dispel much of the suspicion embedded within the cultures, societies, and historical experiences of the EACs, and weakened the historical basis for political resistance to growth under modern institutions.

However, the wholehearted embrace of modern institutions did not follow naturally from the acceptance of the values of industrialization and modernization. For many in the EACs, modernization simply meant rapid and large-scale economic growth, social development, and a rise in living standards. The mindset of the policy makers and national elites was occupied with only a very few indicators, often primarily with GDP itself. For them, GDP is the only respectable measure of growth, as it matches perfectly their notion of the national economy. The privileging of GDP over other indicators, such as corporate profits, labor productivity, human development, the GINI index, environment quality, etc., led to an even narrower pursuit of growth – one that concentrated solely upon the amount and speed of the increase in the nation's total annual volume of production and services. This, in turn, affected – among other things – the direction of capital flows, the purposes of investment, and the functions of financial institutions.

Given such a simple-minded pursuit of growth and development, rules and norms – considered an indispensable part of modern conditions by the early industrialized countries – were vaguely seen as means of achieving the goals of growth and development. Most policy makers in the EACs, along with the social and business elites, entertained such a narrow vision of modernization at the onset of their growth endeavor, and treated economic growth – and its supporting institutions – as separate matters, often with a determination for the former, and an opportunistic attitude toward the latter. In a society where traditional institutions were considered to be the source of backwardness, the utilitarian nature of alternative institutions were taken for granted, and opportunism regarding these alternative institutions followed naturally.

The growth mentality, in essence, helped forge a consensus among people in the EACs that nationwide unity was necessary and collective cooperation among fellow countrymen and women was called for if the country was to advance. It led people to think economic growth is primarily a national issue, a national project, and a national mission, and should thus, naturally, be organized and promoted at the national level. It helped create the sense of a mandate for the political leadership and elites that they should and could do what it takes to promote rapid economic growth. Moreover, growth mentality focused upon rapid industrialization and modernization as a matter of economic growth and, ultimately, of wealth-generation. The value of institutions in economic growth is seen as contingent upon whether they facilitate growth. This institutional opportunism underlay many of the institutional innovations and manipulations found across the EACs, particularly during their rapid growth periods.

### General structural features of the growth system

Underlying the emergent institutional framework for East Asian Growth was the national incorporation of various productive and social forces into a coherent system, along the lines of a conventional business corporation. Such national incorporation led to changes, adjustments, and modifications in relations within and among corporations, between the business community and government, between the economic sector and other sectors of society, and between the national economy and the world economic system, and, further, to the redefinition of the functions of many conventional institutions, such as the government, corporations, financial institutions, etc.

This process of national incorporation occurred in all the EACs, though in different forms and to different extents. Japan is an example where a government–corporate alliance was at the core of national incorporation. Korea, Taiwan, and Singapore form a group where government dominated the national organization of production and distribution. China resembled this second group in terms of the dominance of government. But this government dominance – and the consequent systemic incorporation of national economic activity – was the product of a very different political and historical experience.

There were, however, several features shared by the EACs. First, government was transformed into an entity, similar to the management of a business corporation, which tended to be dominated by a powerful economic decision-making body. The overall structure of decision-making within government and the division of labor between political leadership and the bureaucracy, though, varied among the EACs, and was certainly more complicated than that of corporate management.

Second, there was a close confrontation-suppressing relationship between the state and society, dominated by an even closer, almost collaborative, relationship between government and the business community. Within the business community itself, relations among corporations also experienced significant alternations, and semi-corporate relations developed among individual corporations.

Third, there was the incorporation of individuals into the growth process through two unique mechanisms: the further strengthening of the family and its role as the primary connecting and supporting point for the members of society; and an environment in which the attitudes and interests of individuals were encouraged to change or adapt, allowing them to live, survive, and triumph under the new competitive economic and social conditions. The new institutional arrangements that emerged during the rapid growth period were the consequence of a complex combination of the alternation in existing arrangements and change in the attitude and behavior of individuals on the one hand, and the utilization of the existing conditions, attitudes, and habits on the other.

Finally, a clear boundary between domestic and international market, or between the national economy and the global economy, was aggressively promoted, firmly established, and effectively utilized. It was a delicate exercise, aimed both at creating a managed domestic market and pushing for free trade in the international market in this dual market system.

The following sections will involve an in-depth discussion of each of these aspects, with a focus on how these new arrangements emerged under the combined effects of the growth imperatives, the initial and subsequent responses of growth participants, and the cultural and social conditions.

## Building the three-tier structure of state management

Chalmers Johnson (1982, 1987) identifies four "essential features of the Japanese developmental state" (1982: 315–20): elite bureaucracy, "safety valve" political system, market-conforming state intervention, and a pilot organization like MITI. Here, in terms of the organization structure, elite bureaucracy, political system, and pilot organization are relevant. It seems, however, that the notion of political system is too loose to allow a clearer depiction of the sources of the authority the elite bureaucracy enjoyed and the constraints that were effectively placed on them. Also the pilot organization appears to be part of the elite bureaucracy. There is a need for a distinct concept to cover the gray area between the state and business community. The notion of a three-tier structure of state management presented here takes these factors into consideration.

East Asian Growth required a central role of the state – not only as the principal organizer and effective promoter of the national economy, but also as the primary shaper of the new national incorporation. Early discussions have also shown that the cultural and social settings present in the EACs were conducive to the emergence and function of such a state. But because of the historical circumstances of the EAEs prior to their takeoffs, perhaps with the exception of China, a strong and effective state was not an automatic reality. The end of colonial rule and civil conflicts, in the case of Korea, Singapore, and Taiwan, and the collapse of the wartime state machinery in the case of Japan, left a political vacuum at top of their authority structures. In each of these cases, a new, strong, and even authoritarian state was restored through unique subsequent developments in each of the EACs. In China, such a state simply carried on and took advantage of the existing state machinery.

Moreover, once the political authority was in place, there was also a process of delegating economic policy-making to core bureaucratic operators. Finally, the effectiveness of the state's policy and operation was enhanced through the facilitation of peripheral organizations, which served as a bridge between the government and industrial groups. Political authority, bureaucratic autonomy, and growth alliance were critical parts of the management of the growth system. The following discussion will examine this three-tier structure, and trace the process in which these three components emerged to form the managing structure.

### The rise of political authority

As suggested earlier, it is important to distinguish (in the overall conception of the strong and interventionist state) between the political authority and bureaucratic operators. Often, discussions regarding the strong and interventionist state concern the latter part. Given that strong state capacity can be forged within various authority structures, one cannot arrive at a direct causal link between economic performance and a particular authority structure, much less the type of authority structures perceived to be prevalent in the EACs. Instead, we must explore the various authority structures present in the EACs, both before and during their growth periods, to determine how a particular authority structure (or its reconstruction) led to effective operational capacity at the bureaucratic level.

*Political authority* here refers to the highest political power within the growth system, which monopolizes resources and decision-making on economic policy and possesses exclusive access to a wide range of methods in economic, social, and political mobilization and control. Political authority in East Asian Growth came in various forms: the prolonged rule over the state by one dominant political party, the authoritarian military party-state, or the communist party-state.

In Japan, for example, under what is called "the 1955 system" (Junnosuke 1995, for example), established with the creation of the Liberal Democratic Party (LDP), the LPD maintained a majority in the Diet for 37 years following its creation in 1955. Consequently, it also controlled the cabinets during this period. The prolonged dominance of the ruling party over the state, the state's monopoly of national resources, factional politics within the ruling party, and a lack of effective political challenges to its policy-making determination and capacity, were all as real as anywhere else in the EACs.

In Korea, Singapore, and Taiwan, the political authority took a more authoritarian form. In Korea, its rapid growth period was dominated by the 27-year rule of the military government. Taiwan's rapid growth period was dominated by the even longer rule of the Kuomintang (KMT) "semi-Leninist" (Cheng *et al.* 1989) party-state. The KMT had controlled the state machinery ever since it established itself on the island in 1949, until it was voted out of power in 2000. The same was true with Singapore. The ruling People's Action Party (PAP) has controlled the government since the very first elections in Singapore in 1959.

In China, the communist system offered an extreme example of such political authority. Within this system, the Chinese Communist Party (CCP), the state, and the military were simply one ruling structure, and the domination of this ruling structure has continued since 1949, when the communists took power. For much of its rapid growth period since 1979, this political authority has been effective in the control of resources and the decision-making process, and capable of mobilizing and directing productive, social, and political forces.

These political regimes established not only a well-disciplined bureaucracy focused on policy design and implementation, but also a tightly suppressed society, where dissenting interests were marginalized – if not eliminated. Like China, the political authority in these EACs often tended to be personalized, with a charismatic leader at the top.

The primary function of the political authority in East Asian Growth, however, was not intervention, as many conveniently believe. Intervention becomes a relevant concept in an environment where the intervener is not a legitimate part of the operation, and the intervention is not a function legitimately prescribed for the intervener. In the EACs, the case was the opposite. The state was considered – and expected – to be, and indeed has always been, an active player in the national economy. The primary function of the political authority was, rather, to provide general policy guidance and discipline for growth participants, along with political protection and support for the bureaucratic operators – insulated from possible attempts to influence policy by the general public, social elites, and politicians themselves. It was the ensured continual rule of the dominant party that provided predictability in the direction of government policy, certainty in calculation by growth participants in growth activity, and reliable protection for bureaucratic operators. Political protection and support was necessary for the "insulation" of bureaucratic operators from distributive and political interests generated by the state's policy moves.

While there is some kind of division of labor between the political authority and bureaucratic operators, EACs varied as to how far the political authority kept itself from the technical management of the economy, particularly where the political authority had personal stakes in policy issues. Yun-han Chu, in his study of the state structures of the EACs, found that, in Korea, the political authority in the 1960s, established by the military through a coup d'état, was more closely engaged in technical management than their counterpart in Taiwan (Chu 1989). President Park himself, for example, personally supervised the export promotion drive by sitting on the committee on a regular basis. This view is echoed by Ungson, *et al.* on the Korean side that President Park, for example, "secured his control over the entire financial system by confiscating large shareholdings in banks" and placed "the Bank of Korea under the control of the Ministry of Finance" (1997: 250). President Chiang Kai-shek of Taiwan in the 1950s through the mid-1970s, on the other hand, left much of the business of running the national economy to his close associates.

Several mechanisms are identifiable among the EACs that proved critical to the capacity of political authority to provide insulation for, and impose discipline upon, bureaucratic operators. First, there was *one-party rule* among the EACs during their rapid growth periods. While the reasons for one-party rule – and its form – varied, it allowed the holding of offices consistently by people possessing the same political, economic, and social interests. With the expectation that policy-making power would remain in the hands of the same few indefinitely, it became easy – if not necessary – for the political authority and bureaucratic operators to build trust and nurture a working relationship.

Second, an integration of the party apparatus and the state machinery, and thus of their functions, often accompanies one-party rule. In China, Taiwan, and Korea during their rapid growth periods, the ruling party and the state almost became one – or "one structure, two faces." In China, the party's unified leadership was the idea of combining the functions of the party and the state under the decisive directorship of the party. In Taiwan, there was a long tradition of referring to the ruling Nationalist Party and the state as, literally, the party-state (or *dangguo*).

In the case of Korea, one-party rule was very much the result of the dominance of the military junta led by General Park Chung Hee, General Chun Doo Hwan, and General Roh Tae Woo consecutively from 1961 to 1987. One-party rule in Japan and Singapore was mainly the effect of the consistent control of Parliament by the LDP and the PAP respectively. The LDP's dominance came to an end only after 37 years in power, while the PAP has maintained power since 1959.

The single most important advantage that the integrated party-state system brought to the ruling elites was the monopoly over national resources accorded to the ruling party, through the state machinery. The integration of the party with the state also helped legitimatize the interests and activities of the party.

Third, with the dominance of one ruling party and the integrated party-state, *factionalism* within the ruling party became inevitable. This was just as true for Japan's LDP as it was for China's CCP. Because of the monopolization of national resources by the ruling party, and the impossibility for outsiders to challenge the party – either through the existing electoral system as in Japan, or using methods of open opposition within an authoritarian environment as in the post-war Taiwan – social elites often opted to join the party as an effective way of advancing their careers and political interests.

On the other hand, within the large tent of the ruling party, there must be a variety of interests concerned with any particular policy, along with personnel issues. Factions were the embodiment of cleavages within the giant ruling party. Factionalism in the EACs was a semi-institutionalized representation of differing interests within a political party, where splitting into different political parties was not a feasible option. Whatever the other effects factionalism may have brought to national politics, it facilitated policy debate and deliberation to a measurable extent.

While there was a distinct level of strong political authority accompanying rapid growth in the EACs, such political authority had not necessarily existed prior to their rapid growth. A major aspect of the "institutional reconditioning" across the EACs in their early years of rapid growth was the establishment, imposition, or privileging, of a strong, assertive, and stable political authority. In Taiwan, the end of Japanese rule saw the arrival of the KMT government, retreating from mainland China, and the swift installation of a harsh authoritarian regime under martial law, following – exactly – the Chinese centralized state model, dominated by the KMT, the military, and the secret police.

As soon as the KMT government was re-established, efforts were made to impose this authoritarian regime on the island, where the collapse of Japanese rule left an uncertain political vacuum. The 2.28 Incident of 1947, where government troops violently suppressed rebellions against Nationalist rule, was the first of a series of government actions that established the unchallenged rule of the KMT government. Martial law was declared, followed by the prolonged extension of emergency measures, the Temporary Provisions, which suspended the Constitution, banned political parties and opposition activities, and gave the President and the ruling KMT almost unlimited powers. "A quasi-Leninist authoritarian regime" (Cheng 1989: 471) was firmly in place. On the other hand, land reforms in the early 1950s effectively weakened the power base of local landed elites. By the late 1950s and early 1960s, when Taiwan started to embark on its rapid growth, the KMT government had recovered from defeat by the communists on the mainland, and had firmly established its grip over the island under the authority structure.

In Korea, a similar authoritarian regime was established after a period of experimentation with a competitive, pluralist political system in the 1950s. The new pluralist institutions failed to take hold, and the political leadership was not able to effectively engage with the dominant societal elites – most notably business groups. Instead, the state came to be penetrated and dominated by major business interests and dominant social groups. Before taking on economic growth in the early 1960s, the system was paralyzed by contested business interests and competing social groups. With the imminent threat from the North, the survival of the new Republic at stake, and perhaps the concerns of the Allies regarding the stability of the regional security structure, the military took action.

The coup of 1960 installed General Park Chung Hee as Chairman of the Supreme Council for National Reconstruction (SCNR). He soon revised the constitution and gave "much stronger power" to the presidency over the cabinet and the legislature, before he called for – and won – the presidential election in 1963. As in Taiwan, the notorious KCIA (Korean Central Intelligence Agency) was established right after the military coup. The country was run in the only style familiar to General Park. Opposition to the regime was rounded up in operations designed to clean up government and the business community. New laws were passed restricting citizens' movement and activity. Finally, in 1972 martial law was declared, the National Assembly was dissolved, colleges and universities were closed, and Kim Dae-jung – "a sworn nemesis of Park" (Oh 1999: 60) and opposition leader – was kidnapped. Park became a military dictator, and turned the country into a military machine.

In Singapore, the birth of the new state – in the late 1950s and early 1960s – was a difficult process. After breaking away from the Malay Union in 1965, Lee Kuan Yew (and his People's Action Party) was quick to establish a harsh rule, which was both willing and capable of imposing the state's agenda and suppressing other interests and opposing views, though in a more subtle way. The PAP managed to control the state machinery, monopolize resources, marginalize the oppositions, and gradually establish its unchallenged rule in the government, and then in society. The PAP government justified their moves through the communist threat, as in the cases in Taiwan and Korea. The problem of ethnicity in building a new state of Singapore was treated mainly as a communist threat. Early efforts to build a strong government were targeted mainly at the Chinese. Chinese schools were banned, along with Chinese language learning. The Emergency Act was implemented, enabling the government to detain, arrest, and try anyone found to be sympathetic to communism and China, and restrict the freedom of press and assembly. The PAP has remained the ruling party since then.

Unlike the three former colonies, the emergence of strong political authority in Japan was much more subtle, particularly as it arose within an constitutional order of multi-party open competition.[2] The unique design of its electoral system, the political culture of the populace, and the main interests of its chief international patron facilitated the rise of strong, assertive, and stable political authority in post-war Japan. Particularly important was its single nontransferable vote (SNTV) electoral system, or what J. Mark Ramseyer and Frances M. Rosenbluth called the "two-to-six district model" (1993: 16), and what Abe called the "medium-sized-district (MSD) electoral system" (1994: v) before 1993, where there were multiple seats allocated for each electoral district. Under this system, the maintenance of a majority in the Parliament, and the Party's main purpose of seeking a majority, worked for each other, and led to an uninterruptible majority. The great voter appeal of the ruling LDP attracted the brightest candidates to work, and campaign, under the LDP banner. However, the multi-member districts forced LDP candidates to fight among themselves. Thus, instead of debating the party's ideology and national policies, where party identity matters, LDP candidates tended to focus their campaign on community service issues, to distinguish themselves from other LDP candidates. Moreover, because the LDP was able to maintain power and control over much of the services-related resources of the state, the LDP was able to support its candidates on an individual basis. In the end, while voters vote for individual candidates according to their preferences, it was the

LDP that always collected the majority of winning candidates. This is a form of political authority building that led to a similar effect found in the other EACs: prolonged single-party rule.

The consistent and stable rule of the LDP went comfortably with the prevalent political culture of Japanese society. Given the dependent expectations of the populace, strong political authority is seen as a value, if not a necessity, demonstrating the sense of responsibility and governing capability of the political leadership. Finally, as in Taiwan and Korea, having the government in the hands of a trusted political party in Japan was very much in the interest of the USA, which had a decisive influence upon the politics and policies of the country, particularly in the early decades of the Cold War era, and was seen as a necessity – if not an inevitability – considering the serious security problems with Japan's Communist neighbors.

The Chinese case differed somewhat. Instead of moving the system from a more pluralistic one to a more authoritarian one, as was the case in its fellow EACs, China – in the late 1970s and early 1980s – was moving from an extreme authoritarian regime to a less authoritarian, and less centralized, system. For the Chinese, the issue – in terms of the relation between political authority and growth interests – was, on the one hand, to open up its economic system and introduce mechanisms that could generate growth, and, on the other hand, to retain a level of political authority that would keep the process of change and growth in its hands. It was a delicate process of separating the economic process from the political one, and transforming the system of "two hard hands," in both the economy and politics, to a more East Asian Growth-type of system, with "one soft hand" in the economy and another hard hand in politics – "one country, two systems," if you will, but in a very different sense. The Tiananmen violence, and Deng's moves afterwards, finalized the demarcation between the two. As a consequence, political authority has remained both effective and pervasive throughout the two decades of rapid economic growth.

What we have seen from the above discussion is that there was a general movement in the EACs, around the time of the takeoff of their rapid growth periods, toward a system of strong political authority. Strong political authority, while in various ideological guises, created – in essence – a national political environment where government policies and programs could be implemented without the challenges or interruptions that might otherwise be the case. Its features include stable control of government by senior politicians with consistent interests (as in the form of one-party rule), deliberation and policy formulation mainly within the ruling party (through the functioning of factions), the monopolization of state resources by the ruling party (with the aid of party–state integration), and the lack of effective challenges to the sustained power of the ruling party (both within, and outside of, the constitutional order). While the establishment of political authority in the EACs was not necessarily driven by the growth agenda of some political, or even military, elite, as some have suggested,[3] the presence and effective functioning of this political authority, indeed, provided the first layer of the management structure for subsequent rapid economic growth.

Moreover, even though the path to such political authority varied among the EACs, the conditions for the movement seem to be similar. The ability of political authority to come to predominance and to exercise power, uninterrupted for a considerable length of time, reflected the paternalistic nature of the cultural and social conditions; the anxiety of the general public and dominant social and corporate forces for a determined political leadership to lead a focused national campaign for rapid economic recovery, growth, and industrialization; and the internal and external security environment of the time, not to mention the effects of the harsh methods applied in most of the EACs to establish and maintain such political authority.

### The shaping of bureaucratic autonomy and capacity

If conditions for political authority, and its operating form, varied among the EACs, their bureaucracies were very much alike. Across the EACs during their rapid growth periods, bureaucratic operators emerged to be the most critical core structure for growth planning and decision-making, the coordination and implementation of growth policies, and the monitoring, promoting, and disciplining of growth activities. If growth was, to a considerable extent, driven by government growth policy in the EAEs, these bureaucratic operators were the soul of policy-making and implementation, whether they were long-term or short-term policies, and at macro or micro levels. The study by Cheng *et al.* (1998) demonstrated how the "unusual organizational independence" of the bureaucracy was instrumental for the success of industrial policy in East Asian Growth.

There are two levels to be considered: bureaucratic operators and the core economic decision-making structure. The first are the ministers with responsibilities for specific sectors. As the key aspects of the EAEs' rapid growth was industrialization and manufacturing upgrading, the organizing of growth financing and the promoting of exports, ministries of industry, state development banks, export and import banks, and boards of export promotion all became the most powerful bureaucratic agents in the growth management apparatus. This is the case with the Ministry of International Trade and Industry (MITI), the Japan Development Bank (JDB), and the Japan Import-Export Bank (JIEB) for Japan; the State Development Bank (SDB), and ministries for industries and external trade for China; the Korea Development Bank (KDB) and the Korea Foreign Exchange Bank for Korea; the Industrial Development Bureau (IDB) and the China External Trade Development Council for Taiwan (CETRA); and the Development Bank of Singapore (MAS), the Singapore Industrial Promotion Board (SIPB), and the Singapore Trade and Development Board

(STDB) for Singapore. These agents provided the hands-on management, coordination, and promotion of nationwide growth activities. They provided the macro control and micro management of particular industries. They provided guidance and assistance, as well as discipline.

There is another level – the core structure of economic policy-making and implementation. This level consisted either of a single powerful planning and decision-making body, such as the Economic Planning Board (EPB) in Korea and the Economic Development Board (EDB) in Singapore; or several key agencies forming an interconnected structure. In Taiwan, the KMT's Economic and Financial Special Group, Council for Economic Planning and Development, and Industrial Development Bureau were important agencies in the making and implementation of economic and industrial policy. In Japan, there was "the Economic Council (Keuizai Shingikai) attached to the Economic Planning Agency, the Industrial Structural Council (Sanhyo Kozo Shingokai) attached to MITI, and the Foreign Capital Council (Gaishi Shingikai) attached to the Ministry of Finance" (Johnson 1982: 48). In China, under the Leading Group for Economic Affairs, led by a standing Politburo member of the CCP, there existed the State Commission on Development and Planning (SCDP) for planning, and the State Economic Commission (SEC) for operations. The names and functions of these agencies changed over time. For example, Taiwan's Council for Economic Planning and Development originated from its Council on Use of US Aid (CUSA) in 1948, then changed to Council on International Economic Cooperation (CIEC) in 1963, then to Council on Economic Planning (CEP) in 1973, and finally to its current name and functions in 1977. The periods in which these economic decision-making cores were most influential often coincided with the rapid growth periods in the respective EAEs.

Such a decision-making body often served as a bridge between the highest level of political leadership and the bureaucracy at the ministerial level. It incorporated the growth goals and determination of the political leadership into an operational blueprint in the form of short, medium, and long-term economic development plans, general guidelines and directives for individual industries to implement these plans, and inter-ministerial coordination. It also served as a primary window for the political leadership to grasp the growth reality. This core of growth management was often an ad hoc group, trusted by senior politicians in the early stages of the rapid growth period (such as in Korea and Taiwan in the 1960s), and increasingly more institutionalized in the latter stages.

The building of the bureaucratic core structures should have been quite natural for the EACs because of their well-established tradition of centralized states. In fact, the civil service system, the examination system, and the values in study-to-work-for-government in society did make the power and prestige of bureaucracy much easier to develop in the EACs. But, at the time of their takeoffs, there were additional factors that required extra efforts to reinforce the power of the bureaucratic operators and shape their roles and functions to the specific needs of East Asian Growth.

The first is a clear division of labor between political authority and the bureaucratic operators. Political authority has a genuine interest, and is often in an advantageous position to penetrate and control the bureaucratic process for political purposes, and the bureaucracy also has a natural tendency to be co-opted and submit itself to the purposes and interests of political authority. Because of the overall non-competitive nature of the system, and the way political authority came about – and managed to hold on to power – this was a particular challenge for the EACs. This challenge, however, was met by the delegation of authority to the bureaucratic operators by the political leadership.

Cheng *et al.* (1998) observed in the case of Korea, for example, that the initial reform of the economic decision-making structure "was typically preceded by a concentration of political power in the executive." However, the "executive also delegated some independent decision-making authority to relatively insulated technocratic agencies. . . . Delegation signaled the government's willingness to make certain policy decisions on the basis of economic criteria" (1998: 98). The bureaucracy under Syngman Rhee was "ineffective and disorganized, characterized by widespread corruption and patronage" (1998: 94). As soon as Park Chung Hee seized power

> the military undertook a substantial restructuring of the bureaucracy and the economic decision-making structure . . . resulting in a ministry that had an unusual level of intra-bureaucratic independence and control over the activities of other ministries. The bureaucratic reform centralized control over a variety of policy instruments, including control over foreign exchange, finance, trade policy and the budget.
>
> (Cheng *et al.* 1998: 85)

Across the EACs, authority was delegated through the establishment, around the time of their takeoffs, of supreme government agencies for economic planning, policy formulation and implementation, and inter-agency coordination, such as the EPB (Korea), the EDB (Singapore), the Council for Economic Planning and Development (Taiwan), the SCDP (China), and the Economic Planning Agency (Japan), as discussed earlier. These agencies usually operated directly beneath the political authority, were given powers over ministries, and enjoyed unlimited resources and access. They were effective through the rapid growth periods in each EAE.

The delegation of authority, in essence, was aimed at nurturing a level of bureaucratic autonomy or insulation, which in turn helped ensure the *apolitical* nature of economic policy-making, in the face of politicking on economic policy from various directions. First, the delegation of authority created a higher level of coherence in policy-making within government, and thus reduced the damaging impact of inter-departmental politics on the quality of growth policy management. Ministries of Finance and Tax tended to have a very different view from the Ministry of Economy, for example, on whether government should provide tax breaks for some industries, and on the level of such tax breaks. As a result, it could be more costly for the government to get a decision on the issue. Often, the centralized economic decision-making structure gave powers of this nature to a "super-ministry" (Cheng *et al.* 1998: 92), which, with the blessing of the political authority, could override interests at the ministerial level.

Political challenges to the power of the bureaucracy came, also, from wide-ranging distributive interests within society, such as industrial capital, labor unions, social elites, and various other interest groups. The exercise of power would certainly affect these interests, and move them to challenge the legitimacy and soundness of government policy. Authority delegation provided an authorizing relationship between senior politicians and the bureaucracy, in which the senior politicians would deal with societal dissent politically, and allow bureaucratic operators a political concern-free environment, in considering and carrying out (often unpopular) economic policies.

Finally, authority delegation and the insulation of the bureaucracy also added a form of protection, however fragile, from unwanted intervention from the political authority itself. While growth have been the original concern of the political authority, and while senior politicians may have chosen to refrain from being technically involved in economic policy-making, due to their lack of necessary expertise and experience, there were – it must be said – conditions under which the political authority had a greater political agenda, or personal interests, incompatible with the professional preferences of the economic decision-making body. When Prime Minister Tanaka of Japan decided to go ahead with Lockheed purchases in the 1970s, when Prime Minister Hao Pei-chung of Taiwan decided to purchase warships from France instead of from South Korea in the early 1990s, and when Prime Minister Zhu Rongji of China decided to take a concessionary WTO package to Washington in 1999, the bureaucracy often ended up compromising their professional position to accommodate political pressures. The delegation of authority helped balance the asymmetric dynamics between senior politicians and core economic policy operators. It was here that the EACs distinguished themselves from other strong states, and this issue should shed light upon whether a strong state will lead to growth.

The acquisition of authority from the political leadership itself is not sufficient for optimal bureaucratic performance. Trust itself does not necessarily lead to effective growth performance. For this to happen, bureaucrats not only need to be trusted with economic decision-making powers, but must also be capable of exercising these powers effectively. *Operational capacity* is the ability of bureaucratic operators to reach policy targets. It involves the capability and skills of the bureaucratic operators to operate effectively and efficiently, as well as their determination, loyalty, and sense of responsibility in carrying out assignments.

The operational capacity of the bureaucratic operators in the EAEs benefited greatly from their education and career systems. There was a social class of bureaucratic elites in the EACs who received the best education, followed a narrow path of career development that was established and privileged within society, and who had a life-long commitment to government service. Unique regarding the role of education in East Asian Growth was more than the number of years spent in school, seen by many as a primary indicator of the level of education – and thus the "role of human capital in economic development" (Barro and Lee 1993)[4] – and of the level of pay for those working for the government, considered by many as a factor contributing to the high quality, low corruption, and career stability of the government bureaucracy in the EACs (*The Economist*, November 26, 1994; *Straits Times*, August 19, 1997).[5] It was the general social values in education, as the only way to get oneself ready for a challenging career in government, and in the notion that working for government is glorious, that constantly brought in government generations of the most talented, with the same mindset, the same set of skills and attitudes, and the same sense of obligation, responsibility, and proper behavior. These social values had deep roots in the traditional education, examination, and government career systems in the EACs.

Unique also, for the operational capacity of the bureaucratic operators in the EACs, was the wave of overseas-trained students returning to their birth country during their rapid growth periods. This was particularly evident in Korea and Taiwan in the 1970s and 1980s, and China in the 1990s. Modern education in these EACs, in the early stage of their rapid growth periods, lagged well behind the level Japan enjoyed at the same stage of its rapid growth period. The number of overseas-trained professionals returning to work for the government – as well as for law firms, accounting offices, and corporate management – provided the much-needed skilled professionals for increasingly sophisticated economies. More importantly, many of the returnees working in government soon rose above their colleagues, and, with their international outlook and connections, as well as knowledge and operation style, became a critical part of the economic decision-making structure upon which senior politicians relied heavily.

Operational capacity was also enhanced through the, often ambiguously prescribed, powers of government agencies, and thus often their discretional exercise. The institutional setting was intentionally made ambiguous, leaving room for bureaucratic manipulation. This was reflected in the budget process, the discretional powers of bureaucratic departments, and the usually unspecified legal obligations among government departments, and in their relations to the legislative branch. In a typical OECD environment, for example, procedures and obligations regarding government operations, such as budgeting processes, are legally prescribed and have disciplinary power over government. But in an EAE, these procedures and obligations could well be practiced according to the discretion of government. In the Chinese government's efforts to reach 8 percent GDP growth in 1998, for example, senior politicians decided on the target, and allowed the Ministry of Finance to revisit the budget, significantly altering it with more "deficit spending " to increase "internal market demands" and keep the economy "stimulated." Similarly, in Taiwan, at the same time as dealing with an increasingly high level of bank insolvency, the Ministry of Finance was encouraged to instruct banks, through "moral persuasion," to delay seeking the repayment of loans made to troubled businesses.

Legally, the Ministry in Beijing probably had obligations to the National Congress in following the budget, but existing relations between the executive branch and the legislative branch made it all too easy for government to circumvent these obligations. Similarly, the Ministry in Taipei probably had no legal authority over banks, particularly private ones. However, due to the historical circumstances in which the relations evolved, such an exercise of power was often accepted, and even expected. Ambiguity in the legal boundaries of the powers of government agencies led to greater room for policy manipulation by government, and added significantly to the operational capacity of bureaucratic operators.

In terms of organizational effectiveness, the traditional bureaucratic system in the EACs was known for its level of sophistication in specialized government functions and inter-agency cooperation. Strictly enforced systems of punishment and incentive – and unpredictable levels of involvement and expectation from the political authority – further enhanced such effectiveness. Finally, the work culture and ethics within the bureaucracy were very competitive, due to the political nature of the operational environment, the nature of the career promotion scheme, and, particularly, due to the anxiety of the bureaucrats themselves in seeking recognition from their supervisors on the basis of often unspecified standards and criteria.

Like the rise of political authority in the post-war EACs, the sustained power and capacity of the economic policy bureaucracy reflected long-held traditions, where the young and brightest were brought to working for government through the narrow path of education and public career, and where bureaucrats committed themselves to the nation, the state machinery, and the political leadership itself. Long and uninterrupted collaboration between political authority and bureaucratic operators formed the core of the structure of growth management.

### *Incorporation of industrial capital*

The last element of the three-tier management structure is the *peripheral organizations*, with or through which government reached out to the various sectors of society. A capable bureaucracy, with a political mandate, is further aided by a set of collaborative relations with the movers and shapers of the national economy. A collaborative relationship between government and dominant industrial capital may be seen as "ethically wrong" or "technically unhelpful" in an ideal market-driven economic environment. But, in reality, it is hard to argue that such relationships could ever be avoided. In the EACs, this was a critical mechanism, upon which the effectiveness of both the engagement of the national economy by government, and the efforts to shape government policy by dominant societal forces, was based.

There are two different kinds of peripheral organizations. The first type function as an intermediate layer between government and the various industrial sectors. They concern, in the main, government's relations with key industries. A peripheral organization in that sense, as was seen in Japan during the growth period, was typically the primary association of key actors in an industry. Members of the association maintained a very close relationship with government, through their personal and social connections with bureaucratic operators within government. This close relationship was also facilitated by a high frequency in the exchange of career positions, and intensity in the exchange of privileged information between members of a peripheral organization and government officials. Effectively, a peripheral organization could function in both ways: to carry out the government's interests and agenda and see them through in the industry it represents, and to convey the particular interests and concerns of the industry to the government, making sure they are reflected in government policy.

This same type of peripheral organization could also be found in other EACs. In China, for example, their function used to be integrated into formal government ministries for individual industries, such as the Ministry of the Textile Industry, the Ministry of the Petroleum Industry, etc. In the restructuring of government organization in 1998, these specific-industry-targeting ministries were decommissioned and converted into semi-government associations, with purposes and functions similar to the peripheral organizations found in Japan (for example, the *Association of the Textile Industry*).

In addition to peripheral organizations closely related to individual industries, there are also national organizations of commerce and trade that have memberships across industries. For example, in Japan, there exists the the Japan Federation of Economic Organizations (Keidanren) (a nationwide business association), the Japan Federation of Employers' Associations (Nikkeiren), the Japan Chamber of Commerce and Industry (JCCI), and the Japan Association of Corporate Executives (JACE) (a business forum where leading executives develop and propose economic and social initiatives, as examples of prominent national industrial associations).

In Taiwan, three major industrial associations represented industrial interests – the National Council of Commerce (NCC), the Chinese National Federation of Industries (CNFI), and the Chinese National Association of

Industry and Commerce (CNAIC). There were similar industrial associations in Korea and Singapore, such as the Federation of Korean Industries (FKI) (an organization of Korea's leading business and industrial associations), the Korea Chamber of Commerce and Industry (KCCI) (a national federation of leading Korean businessmen devoted to the development of commerce and industry, the promotion and protection of the interests of those engaged in business, and the strengthening of international economic relations), and the Korean Trade Promotion Corporation (KTPC) (a national organization promoting the country's external trade).

These peripheral organizations concerned themselves with broad strategic issues regarding national economic conditions and the general direction of government industrial policy. They were, indeed, the backbone of the business community in these countries, and thus a cornerstone in governments' relations with industrial capital.

In addition to providing mutual support for members, and representing their interests to government and the public, industrial associations acquired a more critical function – conveying government messages, directives, plans, or policy positions to the business community in a more informal and subtle, but perhaps more effective, way. They became a clearing-house for messages, ideas, plans, or positions from both directions between government and the business community. This mechanism helped both sides make informed assessments and decisions about each other and, therefore, reduced the costs that may have resulted from exploring and testing – possibly uninformed – decisions if this mechanism did not exist.

These chamber of commerce-type peripheral organizations were weaker in China and Singapore. In China, private enterprises are only a recent phenomenon. Their interests have yet to arrive at a point where their independent representation at the national level is necessary. Furthermore, the government had already established mechanisms for channeling industrial interests and government intentions, along the lines of the state-owned enterprise (SOE) system. Moreover, organized representation at the collective level, beyond government sanctioned processes and procedures, is still taboo, barring significant associational activities at the national level. For Singapore, much of the industrial and commercial activities that have been manifested are managed from outside the country, and the concept of "national industries" is obviously weak. In both cases, however, many of the functions performed by this type of peripheral organization were, indeed, overseen by the government. The political culture there has always been suspicious of associational activities.

The collaboration of industrial capital is as important as the role of bureaucratic operators. The very nature of the growth imperatives and the pursuit of the international competitiveness of the national economy required the satisfaction, as well as the sacrifice, of the interests of industrial capital. The satisfaction of these interests became an essential way to mobilize the business community and gain their compliance with the growth requirements. Moreover, as the governments of the EACs were not a product of genuine pluralism and open political competition, the public's mandate tended to be unclear. The support of the business community, therefore, was always perceived as an essential indicator of the legitimacy of the government, and as a key component of the popular mandate for the government.

However, growth as a national campaign – and the need for competitiveness at the national level – imposed a set of interests larger than those of individual corporations and industries. There must be mechanisms with which the compliance of industrial capital could be ensured. In the EACs, such compliance was ensured through the incorporation of industrial capital into the national growth-managing structure, and thus their interests into the growth interests at the national level.

On the basis of the traditional close relationship between government and business community in the EACs, the incorporation was further enhanced during their rapid growth periods in several ways. First, government used various "policy instruments" to lure – or force – industrial capital to be an integral part of government growth programs. An obvious case, for example, concerns how the Korean government, initially under the Park regime, managed to place the powerful and predatory *chaebol* firmly within its grip. After the initial purge of prominent *chaebol* leaders, the Park regime used capital and other resources "in the form of preferential interest rates on commercial bank loans and chaebol access to scarce foreign exchange and the government's own substantial development funds" (Fields 1995: 53; see also Kim 1987) in disciplining the *chaebol* and integrating their growth activities. Fields observed that the "highly leveraged chaebol reaped the benefits of this risk socialization when they complied, but also experienced the costs of noncompliance in terms of called in loans and in some cases even receivership." By the mid-1960s, the Park regime reached its " 'apex of unilateralism' vis-à-vis the chaebol" (Fields 1995: 53).

In addition to government leverage over corporate groups, the integration of industrial capital also came in a more formal form, concerning government's courted relations with industrial associations. While corporate groups were essential in bringing about growth activity, industrial associations were crucial in bringing corporations into line with government. As the result of government's deliberate efforts, the function of corporate culture, and "mutual career opportunities" between government and industrial associations, these associations emerged in the EACs as the most important "intermediate layer" between government and the industries these associations represented. The emergence of the vital role of industrial associations resulted from the desire of the industries to be collectively represented, and the need to enhance their collective bargaining power in the decision-making process concerning national economic policy, as much as from government's courtship.

The close collaboration between government and industrial capital formed a key cornerstone for what is called "growth alliance" (Rowen 1998: 51). Growth alliance provided effective constraints on various growth participants, and served as a mechanism where the interests of those involved could be mutually satisfied. More importantly for the growth imperatives, with the cooperation of industrial capital, the government faced less resistance in reorganizing production, restructuring industries, and centralizing growth activities. It became relatively easy to generate compromises from individual corporations and industries.

In summary, the emergence of the management structure was the combined effect of the existing cultural and social conditions, and of historical events and circumstances, and serious, painstaking, and sometimes disturbing efforts of institutional innovation and manipulation were made to reshape existing arrangements to the satisfaction of the effective and dominant interests in the growth process, and bring their state structures closer to the three-tier structure. The three-tier structure of national management was at the core of the growth system, and played a critical role in organizing rapid growth.

## Internalizing productional and social forces

In addition to the structure of state management, there was a huge arena in society where a wide range of growth participants came to confront the opportunities and constraints resulting from the growth imperatives and the striving for international competitiveness. Families, enterprises and corporations, labor unions, and grass-roots social groups were some of the most critical ones. In the process of taking advantage of the new growth environment and adjusting to the emergent institutional setting, these growth participants transformed themselves.

There were two dimensions to this transformation. On the one hand, some aspects of the existing infra-structural arrangements were facilitative to the growth imperatives and the methods for international competitiveness. The economic functions of the family and the social functions of the company were good examples. These aspects were greatly strengthened and further promoted in East Asian Growth.

Others, such as competitive inter-corporate relations, confrontational labor–management relations, and the centrifugal tendency of social forces in the market economy, were incompatible with East Asian Growth. Because the international competitiveness of the EAEs was to be derived, largely, from institutional efficiency, adjustment and reform in these relations became crucial for East Asian Growth. Consequently, new arrangements emerged, either through the coercive and suppressive efforts of "the management," as in the case of labor subordination, or through subtle negotiation and compromise, as in the case of corporate grouping. Corporations formed collaborative relations among themselves. Labor and management were forced into a new set of rules and procedures. Social forces were incorporated into a comprehensive and coherent system of social management. The overall effects of the institutional adjustments and reforms were the confinement and reduction of competition among fellow corporations, confrontation between labor and management, and the centrifugal dynamics in society.

For the growth imperatives and the striving for international competitiveness, this reorganization of production and distribution ultimately reduced transaction, as well as social, costs associated with the function of the market economy; internalized the relations between family and enterprises, among corporations, between labor and industrial capital, and between state and society; and thus helped enhance the institutional efficiency of the overall growth efforts. The emergent arrangements in East Asian Growth redefined the functions and purposes of the family and enterprises, redrew the boundaries of individual corporations, reconfigured the relationship between government and the corporate sector, and redefined the relationship between state and society. The blurring of conventional boundaries led to the incorporation of those elements of society deemed critical for growth into the growth process, and the establishment of the national economy as the primary unit of production, distribution, and international competition.

### The economic family

It was observed earlier – in discussing cultural and social conditions – that the family as an economic unit is an important aspect of traditional society. In a competitive market economy, upon which the EACs' rapid economic growth has been built, this tradition has been largely preserved. In discussing tradition in Japan, for example, Thomas C. Smith argued that early industrialization in Japan had impacted little upon the various aspects of traditional society:

> The most important were the small size of the farming unit, family organization of production, and the unsparing use of hand labor. Whatever the reasons for these extraordinary continuities – and they are hotly debated – they had the effect of perpetuating the peasant family as an economic unit, thus allowing little change in its social character. The family's welfare continued to be of transcendent value, its authority immense. Solidarity and obedience were taught to the young as conditions of survival, and these traditional values carried over to behavior outside the family.
>
> (Smith 1959: 208)

They were certainly carried over to behavior outside the rural areas.

The role of family in post-war East Asian Growth can be demonstrated in several aspects. First, the family served as *a natural unit for primitive economic activity* – a legacy of the agrarian society, but well practiced in the urban industrialization of the EACs. Household manufacturing and trade was a unique phenomenon in developing countries – and certainly in the EACs – particularly in the early stage of growth, where the labor market was poorly developed, and mass manufacturing had just started to take form. The subcontracting of manufacturing work to household labor, particularly in labor-intensive industries, such as those making cloths or toys, was widely practiced in Japan in the 1950s, in Korea, Taiwan, and Singapore in the 1950s and 1960s, and in China in the 1980s (for more on this, see Saptari 1999). Household subcontracting gave the employer a cost-saving advantage: it normally operated on a piece-rate wage system, with no costs associated with the provision of labor standards, and manufacturing equipment and facilities.

A report in 1978, in *Focus Japan*, gave a picture of the role subcontracted household employment played in the Japanese economy. It described the workforce of one large manufacturing subcontractor:

> 80 percent of whom are housewives from nearby farming communities who work on a part-time basis [at home]. . . . These housewives are the first to lose their jobs when the demand for televisions and stereos drops. But since many work only to supplement the main household income, unemployment causes less serious consequences than when the main household income is cut off.

Nationally:

> the total number of households where at least one member was working on a subcontracting basis at home was 1.4 million in 1977 (about 4 percent of all Japanese households). Many household subcontractors are engaged in apparel (sewing, lacing, darting), textiles (weaving, knitting), mechanical assembly (assembling parts for electrical appliances), and sundry assembly work (dolls, toys, artificial flowers, and fireworks).
>
> (Cited in Okimoto and Rohlen 1988: 83–5)

At the level of the national economy, this part of the growth activity – the informal economy, if you will – was often outside mainstream economic models, but accounted for a substantial part of the national economy in the EACs.

Related to its role as a unit for primitive economic activities, the family also functioned as a *mini provider of welfare* for family members. Family members considered it their moral obligation to provide emotional and financial support, as well as temporary shelter, for family members in times of trouble. In contrast to a widely perceived image that the governments in the EACs provided more welfare benefits – such as those for unemployment or retirement – to their citizens, the provisions were very limited (Taiwan and Korea), at least during their rapid growth periods, and mostly tied to recipients' work contributions (Singapore) (White *et al.* 1998). There were times when children might fail in their struggle to survive in their jobs. The family would serve as a shelter for them between jobs, or even without a job. On the other hand, parents would expect their children to support and take care of them after they became unable to support themselves.

From the point of view of the national economy, support from the family absorbed the destructive effects of the fluctuations of a market economy, and evened out the burdens on society of human development cycles. Particularly in East Asian Growth – where social welfare systems were either poorly developed, or were shaped by the distributional imperatives of growth interests – the support function of the family provided valuable relief for government, corporations, and family members. It contributed to the growth process by helping to absorb the demands for support and assistance for affected employees that rapid economic growth inevitably brought upon the state. This, again, stands in contrast to the social practices in many OECDCs, where the state has been the primary – and often the only – provider of such support and assistance.

Third, the family was also *an organizational basis for business*. This is the focus of quite a number of studies on the importance of family-run business in East Asian Growth, especially in Taiwan, China, and Korea (Hamilton and Gao 1990; Kim 1998; Okochi and Yasuoka 1984) as discussed earlier. In a society where the legal system was not necessarily neutral, and often not effective, trust among family members became a critical factor for the security of business operations.

Added to the family factor were valuable international family connections, which facilitated the initial movement of business into international export markets. This was particularly important for the second and third waves of industrializers (Taiwan, Korea, Singapore, and China). Each "wave" faced, initially, a daunting challenge to compete with their fellow EACs, which had established themselves in the markets earlier. These "new Asian emperors" (Haley *et al.* 1998) not only helped Asian businesses with market information, local networks, language, law and regulations, consumer preferences, customs and transportation, and even start-up funds, but also effectively reduced the heavy transaction costs facing new businesses.

From the perspective of the national economy, these international family connections provided invaluable human resources for the economy, in its transition from an inward-looking agrarian one to an outward-looking, industrial, and export-oriented one.

In summary, the family in the EACs undertook various unusual economic functions. In general, this wide range of unusual functions was very much in line with the social traditions of the EACs. Many of these family-supported economic functions were preserved, and further enhanced, in post-World War II growth.

## The company as family

The concept of enterprise is also troubling in East Asian Growth. Early investigations regarding the uniqueness of Japan's economic success concerned the nature and function of the Japanese company (Aoki and Dore 1994; Fallows 1994; Redding 1993; Tai 1989; Vogel 1979).[6] The Japanese company provided job security, a sense of family, and various welfare benefits to the employees, and in return the employees were devoted and loyal to the company, and worked harder and longer under the labor conditions set by the employer. As Tai puts it:

> To Western countries, the company is considered an economic enterprise pure and simple. It aims at profit making through efficient production of goods and services. In contrast, the Oriental company functions not only as an economic enterprise but also a social entity. It is an organization to produce goods and services, but it is also an institution reinforcing social values.
>
> (Tai 1989: 19)

The family-patterned company, as Tai points out, was a phenomenon not limited to Japan. The same company model can be found across the EACs. Particularly worth mentioning are the enterprises formed under China's socialist system. While the socialist system fundamentally changed the social and corporate structure, the tradition of the family-patterned company was well preserved. In fact, it became an integral part of the overall social and industrial management under Mao and Deng.

Under the system, *danwei*, as the basic work unit was called in China, provided wages, medical care, retirement pension, and life-long employment, as well as social functions, the mediation of civic disputes, "moral guidance," and political monitoring and discipline. All the government-led peripheral organizations, along with the Communist Party, maintained branches down to the *danwei* level. A *danwei*, therefore, not only organized production and acted as an economic agent in the economic system, but also organized employees' lives and acted as a mini-society, within which social tensions were confined, and where social demands were accommodated. Recent enterprise reforms in China have been gradually moving away from these various "social functions" of the *danwei*, but family-type rapport has remained. It is even reported that managers from Taiwan who ran companies in China sometimes relied upon the CCP's branch committee or the Workers' Union's branch in the company to deal with relations with employees (*Economy Daily*, June 28, 1990; *Investment in China*, July 1996).

Like the tradition of the economic family, the family-patterned company reflected the social and cultural tradition of the EACs, as Rodney Clark would testify in the case of Japan (1979). However, for most of the EACs, the modern enterprise was new to them, and came at a time when the national campaign for rapid growth and industrialization looked for compromising arrangements in production and distribution. Consequently, a number of social functions were incorporated into the enterprise system as part of the efforts to reduce the transaction and social costs in the rapidly changing and growth rate-driven society. The family does more than the ordinary family would in a Western society. The company also does more than an ordinary company would in a Western society.

Beyond reinforcing social values, as one might think, the family-patterned company was an important institutional basis for the international competitiveness of the EAEs. As has been suggested, the EAEs had to rely, primarily, upon institutional efficiency in their drive for international competitiveness. The family-patterned company helped enhance corporate productivity, whether intentionally or not, by nurturing social capital among the members of the company, thus reducing the costs associated with the management of a modern company operating within a competitive market system.

### Corporate grouping

Among the new institutional arrangements that strengthened the international competitiveness of the EAEs, grouping of individual corporations into a giant network of corporate collaboration was most notable. It is no surprise, therefore, that the subject has dominated the debates concerning the EAEs – whether the concern is the *keiretsu* in Japan, the *chaebol* in Korea, the *guanxi qiye* in Taiwan, or, more recently, the *qiye jituan* in China. Much of the literature concerning the adapted corporate structures, however, seems to have failed to identify the fundamental logic behind their predominance. To understand this logic, we need to take a step back, and explore the conventional notion and practice of the corporation in a modern market economy.

The corporation is the principal organizing form of modern economic activity. Among other things, a corporation is a legal entity that "has its own rights, privileges, and liabilities" and can independently "acquire assets, enter into contracts, sue or be sued, and pay taxes in its own name" (Scott 1997, "corporation"). A corporation, therefore, is designed as legal protection for its members against the possible consequences of changes at the corporate level. This underlying dimension of corporate culture reflects the anxiety and fear of individual capitalist entrepreneurs in the early years of capitalism in the early-industrialized economies, particularly Great Britain and the USA.

What confronted entrepreneurs in the EAEs, however, was not so much the potential risks they might face within their enterprises, as most enterprises in the EAEs were initially family-based businesses, owned and operated by the family members themselves. Instead, what confronted EAE entrepreneurs in the early years of their growth attempts was the very survival of the enterprises themselves. The challenges to their survival were due to the difficult initial conditions they faced, both at home and abroad – such as a lack of capital, having to compete in international markets, etc.

The desperate need for capital, market information (outside the country), and risk- and cost-sharing, forced corporations to develop some form of cooperation. Corporate grouping emerged as a successful form of such cooperation. Rodney Clark described the general nature of corporate grouping in Japan:

> [after the war] the *zaibatsu* were broken up by the Occupation authorities, and the family firms were abolished. But after the Allied troops left and Japan regained her independence [and perhaps the need mentioned above became desperate – author], some of the companies of the pre-War *zaibatsu* began to knit themselves together. They exchanged shares with other firms that bore the common *zaibatsu* name, deliberately relied upon group banks, trust banks, and insurance companies, and did business with each other through trading companies. They also exchanged directors, and set up clubs where the presidents of companies could meet.
>
> (Clark 1979: 73)

In a Western corporate environment, corporations – under such conditions – would seek to merge with one another and form a new, and larger, corporation. A larger corporation has an advantage over a smaller one, in regard to better resource availability, market access, and capital flows. However, in the EAEs there were factors unfavorable for formal legal mergers. First, the family-dominated corporate culture in most EACs rarely allows trust to grow beyond family members. When the corporation expands with the family, the corporation will be split, or new takeovers would take place separately under different family members, in most cases members of the younger generation, who themselves would, in turn, form a new family and control an independent corporation on their own. Relations among these independent corporations of close family members are often a basis for corporate grouping. In the case of Japan, where the family no longer controlled corporations, an "extended family" was in place that played the same role as the genetic family would in the other EACs.

Second, a new larger corporation – as an independent legal entity – would entail legal obligations (taxes, for example) and transaction costs (loan fees, for example, between ordinary corporations) normally associated with an independent corporation. The fact that corporate groups allowed their member corporations to remain one step removed from a formal incorporation had the effect of reducing transaction costs, avoiding various legal obligations, and thus, ultimately, enhancing their market competitiveness.

A *corporate group*, therefore, is a set of informal arrangements, grown from business conventions existing among legally independent corporations, to gain benefits that are often only obtainable for members of a conventional corporation, but without the obligations, costs, and risks associated with such a corporation. These benefits include low-interest – or free – capital lending, cross-shareholding, shared market information and access, a division of labor based upon members' advantage in different phases of production and on different lines of products and services, and reduced – or zero – costs for transactions among associate members.

Corporate grouping, for example, has been an effective vehicle for capital formation in the EAEs. Such a form of capital formation has not only become a major source of growth financing, but has also determined the characteristics of growth. Initially, capital shortages, as found earlier when discussing the initial conditions, were remedied – mainly – through foreign aid and consumption. Juro Teranishi observes, in the case of Japan:

> [the] trade balance was in serious deficit through 1957, and the current account was in deficit in the years 1953–1957 (except 1955) and 1961–1964. . . . Japan's trade deficits before the Korean War were financed by foreign aid . . . and those during 1952–1957 were covered by special US military procurement.
>
> (Teranishi 1994: 29)

As discussed already in Chapter 2, foreign economic and military aid formed a significant part of development financing in Korea and Taiwan.

What happened after the initial period of foreign aid differed from country to country. In Japan, government responded to the decline in foreign aid with a conservative fiscal policy, and the establishment of the Bank of Development and Construction, along with a new set of laws and executive directives to promote banks as the chief financier of growth activities. Land reform, the sell-out of government bonds, profits from Korean War-driven exports, and local consumption by the stationing of US troops, together made government capital-rich. Government channeled capital to designated banks, and created an institutional environment in which capital-hungry individual corporations had to develop a close relationship with banks for financing. Due to its involvement in the actual operation of individual corporations for lending purposes, a bank often became the center of a group of corporations with which it had patron–client relations. This was the background condition allowing the revitalization of industrial groups – now called kereitsu, corporate groupings centered around a bank, over which government had only an indirect influence.

In Korea, the government has, in effect, retained such a central organizing role. Banks – in a way – acted, in the main, as the operational arms of the government's financing authorities, through which the government promoted and controlled the *chaebol*. Unlike Japan, where circumstances had "demonetized" sources of capital sufficient for growth activity, much of the capital needed in Korea for immediate growth came in the form of loans from international financial institutions, as well as continual military and economic aid from the USA. After the Korean War in the early 1950s, and before the military takeover in the early 1960s, there was a period where the relationship between the political leadership and major business players was, to a great extent, corrupted.

After Park Chung Hee took power in 1961, he placed the financing authority in the hands of the government itself, with the creation of the EPB. This environment forced corporations to cling tightly to the government, rather than to a bank, as the chief financier of their growth activity. As a *keiretsu* bank would do, the government became deeply involved in the actual operation of corporations, and used this financial leverage to enforce its growth agenda. This is the background against which the *chaebol* rose. The *chaebol* was organizationally dominated by family-related associates, but financially dependent upon the state. As international financial institutions largely supplied the government's financing capacity, its relations with foreign lenders significantly determined a *chaebol*'s financial fortunes.[7]

The evolution of corporate grouping in Taiwan possessed elements similar to both Japan and Korea. For reasons similar to Japan, plus the huge amount of capital the KMT government took from mainland China, the Taipei government was indigenously capital-rich from the very beginning. However, instead of making banks the center of corporate grouping, the KMT government was, itself, heavily involved in organizing and directing economic activities nationwide. All banks were state owned, and were largely arms of the government's financing authorities, as in the case of Korea. While most businesses were mainly family-dominated, as in the case of Korea, they failed to demonstrate the same level of dynamism to expand as legally independent entities, or in the form of a corporate group. The *guanxi qiye* has been much less dominant in Taiwan, compared with the *keiretsu* in Japan or the *chaebol* in Korea.

Corporate grouping in China arose against a very different historical background. Under the socialist model, before the reforms starting in the late 1970s and early 1980s, the organization of production was "incorporated" at the national level, where the government acted as the management of the *national* corporation. There were no legally independent entities as such. Legally independent corporations now operating in China come from two sources. One is the rapid growth of the private sector since the 1980s, including joint ventures and completely independent corporations, initially based upon foreign investment. The other source is the gradual process of restructuring and transforming SOEs since the 1990s. Many corporate groups, today, emerged from the second process – a form of de-corporation of state enterprises. Integral relations between government ministries, banks, and enterprises have been broken up. Formal government ministries have been transformed into semi-governmental "associations or *qiye jituan*." Banks' relationships with corporations have undergone substantial change, now resting upon the bases of commercial operations, rather than administrative ones. Legal instruments, such as taxes, fees, and monetary and fiscal policies, have being gradually replacing administrative ones, such as directives, quotas, and profits in corporations' relations with the state.

While deriving from an opposite direction, corporate groups in China have increasingly moved closer to those in other EAEs, in terms of the role they play in promoting competitiveness and growth. As China is forced to compete with international capital, following its entry into the World Trade Organization, such corporate grouping will continue, as part of the restructuring of state-dominated enterprises, and as the result of the growth of the private sector itself.

Corporate groups have proved critical to the international competitiveness of the EAEs. In essence, under the conventional corporate structure – with legally independent corporations competing with each other – EAE corporations would have remained weak in terms of international competitiveness, at the very time when competing in international markets was a necessity. Corporate grouping, with a set of unconventional corporate arrangements to reduce costs, risks, and uncertainties, helped reduce domestic competition, marginalize legal, organizational, and transaction costs associated with the conventional corporate structure, and thus forged a new corporate structure, where competitiveness could be enhanced – even without, necessarily, a rise in productivity driven by technology and labor efficiency.

Moreover, the formation of corporate groups in the EAEs suggests the subtleties inherent in the dynamic relationship between a modern institution – in this case, the corporation – and its operational setting and imperatives. It was the growth imperatives and the striving for international competitiveness that made such a twisted corporate structure desirable, and it was the dominant cultural and social setting that made it feasible.

### *Labor subordination*

Another, much debated, aspect of the emergent institutional arrangements was the transformed labor-management relations. Like the incorporation of industrial capital, there were government efforts (and various historic circumstances) that helped incorporate, or – in Frederic C. Deyo's (1989) words – "subordinate" labor forces.

After the initial growth takeoffs, the EACs experienced a period marked by an upsurge in labor unrest. Industrial conflict was widespread in Japan and Singapore in the 1960s, Korea in the 1970s and 1980s, and China in the 1990s, and invoked the government's intensive efforts to restrict labor activities and reduce tensions. Japan, for example, was observed to have reached its highest rate of unionization in the late 1960s (34–5 percent), which has since declined, to 24.2 percent in 1993 (Ichimura 1998: 22). Working days lost amounted to 5,669 thousand in 1965, but only 112 thousand in 1993. A similar pattern is found in Korea, Singapore, and Taiwan,[8] though the intensity of labor conflict was much higher in Korea than the other EACs. While the reasons for the decline of labor conflicts in the EACs varied, one can argue that it was largely the effect of the incorporation of labor interests into the national growth process, and thus the transformed industrial relations.

The incorporation of labor interests can be traced along three lines: co-optation, restriction, and provision. Turning the labor movement into an intermediate organization between government and labor has been achieved across the EACs. In what Deyo called corporatist controls, in which there occurred the mandatory incorporation of labor groups into elite-controlled structures of authority (1989: 107), the key was the nature of the labor unions. In the case of Japan, as Toru Shinoda argues, industrial relations in post-war Japan featured a fundamental transformation from "corporatism without labor" to "corporatism with labor." Shintoda quoted T. J. Pempel and Keiichi Teunekawa as saying:

> the dominant coalition of the state and big business was expanded to include, as minor partners, the agricultural and small business sectors. One of the major political strategies chosen by this coalition was to systematically exclude labor from the national-level organizations and to incorporate them at the individual plant level, thus neutralizing their potentially disturbing influence.
>
> (Pempel and Teunekawa 1979, quoted in
> Shinoda 1997: 187–8)

In contrast to Japan's enterprise corporatism, labor incorporation in the rest of the EACs was much more comprehensive, from the enterprise level to the national level. In China, labor subordination was part of the closed non-competitive political system. Like many institutions under the system, labor unions also acquired a dual function as intermediate organizations between labor and government: conveying the interests and concerns of workers to government on the one hand, and informing workers of government policy and regulations on the other. Because the government set wages and labor conditions centrally, there was no need for the unions to negotiate them with the management, on behalf of workers. Instead, labor unions often became "caretakers," or social "smoothers," that helped the Party committee and management to solve workplace problems among workers. Labor unions in China were, by default, apolitical. Increasingly, however, because of the rapid expansion of employment in the private sector, there has been an increase in genuine organized labor in recent years, particularly in companies with "foreign" ownership and management.

The incorporation of labor unions in Taiwan, Singapore, and Korea did not differ greatly from the experience in China, though the methods and circumstances were different. For various historical, political, and social reasons, labor unions in Taiwan had been insignificant. But, in Korea and Singapore, there existed substantial government intervention in industrial relations and integrated labor activities – in government sanctioned forms – at the enterprise, industrial, regional, and national levels. In both cases, government sought to establish "an authoritarian corporatist union structure" on the one hand, and ban unions uncooperative with government, on the other hand (Deyo 1989: 119). In Korea, the government fought against, and finally banned, the General Council of Korean Trade Unions (GCKTU) in the late 1940s, and promoted the Federation of Korean Trade Unions (FKTU) in the 1950s–1960s. "The FKTU, headed by a leadership whose selection and subsequent behavior were strongly influenced by government, became an important watchdog over local labor affairs" (Deyo 1989: 121). In 1980 the government banned industry-wide national unions and replaced them with enterprise unions following the Japanese model. Further, in 1988, the Labor Management Council Act required every company with more than 50 employees to create a works council as a substitute for a union in handling labor management relations. In reality, "management typically controlled the council" (Ungson *et al.* 1997: 177–80).

Similarly, in Singapore the PAP government "set out to destroy union opposition through deregistration of SATU – affiliated unions, jailing of union leaders, and harassment of leftist union organizers, culminating, in 1963, in major police operations that substantially reduced leftist labor resistance." On the other hand, it also invigorated the "pro-government NTUC" (Deyo 1989: 123–4).

While labor unions were incorporated into growth arrangements, there was a wide range of restrictions on what the legal trade unions could, and could not, do. This was often achieved through special labor legislation. What Deyo found in Taiwan, in this regard, gives an overall picture of these restrictions across the EACs during the rapid growth period:

> Unions were legislatively mandated to play a meditative rather than interest-representational role in disputes. . . . No unions were permitted among government administrative or educational workers, or in military-related business. Union business was to be regulated by local government agencies, and strikes could not be called prior to mediation and arbitration, in effect making strikes illegal. Perhaps most damaging of all, unions could not 'demand an increase in wages to the extent of exceeding the standard wage' . . . unions cannot enter into collective bargaining over wages, which are unilaterally set by management . . .

labor disputes in matters of wages or other compensation were to be referred by government authorities to ad hoc mediation boards for conciliation and thence, if still unresolved, to tripartite arbitration boards. . . . Finally, martial law proscribed the formation of oppositional political parties that might have encouraged labor opposition.

(Deyo 1989: 115–16)

Among other things, restrictions on the collective bargaining process, and its subjection to a government-sanctioned national wage-control body, proved crucial in ensuring that wages would not grow prohibitively in the economy. In Singapore, the National Wage Council was set up especially for national wage management.

Finally, labor incorporation was also facilitated by the provision of a wide range of welfare benefits for workers. Japan and Singapore are known for their employee-centered labor welfare benefits, not necessarily provided by the state, but often closely tied to their growth activities. In Japan, as Katsumi Yakabe finds, labor welfare benefits were "composed of the national social security system and welfare measures carried out by individual companies" (Yakabe 1974: 56). For the social security system, Japan established the national insurance and pension system in 1961, which provided health care, pensions, employment insurance, and accident compensation to the employees of private enterprises. For company-provided welfare benefits, "most (i.e. 93 percent) large enterprises provide family housing, medical check ups for adults, rest homes, cultural clubs, athletic clubs, additional labor accident benefits and supplementary health insurance" (Yakabe 1974: 55–72). These welfare benefits were accompanied by practices of lifetime employment, and in-company training and education.

There was an equivalent of the Japanese labor welfare model in Singapore. Singapore's "central welfare institution" (White *et al.* 1998: 199) is the Central Provident Fund (CPF), set up in 1953. As White *et al.* observe, over the past decades, the CPF "has evolved from a simple compulsory savings scheme to a complex social welfare program." In 1968, a Housing Scheme was introduced. In 1984, the Medisave Scheme was added on. With the contributions from the employee and the employer (20 percent each of the wages), the employee could use his CPF account for purchasing housing and approved investment, for hospitalization expenses, and for old-age pensions and contingencies (White *et al.* 1998: 199). The Fund is managed by the government, and can be used and invested by the government in growth projects or overall economic management.

The levels of labor welfare benefits varied in Korea, Taiwan, and China, and the trends there have also been different.[9] However, in terms of the levels of labor incorporation that these benefits were meant to generate, the differences were less significant among the EACs.

Overall, labor incorporation was a crucial part of the national growth system. It helped control and ease tensions between management and labor, thereby reducing the costs that possible tensions, disruptions, and dispute settlements could bring to the growth process at the national and enterprise levels. As labor costs are a principal component of the cost of production, the contribution of the transformed industrial relations to the EAEs' international competitiveness was significant.

### Engaging with social interests

Last but not least, as growth was pursued as a social movement and a national campaign, there were tremendous efforts in the EACs to incorporate various social groups into the growth process. Taking place at the grassroots level, this incorporation performed two functions in relation to the overall growth efforts: solving tensions or preventing confrontations between the government and social groups, between industrial interests and social interests, as well as among social groups themselves, through civic mediation and intervention; and providing services and training to youth and workforces. This grass-roots incorporation was ultimately an exercise of cost control and efficiency promotion.

Grass-roots incorporation took various forms, by the state or by corporations. A nuclear power company in Taiwan, for example, spent millions of dollars each year – mainly government money, as it was a state enterprise – to support public projects in local communities, as part of a "goodwill" package that secured local communities' acceptance of the storage of nuclear waste in their neighborhood. As another example, a laid-off worker would receive compensation and training services from the former employer and the neighborhood committee as part of the government system.

Comprehensive, and more institutionalized, grass-roots incorporation is found in China and Singapore. In China, beside the National Association of Labor Unions, which deals with labor matters, there is one primary institution – sanctioned by the government and operating from the national level to grass-roots levels – for each "functional group" in society: the Chinese National Association of Women, a national organization for women (CNAW); the Communist Youth League (CYL), a national organization directing and organizing activities of the young; and the Neighborhood Committee, which extended to every street corner, taking on responsibilities ranging from street cleaning to civic mediation between a married couple.

Close to the Chinese system of "mass organizations" is the People's Association in Singapore, consisting of various civil councils and grassroots organizations. The People's Association, in a way, is a government-sponsored "civic society," intended to reduce civic tensions, raise the quality of civic life, and bring the citizenry "close to the government."[10] The organization structure of the People's Association stretched from the Prime Minister at the top to the various Community Development Divisions in the districts. The activities ranged from civil defense to neighborhood engagement; from job training to continual education; from support for senior citizens to support for women, and for Malay, Indian, and youth activity; and from club management to lifestyle services.

Organizations of this nature were an integral part of the national growth campaign. They were effective channels or platforms for mass mobilization, and for growth programs that demanded mass participation, sacrifice, and tolerance. They also helped government control social demands that might otherwise derail its efforts to focus limited resources toward its priorities. Furthermore, these organizations played a positive role in enhancing citizens' abilities to stay abreast with the fast-changing social and work environment, by providing training and consultation. Finally, they helped manage labor costs and general social consequences (such as unemployment) associated with the violent movements of the national economy. One can argue that there was already a strong tradition of centripetal tendencies in the EACs. These deliberate institutional efforts dealt with the centrifugal forces associated with the modern market economy, and thus reinforced the centripetal nature of the society.

## Transforming the Confucian man

As was discussed earlier, East Asian Growth has been achieved through the pursuit of international competitiveness on the basis of the national reorganization of production and the collaborative efforts of growth participants, and the high propensity of the individual in the EACs to comply with collective pressures allowed a high probability of the reorganization and collaborative efforts to work. However, these very same cultural qualities – particularly those values at the core of Confucianism – were indeed incompatible, if not prohibitive, with the modern capitalist economy. The Confucian man is driven by the values of moral perfection rather than efficiency maximization, and responds primarily to personalized relations rather than impersonal institutions. Efficiency maximization and effective institutions are the two cornerstones of the modern political economy.

While it is debatable as to what extent Confucian values and traditions have transformed themselves in each of the individual EACs, a closer examination will confirm that a significant change in primary social values, and a new pattern of social behavior, paralleled, if not preceded, East Asian Growth. Along with this change was the adaptation of the institutional setting that would recognize, promote, and protect the interests and activities generated by these new attitudes.

### *From samurai to capitalist entrepreneur*

The preparation of Japanese society for the modern capital economy took place long before its post-war rapid growth period. Most critical, among other things, was the emergence of a new class of capitalist entrepreneurs from the traditional society – a mixture of feudalism and Confucianism.

Traditional Japanese society was no less rigid, static, and hierarchical than its Asian neighbors. Indeed, pre-Meiji society was, by and large, a replica of the Chinese imperial system, where the samurai enjoyed prestige, and merchant and trade activities were considered the business of the lower classes. In particular, the samurai were mainly warrior-turned-Confucian scholars, who were retainers of the *daimyo* or local governors. Generally, they lived on government stipends and did not normally involve themselves in, what we would today call, value-adding economic activities. Toward the end of the Tokugawa reign, the samurai increasingly became a burden to the government, and the prestigious existence they lived began to marginalize the lower classes, therefore suppressing productive activities within society.

As part of the Meiji reform program, the government determined to change this situation. W. G. Beasley finds that "at the end of 1871 samurai had been given permission to enter farming, commerce and other occupations" (1963: 110). Furthermore, the government allowed them – and later made it "compulsory" for them – to commute their stipends in government bonds at half the rates for *daimyo*, "a great deal less than they could live on (Beasley 1963: 110). The government, through these new initiatives, not only provided "former *daimyo* with substantial capital sums" for capital investment, and "achieved the economy it desired, reducing annual expenditure on this item to about half the cost of the stipends of 1871" (Beasley 1963: 110), but, most importantly, forced the samurai into new entrepreneurial activities.

Johannes Hirschmeier, in examining the origins of entrepreneurship in Meiji Japan, confirms the "drafting of samurai for modern enterprise" and placed the rise of the entrepreneurial class in the larger historical context of industrialization and modernization during the Meiji period, and the role of the government in nurturing the transformation (Hirschmeier 1964). His study documented "the rush of the samurai to found banks," and support for samurai to invest in new enterprises, out of "hard necessity, to avoid starvation," with the government providing sponsorship (Hirschmeier 1964: 56–64). The result was not only the survival of the samurai, but their transformation into a new class of capitalist entrepreneurs, many of whom later became the first generation of the "*zaibatsu* builders."

Consequently, these samurai started new lives as craftsmen, merchants, bankers, company managers, property owners, or traders, and gradually formed a new entrepreneurial class that prepared for the rise of modern capitalism in Japan. Even today, Japanese businessmen can still distinguish themselves with the determination, discipline, precision, and intellectual and moral conscience often associated with the old samurai.

Behind the social change the samurai experienced, however, was the undermining of the core Confucian values that were an important part of traditional Japanese society. Pure moral self-cultivation – as the core of the Confucian tradition, and supposedly practiced by the samurai – was no longer considered sufficient, or even appropriate. One's virtue and knowledge had to be acquired through practical actions, and attested in reality.

## The making of the Singaporean

In addition to the class of capitalist entrepreneurs, the effectiveness of modern institutions requires a civil quality among the population which, in the form of citizenship and national identity, allows the equal interests and capacity of the members of society to respond to modern institutions, without, necessarily, the complications of "primordial bonds." Institutional effectiveness is crucial for East Asian Growth dependent upon institutionally enhanced competitiveness. The civil quality needs to be nurtured for societies such as Singapore's, which used to be fragmented along ethnic lines with each group having primary allegiance, loyalty, and an institutional responsiveness of its own, as well as different social and economic interests in society. The making of the Singaporean is a process of promoting the primacy of state institutions and citizenship, and national allegiance and loyalty.

Singapore, at the time of its independence in the early 1960s, consisted of three major ethnic groups: Chinese, Malays, and Indians. The three groups spoke different languages, practiced different religions, ran different local communities, followed different sets of communal rules, and dominated different social domains. "Cultural distinctiveness is associated with extensive social and spatial segregation" (Chiew 1983: 30). The dominant Chinese, themselves, were seen as operating in secretive wealth-hunting clubs, concentrated mainly within urban areas, and practicing Confucian traditions in family and social life. The Chinese in Singapore, at this point, seemed to display elements of both the Chinaman and the Confucian Man. There was literally no nation, nor state, as we know it – only three ethnic groups that happened to share a geographical area and tried to survive, in one way or another. After an independent nation was achieved, a way for the three groups to live within one political structure – and for the structure to survive challenges from the Malay mainland and from Indochina, where communism was spreading rapidly – needed to be found.

What emerged from the initial survival efforts, however, was more important. It was the emergence of the modern Singaporean that gave the growth efforts in Singapore sustainable cultural and social support. The making of the modern Singaporean can be seen as the result of various efforts and events, along two main lines: the relegation of ethnic cultures and identities, particularly those of the Chinese; and the promotion of citizenship and a Singaporean identity.

Beng Huat Chua and Eddie C. Y. Kuo have observed:

> in the first two decades of the emergence of Singapore as a new nation, a very conscious discursive distinction was maintained between

'national interests' and 'racial culture and racial identity.' Racial cultures and identities, administratively reduced to three discursively constructed units – Chinese, Malays and Indians – were given very high visibility through the concept of multiracialism, but were also relegated to the private sphere of individuals and voluntary groups. The government played a supportive role in the religious holidays and major cultural festivals of each group, policing the limits of such cultural experiences through the elastic idea of 'racial chauvinism.' Furthermore, it actively sought to diffuse the political potential of constructed racial constituencies through the demolition of exclusive racial enclaves, the unintended demise of vernacular schools, and the weakening and replacement of certain traditional values by those necessary for capitalist economic development, such as competitiveness and meritocracy. The combined effect of the policy of multiracialism is, thus, the very visible display of racial constituencies which, at the same time, have 'minimal political effects and efficacy.'"

(Chua and Kuo 1995: 119–20; see also
Hill and Fee 1995: ch. 4)

The Chinese population was, in particular, the target of such relegation. For then Prime Minister Lee Kuan Yew, the real challenge came from within – more precisely, from the Chinese community. Among the three ethnic groups, the Chinese community was the largest and most influential. Like their compatriots in other Southeast Asian countries, they controlled much of the nation's businesses. In addition, the Chinese community could well be linked to the communist movement in the region, supported by communist China. But subtly and more fundamentally – for a political leader trained in Oxford with the idea of a society ruled by modern laws and civility – it was the original qualities of the Chinese that were seen as the ultimate obstacle to the rise of Singapore as a viable nation-state and a competitive economy in the long run.

The initial campaign to erase *Chineseness* involved the policy to promote English over Chinese in the early years, along with the banning of radical political activities by Chinese-educated Chinese. Lee Kuan Yew was quoted as saying that, if "'Chinese chauvinists' ever perceived Chinese culture as being threatened, they 'would crawl out of the woodwork'" (Milne and Mauzy 1990: 27). Further, the PAP government moved to "clean up" Chinese middle schools, and urged officials at Nanyang University to "reform the institution, change its radical image, and use more English to secure its survival" (Milne and Mauzy 1990: 19).

However, the privileging of other ethnic groups – as seen in other countries – did not follow the suppression of Chinese influence. In place of relegated ethnic cultures and identities arose the modern Singaporean identity and citizenship, and the rule of law. In fact, the new national identity, citizenship, civil culture, and the rule of law are all interrelated in the making of the modern Singaporean. While the initial selection of a *Singaporean* identity – over either the *Malay* (repressive of the Chinese) or the *Chinese* (progressive, in association with China) – was only a pragmatic choice for survival (Hill and Fee 1995: 27–8), the result was the construction of a national identity. The national identity provided a basis upon which people of various ethnic backgrounds could relate to each other in the name of citizenship, without necessarily referring back to their ethnic identity, and, further, a basis for the government to claim legitimacy for its operations at the national level.

In place of parochial interests, particularly those of an ethnic nature, laws and rules have been consistently promoted. Citizens are urged to abide by laws, rather than opportunistically play between laws and community rules. The making of the Singaporean has occurred not only through legal enforcement and political coercion, but, more significantly, through the administration of public policy. The government's public housing policy, for example, has the effect of allowing people of different ethnic persuasions to live next to each other and mix in residence, which, in the long run, has helped create local communities without ethnic segregation (Hill and Fee 1995: ch. 5; White *et al.* 1998). This is also true with urban development, which has been designed not only to mix up ethnic groups but also to transform the nature of manufacturing and commerce.

Forty years after its establishment – and shaped through political campaigns, legal enforcement, and policy manipulation – there has emerged a new generation of Singaporeans who are renowned for their law-abiding nature, their high levels of education and skills, and their strong sense of citizenship and national identity – in marked contrast to either the Chinese, Malays, or Indians of 40 years ago.

In essence, the Singaporean experience demonstrated a model where the civic and civil identities of individuals are clearly separable, with each possessing different sets of imperatives. In the private sphere, "primordial" sentiments are well preserved and carefully confined, so that they do not impinge upon national interests. The civic culture sees a manifestation of multiculturalism and community life. In the public sphere, in relation to the nation-state, individuals are Singaporeans, with the same set of rights and responsibilities, and respect the national institutions symbolized by the state. Citizenship, rather than ethnic sentiments, dominates the civil culture. The modern Singaporean is a mixture of national identity, modern citizenship, and civic ethnicity.

The modern Singaporean served as a positive factor in the growth process in two senses. First, with ethnic sentiments confined to the civic level, there were fewer constraints of an ethnic nature upon the national policy process, and lower levels of ethnic tension and conflict, leading to a stable political and social environment. Second, the shared sense of citizenship and national identity enhanced the effectiveness of state institutions. The fact that the relationship of individuals to the nation and the state are based on citizenship and national identity, rather than "primordial interests and culture," enhanced state legitimacy and effectiveness in policy formulation and implementation.

### *"Getting rich is glorious"*

Such a grand transformation of society is also found in Korea, Taiwan, and, more recently, China. Here we will focus on the case of China, and explore how the new class of capitalist entrepreneurs has emerged, and national institutions have been built, in recognizing, promoting, and protecting their interests.

It is ironic that some of the profound values of Confucianism – completely discredited under Mao's reign – were best practiced under Mao's communist system. Confucius' teaching, "from a good scholar to a good official," can be understood as such an example. With the support of China's education and career systems under Mao, it was indeed the best – and one of the few – options available to the young and brightest.

When Deng declared in the early 1980s that "getting rich is glorious," it ran against the long-held ideal that sacrifice for the Communist tomorrow is glorious, as well as deep-rooted egalitarian and collectivist values of Confucianism. The CCP's declaration – and subsequent propaganda drive – promoted an environment in which it became gradually accepted that only a few in society got rich and one worked mainly for one's own enrichment – the foundations of the modern capitalist economy. It took years for society to accept the reality that someone could be richer than you, and that one must work for that oneself.

In the early years of Deng's era, most people would still seek the highest education and then either work for the government or go abroad. In the rural area, growing more crops in government-allocated land seemed to be the only option. Over the years, however, constant government propaganda and new policy initiatives lured hundreds of thousands of those working in the government and universities to give up their prestigious positions and privileges, and join the rapidly growing population of capitalist entrepreneurs. These people possessed the best education, the best knowledge, and valuable government connections that allowed them to break up government monopoly. It also motivated hundreds of thousands of those working on farm land to move into towns and cities, to open their own small businesses, to take over collapsed state enterprises, and to engage in trade, manufacturing, services, and areas other than subsistence farming. They were people who were willing to take the risk that their private businesses may run into the very formidable state enterprises, and that the government may change its mind over new policy initiatives at any time. They owned their businesses and worked for themselves. They became the cornerstone of the fast-growing private sector.

As the reforms went further – and with the growing dominance of the private sector in the economy – public interest and debates shifted to the necessity for institutions that would recognize, promote, and protect private interest and property. This, for example, was reflected in the serious efforts at building institutions concerned with the issue of intellectual property rights. In 1980, China joined the World Intellectual Property Organization (WIPO). Then the National Congress passed a series of laws that recognizes and protects intellectual property rights, such as the Trademarks Law (1982) and the Patent Law (1984). The new General Rule of the Civil Law (1986) stipulates – for the first time – that citizen's copyrights, and their rights to authorship, publication, and consequent profit are protected. In 1990, the new Copyright Law was passed by the National Congress, and, in 1997, Amendments to the Criminal Law defined the violation of intellectual property rights as a punishable crime.

On the broader issue of private property rights, a new constitution became effective in 1982, which stipulates that the state protects citizens' ownership of lawful incomes, savings, houses, and other lawful properties. This general principle was further reinforced with the passing of the new Inheritance Law (1985), Amendments to the Criminal Law (1997), and Amendments to the 1982 Constitution (1988, 1999). The 1988 Amendments permit lawful rental, and transfer for profit, of land use rights – and thus, for the first time, recognizes rights to private property. The 1999 Amendments stipulate the protection of the rights and interests of privately owned businesses. The new Criminal Law of 1997 goes beyond the narrow definition of private property in the 1982 Constitution, and also includes in it rights to privately owned productive materials, as well as shares, stocks, bonds, and other properties. Increasingly, the stipulations on the protection of private property rights in the 1982 Constitution were significantly insufficient. Increasingly, efforts now focus on further amending the Constitution, or passing a stand-alone Property Rights Law, or a broader Civil Code, to have a comprehensive definition of property rights, individual or corporate; state obligations for their protection; and conditions for punishment and remedy on their violation.

It is evident that accompanying the 20 years of rapid economic growth in China has been a significant transformation of society in terms of people's attitudes to what is good for society and what is good for themselves as individuals. Moreover, in response to this, a new institutional setting has gradually but steadily emerged to recognize and protect the new relations driven by these new attitudes and activities. Thus, the essence of the transformation is a move away from a society where centrally articulated collective interests prevailed (through a combination of moral appeal and state coercion), to a society where individual interests occupy a central position, and where these interests respond primarily to effective institutions and are capable of having them recognized and protected by these institutions.

## Separating the markets

Finally, the working of the national unit of growth and competition, or the growth system, required the separation of the domestic market from the international market. However, the shaping of the internal infrastructure (as discussed earlier) was not sufficient for such a dual market[11] regime to emerge. The national growth system would not be complete without the erection of boundaries, and the exercise of control over them by the dual market operators.

National boundaries were critical for the working of the growth system. In a general sense, it was competitiveness at the national level – in relation to competitors in the international markets – that ultimately made East Asian Growth unique. More specifically, it was not merely a protectionist device, as in an import substitution setting. Rather, in export-led growth, it was a growth-promoting regime. It was necessary for the methods of institutionally enhanced international competitiveness. Different sets of prices, demand and supply in two separate markets, and the necessity to capitalize products and services in "external markets," forced internal adjustment in relations between production and distribution in the "internal market," as discussed earlier. National collaboration, however, would not be possible without effective control of the direct access of individual domestic corporations to international markets. Industrial policy aimed at effecting a desirable industrial structure would be ineffective without devices such as exchange rate controls, export subsidy, and import quotas. National boundaries are necessary for these devices to operate. The dual market, operating according to these mechanisms, thus provided a basic foundation for East Asian Growth.

In contrast to the widely circulated view that it was the industrialization vision that led to the adoption of boundary-building regulations, much of the regulations were, in fact, emergency measures inherited from the initial conditions, adjusted and enhanced over time. This was certainly the case with Japan in the late 1940s and early 1950s, and Taiwan, Korea, and Singapore in the late 1950s and early 1960s. Many of the export and import controls – and, in fact, emergency control by the state over the whole national economy – were carried out to meet institutional demands for the bifurcation of the market. After the initial short period of import substitution, these EACs all shifted to export-led growth. The adjustment of international regulations – regarding international flows of commodities and capital in response to the shift in growth orientation – added a promotional element to the regulations. Over the years, the promotional aspect of international regulations gradually surpassed the protectionist aspect, and came to dominate international regulations in the EAEs.

In the case of China, the separation of the national economy from the international economic system was only natural, as from the beginning of the People's Republic's existence it had been under a USA-led international embargo, which lasted until the two sides reproached each other in the 1970s. This international embargo effectively cut China off from the international economic system, and confined it to narrow international contact with the Soviet bloc. By the 1970s, this narrow Soviet connection was long gone. China was in complete isolation.

This complete isolation helped create a very independent economic system, which not only was separated from the rest of the world, but operated on the basis of very different mechanisms and arrangements. Much of this system was built upon socialist economic theory, which does not recognize independent economic agents within the system. Consequently, there was no private ownership, no taxes (personal or corporate), no markets (commodity, capital, or labor), and no government fiscal and monetary policy, as we know it.

For China, therefore, the building of the "bamboo fence" was concerned more with scaling-down internal controls, nurturing domestic capital, and injecting competitiveness into them, rather than erecting new barriers to separate the domestic market from the international market. Economic reforms in the late 1970s and 1980s aimed at revitalizing the national economy, and in the process resulted in the (re-)establishment of various forms of private ownership; the tax system; commodity, capital, and labor markets; and the mechanisms of monetary and fiscal management. Market competition gradually replaced government planning and control in production and distribution.

The establishment of these market arrangements has made possible effective transactions between the national economy and international markets, creditors, and investors. Capital account convertibility between *renminbi* and international currencies was established, along with capital markets. Laws regulating international business were gradually put in place.

At the same time, international transactions grew, from the late 1970s, alongside the mechanisms of heavy government control and regulation inherited from the socialist system. With the controlled process of reform, essential control mechanisms – including quotas and licensing on exports and imports; closed capital, labor and commodity markets; and an inconvertible currency – have largely been preserved for much of the rapid growth period in the 1980s and 1990s.

Many elements of the old socialist economic system were conveniently incorporated into China's emergent East Asian Growth. The government, for example, in concurrence with newly emerging domestic capital and a large population of individual investors, still strongly believes that domestic capital, and the stock market, needs insulation from the movements of international capital, to ensure stable growth and continued functionality.[12] This view has been further reinforced by the region's economic crisis of 1997 and 1998.

The institutional arrangements that have emerged from the reforms and growth of the past 20 years, therefore, are not simply a case of tearing down the iron curtain[13] so that free flows of capital and commodities may take place. Rather, they constitute a case in which the iron curtain has been subtly transformed into "bamboo fences," if you will, within which capital and commodities do flow, but in a controlled fashion underpinned by a consideration for the nation's immediate priorities and long-term interests – a phenomenon that has been found throughout the EACs, particularly during the early stage of their growth periods.

These bamboo fences are a series of government regulations and national conditions that affect international flows of commodities, capital, and labor. There was little international movement of labor in the EAEs during their rapid growth periods. Many of the controlling efforts focused upon the international flows of commodity and capital. The management of international commodity flows consisted of import controls and export promotion. Import controls were exercised, generally, through "fences" at three levels. At the first level, there was a substantial level of tariffs and quotas, particularly heavy concerning consumer products. Across the EAEs – even following the initial import substitution period – import controls were largely preserved, if not enhanced. However, controls during the lengthy period of export-led growth were more selective, and made special allowance for the import of materials for domestic manufacturing. At the second level were so-called non-tariff regulations, ranging from matters regarding packaging, safety, health, and environmental impact, to matters that required complicated certification or verification. Generally speaking, import controls at these two levels have not been confined solely to the EACs. In the early post-war decades, they were part of the international economic system, and were practiced by almost every country.

What was unique for the EAEs, perhaps, were the "fences" at the third level, which cannot strictly be called "controls" as they were the natural effects of the corporate culture in the EACs. In short, fences at this level were invisible cultural barriers that countered "foreign" economic forces. Japanese and Korean consumers, for example, preferred their own products over imported ones. Retailer distribution networks in the EAEs were tightly knit, so that foreign products had extra difficulties in penetrating domestic markets in the EAEs.

In terms of export promotion, a wide range of policy instruments were in action. The ideas behind industrial policy had much to do with the initial drive to encourage exports. Government concentrated limited national resources within certain key industries, which were seen as possessing potential in returning export revenue. Selected industries were entitled to preferential treatment through tax breaks, low-interest loans, expedition in permits, licenses, and other legal requirements, import privileges, and, if necessary, reasonably priced land provisions. In the actual export of related products, government made export quotas exclusively available to these industries, provided export credit and insurance, organized collaboration among domestic producers of the same export products, and promoted these products abroad on behalf of industry.

Export promotion, like import control, was also a boundary-defining regime. It defined what the key industries should be for the country, and subsequently promoted these industries. The bamboo fences here, like the real ones around a house, operated in both directions. They prevented foreign economic forces (unwanted intruders or trespassers) from disturbing the ordering of economic forces within the country (entering the house), but also – as part of the landscape of the property – enhanced the competitiveness of the national economy (the attractiveness of the house, and thus its value).

The management of international capital flows is no less significant than that of commodity flows. This is much more obvious now than it was 50 years ago, as international capital flows have become instantaneous and far more volatile. In the early years, capital control was a less serious problem. Most EACs did not have capital markets until late into their growth. Even with capital markets, there were significant restrictions on foreign listings. National currencies were usually not convertible in current accounts. Much of the capital control in the early years came in the form of control, by the government, of foreign official and private investment.

The experience of China in handling the conversion between the *renminbi* and foreign currencies in the early years, and the separate listing of A and B shares in the stock market, and that of Singapore in its Asian Dollar Market, provide two good examples of how the EACs defined the boundaries of its capital market, and subtly handled its interaction with international capital. When China started to open up its economic system in the late 1970s and early 1980s, there was an urgent need to establish some form of exchange mechanism between the *renminbi* and foreign currencies – mainly the US dollar – to make trade and other international transactions easy. On the other hand, the economic system still followed a socialist model, where the *renminbi* played a role very different from that of a currency in an open world economy. To solve this problem, the government introduced Foreign Exchange Notes, which were made convertible into foreign currencies, but which were also allowed to circulate inside China. This temporary (for much of the 1980s) method still insulated China's currency system from those of open market economies, but at the same time established a useful mechanism facilitating transactions between the two systems.

Later, a similar problem arose concerning the integration of the Chinese capital market with international capital when the stock market was set up in China in early 1990s. There was a need to attract international capital through the stock market, but there were also concerns over the impact of international capital on the domestic economy. A dual capital market was thus put in place, where domestically owned shares and foreign-owned shares are listed and regulated separately. A-shares are reserved for domestic investors and B-shares for foreign investors.

The same practice was found in Singapore, but with a broader agenda behind it. Beginning in the 1980s, Singapore started to position itself as an international financial center. Wide-ranging measures were adopted to attract foreign investment. The Asian Dollar Market is similar to the B-shares in the Chinese case. However, financial institutions in Singapore all have their own Asian Dollar Unit, facing different sets of regulations in taxation, permits and licensing, and capital control. Thus, the Asian Dollar Market is a comprehensive "special financial zone" between the domestic capital market and international capital.

Effective boundary management completes the whole system of East Asian Growth. Boundary management is a key aspect of the efforts of growth management to ensure industrial restructuring and the reorganization of production, distribution, and exchange. It therefore plays an important role in East Asian Growth, where institutions are designed to entice change in industrial behavior. The fact that these boundaries were sustained for a considerable time reflects the unique nature of the societies of the EACs, known for their histories as centralized states and centripetal societies.

## Summary and discussion

In this chapter, I have tried to trace the formation, and basic features, of key components of the growth system in the EAEs and how they related to the working of East Asian Growth. The rise of state management, the incorporation of critical productive and social forces into a national structure, the transformation of individual values and behavioral patterns, and the erection of boundaries around the national economy were all part of the deliberate response to growth imperatives and the need to sustain the initial pattern of response by the growth participants.

In the larger picture of East Asian Growth, the emergent institutional setting was critical, as it translated the growth imperatives into tangible benefits, costs, and opportunities to which growth participants could respond. In doing so, it also allowed the responses of individual growth participants to be channeled to form a concerted and collective response – and thus a more effective one.

Institutional arrangements were also critical for East Asian Growth, due to the systematic nature of the relations among the individual components. Together they formed a coherent system of resource prioritizing, cost reduction, risk sharing, planning, and collaboration. The lack of any aspect of the growth system would weaken its ability to meet the challenge of making the national economy internationally competitive.

There was no inevitability inherent in these new institutional arrangements. The emergence of the institutional setting was both accumulative and path-dependent, one building upon another. The early response of the EAEs, and the subsequent growth promotion institutions, may not be the only possible scenario that the growth imperatives could have generated, as discussed earlier. It was the contingent effects of the initial conditions, historical circumstances and events, early responses, and the cultural and social conditions that allowed the growth system to form itself and operate effectively. In return, its effective functioning has further reshaped the cultural and social conditions and helped promote the type of activity found in East Asian Growth.

In tracing the rise and principal components of the growth system, I have further exposed the underlying logic that connected the key aspects of East Asian Growth we have discussed so far: the initial conditions led to early responses; the early responses required the reorganization of production, distribution, and exchange for their effectiveness and sustenance; and the growth system emerged from such reorganization through institutional innovation and manipulation and was conditioned by the existing cultural and social conditions. This dynamic, interactive, and path-dependent process is important, as it does not allow us to isolate any one aspect and treat it as *the* cause of East Asian Growth. Rather, it urges us to understand that East Asian Growth is not simply a matter of which aspect causes growth, but rather that of the evolution and the function of a system over time where these aspects were made relevant and effective for the rapid growth. In the next chapter, we will see the actual function and further evolution of the growth system, conditioned by two primary mechanisms, and how such function and evolution have eventually negated the growth form itself.

# 6 The dynamism and consequences of East Asian Growth

Previous chapters have established the historical and logical sequence, in which a series of factors, actions, and conditions led to the emergence of the growth pattern and methods, and the rise of the growth system. In this chapter, we will further investigate the operational characteristics of the growth system and the institutional consequences of its prolonged operation. We will particularly focus on the dynamic growth cycles that are universally found with East Asian Growth, and the aging of the institutional setting that supported the growth system in the EAEs. Growth cycles are driven by the constant pursuit of comparative advantage, as explored in Chapter 3, while institutional aging is the accumulative effect of the working of various institutional arrangements, as explored in Chapter 5, in making the pursuit effective. Growth cycles and institutional aging have shaped the general growth pattern of the EAEs, and set the limits for the "life expectancy" of the growth system. To a great extent, they determined the nature of the exit games of the EACs out of the system, and the problems and prospects associated with the ending of East Asian Growth.

## Growth cycles

To understand the problem of growth cycles and institutional aging, we shall begin with the notions of product cycle, business cycle, and comparative advantage. A product has its life cycle, from heavy investment in R&D and market entry to profit peak, and to diminishing marginal profit. This in a market economy could itself cause the rolling of a business cycle when the economy collectively cannot survive profit diminishment and capital demand for a move to new products. A business cycle could also occur due to the way the self-adjusting mechanisms of the market operate.

As a market economy, an EAE should evolve according to such cycles. However, unlike a conventional market economy, market movements in the EAEs are subject to planned and concerted efforts to avoid such cycles in their constant pursuit of comparative advantage. Business cycles fared quite differently in East Asian Growth. In essence, the growth cycle in the EAEs was shaped by two important factors. First, an EAE is, by definition, an economy of comparative advantage, which is built upon generations of internationally competitive products. As such, the EAE has a natural sensitivity to the precise nature of such an advantage, and the signs of its shifting. While the functioning of market forces within the economy would encourage similar cyclical effects, adjustment by private enterprise – supported by government incentives and coercive actions, often before those market forces collide and collapse – ensures a reasonable level of production, employment, and profit in the transition of the economy from one comparative advantage to another. The key to the success of "industrial upgrading" is the emergence of a new generation of strategic products that sustains the international competitiveness of the national economy. In each cycle, there is a range of "strategic products," often at the same level of technological, capital, and labor intensity, that dominate both the economy and exports – from textile garments, toys, and simple tools in the first generation, and later to electronic appliances, heavy and chemical industries, and information and technology.

Second, East Asian Growth incorporated state-centered nationwide management, which made pre-emptive adjustments relatively easy. There are reasons why state-led pre-emptive adjustments are desirable, at least in the case of East Asian Growth. In the first place, what dominate the transition from one business cycle to another – in a normal market economy – are responsive adjustments. But a responsive adjustment tends to incur higher costs and greater disruptions. Moreover, the pre-emptive adjustments necessitated by East Asian Growth at the national level are determined by the nature of the growth driven by international competitiveness. The fact that the magnitude of destructive consequences would be incomparably more severe at this level left no option for the government other than to adjust pre-emptively whenever, and wherever, possible.

It is more appropriate, therefore, to see East Asian Growth not just in product or business cycles in their conventional sense, but in growth cycles as rounds of proactive adjustments to anticipated shifts in comparative advantage and consequent changes in wage, capital, and profit, in the form of product upgrades, new areas of investment, and the expansion and diversification of export markets. It was the circumvention of the possible "creative destruction" in product cycles in a normal market economy that marked the move from one growth cycle to another.

### The dynamics of growth cycles

While the overall dynamism of East Asian Growth is determined by shifts in comparative advantage, rounds of adjustments and restructuring, and thus a series of growth cycles, there are forces that underlay each cycle and, together, drove the procession of East Asian Growth.

Often, a growth cycle is initially driven by opportunities for certain products in international markets and competitive exports from the EAE, and then further by the demand for mass production of the products, which would push the EAE to full employment. Full employment then would lead to a rise in wages and, further, the prices of its export products. This increase in the cost of export products – accompanied by growing competition from fellow EAEs and protection by importing countries – would contribute to the weakening of the EAE's competitiveness in existing exports. To overcome this anticipated downturn, and with a significant level of capital now already accumulated, the EAE would then work hard to open new markets with stronger subsidization and promotion; and, more importantly, to develop, manufacture, and market new strategic products to absorb its market, labor, and capital pressures, and thus to retain its competitiveness.

*Market pressures*

East Asian Growth is renowned for its heavy reliance upon international markets. When Japan started its rapid growth period in the 1950s, international trade was fundamentally unregulated, and, most importantly, there was easy access for foreign products. Since then, products from the EAEs have gradually formed a substantial part of OECD markets. There was an overall pattern of constant shifts by the EAEs, from one generation of export products to another and from one set of destination markets to another. This overall pattern serves as a good indicator of the constant market pressures facing the EAEs. We shall take a look here at destination shifts in the case of Japan and product shifts in the case of the KOST.

Figure 6.1 shows that Japan's exports in the early 1950s went predominantly to Asia, presumably because of the procurement boom associated with the Korean War. The gap between Asian markets and the North American market was soon closed, and for the 1960s (and much of the 1970s) Japan's exports to the North American market surpassed those to the Asian market.

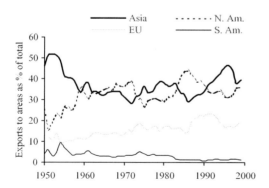

*Figure 6.1* Japan: exports by destinations (1951–2000).

*Source*: JPN-JSY (various years).

Since the 1970s, trade frictions between Japan and the USA have started to challenge Japan's export-led growth. The squeezing effect of these trade frictions forced Japan's export move into other markets – notably to East Asia. Exports to Asia bounced back from the early 1970s, and continued to rise, staying above the level of exports to the North American market. At the same time, exports to Europe also rose from the 1970s.

In 1970 – when the North American market dominated Japanese exports – the North American market took 36.7 percent of Japan's total exports, the Asian market, 31.2 percent, and the European Market, 15.6 percent. In 1996 – before the Asian financial turbulence – the North American market had dropped to 31.5 percent, the Asian market rose to 46.4 percent, and the European market rose to 18.0 percent.

Not only was there constant movement in search of new markets, but there were also frequent migrations to new strategic products to relieve market pressure. Each EAE has shifted its concentration progressively throughout its rapid growth period, from labor-intensive and resource-based products, to metal manufacturing and electrical machinery, then to information and technology products more recently. Peter C. Y. Chow and Mitchell H. Kellman (1993), in their detailed study on the trade patterns of the four NICs in relation to the OECD and Japanese markets, provided strong evidence for the existence of the unique market pressure facing the EAEs – as manifested in the general pattern of progressive shifts, driven by the "revealed comparative advantage" (RCA) of the EAEs, thus by the cycles of their strategic products.

Table 6.1 shows the relative competitiveness – in the OECD markets – of key products of three EAEs at different stages in their rapid growth periods. Almost identically in the three cases, the market strength of textiles in the OECD markets went from strong to weak in terms of competitiveness, and metal manufacturing and electrical machinery from weak to

*Table 6.1* KOST: revealed comparative advantage in OECD markets (1965–90)

| EAEs | | 1965 | 1970 | 1975 | 1980 | 1985 | 1990 |
|------|---|------|------|------|------|------|------|
| KOR | 1 | 3.14 | 2.45 | 2.15 | 1.80 | 1.37 | 1.13 |
|     | 2 | 0.18 | 0.24 | 0.69 | 1.48 | 1.69 | 1.35 |
|     | 3 | 0.17 | 0.86 | 1.44 | 1.52 | 1.64 | 1.67 |
| TWN | 1 | 1.80 | 0.46 | 1.22 | 0.83 | 0.78 | 0.88 |
|     | 2 | 0.15 | 0.28 | 0.40 | 0.69 | 1.01 | 1.16 |
|     | 3 | 0.95 | 2.76 | 2.20 | 2.03 | 1.61 | 1.57 |
| SGP | 1 | 0.90 | 0.74 | 0.27 | 0.32 | 0.07 | 0.07 |
|     | 2 | 1.44 | 0.02 | 0.10 | 0.12 | 0.21 | 0.16 |
|     | 3 | 0.82 | 5.80 | 5.12 | 5.92 | 3.61 | 2.67 |

*Notes*: 1 textiles; 2 metal manufacturing; 3 electricals; unit: revealed comparative advantage index.

*Source*: Chow and Kellman (1993: 16).

strong. This progressive adjustment in export products reflected market congestion as the result of aggressive efforts at market expansion by the EAEs in the OECD markets, and the decline in the competitiveness, and thus profitability, of old products.

Accompanying the progressive movement from one set of strategic products to another in an EAE, there was also the "progressive vacating" of markets by early EAEs, and their replacement by the later comers – the so-called flying geese pattern of growth in East Asia (Akamatsu 1962; Ichimura 1998: 25–8). Again, Chow and Kellman's study finds strong evidence that the structure of KOST exports in 1990 resembled that of Japan's in 1965. The similarity index shows Korea, Taiwan, and Singapore's similarity with Japan in 1990 was 51.4 percent, 46.9 percent, and 45.8 percent respectively, while in 1965 the same similarity index was 29.0 percent, 35.1 percent, and 19.2 percent respectively (Chow and Kellman 1993: 25). In other words, while Japan moved on to capital- and technology-intensive products in the 1960s and 1970s, KOST generally took over the markets vacated by Japan. This same phenomenon happened between KOST and China in the 1980s and 1990s.

### Wage pressures

As discussed in Chapter 2, the EAEs started their rapid growth periods with high levels of unemployment. Naturally, the early stage of their growth was marked by a concentration upon labor-intensive products for external markets. As mass production continued, the labor market reached close-to-full employment. At the same time, international competition demanded higher quality products, and thus more highly skilled workers. Consequently, labor wages rose sharply after roughly 20 years of labor-intensive export-led growth. As Figure 6.2 shows, wages in Japan started to rise in the early 1970s, and in Taiwan, Korea, and Singapore from the early 1980s,

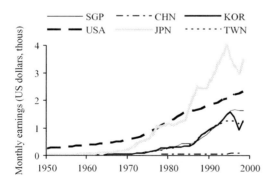

*Figure 6.2* EAEs: monthly wages in manufacturing (1950–99).

*Source*: Appendix A1–5: 7.1

while China, thus far, still enjoys relatively low labor wages. Ample surplus labor in rural areas may give China extra advantage in confining its labor costs, but there will be a point where labor from rural areas would no longer be automatically absorbable by urban manufacturing and service industries, and thus costs will rise for *skilled* labor. Gradually, advantage in cheap labor would become insignificant, and the economy would no longer be able to maintain the international competitiveness based upon it.

### Capital pressures

As was also discussed in Chapter 2, the EAEs started their rapid growth periods with a severe lack of capital. As growth continued, capital was accumulated. However, uniquely, a substantial amount of economic activity was financed through government targeting schemes, informal capital markets heavily dominated by corporate connections, and the open capital market – so much so that financial lending itself became a major element of economic activity (and, indeed, a major form of profit-making) without having to go through the conventional process of manufacturing, marketing, and re-capitalization. Coupled with this was the increasing convenience of simultaneous monetary transactions and financing through open capital markets on a global scale, and increasingly low profit margins from traditional manufacturing.

Consequently, financing occurred at a much greater scale than the "real" economy could actually absorb, with capital going to areas of quick profit, such as real estate or the financial markets themselves. The "bubble economy" became a critical feature of the EAEs toward the later stage of the rapid growth period, being more severe in some EAEs than in others. Figure 6.3 shows that the USA, used here as being representative of a conventional economy, has maintained its gross fixed capital formation at 15.46 percent during the post-war period, while the EAEs reached high levels in the 1960s,

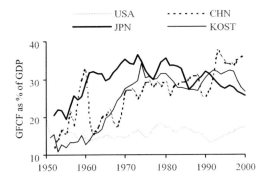

*Figure 6.3* EAEs: gross fixed capital formation as percentage of GDP (1951–2000).
*Source*: Appendix A1–5: 3.1.

and stayed at these high levels. Their average share of gross fixed capital formation in GDP during their rapid growth periods is 26.81 percent. If around 15 percent of gross fixed capital formation in the US economy is taken as a standard, then there is good reason to suspect that a substantial amount of capital in the EAEs is not fixed in "real" economy.

## Cycle management

The three factors identified above: market congestion, rapidly rising labor costs, and hot money overflow, are classical signs of a pending market collapse and recession. In a conventional market economy, these signs are likely to be treated as indicators of an overheated economy, and macro-economic policy would be applied to cool down the economy. For an EAE, however, these factors were more likely to be seen as signs of an industrial structure problem. Thus, in addition to macro-economic policy to temporarily relieve expansion pressures, the EAEs would rely primarily upon market expansion and diversification, and industrial upgrading and restructuring, to accommodate the expansion pressures.

At the core of the industrial structure problem is the maturing of the existing strategic products. The nature of the EAE ensures that it could rise, become competitive, and grow rapidly on its strategic products, and could also decline, become less competitive and no longer grow because the products no longer give it the competitive edge: producing the products is no longer cost-effective (because of labor costs for example), capital is no longer production-generating because alternative forms of investment offer quicker returns, and the limits of established markets were reached (as a result of the maturity of the market and/or competition from fellow EAEs).

Like a product-based company, an East Asian economy reaching maturity on strategic products has to find new outlets for its productive capacity, in terms of profit-hungry capital and a salary-dependent work force. Unlike a single company, an East Asian economy had a much stronger capacity to anticipate such a downturn in product cycle, and, more importantly, to take proactive actions to fashion a transition to a new stage of growth with new market destinations, a new set of strategic products, and a constant level of profitability for circulating capital. All these would lead to further demand for capital, labor, and products.

Thus, the growth system diffused the tensions built up by the movements of product cycles and prolonged continuous high-speed economic growth, by prompt market expansion and diversification, product up-grading, and the redirection of investment capital. This, as we shall see, involved a significant level of exports redirection, industrial restructuring, and other macro-economic policies that reduced the intensity of the impact of product cycles, postponed the release of tension among the factors of economic growth, and transferred key factors – such as capital and labor – into a configuration for new strategic products.

## Market expansion and diversification

Expansion into new markets has been a classical response to a downturn in growth cycles. Such response is natural when there is increasing competition, more protection, and a decline in profits in a market open to products from the EAEs. For government, managing cycle pressures is not simply a matter of backing winners – rather, it involves the redistribution of business opportunities and risks in a broad range of market scenarios, through the targeted taxation, preferential financing, and insurance of selected products and markets.

Under conventional market conditions, mass production would eventually reach a market limit. In the EAEs' expansion into the US market, the different timings of their entries into the same US market, normal product cycles, and the vertical complementariness among the EAEs created a positive condition among the EAEs, which helped them overcome conventional market limits. Structural complementariness allowed "consecutive share" of the market by the EAEs, with one vacating, another taking over, and the "leading goose" continuously exploring new products and expanding new market opportunities.

Besides intra-EAE dynamism, the successful export expansion can be largely attributed to the EAEs' proactive efforts in sustaining high-speed export growth. The careful campaign by the Japanese government and corporations to significantly expand Japan's economic presence in, and divert their exports to, East and Southeast Asia from the 1970s was a good example. The usual export promoting and market targeting measures aside, one key factor that led to the rapid trade and investment relationship between Japan and Asian countries was Japan's Official Development Assistance (ODA). A study by Shinichi Ichimura on Japan and Asian development finds that Japan's ODA jumped from $1.4 billion in 1977 to $9.4 billion in 1996, a 671 percent increase. Of Japan's total ODA in 1996, 88.9 percent of the available funds were disbursed to Asian countries ($8.36 billion), amounting to a 20.4 percent increase from 1980 ($6.94 billion). In 1997, Japan led world ODA to Asia with 53.9 percent of the total, over Germany's 13 percent, France's 4.8 percent, and the USA's 4.6 percent, with other countries contributing 23.7 percent (Ichimura 1998: 111–12).

The role of ODA in promoting Japan's economic presence in Asia in general – and its market share in particular – was critical. The inflow of Japanese government assistance was often accompanied by private investment and trade activities. Often, there was a preference to use such assistance to purchase Japanese products and equipment. The ODA could also be directly pledged in support of Japanese exports in the recipient countries.

Another unique case of market expansion and diversification is the move of Taiwan's products and investment into China – even though it was not necessarily the effect of government policy. It was the rapidly growing market and manufacturing bases in mainland China in the 1980s and 1990s that absorbed much of the overcapacity in production and investment in Taiwan. Taiwan's exports to China (via Hong Kong) have rapidly expanded over the past decade – even under the overall government policy setting, which allows no direct trade with China – from about 10 percent in its total exports in 1990, to between 17.45 percent (Taiwan: MEA 2001) to 24.61 percent (China: CSY 2000) in 1999, depending whose estimate one uses. For a median figure of 20 percent, it would be about $25 billion in 1999, or about 10.4 percent of its total GDP.

On capital investment, the situation is even more illuminating. Taiwan's officially approved investment to China (including Hong Kong) has risen from 0.4 percent of its total gross fixed capital formation in 1990, to 2.2 percent in 1999, with two peaks recorded in 1993 (5.8 percent) and 1997 (7.3 percent) (Taiwan: MEA 2001). However, according to China's official figure, contracted investment in China from Taiwan has jumped from 2.5 percent of Taiwan's total gross fixed capital formation in 1990, to 5.1 percent in 1999, with the highest level occurring in 1993 (17.9 percent) (China: MOFET 2001). With an equivalent of almost one-fifth of its gross fixed capital formation invested in China, this has provided decisive relief for Taiwan's overcapacity.

### Industrial upgrading and restructuring

Of all the measures of cycle management, industrial policy has emerged as a principal one, and is considered unique among the EAEs. The term "industrial," here, is not necessarily confined to manufacture, despite the fact that this was the primary target of industrial policy for the EAEs. Strategic planning, sectoral nurturing, and structural transformation concerned all the major sectors of the economy (primary, manufacturing, services, etc.), was often concentrated on industries at the sub-sector level (promoting chemical and heavy industry, or IT, for example), and effected movements between the sunset and sunrise industries of the time (protecting the former and promoting the latter). The promotion of Japan's semi-conductor industry in the 1960s, Korea's chemical and heavy industry in the 1970s, China's primary exporting products for China in the 1980s, and Singapore's international financial services in the 1990s were all the examples of the working of industrial policy.

As a national policy that shapes the sectoral structure of an economy in the medium and long term, industrial policy in the EAEs has several common features. First, it is usually based upon some form of governmental medium- and long-term planning. Government industrial plans took into consideration, among other things, the competitiveness of national products within established and potential markets and the structural soundness of each individual sector or industry, and, further, set the targets, directions and pace of change in industrial structure, and the guidelines in promoting (or demoting) specific sectors or sub-sectors for a specified period. A closer look at the post-war history of the Japanese economy will find that each industrial boom, from the Jimmu boom of 1956–7, to the Iwato boom of 1959–61, to the Izanagi boom of 1967–9, to the "bubble boom " of 1989–90, was accompanied – and perhaps preceded – by a government economic and industrial development plan (Nakamura 1995: 57, 92–3).

Second, industrial policy is, mainly, a government policy aimed at the "industrial" behaviors of the business community. East Asian Growth incurs a need to pursue competitiveness at the national level, which creates a significant problem concerning collective action. In particular, the management of growth cycles raises the question of forming an interest at the national level over the changing conditions for competitiveness and translating it into tangible benefits for growth participants to actively engage in new growth activity anticipated by the need to sustain competitiveness.

Industrial policy, thus, through various policy instruments, serves as a bridge between the national interest and the interest of private growth participants. It is a critical – and often very manipulative – layer of the institutional setting that encourages a pattern of industrial behavior (where to invest, whether to export, what to produce, etc.) to emerge on strategic products or industries. Here we will look at two specific examples of industrial policy to illustrate these points: one involving Korea's drive to promote chemical and heavy industries in the 1970s, and the other involving efforts by the Singaporean government to promote Singapore as an international financial and service center.

In the case of Korea's drive for "strong chemical and heavy industries," the collective interest for the national economy at the time was, as summarized in a World Bank study on structural change in Korean industries (Corbo and Suh 1992), that there was a strong need to develop "new strategic export industries," promote the production of intermediate materials and capital goods for sustained growth, and close the emergent gap between rural and urban areas; that there was an urgent need to combat a reversionary movement in the economy as the result of the oil shock in the early 1970s; that the reduction of US troops in Korea in the early 1970s "raised concern about the need for a strong defense industry to protect national security"; and that "there was also concern that Korea might lose its comparative advantage in light manufacturing exports" (Suh 1992: 18).

These concerns, however, could not possibly be addressed by the private sector alone. It is not in the direct and tangible interest of the private sector to promote national security, close the rural–urban gap, or fight recession. Here, the government served as a provider or generator of the public good through its industrial policy – in this case, the drive for chemical and heavy industry. The government produced the *Heavy and Chemical Industry Development Plan* in 1973, which, as Suh's study finds:

> favored such industries as shipbuilding, automobiles, steel products, nonferrous metals, and petrochemicals. It encouraged large-scale

investment projects in these industries through special tax incentives, preferential credit allocation, and negative real interest rates under a system of widespread credit rationing. The government also resorted to heavy foreign borrowing. To make economies of scale possible in a limited domestic market, monopolistic production was permitted in a few industries. A new National Investment Fund provided financial resources at lower interests rates to meet the large investment requirements of the new enterprises. The fund helped mobilize public employee pension resources and a substantial portion of private savings at regular banking institutions. These funds were channeled into heavy industry projects favored by the government. The administration also set up high protective barriers for these infant industries and maintained the protection until the industries became internationally competitive. Finally, the government provided many incentives for worker training and research and development.

(Suh 1992: 18)

The government not only used policy instruments to promote a new industrial sector, but also reduced its support for exports from "sunset" labor-intensive industries. The government revoked the 50 percent corporate and income tax break on export earnings. Tariff exemptions for capital equipment imported for the production of exports were changed.

The foundation of Korea's emergent leadership in world chemical and heavy industry was laid, and continued rapid growth after the early phase of labor-intensive exporting industries was ensured. The Korean economy moved to a new level of capital concentration, technological sophistication, and labor quality. In the short term, as Suh reports, the recessionary effects of the early 1970s were "sufficiently" neutralized, and export growth continued.

From our point of view, the government's industrial policy altered the institutional setting, through tax regulations, financing schemes, and the manipulation of credit and interest rates, that allowed a different set of calculations by private growth participants and effected their movement to the new industries and products. It provided the capital needed by the private sector to develop new capital-intensive products, helped the private sector to connect their production activity with anticipated new strategic products, and ensured a reduced level of risk and high rates of investment returns. It also discouraged investment in non-strategic sectors. In the end, both the national interest and the interests of the private sector were served.

Regarding Singapore's efforts to promote itself as an international financial center, the Singaporean government had, since the 1970s, sought to develop its financial sector as a strategic industry and, upon this basis, to further position Singapore itself as an international financial and service center. Unlike the other EAEs, Singapore is a city-state and has a less competitive physical base to build chemical and heavy industry, as Korea did. The government's plan to reconstruct Singapore as an operational center for international finance and services recognized the challenges facing Singapore, and rested upon the idea of the global hub economy. Once again, this vision was seen as beneficial for the economy as a whole in the long term. However, for individual investors, both inside and outside Singapore, the financial sector is risky, investment returns are uncertain, and the move to Singapore – rather than, for example, Hong Kong – needs to be justified.

Moreover, instead of possible inaction toward government initiatives (due to the aforementioned reasons), individual investors may opt to compete with the government within the financial markets, and profit in a way that is not positively related to the desired interest.

The government's industrial policy in nurturing the financial center, therefore, had two aspects: to attract international capital to Singapore and, at the same time, to insulate domestic markets from the impact of the activities of offshore international capital. To attract international capital, the Singaporean government set up a special Asian Dollar Market where, as found in a study by Cheng Yuk-shing, Chia Siow Yue, and Christopher Findlay, "various incentives" have been utilized. "These incentives include various tax concessions and exemptions from reserve and liquid asset ratio. [Within the Asian Dollar Market], there is free convertibility of deposits between local and foreign currencies" (Cheng *et al.* 2000: 235).

On the other hand, to protect the domestic economy, various policies "have been introduced to insulate domestic economy from the financial center's offshore activities. ACUs (Asian Currency Units permitted to operate in the Asian Dollar Market) are strictly demarcated from the banks' domestic operations under domestic banking units (DBUs), enabling the official monitoring of the use of ACU funds, especially the extent to which they are lent to domestic operations. ACU activities are confined to non-Singapore dollar transactions, whereas DBUs are able to engage in foreign currency transactions. The Monetary Authority of Singapore (MAS) imposes an upper limit on ACUs but not on DBUs, except for banks with restricted and offshore licenses whose domestic activities are confined mainly to wholesale banking. Tax and regulatory measures favor ACUs, so banks find it more profitable to book a large part of their business through ACUs rather than DBUs. Foreign residents also prefer to deal with ACUs because of the absence of withholding tax on interests and because of the exemption from Singapore estate and stamp duties" (Cheng *et al.* 2000: 235).

Here, the tax codes, licensing regulations, banking system, and market rules, are all part of the institutional setting affecting the industrial behavior and business decisions of the private sector. This aspect of the institutional setting introduced a new calculation matrix for individual investors and industrial entrepreneurs, so that moving in the desirable directions would be in the interest of these investors and entrepreneurs themselves.

Industrial upgrading and restructuring moved growth activity on to new strategic products and industries, and thus ensured the continual competitiveness of the national economy. At the same time, it helped release pressures built up in growth cycles and thus was a critical method of cycle management.

*Macro-economic policies*

There were further policy instruments employed by the EAEs to contain, or diffuse, tensions in growth cycles. These instruments – namely fiscal policy, monetary policy, interest rates, exchange rates, and the stock market – cannot be seen as industrial policy. In fact, many of these instruments did not exist in the EAEs for much of their rapid growth periods. Only in the later stage of the rapid growth periods did these instruments start to become integrated into economic management.

While these policy instruments are normal macro-economic tools, widely employed in contemporary economies, the actual operation of these instruments in the EAEs (and, consequently, their effectiveness to achieve desired outcomes) has been unique, because of the overall setting in which these instruments operate. I will not dwell here on how these instruments were used in the EAEs for growth cycle management, as the general characteristics of these instruments are familiar to us. Rather, what interests us here is how these policy instruments were "twisted" in practice, beyond their normal terms of operation, which made the EAEs' cycle management a unique experience.

Of the policy instruments, interest rate policy and monetary policy were least effective in the EAEs, if compared to the extent to which these instruments affect the economy in the USA. Fiscal policy was a major tool, as the EAEs were severely dominated by the government and its economic

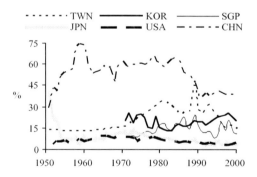

*Figure 6.4* EAEs: government expenditure on economic affairs as percentage of total expenditure (1950–2000).

*Source*: Appendix A1–5: 6.4.4.

activity. As illustrated by Figure 6.4, government expenditure on the economic affairs of the EAEs – as a share of total government expenditure during their rapid growth periods – was, on average, 21.95 percent, while the share in the USA – over the post-war period – was, on average, 7.17 percent. The government's spending, in forms of state enterprise operations, transfers and subsidies, partly financed its directive economic policy, and in part contributed substantially to domestic consumption.

In Figure 6.5, we find that most EAEs maintained a conservative fiscal policy during their rapid growth period (0.95 expenditure over revenue ratio, compared to the USA's 1.09). Korea had a very high ratio before its rapid growth period but brought it down dramatically soon after the rapid growth period started. Singapore and Japan performed best in keeping a conservative fiscal policy. The ratio of many EAEs rose in the 1990s, due to a more "liberal" use of fiscal policy.

The EAEs' exchange rate regimes are very different. Most of them had a fixed exchange rate during their rapid growth period, particularly during the early decades. There is no "across-the-board" evidence that currency devaluation was behind export expansion. China and Korea saw a steady decline in the US dollar exchange value of their currencies, while those of Japan and Singapore moved in the opposite direction, with a more complex pattern found in the movement of Taiwan's exchange rate. The exchange rate became an issue for the EAEs when their currencies were allowed to float, in the wake of financial liberalization in the latter stages of the rapid growth periods and the growing impact of global markets. The nature of the EAEs ensured that their priority, with regard to the exchange rate, was to protect the domestic economy.

Various regimes were developed to meet this concern. In Singapore, as the study by Cheng *et al.* points out, the main issue "was to reconcile Singapore's ambitions to extend its entrepôt role to financial markets and the

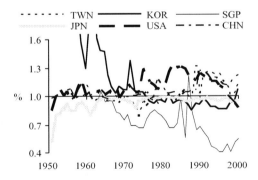

*Figure 6.5* EAEs: ratio of government expenditure over revenue (1951–2000).

*Source*: Appendix A1–5: 6.2.

desire to reduce the risks faced by business in markets for foreign exchange" (2000: 234). Singapore has adopted a "managed floating regime" since 1973, whereby the range in which the Singapore dollar is allowed to float is determined by the averaged exchange rate of a basket of international currencies. While some form of floating is allowed for the Singapore dollar, various restrictive rules were put in place to ensure the "safe" movement of the currency. Non-residents, for example, were not allowed to borrow in Singapore dollars. Banks were required to "consult" the MAS before lending Singapore dollars for use outside Singapore (Cheng *et al.* 1998: 173–4).

Similar to this managed floating regime were the regimes of Korea and Taiwan – although the actual methods of "managing" could be very different. Korea, for example, replaced its "basket" regime in 1990 with a more liberal, but more complicated, "market average system," "where the official won–dollar rate was determined by market forces in the interbank foreign exchange market" (Smith 1998: 76). In Taiwan, however, the exchange regime was only semi-liberalized, with various restrictions imposed upon capital transactions. In all cases, heavy government intervention was a normal part of the operation of the foreign exchange market, and the stock market. Besides these various forms of managed floating regimes, there was a more liberal regime in Japan, and a controlled regime in China.

The levels of control or management in the foreign exchange markets of the EAEs differed, and were determined, primarily, by how a particular regime would affect the domestic economy. Here, an exchange rate regime of some degree of flotation was not in itself a value, but rather a tool in facilitating capital accumulation, reducing costs in capital transactions, and meeting the challenge of a global capital market, while, at the same time, preventing capital flows in the reverse direction, fencing off the destructive impact of fluctuations in the global capital market, and ensuring smooth and safe contact between domestic and international capital markets.

The various instruments of macro-economic policy in the EAEs have increasingly become an important part of the cycle management toward the latter stages of their rapid growth periods. This resulted, partly, from growing overcapacity beyond the levels that market expansion and industrial upgrading could help absorb. Macro-economic instruments, here, were utilized to restrict the movement of profit-hungry capital, direct it back to production, and manage their interaction with international capital.

Market expansion and diversification, industrial upgrading and restructuring, and macro-economic policy have been important mechanisms through which market, wage, and capital pressures – brought upon by growth cycles – were defused, deferred, or redirected to new strategic products and industries. However, all these mechanisms operated at a cost to the overall growth system. The longer the growth pattern is sustained, the less effective these methods of cycle management would become. Eventually, the rapid growth period would end. Perhaps the EAEs would mature to become a developed economies Let us now look at why this has been the case with the EAEs.

# Institutional aging

In an ideal situation – where the potential for market creation and expansion, capital formation and investment, the development of strategic products, and the provision of human resources were sufficient, and the directive institutions were capable and effective, as designed – East Asian Growth would be able to go on indefinitely. Generally speaking, the ability of the EAEs to sustain their rapid growth over a long period reflected, as discussed earlier, their ability to respond, and adjust, to the changing conditions for their international competitiveness, and to bear the burdens – and absorb the costs – arising from their constant response and adjustment.

However, there are fundamental limits to their sustaining capacity, beyond which the growth system would fail to function effectively – where rapid growth would cease to continue, or limits to their adaptive capacity would become obvious – and beyond which East Asian Growth would have to become something else. The first scenario explains the ending of the rapid growth period. The second scenario calls for fundamental reform and restructuring of the growth system itself. In either case, East Asian Growth would come to an end in due time.

Besides the internal logic of East Asian Growth, its ending – and perhaps the variations in the circumstances for its ending, and the respective exit strategies of the EAEs – were also affected by extra-institutional pressures, from both within and outside the country. Domestic demand for political liberalization, and international pressures for both a market economy and democratic politics, in the 1980s and 1990s put critical pressure on the growth system. To explain the aging, we will discuss the internal and external conditions first, then the decay of the institutional arrangements and how the process was intensified by the global movements of economic and political liberalization in the 1990s, as part of the change in the operational environment of the growth system.

## *Operational conditions for East Asian Growth*

From an institutionalist point of view, the effective working of the growth system during the rapid growth period relied upon three operational conditions, some of which were found only in the social and cultural setting of the EACs at the time. First, there were sufficient resources at the disposal of the chief organizer. The chief organizer in all these EAEs was the state, or some form of elitist and corporatist structure dominating the state. This can be further divided into three subcategories: the chief organizer was the primary distributor of growth resources and benefits (monopoly); the chief organizer was able to limit demands for resources (discretion); and the chief organizer had resources at its disposal (resourcefulness).

Monopoly was preferable, if not necessary, as it guaranteed that growth participants would respond to institutional manipulation, when not responding to such manipulation would surely affect their access to the necessities and benefits of growth. Monopoly ensured such a manipulative link. Across the EAEs, particularly in the early stage of their rapid growth periods, some form of government monopoly existed, or was created at the start of the rapid growth period: the government monopolized growth financing, export and import quota and licensing, financial institutions, and key industries (via state ownership and management). Korea, in the early 1960s, created such a monopoly by establishing exclusive control over national decision-making regarding economic growth, subduing powerful but corrupt political and corporate forces, and directly managing the key institutions of economic management (such as banks) and key aspects of economic activity (such as exports and imports, lending and financing, international interactions, and industrial planning and regulation). The pre-existing conditions in the other EACs were much more conducive for such monopoly.

Discretion in decision-making, regarding resource allocation, was critical when demand surpassed distributable resources. This was particularly a problem in the early stage of the rapid growth periods, when initial conditions created a de facto economy of scarcity. The discretional power of the chief organizer in the EAEs in allocating scarce resources in a "growth-friendly" fashion was nurtured, or made possible, by three main factors: the elitist nature of the process of national and corporate policy-making, the centripetal nature of society, and the authoritarian political setting of the time. These factors – together with other historic conditions present at the time – led to a reduced level of open competition within the broad conception of the policy formulation process. The discretional power of the chief organizer found a supportive environment within the EACs, where policy-making had been traditionally autocratic, and authoritarian governance of one form or another dominated national politics during their rapid growth periods.

The chief organizer also required disposable resources, to back up its institutional initiatives and policies. These resources could be direct or tangible ones, such as loans, credits, subsidies, tax cuts and breaks, and budget allocation, etc., which often required the support of actual capital. They could also be indirect or invisible resources, such as privileges, accesses, permits, quotas, and institutional powers such as economic planning, monitoring, and disciplining. The EAEs had sufficient resources of both types in their rapid growth periods. In terms of tangible resources the EAEs relied particularly heavily upon foreign capital (official assistance, private investment, international procurements, etc.) in the early stage of their rapid growth periods. Soon, however, the source of such resources was replaced by capital earned from booming exports. A significant amount of resources for the Singaporean government's development purposes came from taxation, private savings, and the CPF. The government may or may not own these resources, but the operating forms of these resources

– such as the Post Office Savings Bank and the CPF – ensured that the government has been able to use them for defined purposes.

The second condition was the life cycle of the effective institutions – a subtler problem, but profoundly related to the rise and fall of the growth system. We will explore this in depth shortly. Institutional arrangements are designed to achieve certain effects. However, the operation of a set of institutions is never a one-way street. While the chief organizer may have its own expectations and methods, those affected by its actions also have their own expectations and methods. The government, for example, can design an industrial promotion scheme, under which certain strategic industries enjoy privileges and preferential treatments. For a while, this scheme will attract investment in the targeted industries. However, once the investors have established themselves within this scheme, the preferential treatment would, gradually, be taken for granted. Instead of continuing to operate in the direction desired by the preference provider, those benefiting from the arrangements would increasingly consider the preferential treatment as an entitlement, play with the anticipated government actions, seek to "monopolize" preferential benefits, and thus effectively corrupt the scheme.[1] The scheme would no longer function to the effect initially designed.

As another example, in battling the volatile movements of the stock and foreign exchange markets in the 1990s, the government of Taiwan, at some point, decided to give up their long-held practice of market intervention through pouring in huge amounts of funds to "stabilize" the markets every time they were in trouble – a practice established over the years, and anticipated in the speculative game played by investors. The reaction of the business community was: isn't the government supposed to support and protect us? Here, the rule – in the course of government action – was designed and offered as a market adjustment arrangement. However, over time it transformed into a distributional arrangement. Private investors understood government intervention to be a standard part of market calculations, and the policy gradually lost the effectiveness of its redirective function.

Like the previous example, this one shows that, under an institutional framework substantiated by general rules and policies, a responsive culture of actions by those operating under the new institutional setting eventually forms. Once "culturally" conditioned, those operating under the setting took it for granted, seeking the best option for them to fare well under the setting, and becoming unresponsive to the utilitarian effects of the setting. The government's promotional course of action was no longer effective in promoting desired business activity. Rather, it itself became the target of corporate manipulation. Moreover, the government's intervention in the stock market was no longer effective in fighting speculative activities. Instead, it itself became the target of speculation.

The phenomenon that an institution, such as these schemes, loses its designed effectiveness over time is what I call *institutional aging*. At the core of this problem is a subtle, dynamic, and often ambivalent, boundary between institutions and culture, and thus the ultimate limits to the power of the institutional setting. If a redirective arrangement (institution) is designed to alter or secure a pattern of behavior (culture), then, over time, the arrangement – however effective in redirecting at the beginning – would forge a new culture that tends to reduce the effectiveness of the institution concerned, as an institution-induced culture tends to marginalize the public good effect of the institution, and tilt its functions toward the satisfaction of individual interests.

If institutional aging happens to a single arrangement on a small scale, a new arrangement can be easily developed to carry on the redirective function. But for a comprehensive and systemic range of arrangements, such as those developed in the EAEs, there is no viable alternative to them carrying on the redirective functions established in the system. The result is the decline of the effectiveness of the growth system. In other words, it is the working of the internal logic of the dynamic institution-cultural interaction that a system of definitive institutional arrangements, such as those in the growth system, would have to cease to function effectively. The ending could take the form of the collapse of the whole system, or piecemeal change and transformation.

A third condition is considered historically unique for the working of the growth system. The growth system, as an economic system, depended greatly upon the support of the operating environment. Besides heavy reliance upon export markets, the working of the growth system during the second half of the last century gained much of its sustaining capacity from the global political, security, and economic regimes of the time. Politically, from Japan to Singapore, and from Taiwan to Korea, a strong (by whatever means), suppressive (against the communist movements), and supportive (of the Cold War world order and the regional security imperatives) political regime was very much in the greater geopolitical interest of the USA, who, in turn, unswervingly supported (by almost whatever means possible) those political regimes in doing whatever was necessary internally. Whether or not the USA had clear ideological intentions in effecting or supporting "hard" or "soft" authoritarian regimes in these EACs, these regimes were critical in supporting the geopolitical interests of the USA in the region.

On the other hand, such an external political and security environment also provided these political regimes with valuable support for them to effectively perform the functions essential to the working of the growth system: the monopolizing of national resources, the prioritizing of social interests, and, last but not least, the suppression of "disruptive" political forces. We might engage in an endless debate concerning whether there was a direct link between the type of political regime and the rapid economic growth within these EACs (Olson 1993; Roy 1994), but there is, at least, a pattern that emerges showing that the rapid growth periods of the EAEs coincided with the type of the regime prevalent in the recent political history of these EACs, with China still serving as an example.

Economically, the international trade, monetary, and financial regimes of the time were also supportive of the working of the growth system. A high level of trade protectionism was not initially present. When floods of products from the EAEs caused the rise of protectionism in targeted markets, these products had already become a part of the daily life of the local people, and it became hard to stop them at the borders. In terms of monetary regime, the global exchange rate system, for example, was centered on the Bretton Woods system until 1971, where the value of the US dollar – and the rest of world currencies – was fixed. Fixed exchange rates greatly facilitated the growth of international trade. For the EAEs, in particular Japan and KOST in the early stage of their rapid growth periods, the success of export-led growth can be credited, to a great extent, to the stability, reliability, and predictability of the values of major international currencies.

The world financial regime was also supportive of the growth system. In growth financing, in particular, there was a wide range of sources and methods of international financing. Up until very recently, the global financial system was still divided along national lines, and much of the growth financing from external sources was provided by foreign governments, international financial institutions, and multinational corporations, and channeled through the government of the recipient country. Such a regime of international financing gave great power and leverage to the government over the domestic end-users of the funds, and helped gear the funding to the national growth agenda. The capacity of the developmental state partly depended upon such a regime of international financing.

Finally, as shown earlier, there was a dynamic and complementary relationship, both among the EAEs themselves and in the region as a whole. The unique historical sequence of the waves of their rapid growth periods provided each with unique support, in terms of the capital, labor, and markets necessary for sustaining East Asian Growth, which might not be available otherwise.

In summary, the dynamics of growth cycles demanded the constant adjustment of, and innovation in, the institutional framework. However, there are limits to the extent that the institutional framework could evolve without losing the initial qualities supporting its purposes and functions. The interaction between growth cycles, the evolving institutional framework, and the operational conditions determined the rise and fall of the growth system.

### The aging of the growth system

The aging of institutions, therefore, concerns the decline of their effectiveness in altering or preserving a targeted culture, due to the tensions accumulated in their configuration and operation, and is intensified by changes in the conditions that initially led to the institutions themselves.

To understand the aging of the growth system, we need to understand the unique process of the formation of the growth system itself.

There are some key features of this process. First, in contrast to the notion of institutional design, where one has a clear vision of the desirable set of institutions for clearly defined functional purposes, and a comprehensive plan of installing them, the formation of the growth system was ad hoc, piecemeal, reactive, and reparative, as was demonstrated in Chapters 2 and 3. It was the initial conditions that encouraged the EAEs into a dependent path of growth, more than any particular industrial vision and strategic plan. In a sense, the formation of the growth system has been a process of the constant search for a better institutional setting for the desired growth effects – that is, the international competitiveness of the national economy. Thus, it is historically false to argue that someone – be they the MITI, Park Chung Hee, Lee Kuo-ting, Lee Kuan Yew, or Deng Xiaoping – had a vision of the system, and that the formation was just the unfolding of such a vision.

Since East Asian Growth has always been a process of reactive adjustments, piecemeal adaptations, and pragmatic changes, over the long-run incremental institutional changes and innovations would gradually deform the principal framework of the growth system. Today, many of the EAEs are no longer export-concentrated, movements of capital, products, and labor are no longer controlled as much as in their earlier times, and growth alliances and corporate groups have yielded to more competitive forms of production and distribution. More importantly, the government is no longer as capable and effective as it was 20 or 30 years ago in "governing" the market.

Second, the growth system that gradually took shape instigated profound changes in production, distribution, and social relations, which – over the long term – built up tensions in the dominant arrangements. The institutional response to the initial conditions catered to the fact that the corporate sector was internationally uncompetitive, the society was over-dependent and expectant upon the state and the corporate community, and the international environment was, by and large, supportive of nationalistic plans and agendas.

The emergent growth system functioned to forge a close collaboration between government, industrial capital, and social elites; marginalize "non-essential" societal interests; and organize internationally competitive production and distribution in a nationalistic fashion. It was, in this long process, the strengthened competitiveness and political and economic power of industrial capital, the transformation of social values and relations, and the international environment's growing suspicion of – if not hostility to – nationalistic aspirations, that has gradually weakened the very fabric, or operative fundamentals, of the growth system.

Third, the growth system evolved to confine or redirect the natural movements of market dynamics. It was designed to "govern" the market (Wade

1990), so to speak. As such, it was a very costly operation. The effective function of the growth system required, first, a significant amount of resources to be at the disposal of the chief organizer. Government needed operational resources to back up its programs for subsidies, tax cuts, public works spending, and other operational costs for the centralized management of the national economy. Redirective arrangements put huge burdens upon government. Export subsidies and industrial upgrading cost government tax revenue and budget expenditure. Intervention in financial markets cost government a substantial amount of capital. State-owned enterprises placed a burden upon the government budget, particularly when they were not performing. Efforts by government to bail out failed businesses, as part of cycle suppression, cost the government. The funds government spent to maintain a social setting supportive of the government growth agenda also cost.

Burdens also fell upon the corporations themselves, as they had to build and operate corporate networks, and share the risks and costs that came with it. Corporations also had to build and operate costly relations with government. Finally, there were burdens and sufferings on the part of the labor force – and the general public – given the institutional framework. The construction of the system enabled various participants within the growth process to sustain such a costly operation for a period of time. However, in the long term, these burdens and sufferings accumulated to limit the capacity of the system to continue functioning effectively.

### The impact of political liberalization

Beyond its internal dynamics, the fate of the growth system in the 1990s also concerned the drastically changing environment in general, and *political liberalization* and *globalization* in particular. Explaining the profoundly different economic performance of Japan in the 1990s from that of the 1960s, T. J. Pempel identifies a "regime shift" in which "the present political economy deviates profoundly from earlier forms," "rendering Japanese politics far less predictable than in the past" (Pempel 1998: back cover). Indeed this has been a wider spread phenomenon in the EACs. Since the 1980s, there has been a widespread movement toward political liberalization in the EACs, against the background of such a movement on a global scale.[2] Korea held an open competitive presidential election in 1987 – the first since the military took power in 1961 – and had a new Constitution in 1991. In Taiwan, after the initial relaxing of political controls in the late 1980s, a series of constitutional reforms took place in the 1990s, which turned a hard-core authoritarian party-state into a new democratic state. Opposition parties were legalized in 1986. Martial law was formally lifted in 1991. The first direct Presidential election was held 1996, and an opposition party, the Democratic Progressive Party (DPP), won the Presidential election in 2000. A level of legislative and judicial checks and balances on executive powers has been established.

Similar momentum was also seen in China in the 1980s and 1990s. Though the attempt to achieve immediate and comprehensive political reform failed, in the wake of the Tiananmen movement, elements of pluralist politics have been growing since then, with a more open and competitive society, more transparent policy processes, a relatively freer press, and a limited level of grass-roots experimentation in open competitive politics. The level of political liberalization in China cannot be compared with that of Taiwan or Korea, at the fundamental level of democratic institutions. But a more competitive political and policy environment is taking shape.

The cases of Japan and Singapore are somewhat different, even though – in the end – they involve the creation of an open and competitive political and policy environment. Unlike Korea and Taiwan and, in a different way, unlike China, neither country has really formally infringed upon their constitutional stipulation of democratic principles, even during the darkest period of the Cold War, nor during the heydays of their rapid growth periods. Elections have been held according to their constitutions. However, both countries turned out to be one-party states, with the ruling party being continuously voted back into office, often with an overwhelming majority of the vote.

The dominance of the LDP, which had ruled Japan since 1947, came to an end in the early 1990s, after the party split into two in 1991. Since then, there has rarely been a majority party that can control government, and a coalition government of one combination or another has been the norm. In addition to the usual vulnerability and instability associated with coalition government, national politics and public policy in Japan have certainly become more competitive, and the various societal interests more demanding and assertive.

In Singapore, PAP has maintained power since 1959. Civil society is growing in its own fashion, and political oppositions have not formed a viable force. The state has firmly incorporated society. Within this fundamental framework, however, society is open and competitive. Political and policy processes are merit-based, efficient, uncorrupted, and transparent.

This more competitive political environment in the EACs allows increased inputs into the political and policy process, from a broader range of societal interests, both old and new. In particular, those interests that were marginalized, ignored, or suppressed during the rapid growth period have become a major voice in the reshaping of their relations with the major forces of the old growth regime. From hospital workers or Hyundai employees in Korea, to state enterprise employees and farmers in China, workers demand better work entitlements and conditions, and the continual support and protection of government. Work forces in Taiwan, for example, are demanding state provision of superannuation, shorter working hours, more paid holidays, and better working conditions. Particularly during competitive elections, political promises often carry financial implications.

In national elections over the past ten years, major political parties have promised to introduce a government-sponsored elderly pension fund if elected. And every politician knows that the government does not have the money for that.

Special interest groups have also become more assertive, and more effective on government policy. Environment conservation groups in China, for example, called on the government to reconsider its flagship growth project, the Three Gorge Dam project, and – once the project was put in place – to spend more money on environmental preservation.

The movement of political liberalization in the 1980s and 1990s across the EACs led to calls for alternative forms of organization of production, exchange, and distribution, and challenged almost every aspect of the growth system: from the centralization of power to elite policy-making, and from growth as priority to marginalization of social and political interests. The growth system with a strong state at its core could no longer sustain itself.

## Globalization and international pressures

The growing pressure for alternative forms of organization of production and distribution, and demand for resources and reprioritizing, has not only been the result of the working of the internal dynamics of the EACs themselves, but the effects of international economic dynamics, not only because of the nature of the EAEs that depend so much on the world economy, but also because of the significant change of the world economy itself in the 1980s and 1990s, a process often dubbed as globalization.

The international dimension has always been prominent in East Asian Growth and most people would agree that such prominence is for the most part positive. Without the relatively free world markets, East Asian Growth would have been much more difficult, if possible at all. Exports-as-engine theorists, as well as neoclassical economists in general, would go as far as to say that it is the demands in world markets and the facilitating world trade and financial regimes of the time that made East Asian Growth possible. In the early discussion of the initial conditions for East Asian Growth, I have tried to demonstrate that the international demand and supply of the time was critical in shaping the general directions of the initial rapid growth in the EAEs and subsequent methods of sustaining this form of growth.

From the 1980s onwards, however, the nature of the international dimension in East Asian Growth has changed and become more complicated. On the one hand, the economic thinking in Washington and London came to be dominated by what is called *Reaganomics* and *Thatcherism*, which, among other things, challenged the role of government in national and international economic activity. This new economic philosophy and policy laid the seeds of the new global movement in the 1990s, pushing for open national markets, fair trade practices, and global business and labor standards. Multinational corporations became more active and aggressive under this new changing world economic environment. On the other hand, the rising competitiveness of EAE products caused the USA and Europe to move to protect their national industries and consequently a "less friendly" world economic system resulted for the EAEs. Both trends seemed to be particularly detrimental to East Asian Growth.

There is a large body of literature on globalization and the EAEs (for example, Kim 2002; Le Heron and Park 1995; Lee 2002; Noland and Pack 2003; and many others on individual EAEs). Many of them link the 1997–8 financial crisis to the puzzling relationship between globalization and East Asian countries. Globalization is both an opportunity and a challenge for the EAEs. It is clear that, on the wagon of globalization, the EAEs have been able to expand their economic presence around the world. To people in many parts of the world, the EAEs are one of the principal forces behind the disruption and dislocation caused by globalization.

Globalization, as widely recognized, also forces EAEs to open their own doors for foreign products, services, and investment. But the most significant impact of globalization on EAEs is the detrimental effects it has on the growth system itself. The increasing interaction and integration with world economic systems has forced the EAEs to confront different ideas of organization and management, different standards of business and society, and the different values placed on human life held by the countries they trade with. The impact of this interaction was significantly intensified in the wake of the global movement of political and economic liberalization in the late 1980s and 1990s. With regard to the function of the growth system, two particular aspects of this global pressure were most relevant: labor standards and business practices – each of which has the potential to affect the production costs of the EACs, and thus their international competitiveness.

A significant gap in labor standards – such as the minimum wage, worker age, and employment benefits – were found between the EAEs and their economically more advanced trading partners, particularly during their rapid growth periods. East Asian Growth was, in part, built upon the control and suppression of labor demands, as a form of cost reduction and competitiveness enhancement.

As part of the historical dynamism of international political economy, nations have developed various systems of labor standards, and have to compete with each other on different cost bases. CEOs in non-EAE advanced economies may be no less enthusiastic about cost reduction, in whatever way, than their EAE counterparts. It is just that there exist legal and moral limits to what they may pursue along that line in their local environment. There were two consequences of the tensions in national labor standards. First, we have seen an increasingly large number of businesses, in countries where high standards are the norm, move to many

EAEs, where labor standards are relatively low, and where the growth arrangements established there are able to keep it that way. This accounts for much of the business relocation from the USA and Europe to Asia, and from the EAEs in the later stages of their rapid growth periods to those in the earlier stages (Japan to KOST in the 1970s, and Japan and KOST to China in the 1980s and 1990s). Some of this relocation occurred in the form of global deployment and division of labor within giant multinational corporations.

Second, this "vacating" of businesses from economies with higher labor standards has created tensions within these economies themselves. Low labor standards in other countries, particularly in the EAEs, are seen as the direct cause for the decline of business in certain industrial areas, and therefore the rise of unemployment. Thus, the debate over labor standards across national boundaries has mixed real economic interests with moral arguments. Demands for global labor standards are transformed into political pressure on the EAEs, through the representative governments in the affected countries. The most notable case is the one between the USA and its Asian trading partners – initially with Japan, then with KOST, and now increasingly with China.

Related to this problem of labor standards is another aspect of international pressure: business practices – that is, the international rules and norms of business operation, an issue facing the CEOs of international businesses operating in the EAEs, rather than labor forces back home. This problem involves a wide range of issues, including export subsidies, ambiguous methods of dispute resolution, "corrupt" forms of business decision-making, and selective and opportunistic attitudes toward international organizations. In the past, particularly when this problem concerned – in the main – Japan, the issue was treated, more or less, as one of cross-cultural difference, so that international businesses needed to get used to, adjust themselves to, and learn to act like locals if they were to succeed there.

Increasingly, however, this problem has been seen more as an issue of the quality of institutions, or the lack of institutionalization in business operation in the EAEs. Over the past decade or two, with international businesses increasingly active in the EAEs, and the growing arbitrating power of international functional organizations – such as the International Monetary Fund (IMF), the World Bank, the World Trade Organization (WTO), and GATT (General Agreement on Tariffs and Trade) before that – the business practices of the EAEs are increasingly seen as something that the EAEs themselves need to change or adapt. There are three major trends in which this view, and the pressure it has brought on the EAEs, has become dominant. First is the *increasing integration of domestic and international economy*, in which common business standards have become both necessary and possible. International property rights, for example, are increasingly promoted, and accepted, as a necessary component in the modern economy, and their protection as a national and international business standard deemed necessary. Through bilateral trade negotiations and unilateral acts of trade sanction, such as the 301 List, the USA has been able to compel the EAEs to come to terms with trading with it.

Second, *major international financial institutions* have been aggressively involved in the operation of the national economies of the EAEs at times of crises and difficulties, and have imposed transparency, corporate restructuring, global standards of accounting and legal process, arbitrating powers of international financial institutions, and the principles of monetary and financial policy as conditions for their assistance. Most notable was the case involving the IMF at the time of the Asian financial crisis in the late 1990s.

Third, the *building of international institutions* at the global and regional levels has had a considerable effect upon the EAEs, particularly on countries like China, whose entry into these newly empowered international organizations and arrangements has proved to be a transformative mechanism, compelling it to change the way it does business and runs the economy. In the case of China's entry to the WTO, for example, the final deal with the USA, as the benchmark for conditions set for other countries to approve China's membership, is expected to lead to changes in a wide range of "business practices " that have been essential to the country's rapid economic growth in recent decades, including various forms of trade barriers, the dual market structure, intellectual property rights practice, dispute settlement, the control of capital flows and international transactions, etc.

Some international arrangements do not necessarily impose strict entry requirements, but the participation of the EAEs in these arrangements has been gradually intertwined into a web of benefits and obligations, and a set of behavioral codes. The Asia Pacific Economic Cooperation (APEC) is one such example. Initially, this was seen by many EAEs as, in the main, a source of potential export opportunities in the late 1980s and early 1990s. However, as global and regional conditions changed, APEC has turned itself into an international standard-setting body, through its sub-committees in various functional areas.

These international pressures, together with domestic political change, have been translated into forces within the EAEs that have not only further weakened the resource base of their governments' capacity and increased demands on available resources. More importantly, these forces seriously challenge the institutional arrangements at the core of the growth system: from corporate structure to competition-suppressing measures, and from export promoting subsidies to accounting and legal practices. In the end, they have de-legitimized the working of the growth system, and have helped accelerate the process of its aging.

## The end games

In the 1990s the EAEs were struggling to fashion a form of post-rapid growth period growth, experiencing the ending of their rapid growth periods, or moving into its late stage. There were different ending experiences observed among the EAEs. But, before getting into the specifics, let us look at the general pattern of the ending stage of the rapid growth period. Toward the later stage of the rapid growth period, the signs of institutional aging systematically occurred, and the burdens placed upon government and key institutional players in the growth process became difficult to sustain. At this stage, various efforts were made to ease the burden and strengthen the sustainability of the institutional arrangements. The government, for example, would increase capital injection into major domestic projects to create internal demands in response to the shrinking international market. This was called "internal demand stimulation," and was practiced from Japan to Korea, and from Taiwan to China.

In addition to the search for new market outlets, there was also the problem of capital circulation. A substantial part of an EAE is embedded in a multi-player, sophisticated, gradually accumulated, and legally ambiguous relationship of borrowing and lending – and buying and selling – perhaps more so than any other type of economy. This type of permissive and flexible financial network would absorb fluctuations in growth cycles. However, there are limits to the extent that fluctuations can be absorbed. In the later stage of the rapid growth period, corporate chains of financing tended to become overloaded with unpaid debts and overdue loans. The business community would look to the government and international financial institutions for temporary relief and bailouts. Before resorting to international financial institutions for help, the government tended to act as the primary facilitator in revitalizing the financing chains.

In addition, as profits from production – particularly from manufacturing – declined in the later stage, with the shrinking of market advantage, investment capital increasingly moved into certain sectors, which still entertained hopes for both rapid and high returns. From Japan to China, and from Taiwan to Korea, the real estate industry and stock markets became the two major battlegrounds for anxious capital. These are other forms of financing chains, the risk of which did not concern the institutional basis of the growth system, but, rather, the volatility of the global capital market and the nature of "hot money" itself. The combined effect of these factors confronted the EAEs during much of the 1990s. Different combinations of these factors, however, led to different ending experiences.

### Ending of the rapid growth period

After decades of rapid growth, the EAEs found themselves marching toward the end of their rapid growth periods. In looking at the evidence of the ending, I examine three key indicators that are principal in East Asian Growth: GDP growth rate, export growth rate, and labor cost. For both growth rates, I have established in early discussions 7.85 percent, the EAEs' average growth rate for the 50-year period, as the threshold, above which the EAEs enjoyed their rapid growth periods. The rapid growth period is considered to end when the growth rate has "permanently" moved below this threshold. For labor cost, we will identify a similar threshold.

The end of Japan's rapid growth period in the early 1970s was sudden and unexpected, particularly in view of the general length of the rapid growth periods of the other EAEs – around 30 years. Japan's growth rate "permanently" dropped below the average rate in 1974, and has never returned. The average grow rate in the 1980s was a reasonable 4.55 percent. From the end of 1980s, the Japanese economy had a close-to-zero growth rate.

However, the early ending of East Asian Growth in Japan was driven more by external events than by the maturation of its growth. It started with the oil crisis in 1973, which seriously weakened the strategic advantage Japan had established over the years in its institutionally enhanced international competitiveness. Then, the Plaza Accord of 1985 further seriously eroded its competitiveness. Then, the waves of the rise of other EAEs further eroded the international competitiveness of the Japanese economy. Since then, Japan has never really found a solid, alternative basis for competitiveness.

At the same time, many of the internal arrangements remained in place, working for the interests of the established competitiveness model. With the decline in international competitiveness, and thus the level of profitability in established export markets, a large amount of capital moved to non-productive sectors, such as real estate development and financial markets, for quicker and safer returns. What has happened in Japan since 1973 is that, on the one hand, its potential for East Asian Growth was not exhausted, and continued to claim resources and support, while, on the other hand, many of the conditions – particularly international ones – supportive of East Asian Growth's continued operating in Japan, gradually disappeared over the years. Japan has been working hard for a number of years to develop a new basis for competitiveness, but growth benefits have not yet become apparent.

Korea's growth rate moved above the EAEs' 50-year average from 1963, and maintained an average of 8.52 percent during its rapid growth period, from 1963 to 1992. A major disturbance occurred around 1980, when the country experienced political turmoil surrounding the power transition from President Park to General Chun Doo Hwan. After 30 years of "rapid growth," Korea's growth rate dropped to below the threshold in 1993, and the average growth rate in the 1990s was 5.92 percent. The aging of the growth system was clearly reflected in the slowdown of its growth rate.

The same pattern is also found in the case of Taiwan. Taiwan's growth rate rose above the benchmark in 1962, and its 30-year rapid growth period average was 9.36 percent from 1962 to 1989. Its growth rate has dropped below the threshold since 1990. Taiwan had neither a dramatic start to its rapid growth period, nor a dramatic end, as in the case of Japan and Korea. Thus, before and after its rapid growth period, Taiwan still maintained reasonable levels of growth.

Like Japan and Korea, the movement of Singapore's growth rate has been more dramatic, particularly in the mid-1960s, when its rapid growth period started, and in the mid-1980s, when Singapore experienced difficulties as a result of its high wage policy. Singapore moved above the threshold in 1968, and "permanently" dropped below it in 1998, after 30-year rapid growth at an average growth rate of 8.88 percent.

On both counts of the general pattern of the rapid growth period identified here among the EAEs, and the empirical evidence provided by the Chinese economy in the last several years, China's rapid growth period appears to have not ended yet. China's rapid growth period saw its growth rate rise above the threshold in 1982, and it has maintained an average of 9.98 percent since then, with a disturbance occurring around 1990. We will have to wait and see whether China will continue to be able to maintain its growth level above the EAEs' 50-year average for the rest of the decade. There are theoretical and empirical reasons, however, to be confident about the unfolding of the projected pattern within China for the next few years.

Along with a permanent drop in the GDP growth rate below the threshold, there is also a significant drop in the growth rate of exports, which is another principal indicator of East Asian Growth where exports dominate. Japan's post-rapid growth period exports, for example, grew at 10.53 percent on average in the 1980s and 1990s, and 5.49 percent in the 1990s, while during its rapid growth period in the 1950s and 1960s its export growth rate was 18.7 percent. It's export growth rate dropped sharply after the oil shock in 1973, and moved around the 8 percent threshold between.

Data on Korea, Singapore, and Taiwan provide stronger evidence for export growth rate change as an indicator for the ending (as well as starting) of their East Asian Growth. Both Korea's and Taiwan's exports started to grow above 8 percent in the early 1960s and moved below that threshold in the 1990s. In the case of Singapore, its exports started to grow above the threshold in the late 1960s and moved below it in the late 1990s, very much coinciding with its rapid growth period. During their rapid growth periods, exports grew, on average, at 29.46 percent (Korea), 23.34 percent (Taiwan), and 18.76 percent (Singapore) respectively. In their post-rapid growth period in the 1990s, export growth slowed to 10.59 percent (Korea), 7.99 percent (Taiwan), and 3.11 percent (Singapore). As for China, its exports have been continuously growing at an average rate of 14.02 percent annually since 1982, still firmly above the threshold.

Finally, labor wages in manufacturing, measured in monthly wage earnings (MWE) in US dollars, are used as indicators for change in labor cost. There was a rapid growth in labor wages toward the later stage of KOST's rapid growth periods. In the early 1990s, when their rapid growth periods drew toward a close, their MWE reached around US$1,000. If we take this as a benchmark, then Japan was an exception. In fact, Japan's MWE reached US$1,000 around 1978. One can argue that this is a further piece of evidence suggesting that, as a related movement of various variables in a growth system, Japan's rapid growth period should have ended in the late 1970s and early 1980s, had there been no oil shock in the early 1970s. According to this same logic, we can argue that MWE in China, still very early in its rapid growth period, will steadily rise over the next decade, and reached US$1,000 by the end of its rapid growth period.

### The exit moves

The 1997–8 Asian economic crisis helped us recognize the dependence of East Asian Growth on the international economic system and its consequent vulnerability. However, problematic claims were made in achieving this recognition. As such, we have been led to find the answer to the problems facing the EAEs more in their contemporary imperatives than in historical dynamics, and more in external conditions than in their internal logic. Consequently, solutions to the difficulties experienced by the EAEs in the 1990s sought to encourage them to adopt the new framework, without necessarily understanding how the existing framework has operated in the first place.

What happened in each of the EAEs in the 1990s – and their subsequent responses – formed a pattern in the end game in which, instead of subjecting themselves to a campaign aimed at dragging them out of the growth system, with the accompanying drastic short-term costs and consequences to be borne by the economy and society, the EAEs – with the ostensible exception of Korea – have been trying to "grow out of the system"[3] over a reasonably long period of time, with far less disruption to the existing arrangements and the interests associated with them, and, perhaps, a far smoother transition in the end.

The exit moves by the EAEs discussed here reflect several key aspects of the deformation of the growth system in the EAEs. We will look at the domestic demand stimulation programs in Japan, China, and Taiwan, which deal with the tension between increasing competitive international markets on the one hand, and growing overcapacity in these EAEs on the other. Moreover, efforts in Singapore and Taiwan to reshape themselves as global hubs of international operations will be viewed as another major indicator of their moving away from the growth form, which focused primarily upon manufacturing exports. Third, along with these new developments, piecemeal and delicate efforts are observed in the EAEs, aimed at watering down the institutional set-up in the growth system, and, gradually – and in a more controlled fashion – to develop a manageable level of integration with the world economic system. For East Asian Growth, which operates on institutionally enhanced competitiveness for manufacturing exports to international markets, these new developments amount to a significant transformation of the growth system.

*Domestic demand stimulation*

There have been clear movements in recent years in the EAEs to seek internal market expansion. The EAEs have been uniquely reliant upon international markets, and East Asian Growth is seen as robust in exporting industries, and rusty within the domestic infrastructure and markets. With international markets having reached their limits, their fluctuations impacted by exchange rate volatilities, and difficulties in fashioning a new comparative advantage, the EAEs gradually became unable to sustain their economies purely upon export markets. While continuing their conventional methods of expansion in new international expansions, the EAEs have begun to pay more attention to their domestic markets.

The Japanese government, for example, has – several times over the 1990s – implemented packages of huge tax cuts and public spending, to "stimulate domestic demand" in order to "re-jumpstart" the stagnating economy. In 1997, facing the shock wave of the regional financial crisis, the Hashimoto government announced a stimulus package worth around US$38 billion, including $15.75 billion spending for public works, and US$6.6 billion in tax cuts for corporations, landowners, and investors (*The New York Times*, December 18, 1997). In April 1997, a new package of US$137 billion was announced. In the following December, a much larger "giant package" of tax cuts, spending, and lending was announced, which brought "total spending on stimulus since 1992 to more than $800 billion," including US$50 billion long-term tax cuts, $10 billion to promote housing investment, and US$8 billion to create one million jobs (*The New York Times*, November 17, 1998). A year later another new stimulus package was implemented, this time amounting to a further US$172 billion.

Domestic demand stimulation has also fared well in China and Taiwan. The Chinese government, for example, introduced a "proactive fiscal policy" in the wake of the Asian financial crisis and troubled export markets, to boost internal markets for the existing, and continuously expanding, productive capacity. In March, 1998, the government introduced a US$1 trillion construction plan to boost "internal demands," drawn from "domestic bonds, domestic loans, foreign bonds, foreign loans, and direct allocations from the central government and contributions from provincial governments." This policy has not been abandoned with the stabilization and revitalization of exports markets after the crisis. Instead, it is upheld as a core element of the new government five-year plan for 2001–5, and has increasingly come to be seen as the long-term direction of the national economy.

Domestic demand stimulation, or expansionary fiscal policy, is useful, as relief from the overcapacity problem uniquely built up in the EAEs. Anticipating the ending of East Asian Growth, such overcapacity will adjust itself over time. But domestic demand stimulation would help ease out overcapacity and prevent it from collapsing the supporting system.

*Global hub drive*

Another trend in reducing dependence on manufacturing exports to international markets in the EAEs is to recast their economies as centers of global growth activities, rather than mainly as manufacturers and exporters. KOST have been at the forefront in pursuing this new growth basis, with Singapore's efforts being most comprehensive and effective.

Taiwan, for example, proposed in the early 1990s to transform itself into an Asian-Pacific center for operation and management. But, perhaps due to the uncertainty of its domestic setting, and the technical problems involved in the concept – in terms of the potential competition with nearby Hong Kong and, increasingly, with Shanghai, and, more importantly, its unsettled relations with China – the project has not really taken off. The Korean government also developed various plans intended to turn Korea into a global hub of some kind for global manufacturing, R&D, tourism, and logistic support, with its newly opened Inchon international airport and its designated "heart of Asia," Jeju Island.

In the case of Singapore, movement in this direction has been more substantial. Since the mid-1980s – facing the drastic rise in labor costs, structural constraints upon further growth in manufacturing, and the slowdown in both its traditional markets in Southeast Asia and the oil industry – Singapore has taken a series of steps to push the idea of the city-state as an entrepôt economy one step further, with a focus upon the promotion of its services sector. As Lee Lai-To noted:

> while maintaining the importance of the manufacturing sector, Singapore wished to move beyond manufacturing to become an international total business center. It wanted to attract MNCs to establish their operational headquarters in the city-state. In addition, Singapore decided to become a major global provider of services. In this connection, tradable services like financial services, computer services, tourism, hotel management, air and seaport management, and town and city planning would be systematically marketed.
>
> (Lee 2000: 41)

To promote Singapore as a "strategic hub for manufacturing and services," a series of initiatives were introduced. In 1983, the Trade Development Board (TDB) was set up to develop Singapore as an international trading hub, and to promote the export of goods and services. In 1985, the Economic Committee was set up, and major initiatives to cut wage costs and improve flexibility in the remuneration system helped to restore Singapore's cost competitiveness. In 1986, the Overseas HQ (OHQ) incentive was introduced to promote Singapore as a strategic hub for manufacturing and services operations. In 1989, the Productivity 2000 initiative was launched to steer the Productivity Movement through the 1990s and into the twenty-first century. In 1991, the National Science and Technology Board (NSTB) was formed to develop Singapore into a center of excellence in science and technology. The National Technology Plan was formulated, setting out the direction for the promotion of R&D in Singapore. In 1993, the S$1 billion Cluster Development Fund (CDF) was launched to catalyze the development of indigenous industries in high-growth clusters. In 1996, the National Science and Technology Plan 2000 (NSTP), and a S$4 billion Research and Development Fund, were launched to facilitate the development of science and technology in Singapore from 1996 to 2000. Also launched were International Business Hub 2000, Rationalization 2000 and the Promising Local Enterprise Program (PLEP). In 1997, the Committee on Singapore's Competitiveness (CSC) was formed to examine strategies to sustain competitiveness in the medium to long term. Industrial Land Plan 21 (IP21) was launched to ensure a continued supply of affordable industrial land to meet industries future needs (SMTI 2001).

On the surface this is, perhaps, another form of "industrial restructuring" in response to shifts in comparative advantage. But the move to build Singapore as a global hub is much more significant than its early campaigns in industrial restructuring had been. The current campaign, if successful, would move Singapore out of its 30-year pattern of rapid economic growth, which relied upon the separation of the national economy from the global market, and the sustaining of international competitiveness – primarily through the internal reorganization of production, distribution, and exchange. The new global hub model, instead of promoting manufacturing products in international markets, aims to attract investment and activities into Singapore. Taking advantage of its location, human capital, positive business environment, and effective and efficient government, Singapore would need to rely less upon external markets, and would have less need for nationalistic protectionism, but, instead, would rely upon the increasing globalization of the world economic system.

Whether these global hub campaigns can succeed depends on many factors, first and foremost of which concerns China. In fact, even without a concerted efforts to campaign for being a global hub, China is likely to become one on its own because of the snowballing effects of its economy in scale and growing speed. This will have a suppressing impact on its fellow EAEs' global hub efforts.

## Growing out of the system

While domestic demand stimulation is generally a response to the tensions built up in the system to prevent it from collapsing, there are many factors working together that would allow some of the EAEs, such as China, Taiwan, and Singapore, to *grow out of the system*, rather than collapse under it: the exit would not be dramatic, clear-cut, and achieved through "overnight" institutional restructuring. Many of the forces that Barry

Naughton identified for China's ability to grow out of the plan in its early growth efforts (Naughton 1996) are still effective. This has much to do with the EAEs' economic decision-making structure and capacity, unique state–society relations, and general conservatism in economic policy. In addition, Taiwan's relatively smoother post-East Asian Growth transition in the 1990s benefited largely from the rapid expansion of its trade, manufacturing, and investment in China. Singapore's transition has been facilitated by its decades-long efforts to transform Singapore from a manufacturing exporter to a global hub of services and operations.

Many trends in China's growth activity in the 1990s suggested that there exists a constellation of conditions unfolding that would allow China a less destructive passage out of its East Asian Growth, while still maintaining a relatively good level of growth. On the basis of the findings of this study (Table 6.2), China's East Asian Growth could continue for a few more years. From 1998 to 2000, China's average growth rate was 7.63 percent (considering the effects of the Asian financial crisis) and, without major interruptions, it seems China will be able to have its economy move around the EAE threshold. As is shown in Table 6.3, its growth rate at

*Table 6.2* China: key indicators compared with other EAEs at 2000

|  | GDP | GDPPC | Wages |
| --- | --- | --- | --- |
| CHN | 7.63 | 3,548 | 79 |
| JPN | 0.60 | 25,188 | 3,372 |
| KOR | 4.51 | 14,362 | 1,191 |
| SGP | 4.97 | 27,145 | 1.679 |
| TWN | 5.28 | 18,826 | 1,145 |

*Notes*: GDP: GDP annual growth rate; GDPPC: GDP per capita in current international prices; wages: monthly earnings in manufacturing in US dollars. Data are averages of the three years leading to the year.

*Source*: Appendix A1–5: 1.3, 1.2, 7.1.

*Table 6.3* China: key indicators in 2000 compared with other EAEs at the ends of their rapid growth periods

|  | Year | GDP | GDPPC | Wages |
| --- | --- | --- | --- | --- |
| CHN | 2000 | 7.63 | 3,548 | 79 |
| JPN | 1973 | 6.95 | 4,306 | 323 |
| KOR | 1992 | 7.88 | 9,819 | 933 |
| SGP | 1997 | 8.20 | 25,000 | 1,614 |
| TWN | 1992 | 6.81 | 10,641 | 935 |

*Notes*: GDP: GDP annual growth rate; GDPPC: GDP per capita in current international prices; wages: monthly earnings in manufacturing in US dollars. Data are averages of the three years leading to the year.

*Source*: Appendix A1–5: 1.3, 1.2, 7.1.

2000 is somewhere between the rates of the other EAEs at their respective rapid growth periods. It would be reasonable to believe that China's growth rate will move below the EAE ORP (overall research period) average "permanently" earlier than the other EAEs.

Regarding GDP per capita, however, China's level is much lower than those of the other EAEs, indicating great potential for further growth. The same is true of the wage level. China's monthly earnings in manufacturing in 2000 were significantly lower than those recorded in the other EAEs (Table 6.3). If we take Korea and Taiwan as a benchmark, their monthly earnings toward the end of their rapid growth periods were close to US$1,000, and it took them about 15 years to move from the level of US$75, in 1975, to the level of US$1,000.

While there is still potential for China to grow under the system, there are some unique factors that affect the procession of the ending phase of China's East Asian Growth, including the scale of its economy, the intensity of its international integration, the size of its agricultural sector, and the transformation of its SOEs. A decisive factor in a smooth exit from its East Asian Growth, however, is the emergence of a new growth basis with a much lower reliance upon external markets – one that is able to absorb over-investment in human and physical resources in the declining SOEs and the rapidly growing capacity in the private sector. Such a new growth basis incorporates many of the new trends already identified in Japan, Taiwan, and Singapore, which emphasize generating domestic demand and transforming the economy from a manufacturing exporter into a global center of economic activity.

Critical in crystallizing these dynamics into growth momentum is the drastic increase of capital injection into the economy from both foreign and domestic sources – not only into manufacturing, but also into the wider service sector, including banking, insurance, distribution and retail, the entertainment industry, R&D, and the regional operations of multinational corporations. It helped push up consumption within the economy itself, and facilitated the development of new areas and sectors of growth. As Singapore's experience indicates, these new developments are not simply the manipulation of another growth cycle within the growth system, but, rather, are qualitatively different efforts to transform the nature of the economy and the growth system itself.

In terms of the influx of foreign capital and business into China, the share of the industrial output of foreign capital enterprises in China's total industrial output is of interest. It has steadily grown in the 1990s, from 2.28 percent in 1990 to 27.75 percent in 1999. By 1999, one third of industrial output was from enterprise owned by foreign capital (MOFET data 2001).

Reflecting the influx of foreign capital, and an injection of capital from the government's proactive fiscal policy, was the significant increase in gross fixed capital formation (GFCF). China's GFCF as a percentage of

GDP leapt from 25.5 percent in 1990 to 36.5 percent in 2000. It grew at an average annual rate of 20.99 percent, and increased 6.9 times within ten years. The same is true for gross domestic consumption, both government and private. China's gross private consumption rose from 911 billion yuan (and government consumption from 225 billion yuan) in 1990, to 4,291 and 1,171 billion yuan respectively in 2000, and at average annual rates of 16.2 percent and 17.53 percent.

The influx of foreign capital and businesses – and the rapid expansion of the domestic market – should pave the way for the Chinese economy to transform itself from one dependent upon markets and centers of economic transactions elsewhere, to one able to attract global economic activity concentrated upon China on its own merits. Whether China can successfully transform its economy into a global hub (or several global hubs) of manufacturing, services, and operations – as Singapore intends to do – depends largely upon how these emerging trends unfold, bringing other economic forces along with them.

## Hard landing and the 1997–8 Asian financial crisis

The EAEs have not been immune from systemic collapse as a form of tension release. But before we discuss hard landing in the case of Korea, let us first take a general look at the 1997–8 Asian financial crisis, various theories about its nature and causes, and how it relates to what we discuss here. The Asian financial crisis in 1997 and 1998 proved to be quite a surprise to many. It consequently caused an unprecedented high volume of scholarly activities: conferences, workshops, articles, books, speeches, etc., which themselves became an interesting phenomenon. Besides the reactions of those who might say "I told you so" (most likely proponents of the looters' game theory and economic nationalism theory) and those who were too quick to make profound judgments, debates and discussion have mostly focused on the nature and causes of the crisis and logically its cures and future prospects.

From many of the works on the causes of the financial crisis, one can discern three general views. The first one puts the blame on the domestic conditions of the EAEs – either those problems long claimed by some, such as corporate malpractices, cronyism, authoritarian regimes, corruption, etc. (for example, Clifford and Engardio, 1999), or the failure of the development model (Richter 2000, for example). Those in the first group have always been pessimistic and suspicious of East Asian Growth, and the financial crisis was just seen as a good vindication of their long-held views. For them, the question is not whether this is the end of the miracle, as, in their view, it never was one. Nor is it a question of whether there is a cure to the problems, as the problems are not curable.

The second group sees the crisis more as the problem of global governance in general and the international financial regimes in particular (Sharma

2003; Noble and Ravenhill 2000; Lee and Bohm 2002). For them, the urgent task to avoid another such crisis is to reform the existing international financial system and build an architecture of good global financial governance. Those in this second group are more ambivalent about the future prospects of East Asian Growth. They seem to understand where the problem is, but are not quite confident about whether the problem can be remedied any time soon, as it is much easier said than done to build the architecture of good global governance.

The third group, typically represented by specialists at the World Bank and IMF, favors technical analysis and solutions. For them the causes of the crisis are found in the problems in capital markets, banking institutions, assets management, monetary and fiscal policy, currency systems, corporate governance, social policy, exchange rates, trade policies, and regulatory capability (Agenor *et al.* 1999; Hunter *et al.* 1999; Stiglitz and Yusuf 2001; Woo *et al.* 2000; World Bank 2000). Once these problems are corrected, the growth will be back on track, and, as the World Bank study puts it, "a new miracle" is possible (World Bank 2000).

Those in the third group are more optimistic about the future of the EAEs, as they believe cures come naturally once the causes are correctly diagnosed. But views vary as to what strategy to take to turn things around. Yung Chul Park, in his East Asian dilemma study, presents a good discussion of the different views (Park 2001). Those for "structuring out" argue that, since the problems are structural in nature, there is a need to completely "dismantle the East Asian Model" (Park 2001: 32) by operationally restructuring "insolvent financial institutions and firms to improving corporate governance, addressing labor market rigidities, opening domestic markets, and introducing a free floating exchange rate system" (Park 2001: 2), things often dubbed as "structural reforms." Those for "growing out," on the other hand, advocate:

> substantially reducing the scope of government involvement and . . . leaving the bulk of the operation restructuring task to the market, relying on the existing and newly developed framework for crisis resolution. There are also grounds for a more expansionary macroeconomic policy, because investment demand has become stagnant.
>
> (Park 2001: 56)

While these views all have good intentions in helping us understand the significant event, and we indeed learn things from many serious, in-depth analyses and explanations, particularly at the technical levels, as to how the half a century-long growth experiences met with the new global economic dynamics, there is much to be desired in many of the observations and explanations. Some of them are too fragile, wavering with the unfolding of events over time, and are too quick to be colored by the established theories and ideologies.

Of particular significance for our discussion here is the fact that many of these "timely" declarations and explanations fail to see the event as an effect of the unfolding of the institutional logic of the growth system. Seen from the latter perspective as articulated in this study, the Asian financial crisis was likely at the time, though not inevitable. The crisis can be seen as a sudden collapse of the aging system (or just parts of it). However, as discussed in this chapter, the aging of the system and an exit out of it can take many forms. A violent one such as the financial crisis in 1997 and 1998 would happen when certain domestic and international conditions were met. The Asian financial crisis did not cause the end of rapid economic growth, but was merely one of its probable consequences. It came not as a final judgment of what's wrong with the system, but rather as a vivid indication of how the system evolved at that particular juncture. It occurred not because of some technical problems, a cure of which can lead to resumption of high-speed growth, but because the system has lived out its life cycle and the time for high-speed growth is over.

Korea's collapse during the Asian financial crisis of 1997–8 reflected the unique characteristics of the Korean economy, the overall problem of East Asian Growth, and the contingent impact of the global dynamics of the time – financial and otherwise. In contrast to the soft landing in Japan, where the fall of the growth rate below the EAEs' ORP average has been a long and gradual process, a hard landing – as occurred in Korea – carried with it a sudden drop in the growth rate, perhaps permanently below the EAEs' ORP average, and the impact of dramatic economic change on existing institutions.

Korea has been renowned for the higher costs of its competitiveness – both in export prices and monthly wages (Smith 1998). Moreover, the financing of Korea's growth expansion has, to a large extent, come from external sources. Over the years, these problems have been, in part, suppressed by the aggressive growth expansion programs of the government and corporations, and partially absorbed in the growth arrangements between government and the corporations, and among the corporations themselves. Korea's problem in the 1990s, like Japan's, was an over-expansion in growth capacity, plus a very vulnerable structure of industrial financing. Many of the problems they faced – such as insolvency – were the effects of an unrealizable production capacity. What made Korea's exit experience unique among the EAEs was that its overcapacity was built upon a less solid financial basis.

While the 1997–8 crisis was not necessarily inevitable for Korea, once it happened its options were limited. Once the government made the decision to let the system stand on its own, many of the subsequent developments followed a unique course of action. While the government and corporate groups were unable to sustain the maintenance of the existing arrangements, the intervention of the IMF was conditional upon the further weakening of these arrangements. A considerable proportion of corporate financing in Korea was provided through international financial institutions. Once confidence at the sources of the financing chains collapsed, the chains themselves collapsed. The ending experience in Korea is viewed as a *hard ending*, as it involved the collapse of markets, the systematic discontinuation of the financing chains, sudden disruptions in the working of the existing growth regimes, and the dislocation of various industrial and labor forces from their established positions in the growth system.

## Future prospects

East Asian Growth has dominated the world economic scene for the past 50 years. By the end of the 1990s, all the EAEs, except for China, had passed through their rapid growth periods. There are several lines along which we could ponder the post-rapid growth period prospects of the EAEs. First, when the economy has grown to a certain level of development (toward the end of East Asian Growth, for example), further high-speed growth would, logically, be very difficult, simply due to marginal costs. If the American economy of the past 50 years can be taken as a "mature" economy, then post-rapid growth period growth in the EAEs is likely to move to around 3 percent, as Japan has shown during the 1990s, and KOST in more recent years – and perhaps China in the not too distant future. One may be forced to accept that this is simply part of the maturation process of the EAEs growing out of the system.

Second, because the responses to the institutional aging by the EACs have varied, the ending of their East Asian Growth – or their transition to a "mature" economy – has been, and will continue to be, different. With these somewhat different exit experiences, there is reason to believe that the EAEs will consider the difficulties they are currently experiencing within the larger context of the growth experiences. In particular, it would be useful to understand the foundations of their rapid growth experience over the past decades; what the essential consequences of the working of these foundation forces are; to what extent they are still effective, relevant, and desirable; and what the fundamental challenges are for them in managing the process of maturation out of the system. On the basis of the findings in this study, the following issues – and how the EAEs might handle them – would be critical for them in making a successful and smooth transition from an East Asian economy to a mature economy.

### Developing new bases of competitiveness

East Asian Growth is built, primarily, upon the basis of institutionally enhanced competitiveness. The institutional arrangements for the sustaining of such competitiveness have become significantly less effective, after decades of bearing the burdens and costs associated with growth. Moreover, with the collapse, weakening, and transformation of the original domestic and international interests behind these arrangements, they have gradually lost both their purpose and value.

Without an institutional basis for its competitiveness, the EAEs would need to find a new basis for reasonable growth as a mature economy. The knowledge economy, as an idea, holds great appeal. If successful, it would allow the EAEs to move beyond an economy based upon institutional competitiveness, to one based upon technological competitiveness, thus placing them on the same footing as other competitive and mature economies.

The promotion of a knowledge economy, however, requires certain conditions that are, intrinsically, part of the growth system: having a set of strategic products, and the support of government in the provision of public goods. In this context, the challenge for the EAEs is twofold. On the one hand, with the new environment in the EAEs supporting a less centripetal society and a less consensual government, the effectiveness of their efforts in promoting the new economy is questionable. On the other hand, if the EAEs must rely upon old mechanisms of institutional manipulation, based upon their past East Asian Growth experiences, there would be concern regarding whether the movement toward a new economy would, simultaneously, help them transform their aging system.

### Overcoming the national framework

The second issue concerns the fact that East Asian Growth has been made possible by treating the nation-state as the primary growth unit, separating the national market from the world market, and incorporating the various facilitators and participants into a giant "Nation Inc." Much has been said about the insurmountable difficulties faced in continuing to sustain such arrangements, dominated by national boundaries and the government's control over them. Without the national organization of production, distribution, and exchange, the notion of institutionally enhanced international competitiveness would become irrelevant.

For the EAEs to find a new framework for sustainable growth under the emerging conditions, much of the original thinking needs to be adjusted. The conception of East Asian Growth concentrated upon the restriction of the international movement of products and capital, and the reorganization of production, distribution, and exchange within the national boundaries, thus creating international competitiveness. In the new environment, where the dynamic movement of products, capital, and human resources on a global scale has become an operational parameter, such manipulative restriction – and consequently internal reorganization – would be hard to sustain. Given that value-addition cannot continue to be derived, in the main, from the institutional manipulation of the national economy against the world economic system, but, rather, must increasingly be derived from the high intensity of economic activity in a particular location on the global scale, the EAEs would have to plan how to attract the inward movement of capital and economic activities. Given this environment, the nation-state is no longer able to serve as the optional growth unit. What we have seen emerge as a trend among the EAEs, in recent years, is the rise of regional centers – such as Singapore, Shanghai, Tokyo, and Hong Kong – as global hubs of manufacturing, services, and operations, attracting investment, technology transfer, and business traffic from around the globe. In turn, these hubs would become the engine of growth for their respective adjacent regions.

In this new framework of global hubs of investment, operation, transaction, and management, the potential for growth does not come from comparative advantage defined by national boundaries and institutional manipulation, but from *comparative attractiveness*, affected by the worldwide freedom of movement in capital, technology, human resources, and products. This regime is in line with the emerging system of global production, distribution, and consumption. There is reason to be optimistic about the prospects of the EACs' move in such a direction, and their chances at excelling under this new regime.

### *Managing institutional transformation*

Within the growth system, one often found close government–business collaboration, a centripetal society, a controlled labor market, and an incorporated nation. Under the new regime discussed above, there is much to be expected from the restructuring of the "internal" organization for growth. One will, most probably, see the leading role claimed by corporations with few national characteristics. Labor conditions, corporate management, and corporate–government relations would steadily adjust to the new global imperatives. The "advantage" one gained from the manipulation of these conditions, as the EACs did in the past, would be severely limited. Corporations themselves will rapidly form and reform, as new technologies rise and fall as the primary capital attractor – and thus advantage creator – along with production driven by these technologies.

In this area, the EACs face the most difficult challenge. The old growth regimes – such as close government–business collaboration, the centripetal society, the controlled labor market, and the incorporated nation as a whole – not only promoted growth, but also the interests of those favorably positioned in the growth arrangements. In other words, change to the existing growth regimes, unlike change in other areas, would most likely affect those favorably positioned. Delicate national politics and policy have to be played out to prevent the possibility that those favorably positioned both resist change in their position – and thus derail the process of reform and adjustment – or relocate themselves within the new growth structure dominated by major corporations, allowing the growth process to be narrowly dictated by corporate interests.

It appears that a gradual and piecemeal process of institutional transformation has prevailed in the EAEs. Such a process allows compromise and negotiation between old and new interests in pursuing a new institutional framework, and room for the old interests and their supporting arrangements to adjust.

### Broadening development agenda

Finally, there is a problem that must be faced by the EAEs. East Asian Growth has been narrowly pursued for decades, arguably at the expense of various other values that a mature economy, or a civilized society, should honor. These include the values of environmental harmony, basic human entitlements and well-being, rules of conflict resolution and dispute settlement, civic standards, legitimacy, fairness, and accountability in decision-making and management in a given organizational environment. In other words, there is a challenge confronting the EAEs – to transform both the economy and the society that has collaborated for growth at any cost, and by any means, into an economy and society that grow with sensitivity toward interests of greater significance in social development.

The EACs have both favorable and unfavorable conditions in this regard. Toward the latter stages, East Asian Growth has reached a point where suppressed and marginalized interests concerned with the promotion of broader development values have surfaced, and demand recognition and proper resources. Whether the key growth facilitators like it or not, the demand for a fairer, more just, and more accountable economic process – and society as a whole – will prevail.

On the other hand, the demands of a wider development agenda come with a price. There is no guarantee that the EAEs will be able to restructure their resource frameworks to meet the growing development demands, while at the same time remain capable of pursuing effective growth. Particularly within a political environment where accountability mechanisms have not been effectively established, the pressures for such a significant shift in resource distribution will be low, and will only arise slowly.

## Summary and discussion

East Asian Growth is a dynamic process, where the striving for international competitiveness led to the formation of a set of institutional arrangements that facilitated the reorganization of production and distribution within the economy, and the constant promotion and expansion of strategic products to international markets.

Like any other market economy, there are inherent business cycles in the EAEs. But the growth system and market-consumption separation enabled the EAEs to defuse tensions in the cycles through aggressive market expansion and diversification, cost suppression, industrial restructuring, and the upgrading of strategic products. The resultant growth cycles thus smoothed out periodic disruptions in business cycles, ensured continuous high-speed growth, and paved the way for advances in industrial capacity and technology sophistication.

There are, however, limits to what the growth system can do to sustain constant cycle management. The management of growth cycles *within* the growth system proved to be both effective and costly. These costs have accumulated over time, increasing the tensions between the various arrangements within the system, and reducing the effectiveness of the overall system. The aging of the institutional setting, and the continual build-up of tensions within the system, will inevitably bring rapid growth to an end and cause the growth system itself either to collapse or negate itself.

The end games of the EAEs have been complicated by the internal and historical conditions in each of the EAEs, but also the new global dynamics of the 1980s and 1990s. While the ending of East Asian Growth should not be a surprise, it doesn't have to end in violent collapse. A smooth transition by the EAEs to a mature economy requires the development of a new basis for competitiveness; overcoming of the obsession with the national unit and its associated structure and arrangements; broadening of the social and political basis of development; and careful management along with the striking of a better balance between various interests in the process – old and new, domestic and international. The emerging new framework in the EAEs, thus conceived, is less likely to be a complete replacement of the growth system, but, rather, one that reflects the mixed conditions and complex interests of the present time, some of which are, naturally, the legacy of the growth system.

# 7   Conclusion

## Institutional competitiveness and East Asian Growth

East Asian Growth is a process and historical experience of rapid industrialization and prolonged high-speed economic growth in the EACs, which has materialized under their unique system of production, distribution, and exchange over the 50 years in the second half of the twentieth century. This final chapter will summarize our discussion of the growth pattern and the defining character of the growth system.

## The pattern of rapid economic growth

Discussions in the early chapters allow us to define the pattern of rapid economic growth in terms of a clearly definable rapid growth period, a set of distinct growth indicators, a unique pattern of government activity, and a shared pattern of how crucial growth inputs related to growth outputs, as well as a country-specific historical sequence where growth-defining, path-dependent events, policies, conditions, and developments have unfolded and led to the rise and fall of the growth system. Evidence, as summarized below, allows us to conclude that this general pattern is shared by the EAEs.

### *Rapid growth periods*

East Asian Growth can be defined first by the fact that each EAE had around 30 years of rapid economic growth, when annual growth rates were generally[1] above the 7.85 percent threshold (the EAEs' average for the overall research period from 1951 to 2000). While the timings, and even the durations, of these rapid growth periods varied, there was, generally, a shared pattern of prolonged high-speed growth, in terms of a clearly identifiable beginning and end of the rapid growth periods, and principal indicators of growth output.

### *Japan*

Japan's rapid growth started after the settlement of war issues in 1951, with the San Francisco Peace Treaty. In addition to the start of the distinct growth rate, there were three additional reasons for using 1952 as the starting point of Japan's rapid growth period. First, between the end of World War II and the early 1950s, the general direction of the government's economic policy was very different from the one that dominated much of the rapid growth period that followed. Under the so-called Dodge Plan,[2] the government pursued a "full-scale deflationary policy" that sought a balanced budget, suspended new loans from the Reconstruction Bank, and reduced and abolished subsidies. Changes came in 1951 and 1952, when "capital accumulation promotion policies for industrial reconstruction were hammered out in quick succession." These, according to Nakamura, "became the prototype for Japan's postwar industrial policies" (Nakamura 1981: 43–6).

Second, the early 1950s were also dominated by a major regional event that generated the initial traffic that ultimately led to Japan's export-led growth – another prominent feature of East Asian Growth. Following the outbreak of the Korean War in 1950, Japan's "wartime" measures to promote exports to keep up with US military orders started to take root in 1952. It is, therefore, appropriate that 1952 is used as the starting point of Japan's rapid growth period.

Third, 1952 also saw the establishment of the JDB and the JIEB, using "national funds" to supply exporting industries with low-interest funds for plant and equipment; tax reform that adopted a progressive corporate tax system for the promotion of plant and equipment investment and exports; the establishment of a foreign exchange allocation system that protected national industries; and the first *Five-Year Economic* Plan. These operational mechanisms became key components of the institutional basis for international competitiveness.

There doesn't seem to be any significant disagreement regarding the ending point of Japan's post-war rapid growth period – despite the fact that it was not the expected point, given the general pattern established in this study across the EACs. According to this general pattern, Japan's rapid growth would have come to an end in the early 1980s. Indeed, many of its growth indicators reached the ending levels of the other EAEs only in the early 1980s. But the 1973 oil crisis shortened Japan's rapid growth period. The effects of higher oil prices deprived Japan of the very conditions for East Asian Growth to work. The importing (of raw materials)–manufacturing–exporting chain was interrupted. The situation was worsened by the rise in the value of Japanese yen against US dollars after 1970. From 1970 to 1973, the yen rose 32 percent. This further weakened the exporting capacity, already under threat from the oil crises.

Alternatively, one can argue that – unlike any other EAEs – Japan had a substantial level of growth and development before World War II. Its post-war growth can be seen, in part, as a continuation of its pre-War growth, and thus did not require the post-war 30 years that other EAEs went through to reach the maturation of East Asian Growth. Whatever the explanations, there was a 22-year period from 1952 to 1973 when Japan's GDP growth rate ran above the 7.85 percent threshold, with an average annual growth rate at 11.93 percent.

### *Korea, Singapore, and Taiwan*

The second wave EAEs cannot be seen as sharing the same period of rapid growth, as some may imagine. Singapore, for example, did not have a real existence as a sovereign country until after its break from the Malay Union in 1965. Not only did the entity of Singapore begin to exist only in 1965, but also it was only after this that the government took a series of promotional measures in an effort to rescue the economy. For 30 years, from 1968 to 1997, Singapore's annual growth rates were generally above the threshold, with an average rate at 8.88 percent.

The Korean case was also unique. Indicators of East Asian Growth – a high growth rate, government's industrial policy, national reorganization of production, exports concentration, a core economic decision-making structure, growth alliance, etc. – only began in the early 1960s. In much of the 1950s, Korea lived under the shadow of the Korean War. After the war, different political forces competed for control of the nation. The competitive politics of the time led to a chaotic political environment, where politicians relied heavily upon business elites to support their political ambitions. Unlike the government–business alliance that formed later under East Asian Growth, government–business relations in the 1950s featured corruption on both sides, without a clear, central, and positive purpose for much of the interaction between political and business elites, much less their subjection to developmental discipline.

Dramatic change took place after 1961, when General Park took control of the government, and put in place a harsh authoritarian military regime. Among the measures taken by the regime to reshape the country, President Park rebuilt government relations with the business community, and subordinated them to the government's political and developmental agenda. The military government immediately announced the first *Five Year Economic Development Plan* (FYEDP). Along with this, it also established the EPB, which would become the central organizer and disciplinary force behind the nation's development activities. Industrial policy, similar to that in Japan, also began to be introduced. The basic elements of East Asian Growth came into existence from 1962. The annual growth rates were largely above the threshold from 1963 to 1992, with an average growth rate at 8.52 percent.

The situation in Taiwan was rather different. There was no clear turning point, like the Korean War in the early 1950s for Japan, the military coup in 1961 in Korea, or a new state in 1965 in Singapore. In Taiwan, reasonably good growth rates were experienced in the 1950s. However, there is evidence that much of the early high growth rate was due to massive capital inflows from the mainland. In addition, tensions and crises over Jinmen and Mazhu islands in 1958, involving large-scale military operations from both sides of the Strait, suggest that the Nationalist government was still occupied with the idea of recovering the mainland from the hands of the communists, and was not ready to settle on Taiwan, much less be able to focus upon economic development. In the early 1960s it became apparent to President Chiang that the USA no longer supported the Nationalists' full-scale campaign to return to the mainland, and the Nationalists began to face up to the reality that they would have to build upon what they had for a long time to come.

Moreover, like many of its neighbors, during much of the 1950s Taiwan saw a period of import substitution (Haggard 1990). By the mid-1950s, the suppressive consequences of import substitution became clear. The economy "turned sluggish," and the government was "forced to rethink and to modify its industrialization strategy" (Ho 1978: 106). According to Ho, in the early 1960s a new strategy took shape, and "is aptly described by the government's new slogan 'Developing agriculture by virtue of industry, and fostering industry by virtue of foreign trade'" (Ho 1978: 106). Between 1958 and 1963, "the government initiated numerous reforms and new programs to stimulate industrialization and export" (Ho 1978: 196). The turn to export-led growth, with a new set of government policies, occurred in the late 1950s and early 1960s. Just as in the Korean case, Taiwan's rapid growth period started in 1962, which produced an average growth rate of 9.17 percent over three decades.

## China

China's case is perhaps the easiest among the EAEs. After 30 years of Mao's romantic experimentation with his socialist utopia, the communist leadership finally realized, in the late 1970s, that the Maoist economic model didn't work. Despite the fact that the leadership was suspicious of the four Asian dragons, and saw heated debates among themselves as to which direction China should take, much of what has followed since the Communist Party's historic meeting at the end of 1978, in terms of the purposes and methods of economic growth, has evolved, generally, along the lines of the growth system. As indicated in earlier discussions, China's rapid growth period continues, and the form of growth remains effective within the Chinese economy. Since China first registered an annual growth rate above the threshold in 1982 under the economic regime, it has since maintained an average growth rate at 9.98 percent.

## Key growth indicators

In addition to the similar durations of the rapid growth periods, East Asian Growth can be further defined by the EAEs' significantly higher GDP growth rates in the rapid growth periods, compared with those outside the rapid growth periods, and the levels of major growth indicators. As shown in Table 7.1, the average growth rate among the EAEs during their respective rapid growth periods is 9.69 percent, while for the overall 50-year period from 1951 to 2000, the average has been 7.85 percent. For the years outside the rapid growth periods, the average growth rate is 5.63 percent. The difference between the rapid growth period and non-rapid growth period is clear and significant.

Other major growth indicators that can help define the boundaries of the rapid growth period provide further substance to the overall pattern of the rapid growth periods (Table 7.2). In addition to annual GDP growth rates and GDP per capital levels, I use five more indicators, considered essential in the facilitation of East Asian Growth: manufacturing output in total GDP, investment share of GDP, total exports as a percentage of GDP, government consumption as a percentage of GDP, and monthly wages in US dollars. In simple economic terms, these five indicators show factor contributions to GDP. In the narrow terms of East Asian Growth, these indicators – together with GDP growth rates and GDP-PC – define the general characteristics of the rapid growth periods, and thus the pattern of East Asian Growth.

The average growth rate at the start of the rapid growth periods, for example, is 13.93 percent. If the abnormal Japan is taken out (the shaded cell), then the average rate is 10.78 percent (EAEs-1), much higher than the 50-year average; while that for the end year, 7.38 percent, is lower than the 50-year average. As far as the levels of GDP per capita are concerned, the average level among the EAEs at their start year was $2,528 in international dollars, and $12,481 for the end year. Again, with the abnormal Singapore taken out, the levels settle at $1,965 for the start year and $9,455 for the end year. Here, it shows that China still has a long way to go to reach the ending level of GDP per capita.

There is a distinct pattern among these indicators, particularly when compared to those of a non-EAE – the USA, as also presented in the table. The EAEs' rapid growth periods had significantly higher GDP growth

*Table 7.1* EAEs: GDP average annual change over three periods

|        | *ORP* | *RGP* | *NRGP* |
|--------|-------|-------|--------|
| CHN    | 7.93  | 9.98  | 6.60   |
| JPN    | 7.23  | 11.93 | 3.20   |
| KOR    | 7.28  | 8.52  | 5.11   |
| SGP    | 8.39  | 9.17  | 7.16   |
| TWN    | 8.39  | 9.17  | 7.16   |
| EAEs   | 7.85  | 9.69  | 5.63   |

*Notes*: ORP: overall research period (1951–2000); RGP: rapid growth period; NRGP: non-RGP (years outside RGP); data are averages over the period; unit: percentage.

*Source*: Appendix A1–5: 1.3.

*Table 7.2* EAEs: major indicators at the start and end of rapid growth periods

| | GDP-rates | | GDP-PC | | M-GDP | | I-GDP | | E-GDP | | G-GDP | | M-wages | |
| | S-year | E-year | Start | End | Start | End | Start | End | Start | End | Start | End | Start | End |
|---|---|---|---|---|---|---|---|---|---|---|---|---|---|---|
| CHN | 11.73 | 7.63 | 1,322 | 3,479 | 39.9 | 42.6 | 16.7 | 21.2 | 8.4 | 23.3 | 14.3 | 12.6 | 35 | 79 |
| JPN | 26.51 | 6.95 | 3,019 | 12,580 | 33.1 | 42.4 | 20.1 | 37.2 | 12.1 | 10.8 | 10.9 | 8.1 | 37 | 323 |
| KOR | 7.82 | 7.88 | 1,804 | 10,669 | 16.1 | 31.6 | 17.4 | 40.3 | 6.4 | 28.0 | 9.6 | 10.6 | 20 | 933 |
| SGP | 13.76 | 8.20 | 4,781 | 24,585 | 19.5 | 25.8 | 49.0 | 43.6 | 114.6 | 171.6 | 11.4 | 9.2 | 67 | 1,614 |
| TWN | 9.82 | 7.06 | 1,714 | 11,092 | 30.3 | 40.8 | 12.7 | 19.8 | 19.1 | 45.8 | 17.7 | 17.1 | 57 | 935 |
| USA | 5.40 | 4.05 | 11,582 | 32,178 | 30.8 | 15.9 | 18.1 | 23.4 | 3.8 | 13.0 | 20.5 | 17.7 | 274 | 2,280 |
| EAEs | 13.93 | 7.54 | 2,528 | 12,481 | 27.8 | 36.6 | 23.2 | 32.4 | 32.1 | 55.9 | 12.8 | 11.5 | 43 | 777 |
| EAEs-1 | 10.78 | 7.38 | 1,965 | 9,455 | 24.7 | 35.2 | 16.7 | 29.6 | 11.5 | 27.0 | 11.6 | 10.1 | 37 | 568 |

*Notes:*
GDP-Rates: GDP annual growth rates in percentages; GDP-PC: GDP per capita in constant international dollars.
M-GDP: manufacturing output as percentage of GDP.
I-GDP: investment share of GDP.
E-GDP: total exports as percentage of GDP.
G-GDP: government consumption as percentage of GDP.
M-wages: monthly wages in manufacturing in US dollars (Singapore 1970, Taiwan 1973 for start year).
S-year: start year–average of the three years leading to rapid growth period.
E-year: end year–average of the last three years of the rapid growth period.
EAEs: average among EAEs; EAEs-1: EASs without the one with largest abnormalities (shaded).

*Sources:* Appendix A1–5: various entries.

rates, exports, investment share of GDP, but lower GDP per capita levels, government consumption, and monthly wages in manufacturing. Moreover, all indicators – except the shares of government consumption in GDP – had significantly increased from the start year to the end year. Finally, these indicators can serve as technical indicators of a typical EAE: an average 8 percent or above in GDP annual growth; GDP per capita moving from around $2,000 in international dollars to about $10,000; share of manufacturing output in GDP moving from 25 percent to 35 percent; investment share of GDP moving from about 15 percent to around 30 percent; share of exports in GDP moving from 10 percent to 25 percent; and monthly wages moving from USD about US$40 to around US$600. The only exception is the government consumption as percentage of GDP, which, at around 10–11 percent, has not changed much.

## *Government activity*

The rapid growth periods are also distinguishable by a unique pattern of growth impacting activity by the government. Given the critical role of government in East Asian Growth, the association of the rapid growth period with a unique pattern of government activity is of special interest. As shown in Table 7.3, the governments of the EAEs generally followed a more conservative fiscal policy during their rapid growth period (average 0.95 in expenditure over revenue ratio, compared to the USA's 1.09 over the whole period). Among them, Singapore has been constantly the most conservative in government fiscal policy. Japan and Korea moved in opposite directions. In total government expenditure as a percentage of GDP, the EAEs' average level has stayed at around 17 percent, lower than that of the USA (19.81 percent). This confirms our early finding in the EAE–OECD comparison: the EAEs' size of government is not necessarily big.

Regarding each category of expenditure, the EAEs' spending in total government expenditure on economic affairs (22.8 percent over the rapid growth period), and education and health (19.98 percent) are significantly higher than those of the USA (7.17 percent on economic affairs, and 12.49 percent on education and health), while spending on social security is much lower (9.34 percent) than the USA's (27.62 percent). Moreover, there is a general pattern of an increase in education and social security expenditure, and a decrease in defense and economic expenditure. The data show that, apart from defense spending, the EAEs devoted a significant proportion of government spending to economic affairs. Government behavior in the early stage of the rapid growth period shows distinct characteristics from the late stage on the different categories of government expenditure.

## *Growth input–output relations*

The pattern of East Asian Growth is also reflected in a shared pattern of how growth inputs related to growth output. There is a general consensus

*Table 7.3* EAEs: government activity and GDP growth (1951–2000)

| | Expenditure/revenue ratio | | | Total gov. expenditure as % of GDP | | | Edu. and health spending as % of total exp. | | |
|---|---|---|---|---|---|---|---|---|---|
| | *RGP* | *S-Year* | *E-Year* | *RGP* | *S-Year* | *E-Year* | *RGP* | *S-Year* | *E-Year* |
| CHN | 1.11 | 1.03 | 1.17 | 17.20 | 21.71 | 16.24 | 23.44 | 21.47 | 26.40 |
| JPN | 0.90 | 0.73 | 0.92 | 11.76 | 12.46 | 12.63 | 11.97 | 9.28 | 12.88 |
| KOR | 1.05 | 1.49 | 0.93 | 15.89 | 10.75 | 16.42 | 18.87 | 18.37 | 18.75 |
| SGP | 0.72 | 0.81 | 0.46 | 19.39 | 16.90 | 17.23 | 27.08 | 26.08 | 25.71 |
| TWN | 0.99 | 0.99 | 1.15 | 21.82 | 18.96 | 27.08 | 18.54 | 16.08 | 21.37 |
| USA | 1.09 | 0.98 | 0.92 | 19.81 | 18.02 | 18.61 | 12.49 | 4.17 | 24.35 |
| EAEs | 0.95 | 1.01 | 0.93 | 17.21 | 16.15 | 17.92 | 19.98 | 18.26 | 21.02 |

| | Defense spending as % of total exp. | | | Social security spending as % of exp. | | | Economic affairs spending as % of exp. | | |
|---|---|---|---|---|---|---|---|---|---|
| | *RGP* | *S-Year* | *E-Year* | *RGP* | *S-Year* | *E-Year* | *RGP* | *S-Year* | *E-Year* |
| CHN | 9.46 | 13.56 | 7.95 | 1.60 | 1.78 | 1.37 | 45.20 | 59.78 | 36.81 |
| JPN | 9.64 | 13.69 | 6.86 | 15.49 | 12.07 | 21.45 | 11.65 | 27.24 | 12.13 |
| KOR | 27.14 | 27.35 | 22.16 | 6.45 | 5.23 | 9.51 | 18.41 | 21.51 | 18.42 |
| SGP | 26.40 | 33.60 | 27.62 | 10.62 | 7.22 | 15.75 | 14.83 | 10.08 | 14.85 |
| TWN | 30.61 | 45.85 | 17.43 | 12.52 | 7.89 | 18.73 | 23.90 | 14.09 | 27.43 |
| USA | 33.69 | 55.45 | 18.17 | 27.62 | 11.45 | 33.20 | 7.17 | 5.60 | 5.30 |
| EAEs | 20.85 | 26.81 | 16.40 | 9.34 | 6.84 | 13.36 | 22.80 | 26.54 | 21.93 |

*Notes:*
RGP: rapid growth period (each EAE respectively).
S-year: start year–average of the three years leading to rapid growth period; E-year: end year–average of the last three years of the rapid growth period; EAEs: average among EAE.
*Source*: Appendix A1–5: 6.2, 6.3.2, 6.4.

that exports, manufacturing, investment, government consumption, wages and exchange rates are significant factors contributing to GDP uniquely in East Asian Growth. Strong and positive relations are found during the EAEs' rapid growth periods between change in manufacturing, exports, capital formation, government consumption, and wages on the one hand, and change in GDP on the other. During non-rapid growth periods, most relations were negative or insignificant. There is no clear pattern between exchange rate change and GDP change.

Figure 7.1 shows the correlation between growth in manufacturing and GDP for each EAE. In this figure and the following five figures, each trend-line represents the correlation for one of the EAEs. The solid trend-lines represent the correlations during the EAEs' rapid growth periods (RGPs in the figures), while the dotted trend-lines represent the correlations during their non-rapid growth periods (NRGPs), as defined above.

As seen in Figure 7.1, there is a clear and strong pattern of positive correlation between growth in manufacturing output and that in total GDP during the rapid growth period. The trends during the non-rapid growth periods are the reverse, and move in different directions – with the exception of Japan, where the correlation during its non-rapid growth period is still positive. This reflects the sudden interruption of Japans' rapid growth period where the rapid growth period has ended, but manufacturing's support for GDP growth has remained. This abnormality also shows up in correlations with other contributing factors.

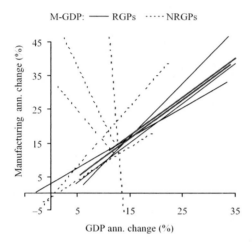

*Figure 7.1*  EAEs: correlation of changes in manufacturing and GDP (1951–2000).

*Source*: Appendix A1–5.

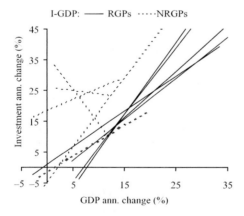

*Figure 7.2*  EAEs: correlation of changes in investment share and GDP (1951–2000).

*Source*: Appendix A1–5.

The general pattern also holds true for other indicators: investment (Figure 7.2), exports (Figure 7.3), government consumption (Figure 7.4), and wages in manufacturing (Figure 7.5). All these factors have a strong positive relation with GDP growth for the rapid growth period, while the relations during the NRGP varied, and, in most cases, are in the reverse. On wage-GDP correlations, however, relations in both the rapid growth periods and the non-rapid growth period are positive, indicating that wage growth always goes with GDP growth.

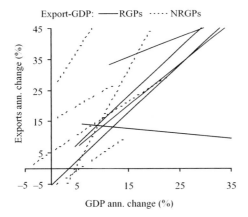

*Figure 7.3* EAEs: correlation of exports and GDP growth correlations (1951–2000).

*Source*: Appendix A1–5.

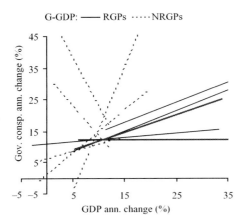

*Figure 7.4* EAEs: correlation of changes in government consumption and GDP (1951–2000).

*Source*: Appendix A1–5.

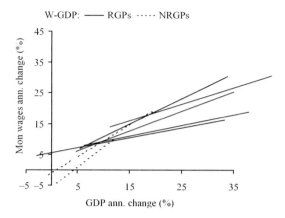

*Figure 7.5* EAEs: correlation of changes in wages in manufacturing and GDP (1951–2000).

*Source*: Appendix A1–5.

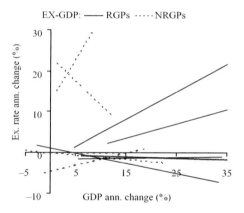

*Figure 7.6* EAEs: correlation of changes in exchange rate and GDP (1951–2000).

*Source*: Appendix A1–5.

As far as the exchange rate is concerned (Figure 7.6), there is little correlation between exchange rate movement and GDP growth. Japan maintained a relatively stable exchange rate during its rapid growth period, while the currencies of Taiwan and Singapore moderately appreciated. On the other hand, Chinese yuan and Korean won experienced a significant devaluation during their rapid growth periods. Interestingly, China and Korea here show slightly positive correlations during their rapid growth periods.

### *Historical sequence and path-dependent dynamism*

Finally, the pattern of East Asian Growth is also defined by the historical sequence where growth-defining, path-dependent events, policies, conditions, and developments have unfolded and led to the rise and fall of the growth system in each EAE. East Asian Growth is not a static framework where one can identify a singular cause–effect relationship. The formation of the growth systems was a dynamic historical process, with one effect or action leading to another. Together, and over time, these effects supported rapid prolonged growth. What is important for East Asian Growth is not so much how important one factor – or a list of factors – are, but, rather, how over time these factors came to be relevant in the growth process, and how they interacted with each other, or were manipulated by growth participants, to create the conditions for rapid growth.

The historical sequence through which the growth system unfolded within each EAE has been shaped, in particular, by two sets of factors. The first involves the unprecedented events that left a significant impact upon the working of the growth arrangements. I have discussed how the initial conditions in the EAEs led to the series of subsequent developments. Even during the rapid growth periods, those unprecedented events and developments continued to leave their mark. In the case of Japan, for example, the oil crises of the 1970s literally ended Japan's post-war rapid growth. In Korea, the political crisis of the late 1970s caused its economy to plunge to a –2.09 percent growth rate in 1980. Similarly, the political crisis of the late 1980s in China led to a drop in its growth rate. Singapore's high-wage policy in the early 1980s was responsible for the plunge of its economy to an unprecedented low growth rate of –1.14 percent. Needless to say, all the EAEs' were affected by the financial crisis of 1997–8.

Also affecting the historical sequence of East Asian Growth were the growth cycles in each growth process. As demonstrated earlier, these growth cycles – driven by product cycles and shifts in comparative advantage – compelled government (and other growth participants) to resort to the same set of industry promoting policies and mechanisms, and determined the actual configuration of the growth arrangements and methods. The progression of East Asian Growth has been a process of constant adjustment, and a series of moves, from concentrating upon labor and primary resource-intensive industries, to capital-intensive industries, and then to technologically sophisticated industries. However, due to differences in the content of the growth cycles, the specific sub-industries to which the EAEs moved into – and the methods for this periodic upgrading and restructuring – differed. The Koreans focused upon the petrochemical, heavy metal, and shipbuilding industries in their second stage of industrialization, borrowing heavily from international financing sources, while Singapore concentrated upon developing its service sector to attract multinational corporations, with a more conservative fiscal and monetary policy.

The historical conditions, out of which East Asian Growth took shape, are critical for our understanding of the rise and fall of the growth system. It was this path-dependent course of action that linked the country-specific conditions of the EAEs to their general pattern of growth, and the specifics in which the general pattern operated in each individual EAE. East Asian Growth, in this sense, is a prolonged process of rapid economic growth, propelled by the relentless efforts of growth participants to combat product cycles with market expansion, industrial upgrading, and cost reduction through institutional innovation and manipulation.

## The growth system

East Asian Growth is not only defined by a distinct level of consistently high GDP growth rates, a set of growth indicators, and the pattern of growth input–output, but also by the onset at the beginning of the rapid growth periods, and the fading out at their end, of some principal features of institutional enhancement for international competitiveness. Fundamentally, East Asian Growth has set itself apart from other forms of growth through the dynamism of prolonged GDP growth, built primarily upon institutionally enhanced international competitiveness, growth-privileged mobilization and distribution of national resources and income, and strategic utilitarianism focused narrowly upon what works in respect to growth demands. What has made all this possible, operative, and relevant, however, are what I would call the *five principal elements* of the growth system: a growth-at-any-cost mentality, a core economic decision-making structure, a national growth unit, an economy based upon strategic product(s) and their constant upgrading, and a centripetally dynamic society. Let us now look at these principal features.

### *Growth-at-any-costs mentality*

The people of the EACs, particularly their elites, developed a predominant sense of purpose, and thus appropriate means and ends, for their growth activities, driven primarily by two major historical conditions. First, there was the overwhelming power and influence of the Western countries in these EACs from the eighteenth century. These EAEs related to the expansion of Western influence in different ways, but whether they would join (or rejoin) the world rank of power and affluence has been an ultimate challenge to the leadership of the EAEs, in terms of their legitimacy and capability; and the ultimate expectation of the general public of the EACs.

Second, there were the initial conditions facing the EACs right before their rapid growth periods, as was discussed earlier. For all the EAEs, facing the initial conditions was a matter of life and death. Growth to survive became an unspoken mandate, for government, corporations, and the general public.

The consequence of such a growth mentality is that growth was promoted and protected at great costs – political, social, human, and organizational. In this sense, East Asian Growth was not a miracle. It came with a huge price tag, which other societies – and even today's EACs – may or may not be able to endure, or consciously accept.

## Core economic decision-making structure

Without exception, the start of the EAEs' rapid growth periods saw the establishment of a core, unconventional decision-making structure of supreme economic powers; and the end of the rapid growth periods saw the crumbling of what Robert Wade calls the "economic general staff" (1990: 196). The function of the core economic decision-making structure is crucial for East Asian Growth. It reduced inter-agency friction and bureaucratic inefficiency within the government; provided a central point for direction and authority in growth activity; and served as a direct converting mechanism between the general policy agenda of the political leadership and the operational details in functional ministries and lower levels of economic operations outside the government. Ultimately, it is this core structure that ensured the technical quality of the engagement of the government in national growth activity.

## The nation as growth unit

The organization of growth at the national level was unique for East Asian Growth. It was necessitated by the pursuit of international competitiveness. The nation, as a growth unit, demanded the reorganization of production, distribution, and exchange for the competitiveness of the overall national economy. It entailed adjustment in productive relations – within the corporation, among corporations, between government and corporations, and between industrial capital and labor forces, etc. – to achieve maximum institutional efficiency.

The nation, as a growth unit, also demanded the separation of the national economy from the world economic system. Such separation was necessary for the effective functioning of the national growth unit. It required the separation of the domestic market from the international market, and mechanisms for the protection and promotion of growth activity across national boundaries. Inside and outside the insulated national growth unit, the EAEs pursued different interests with different methods, and were constrained by different institutional frameworks.

## Strategic products and industrial policy

The phenomenon of large-scale export concentration and the aggressive and effective promotion of successive generations of products in East Asian

Growth shows the determination and capacity of the EAEs to develop and maintain competitiveness in the global market over a set of *strategic products*. The products are strategic as they gave the EAE a profit advantage as the result of their constant pursuit of comparative advantage, against the natural trend of the movement of production factors. The experiences of the EAEs show that they tended to focus, narrowly, upon a set of products, and migrated periodically to new sets of products involving higher levels of labor skills, capital intensiveness, technological sophistication, market exclusiveness, and value-adding margins.

Associated with strategic products – given an edge by human and institutional support – is the ability of the EAEs to periodically adjust the strategic direction of growth activity and refocus their resources in response to shifting comparative advantage. The capital accumulation mentioned earlier reinforced the ability of growth participants to make the necessary adjustments, but government sought – as its primary responsibility – to redirect growth activities through promotional and punitive laws and regulations. This pattern of product upgrading and revolution – driven by shifting comparative advantage – required a significant supporting role of public goods, in R&D, insurance, and the sharing of costs and risks in establishing markets for new products. This is where the industrial policy really fits in.

### Centripetal society

A *centripetal society* is marked by the effective presence of a center, in a broad sense of government and social elites, in the management of both the economy and society at large; a relationship of mutual dependency and expectations between the center and society; and a set of mechanisms supporting consultation, conformation, and accommodation. Despite their varying political regimes, ideological orientations, and contemporary experiences, the EACs can all be seen as centripetal societies. During their rapid growth periods, the center tended to be dominated by one major political party, and staffed by professionally trained, politically loyal technocrats. It monopolized resources and access, controlled resource allocation and wealth distribution, and commanded the capacity to effectively promote, direct, discipline, and punish.

There are several aspects to the role the centripetal society played in the shaping of the growth system, and thus East Asian Growth. First, because of the very nature of the center – where growth opportunities and benefits are ultimately located and authority over society is relentlessly exercised – attentive elements in society tended to do their best to avoid becoming a victim of the center's manipulative activity, but to benefit from the center's sponsored growth process, and, hopefully, to move themselves ultimately into the center. This centripetal mentality – that is, the propensity to conform and the determination to join – underlay much of the hard work and sacrifice of millions of people in the EACs throughout their rapid growth periods, particularly in their early years, and their passive tolerance of various harsh growth regimes, from labor regulations to price controls.

Second, within this overall centripetal environment, the national policy formulation process tended not to be determined by a political process of open competition among major political parties representing the interests of their constituencies, but, rather, was often settled through political negotiations among major factions within the ruling party, and consultative processes involving parties concerned with the issue at hand. The fact that there is a built-in tendency among many in society to lean toward the center allows the use of various leverages by the center to keep significant societal elements focused upon the center, including, primarily, the business sector.

## Final words

East Asian Growth took place in the EACs over the second half of the twentieth century. The EACs "grew" into this unusual path of economic recovery, rapid industrialization, and prolonged economic growth, and, in the process, developed the unique growth system that focused upon the enhancement of their international competitiveness. During this 50-year span, each of the EAEs experienced 20 to 30 years period of rapid growth, with a distinctly high level of annual GDP growth rates, and a unique pattern of relationships between GDP growth on the one hand, and the key growth inputs, government activity, institutional setting, and historical conditions on the other.

At the core of the form of growth, institutional enhancement was made necessary by the need for international competitiveness in these economies, and, at the same time, the lack of competitiveness by other means. It was made possible by a similar set of historical, social, and cultural conditions in each of the countries at the time, and ultimately was driven by the growth-at-any-cost mentality prevalent in these countries.

This institutional enhancement affected state structure and functions, economic policy, corporate arrangements, social structure and relations, individual behavior, and domestic and international interaction. Each of these elements became a critical aspect of the growth system that defined and propelled the rapid growth. The growth experiences of the East Asian Five have demonstrated that rapid industrialization and economic growth are achievable in economies where there is insufficiency in the provision of growth factors often deemed necessary for normal economic growth, and that institutional competitiveness can make up, and, over time, eliminate such insufficiency, and thus create and sustain economic growth.

The dynamic and institutional nature of East Asian Growth determined not only the characteristics of their growth, but also, ultimately, the limits of the growth system. Toward the latter stages of their rapid growth periods, burdens accumulated over the rapid growth period went beyond what the growth system could sustain. At the same time, confrontations with other forms of economic operation intensified as the initial conditions for the rapid growth gradually faded. Together, they led to the declining effectiveness of this form of growth. The ending of the rapid growth period – and thus East Asian Growth – is marked by a significant decline in growth rates, and increasing difficulties in the continual effective operation of the growth system.

The rise and fall of the growth system and the growth pattern it has generated are a good example of how modification in an institutional framework can lead to the desirable behaviors of those effectively located within the framework. Such modifications are inputs from all participants, including government, industrial capital, consumers in markets, and other social forces, on the basis of the impact that their varied capacities have upon the institutional setting. The growth system thus is not a set of "independent variables" that "caused" growth, but rather a system of significant, relevant, and contingent conditions for such growth to occur. It operated on the fundamental value of rapid economic growth. When rapid economic growth became the fundamental value of a society, the society would adjust accordingly. This would affect the means and purposes of social activities in general, and the organization of production, distribution, and exchange within society in particular. In this sense, the growth system is not only one of economic growth, but also that of grand social movement and transformation.

It seems that this book could just stop here. But that would waste much of what has been achieved in this study. The consideration and study of human phenomena should always be aimed at moving us up the "ladder of abstraction" (Rosenau 1971). The theories of institutionalism, historicism, path dependence, comparative advantage, and international competitiveness incorporated within this study are just part of an effort to climb up this ladder. There is something more fundamental about East Asian Growth.

When the nation-state first emerged in Europe centuries ago, Niccolo Machiavelli and Thomas Hobbes advised us that a form of social order – preferably in the form of the state – was necessary for meaningful human existence and progress. Moreover, a social order is not automatic and must be constructed. The construction of social order requires innovation and determination on the part of those participating in the process, and – as conventional reading goes – their skillful handling of the challenge of the prevailing social habits, ethical values, and institutional norms (Hobbes 1651; Goldsmith 1966; Machiavelli 1950; Viroli 1998). Obviously, there is a question of purposes for any "constructed" social order. It is not often that a social order was dictated by a single, very narrow purpose.

Construction of a social order for the narrow purpose of rapid industrialization and economic growth has been at the core of East Asian Growth.

To achieve that, the EACs have challenged not only the economic conditions and popular theories of economic growth and development; they have also challenged themselves and the human condition in general, in terms of the physical limits, prevailing social habits, ethical values, and institutional norms of the time.

In the 1950s and 1960s, when we told millions of those in the developing world, seeking rapid industrialization and modernization, to get their "production factors" right, and to get their "institutions" right, we didn't seem to realize that economic growth can be more than just an adding up of production factors, and institutions can be quite significant in shaping the pattern and methods, and ultimately the possibility of growth. On the other hand, the institutions we understood then are probably too narrow to give a full account of the wider range of "institutions" effectively operating in different historical and social contexts; too static to allow their dynamic and historical nature to be recognized; and too universalistic to accommodate an understanding of how institutions become relevant and effective in a society. We have certainly learned a lot since then through new developments over the decades. In retrospect, East Asian Growth has not only expanded our world of material wealth, but also that of intellectual richness.

# Notes on data and appendices

1   Data used in Appendix A and B tables for the following groups are averaged among group members or over the period:

EAEs (East Asian Economies: China, Japan, Korea, Singapore, and Taiwan);
OECDEs (Economies of original OECD member countries in 1961, excluding Turkey);
KOST (Korea, Singapore, and Taiwan).

2   Keys to data sources used in Appendix A and B tables (years in parentheses indicate the latest edition up to which data are used or, in the case of web-based databases, the dates they were accessed):

| | |
|---|---|
| ILO-EAP | International Labor Organization, *Economically Active Population 1950–2000* (1997). |
| ILO-LABORSTA | International Labor Organization, *Labor Statistics Database* (2003). |
| IMF-GFS: | International Monetary Fund, *Government Financial Statistics Yearbook* (various years). |
| IMF-IFS: | International Monetary Fund, *International Financial Statistics* (CD-ROM, December, 2001; *IMF Online*, 2003; and in some cases, *International Financial Statistics Yearbook*, various years). |
| IMF-WEO: | International Monetary Fund, *World Economic Outlook Database* (2003). |
| OECD-2001 | Statistics Directorate, OECD, *Historical Statistics 1960–1999* (2001). |
| OECD-2003 | Statistics Directorate, *SourceOECD Statistics* (2003). |
| PWT6.1 | Alan Heston, Robert Summers, and Daniel A. Nuxoll, *Penn World Tables* 6.1 (2002). |
| UNDP-HDI | United Nations Development Program, *Human Development Indicators* (2003). |
| WB-GDN | World Bank, *Global Development Finance and World Development Indicators* (2001). |

| | |
|---|---|
| WB-PCSD | World Bank, *A New Database on Physical Capital Stock 1993* (2001). |
| WB-WDI | World Bank, *World Development Indicators Datasets* (2002). |
| WB-WIDER | World Bank, World Institute for Development Economics Research, *World Income Inequality Database* (2001). |
| WEF-GCR | World Economic Forum, *The Global Competitiveness Report* (2003). |

3  In the event data are missing from above datasets, the following national statistics are used (years in parentheses indicate the latest edition up to which data are used, or in the case of web-based data, the year they were accessed):

| | |
|---|---|
| CHN-CSYB | State Bureau of Statistics, China, *China Statistics Yearbook* (2002). |
| CHN-HNAC | State Bureau of Statistics, China, *The Historical National Accounts of China 1952–1995* (1997). |
| JPN-JSY | Statistics Bureau, Government of Japan, *Japan Statistics Yearbook* (2003). |
| JPN-HSJ | Japan Statistical Association, *Historical Statistics of Japan* (1987). |
| KOR-KSY | Economic Planning Board, Korea, *Korea Statistical Yearbook* (various years). |
| KOR-KOSIS | National Statistical Office, Korea, Korean Statistical Information System (2003). |
| SGP-SS | Department of Statistics, Singapore, *Statistics Singapore: Selected Historical Data* (2002). |
| SGP-SYB | Government of Singapore, *Singapore Yearbook* (various years). |
| TWN-DGBAS | Directorate-General of Budget, Accounting and Statistics, Taiwan, *National Statistics Database* (2003). |
| USA-BEA | Bureau of Economic Analysis, US Government, *Dataset* (2003). |

4  For Appendix C:

a  Timelines use year as base unit.

b  All events, activities, or institutions are recorded for the year they first occurred. Some shown in 1951 may have occurred earlier.

c  Please refer to Index for abbreviations.

d  Sources: from a wide range of publications (particularly, Li 1995; Tsuru 1993; Huff 1994; Nakamura 1995; Song 1990; Cheng 1982; Noguchi 1994; Lee 1996; World Bank 1993, 1994; SMTI 2001; 1990; and Peebles and Wilson 1996).

# Appendix A
## Individual EAE datasets

Please refer to "Notes on data and appendices" on pp. 224–5 for sources and keys in this Appendix.

# CHINA DATASET (1)

| | 1951 | 1952 | 1953 | 1954 | 1955 | 1956 | 1957 | 1958 | 1959 | 1960 | 1961 | 1962 | 1963 | 1964 | 1965 | 1966 | 1967 | 1968 | 1969 | 1970 | 1971 | 1972 | 1973 | 1974 |
|---|---|---|---|---|---|---|---|---|---|---|---|---|---|---|---|---|---|---|---|---|---|---|---|---|
| **1. GROSS DOMESTIC PRODUCT (GDP)** | | | | | | | | | | | | | | | | | | | | | | | | |
| 1.1 pc. usd. cr | | 48 | 5? | 58 | 60 | 66 | 6? | 80 | 8? | 93 | 76 | 69 | 7? | 83 | 96 | 102 | 94 | 89 | 98 | 102 | 107 | 121 | 152 | 159 |
| 1.2 pc. id. cr | | 507 | 615 | 601.21 | 630 | 676 | 686 | 715 | 672 | 685 | 685 | 647 | 668 | 724 | ---- | 805 | 786 | 741 | 707 | 820 | 834 | 851 | 884 | 881 |
| 1.3 ac. nc. cs | | | 15.6 | 4.2 | 6.8 | 15.1 | 5.1 | 21.2 | 8.9 | -0.3 | -27.3 | -5.6 | 10.2 | 18.2 | 17.1 | 10.7 | -5.? | -4.1 | 16.9 | 16.2 | 6.9 | 4.6 | 12.8 | 4.0 |
| 1.4.1 Agri (*gdp.nc.cr) | | 50.5 | 45.9 | 45.6 | 46.3 | 43.2 | 40.3 | 34.1 | 26.7 | 23.4 | 36.20 | 39.4 | 40.3 | 38.4 | 37.9 | 37.6 | 40.3 | 42.? | 38.0 | 35.2 | 34.1 | 32.9 | 33.4 | 33.9 |
| 1.4.2 Manuf (*gdp.nc.cr) | | 17.6 | 19.8 | 21.5 | 21.0 | 21.9 | 25.4 | 31.? | 37.4 | 39.0 | 29.70 | 28.3 | 29.6 | 31.? | 30.? | 34.7 | 30.? | 28.5 | 32.3 | 36.8 | 38.2 | 39.3 | 39.4 | 38.8 |
| **2. INTERNATIONAL TRADE** | | | | | | | | | | | | | | | | | | | | | | | | |
| 2.1.1 Exports (ac. usd.cr) | 38.2 | -7.9 | 24.4 | 12.7 | 22.6 | 17.0 | 34.2 | 23.1 | 16.4 | -18.9 | -24.5 | -1.5 | 6.2 | 10.8 | 13.9 | 4.6 | -10.9 | -2.0 | 3.8 | -5.9 | 20.6 | 32.7 | 59.1 | 21.0 |
| 2.1.2 Imports (ac.usd.cr) | 106.9 | -6.7 | 20.5 | -4.4 | 34.1 | -0.8 | 30.2 | 23.4 | 15.4 | -8.4 | -34.0 | -21.4 | 5.6 | 17.9 | 31.3 | 10.5 | -12.6 | -4.7 | -7.3 | 18.9 | -6.6 | 33.9 | 82.7 | 49.6 |
| 2.2.1 Exports (*gdp.nc.cr) | | 2.53 | 2.22 | 2.87 | 3.20 | 3.40 | 3.45 | 3.20 | 3.76 | 4.72 | 4.29 | 4.46 | 4.43 | 4.13 | 4.01 | 3.85 | 3.63 | 3.67 | 3.38 | 3.06 | 3.43 | 3.91 | 4.83 | 5.47 |
| 2.2.2 Imports (*gdp.nc.cr) | | 3.68 | 3.24 | 3.18 | 3.18 | 3.02 | 2.93 | 2.69 | 3.20 | 4.69 | 3.84 | 3.3? | 3.33 | 3.24 | 3.51 | 3.52 | 3.28 | 3.25 | 2.74 | 2.94 | 2.72 | 3.11 | 4.2? | 5.72 |
| 2.3 E/I Ratio (nc. cr) | 0.63 | 0.73 | 0.76 | 0.89 | 0.82 | 1.06 | 1.09 | 1.09 | 1.10 | 0.97 | 1.11 | 1.39 | 1.40 | 1.32 | 1.14 | 1.08 | 1.10 | 1.13 | 1.27 | 1.01 | 1.31 | 1.30 | 1.13 | 0.91 |
| **3. SUPPLY AND DEMAND** | | | | | | | | | | | | | | | | | | | | | | | | |
| 3.1 GFCF (*gdp.nc.cr) | | 11.9 | 14.0 | 16.4 | 16.0 | 21.4 | 17.5 | 25.5 | 30.3 | 32.5 | 18.? | 15.2 | 17.5 | 20.0 | 20.4 | 21.8 | 18.3 | 17.4 | 21.0 | 26.9 | 27.5 | 26.8 | 25.1 | 27.0 |
| 3.2 Invest.ac.nc.cs) | | 28.6 | 28.6 | 13.2 | -3.2 | 15.4 | 0.3 | 39.3 | 39.3 | -8.5 | -53.1 | -33.9 | 45.5 | 32.4 | 30.4 | 22.2 | -24.7 | 10.69 | 13.6 | 50.5 | 9.4 | -3.6 | 12.7 | 3.3 |
| 3.3 Invest (*gdp.id.cr) | | 8.2 | 9.90 | 10.89 | 9.85 | 10.59 | 11.16 | 15.62 | 22.58 | 20.34 | 10.40 | 6.48 | 8.90 | 10.57 | 12.43 | 14.03 | 10.49 | 10.69 | 11.02 | 15.41 | 15.85 | 14.42 | 15.41 | 15.76 |
| 3.4 Invest. (pc. id.cr.) | | 9.21 | 11.69 | 12.84 | 12.32 | 14.55 | 16.17 | 24.54 | 34.23 | 31.33 | 14.84 | 9.58 | 13.71 | 17.93 | 23.15 | 28.13 | 21.14 | 21.17 | 24.55 | 37.45 | 41.20 | 39.70 | 46.04 | 51.41 |
| 3.5 Comp.(*gdp.nc.cr) | | | | | | | | | | | | | | | | | | | | | | | | |
| 3.6.1 Comp.Gov (*gdp) | | | | | | | | | | | | | | | | | | | | | | | | |
| 3.6.2 Comp.Pri (*gdp) | | | | | | | | | | | | | | | | | | | | | | | | |
| 3.7 Comp.(ac. nc. cs) | | | 2.3 | 1.4 | 8.5 | 7.2 | 4.2 | 5.2 | -14.2 | -1.5 | 7.7 | 12.3 | -0.5 | 7.7 | 7.4 | 3.9 | 10.3 | -3.7 | 6.8 | 0.0 | 0.8 | 6.5 | 5.5 | 1.5 |
| 3.8 Comp (pc. id. cr) | | 84.85 | 86.18 | 85.96 | 91.73 | 98.55 | 103.25 | 106.09 | 90.58 | 90.03 | 98.89 | 112 | 109 | 116 | 123 | 128 | 142 | 138 | 150 | 152 | 155 | 167 | 181 | 195 |
| **4. MONEY AND CURRENCY** | | | | | | | | | | | | | | | | | | | | | | | | |
| 4.1 M1=2 (*gdp.nc.cr) | | | | | | | | | | | | | | | | | | | | | | | | |
| 4.2 For.Exch.Reser.(usd) | | | | | | | | | | | | | | | | | | | | | | | | |
| 4.3 Savings(*gdp.id.cr) | | 7.14 | 8.99 | 10.61 | 8.98 | 10.93 | 11.62 | 16.08 | 23.10 | 20.37 | 10.80 | 7.44 | 9.87 | 11.36 | 12.87 | 14.33 | 10.81 | 11.08 | 11.59 | 15.51 | 16.43 | 15.08 | 15.90 | 15.54 |
| 4.4 CPI (1995=100) | | | | | | | | | | | | | | | | | | | | | | | | |
| 4.5 Change in CP (an.*s) | | | | | | | | | | | | | | | | | | | | 1.10 | 1.10 | 1.00 | 1.00 | 0.90 |
| 4.5 Ex. Rate (usd.nc) | | 2.46 | 2.46 | 2.46 | 2.46 | 2.46 | 2.46 | 2.46 | 2.46 | 2.46 | 2.46 | 2.46 | 2.46 | 2.46 | 2.46 | 2.46 | 2.46 | 2.46 | 2.46 | 2.46 | 2.46 | 2.25 | 1.99 | 1.96 |
| **5. BALANCE OF PAYMENTS (usd.cr)** | | | | | | | | | | | | | | | | | | | | | | | | |
| 5.1 Overall | | | | | | | | | | | | | | | | | | | | | | | | |
| 5.1.1 Current | | | | | | | | | | | | | | | | | | | | | | | | |
| 5.1.2 Capital | | | | | | | | | | | | | | | | | | | | | | | | |
| 5.1.3 Financial | | | | | | | | | | | | | | | | | | | | | | | | |
| **6. PUBLIC FINANCE (nc.cr)** | | | | | | | | | | | | | | | | | | | | | | | | |
| 6.1 Balance(*gdp.nc.cr) | 0.98 | 0.28 | -0.72 | 0.12 | -1.48 | -1.78 | 0.68 | -1.59 | -3.90 | -4.90 | 0.00 | 1.62 | 0.83 | 0.40 | 0.78 | 1.13 | -1.16 | 0.20 | 0.05 | 0.66 | 0.57 | 0.03 | 0.03 | -0.26 |
| 6.2 Exp Rev Ratio | 0.98 | 0.99 | 1.03 | 1.00 | 1.05 | 1.07 | 0.98 | 1.05 | 1.12 | 1.12 | 1.00 | 0.94 | 0.97 | 0.99 | 0.97 | 0.96 | 1.05 | 0.99 | 1.00 | 0.98 | 0.98 | 1.00 | 1.00 | 1.01 |
| 6.3.1 Revenue (*gdp) | 25.62 | 25.62 | 25.88 | 28.54 | 25.39 | 27.26 | 28.39 | 29.05 | 33.85 | 39.28 | 29.19 | 25.29 | 25.76 | 25.48 | 25.58 | 29.91 | 23.65 | 20.97 | 27.19 | 32.62 | 33.92 | 33.04 | 30.62 | 28.21 |
| 6.3.2 Exp/ture (*gdp) | 25.34 | 25.34 | 26.60 | 28.42 | 28.87 | 29.04 | 27.71 | 30.63 | 37.75 | 44.18 | 29.19 | 25.66 | 26.93 | 27.08 | 26.80 | 28.78 | 24.81 | 20.77 | 27.15 | 31.95 | 33.35 | 33.01 | 30.58 | 28.47 |
| 6.4.1 Defence (*+tol exp) | 43.12 | 33.61 | 34.39 | 23.81 | 24.74 | 20.49 | 18.62 | 12.49 | 10.68 | 9.01 | 14.04 | 19.31 | 20.00 | 18.50 | 18.86 | 18.79 | 18.88 | 26.29 | 23.99 | 22.37 | 23.15 | 20.81 | 17.98 | 16.88 |
| 6.4.2 Edu. & Health(*s) | 11.01 | 12.27 | 14.80 | 14.18 | 12.14 | 15.40 | 15.69 | 10.88 | 10.79 | 13.51 | 17.20 | 17.54 | 15.49 | 16.78 | 13.63 | 12.47 | 13.83 | 13.38 | 9.46 | 9.33 | 8.71 | 9.33 | 10.95 | 12.02 |
| 6.4.3 Social Security(*s) | 0.00 | 1.71 | 1.65 | 2.47 | 1.88 | 1.90 | 1.79 | 0.80 | 0.81 | 1.23 | 2.83 | 2.76 | 3.06 | 4.33 | 2.38 | 1.71 | 1.86 | 1.57 | 1.27 | 1.01 | 0.93 | 1.06 | 1.23 | 1.16 |
| 6.4.4 Econ. Affairs(*s) | 28.76 | 42.56 | 39.88 | 50.62 | 52.38 | 53.31 | 55.09 | 69.65 | 71.68 | 71.57 | 58.98 | 51.76 | 52.44 | 33.33 | 55.24 | 57.55 | 55.48 | 46.40 | 56.20 | 60.46 | 57.13 | 56.40 | 57.90 | 58.33 |
| 6.5.1 Defence (*gdp) | | 8.52 | 9.13 | 6.77 | 7.14 | 5.93 | 5.16 | 3.83 | 4.03 | 3.98 | 4.10 | 4.50 | 4.17 | 5.01 | 5.06 | 5.41 | 4.68 | 5.46 | 6.51 | 7.15 | 7.72 | 6.87 | 5.50 | 4.81 |
| 6.5.2 Edu.& Health(*s) | | 3.11 | 3.94 | 4.03 | 3.50 | 4.47 | 4.35 | 3.33 | 4.07 | 5.97 | 5.02 | 4.71 | 4.55 | 3.65 | 3.59 | 3.43 | 2.78 | 3.38 | 2.57 | 2.57 | 2.91 | 3.25 | 3.35 | 3.42 |
| 6.5.3 Social Securty(*s) | | 0.43 | 0.44 | 0.70 | 0.54 | 0.55 | 0.50 | 0.25 | 0.33 | 0.83 | 0.71 | 0.82 | 0.83 | 1.17 | 0.64 | 0.49 | 0.33 | 0.33 | 0.31 | 0.31 | 0.31 | 0.33 | 0.38 | 0.33 |
| 6.5.4 Econ. Affairs(*s) | | 10.78 | 10.61 | 14.39 | 15.12 | 15.48 | 15.27 | 21.34 | 27.06 | 31.62 | 17.21 | 13.28 | 14.12 | 14.44 | 14.81 | 16.56 | 13.76 | 9.64 | 15.26 | 19.32 | 19.05 | 18.62 | 17.71 | 16.61 |
| **7. COMPETITIVENESS** | | | | | | | | | | | | | | | | | | | | | | | | |
| 7.1 M Wages Manuf(usd) | | 1,109 | 1,143 | 1,129 | 1,178 | 1,267 | 1,288 | 1,357 | 1,289 | 1,293 | 1,186 | 1,218 | 1,259 | 1,371 | 1,474 | 1,531 | 1,496 | 1,414 | 1,520 | 1,583 | 1,598 | 1,618 | 1,671 | 1,654 |
| 7.2 GDP per Wkr(id.cs) | | 7.07 | 7.07 | 7.16 | 6.37 | 6.32 | 7.10 | 3.36 | 3.15 | -0.2 | 21.32 | -4.2 | -3.9 | 4.86 | 2.84 | 5.09 | 1.41 | 2.17 | 2.22 | 1.68 | 2.65 | 1.76 | 1.70 | 1.91 |
| **8. POPULATION** | | | | | | | | | | | | | | | | | | | | | | | | |
| 8.1 urban(nc) | | | | | | | | | | | | | | | | | | | | | | | | |

keys: volume: billions; *gdp: as % of GDP; ac: annual change; cr: constant prices; cs: current prices; id: international dollars; nc: national currency; pc: per capita; usd: US Dollar.

**CHINA DATASET (2)**

| | | 1975 | 1976 | 1977 | 1978 | 1979 | 1980 | 1981 | 1982 | 1983 | 1984 | 1985 | 1986 | 1987 | 1988 | 1989 | 1990 | 1991 | 1992 | 1993 | 1994 | 1995 | 1996 | 1997 | 1998 | 1999 | 2000 |
|---|---|---|---|---|---|---|---|---|---|---|---|---|---|---|---|---|---|---|---|---|---|---|---|---|---|---|---|
| **1** | **GROSS DOMESTIC PRODUCT (GDP)** | | | | | | | | | | | | | | | | | | | | | | | | | | |
| 1.1 | pc.usd.cr | 178 | 163 | 186 | 230 | 271 | 306 | 285 | 275 | 292 | 296 | 288 | 275 | 294 | 361 | 399 | 339 | 351 | 412 | 507 | 453 | 578 | 667 | 727 | 759 | 788 | 852 |
| 1.2 | pc.id.cr | 912 | 901 | 941 | 926 | 1,026 | 1,072 | 1,131 | 1,216 | 1,295 | 1,456 | 1,477 | 1,607 | 1,711 | 1,755 | 1,673 | 1,790 | 1,977 | 2,204 | 2,455 | 2,645 | 2,818 | 2,969 | 3,110 | 3,276 | 3,415 | 3,747 |
| 1.3 | ac.nc.cs | 6.8 | -2.7 | 8.0 | 7.7 | 7.0 | 7.9 | 9.1 | 10.9 | 10.9 | 15.2 | 13.5 | 8.8 | 11.6 | 11.3 | 4.1 | 3.8 | 9.2 | 14.2 | 13.5 | 12.6 | 10.5 | 9.6 | 8.8 | 7.8 | 7.1 | 8.0 |
| 1.4.1 | Agri (*gdp.nc.cr) | 33.4 | 32.8 | 29.4 | 28.10 | 31.20 | 30.10 | 31.80 | 33.30 | 33.00 | 32.00 | 28.40 | 27.10 | 26.80 | 25.70 | 25.00 | 27.00 | 24.50 | 21.80 | 19.90 | 20.20 | 20.50 | 20.39 | 18.68 | 17.54 | 17.70 | 16.64 |
| 1.4.2 | Manuf (*gdp.nc.cr) | 41.5 | 40.9 | 42.9 | 44.30 | 43.80 | 44.20 | 42.10 | 40.80 | 40.00 | 38.90 | 38.50 | 38.90 | 38.30 | 38.70 | 38.30 | 37.00 | 37.40 | 38.60 | 40.80 | 41.40 | 42.30 | 42.80 | 43.50 | 42.10 | 42.70 | 42.96 |
| **2** | **INTERNATIONAL TRADE** | | | | | | | | | | | | | | | | | | | | | | | | | | |
| 2.1.1 | Exports (ac.usd.cr) | 8.2 | -9.7 | 8.3 | 32.4 | 36.8 | 32.9 | 21.6 | 1.4 | -0.4 | 17.6 | 4.6 | 13.1 | 27.5 | 20.5 | 10.6 | 18.2 | 15.8 | 18.1 | 8.0 | 31.9 | 23.0 | 1.5 | 21.0 | 0.5 | 6.1 | 27.8 |
| 2.1.2 | Imports (ac.usd.cr) | | -16.0 | 7.3 | 55.7 | 40.3 | 27.7 | 10.4 | -12.4 | 10.9 | 28.1 | 54.1 | 1.5 | 0.7 | 27.9 | -9.8 | -9.8 | 19.6 | 26.3 | 29.0 | 11.2 | 14.2 | 5.1 | 2.5 | -1.5 | 18.2 | 35.8 |
| 2.2.1 | Exports (*gdp.nc.cr) | 5.21 | 5.03 | 4.72 | 4.80 | 5.49 | 6.29 | 7.83 | 8.58 | 7.97 | 8.62 | 12.15 | 12.73 | 13.63 | 11.89 | 11.89 | 14.83 | 16.24 | 16.33 | 14.41 | 22.03 | 21.03 | 21.07 | 23.10 | 21.95 | 22.06 | 25.84 |
| 2.2.2 | Imports (*gdp.nc.cr) | 5.18 | 4.74 | 4.40 | 5.11 | 5.97 | 6.61 | 7.60 | 6.86 | 7.12 | 8.61 | 14.06 | 14.70 | 13.46 | 13.80 | 13.01 | 12.02 | 13.37 | 15.28 | 16.37 | 20.57 | 19.32 | 18.86 | 19.20 | 18.00 | 19.98 | 24.30 |
| 2.3 | E'T Ratio (nc.cr) | 0.99 | 1.04 | 1.05 | 0.89 | 0.87 | 0.91 | 1.00 | 1.16 | 1.04 | 0.93 | 0.85 | 0.72 | 0.91 | 0.86 | 0.89 | 1.16 | 1.13 | 1.05 | 0.88 | 1.05 | 1.13 | 1.09 | 1.28 | 1.31 | 1.18 | 1.11 |
| **3** | **SUPPLY AND DEMAND** | | | | | | | | | | | | | | | | | | | | | | | | | | |
| 3.1 | GFCF (*gdp.nc.cr) | 29.4 | 29.6 | 28.1 | 29.3 | 28.2 | 29.2 | 25.8 | 28.2 | 28.8 | 29.6 | 29.5 | 30.4 | 31.3 | 31.0 | 25.7 | 25.5 | 27.5 | 31.2 | 37.5 | 36.0 | 34.7 | 34.4 | 33.8 | 35.3 | 35.9 | 36.5 |
| 3.2 | Invest (ac.nc.cs) | 12.9 | -6.8 | 9.8 | 23.7 | 4.7 | 2.6 | -2.7 | 8.9 | 11.9 | 18.9 | 26.1 | 7.1 | 4.6 | 8.7 | -4.4 | 2.8 | 12.6 | 19.2 | 33.6 | 6.5 | 5.7 | 5.7 | 4.5 | 6.3 | 3.7 | 7.6 |
| 3.3 | Invest*.gdp-id-cr | 17.10 | 15.83 | 16.18 | 20.00 | 18.62 | 17.90 | 16.24 | 16.34 | 16.75 | 17.12 | 20.33 | 20.09 | 19.37 | 20.36 | 20.06 | 18.51 | 19.01 | 19.50 | 23.22 | 22.34 | 22.47 | 22.04 | 21.82 | 21.60 | 21.00 | 21.09 |
| 3.4 | Invest. (pc.id.cr) | 63.90 | 61.14 | 69.27 | 90.50 | 101 | 111 | 115 | 134 | 152 | 179 | 230 | 247 | 260 | 289 | 281 | 290 | 340 | 396 | 535 | 570 | 620 | 655 | 685 | 717 | 732 | 811 |
| 3.5 | Consp. (*ggdp.nc.cr) | | 61.1 | 64.2 | 65.9 | 68.1 | 68.7 | 67.7 | 65.5 | 64.4 | 62.7 | 64.1 | 63.2 | 62.3 | 62.4 | 60.8 | 61.3 | 62.4 | 58.3 | 57.5 | 58.9 | 59.2 | 60.6 | 61.1 | 12.11 | 12.66 | 13.09 |
| 3.6.1 | Consp.Gov. (*gdp) | 13.09 | 15.04 | 14.59 | 14.50 | 14.54 | 14.12 | 14.22 | 13.21 | 13.40 | 12.64 | 11.57 | 12.02 | 12.14 | 12.13 | 13.09 | 13.11 | 12.99 | 13.11 | 12.99 | 12.80 | 11.44 | 11.57 | 11.72 | 12.11 | 12.66 | 13.09 |
| 3.6.2 | Consp.Pri. (*gdp) | 47.97 | 49.12 | 51.29 | 53.56 | 54.17 | 53.63 | 51.24 | 51.19 | 50.72 | 49.83 | 51.13 | 50.41 | 49.13 | 48.00 | 46.81 | 45.28 | 46.7 | 45.28 | 44.50 | 46.08 | 47.36 | 46.81 | 47.13 | 47.93 | 48.00 |
| 3.7 | Consp. (ac.nc.cs) | 3.3 | 1.0 | 3.9 | -6.4 | 13.9 | 5.3 | 9.2 | 8.5 | 14.4 | 6.9 | 6.4 | 6.0 | 6.6 | -4.4 | 4.7 | 8.4 | 12.3 | 9.1 | 6.4 | 10.7 | 6.8 | 6.8 | 0.8 | 3.7 | 6.6 | 6.2 |
| 3.8 | Consp. (pc.id.cr) | 218 | 227 | 246 | 242 | 295 | 336 | 396 | 453 | 505 | 589 | 642 | 692 | 748 | 811 | 790 | 848 | 949 | 1,083 | 1,193 | 1,277 | 1,426 | 1,542 | 1,570 | 1,640 | 1,761 | 1,870 |
| **4** | **MONEY AND CURRENCY** | | | | | | | | | | | | | | | | | | | | | | | | | | |
| 4.1 | M1=2.(*gdp.nc.cr) | | 26.49 | 24.26 | 32.53 | 36.99 | 40.67 | 42.79 | 45.71 | 50.18 | 54.38 | 62.23 | 66.52 | 64.32 | 67.38 | 79.16 | 86.04 | 91.33 | 103 | 100 | 104 | 123 | 112 | 123 | 135 | 147 | 210 |
| 4.2 | For.Exch.R (usd) | | 2.35 | 1.56 | 2.15 | 2.26 | 4.78 | 11.14 | 11.48 | 16.71 | 20.18 | 10.51 | 17.55 | 19.37 | 19.01 | 28.59 | 21.11 | 21.20 | 20.49 | 21.20 | 21.39 | 51.62 | 73.58 | 105 | 140 | 145 | 155 |
| 4.3 | Savings (*gdp.id.cr) | 17.12 | 16.10 | 16.47 | 19.71 | 18.18 | 17.60 | 16.45 | 17.51 | 17.14 | 16.51 | 15.15 | 17.74 | 19.53 | 19.37 | 19.01 | 21.11 | 21.68 | 20.49 | 23.69 | 24.05 | 24.05 | 24.09 | 25.52 | 25.40 | 23.01 | 22.57 |
| 4.4 | CPI (1995=100) | | | | | | | | | | | 35.15 | 37.69 | 44.75 | 56.51 | 54.58 | 58.86 | 68.86 | 85.55 | 89.86 | 100.0 | 108.3 | 109.0 | 109.5 |
| 4.5 | Change in CP(an*s) | 1.10 | 0.30 | 2.50 | 0.70 | 1.90 | 6.00 | 2.40 | 1.90 | 1.50 | 2.80 | 9.30 | 6.50 | 7.30 | 18.80 | 18.00 | 3.10 | 3.40 | 6.40 | 14.70 | 24.10 | 17.10 | 8.30 | 2.80 | -0.80 | -1.40 | 0.40 |
| 4.5 | Ex Rate (usd.nc) | 1.86 | 1.94 | 1.86 | 1.68 | 1.55 | 1.50 | 1.70 | 1.89 | 1.98 | 2.32 | 2.94 | 3.45 | 3.72 | 3.72 | 3.77 | 4.78 | 5.32 | 5.51 | 5.76 | 8.62 | 8.35 | 8.31 | 8.29 | 8.28 | 8.28 | 8.28 |
| **5** | **BALANCE OF PAYMENTS (usd.cr)** | | | | | | | | | | | | | | | | | | | | | | | | | | |
| 5.1 | Overall | | | | | | 6.31 | 5.67 | 0.34 | 4.14 | 0.14 | -2.44 | -2.05 | 4.78 | 2.37 | -0.48 | 12.05 | 14.54 | -2.06 | 1.77 | 10.45 | 22.47 | 31.71 | 35.86 | 6.25 | 8.65 | 10.69 |
| 5.1.1 | Current | | | | | | 5.67 | 4.24 | | 4.14 | 2.03 | -2.44 | -7.03 | 0.30 | -3.80 | -4.32 | 12.00 | 6.40 | -11.61 | 1.62 | 7.24 | 1.62 | -0.02 | 36.96 | 31.47 | 21.12 | 20.52 |
| 5.1.2 | Capital | | | | | | | | | | | | | | | | | | | | | | | -0.02 | -0.05 | -0.03 | -0.04 |
| 5.1.3 | Financial | | | | | | | | 0.34 | -0.23 | -1.00 | 8.97 | 5.94 | 6.00 | 7.13 | 3.72 | 3.26 | 8.03 | -0.25 | 23.47 | 32.65 | 38.67 | 39.97 | 21.04 | -6.28 | 5.20 | 1.96 |
| **6** | **PUBLIC FINANCE (nc.cr)** | | | | | | | | | | | | | | | | | | | | | | | | | | |
| 6.1 | Balance (*gdp.nc.cr) | -0.18 | -1.01 | 0.96 | 0.28 | -4.18 | -2.82 | -0.52 | -0.55 | -0.73 | -0.62 | 0.24 | -0.81 | -0.52 | -0.90 | -0.94 | -3.91 | -3.46 | -2.64 | -2.03 | -2.01 | -1.55 | -1.28 | -1.24 | -1.60 | -2.48 | -3.10 |
| 6.2 | Exp Rev Ratio | 1.01 | 1.04 | 0.96 | 0.99 | 1.15 | 1.12 | 1.02 | 1.03 | 1.03 | 1.03 | 0.99 | 1.04 | 1.03 | 1.06 | 1.06 | 1.25 | 1.24 | 1.20 | 1.16 | 1.18 | 1.15 | 1.12 | 1.11 | 1.13 | 1.18 | 1.21 |
| 6.3.1 | Revenue (*gdp) | 27.21 | 26.53 | 26.99 | 30.57 | 27.03 | 24.02 | 22.41 | 21.23 | 21.05 | 20.94 | 20.82 | 20.80 | 18.39 | 15.79 | 15.76 | 15.84 | 14.57 | 13.08 | 12.56 | 13.17 | 10.67 | 10.91 | 10.91 | 12.61 | 13.94 | 14.98 |
| 6.3.2 | Exp'ture (*gdp) | 27.38 | 27.54 | 26.03 | 30.30 | 31.21 | 26.84 | 22.93 | 21.78 | 21.86 | 21.56 | 20.58 | 21.61 | 18.91 | 16.69 | 16.69 | 19.75 | 18.03 | 15.22 | 14.59 | 13.17 | 12.19 | 12.80 | 12.61 | 16.42 | 18.08 |
| 6.4.1 | Defence (* s td exp) | 17.35 | 16.68 | 17.67 | 15.11 | 17.48 | 15.98 | 15.06 | 15.29 | 13.70 | 11.69 | 10.38 | 9.10 | 9.27 | 8.75 | 8.91 | 7.93 | 8.43 | 9.02 | 8.43 | 8.94 | 8.90 | 8.70 | 8.48 | 8.40 | 7.99 | 7.45 |
| 6.4.2 | Edu.& Health(*s) | 12.61 | 14.89 | 14.16 | 13.23 | 13.75 | 16.41 | 16.41 | 21.07 | 21.86 | 21.47 | 22.14 | 22.00 | 22.36 | 23.33 | 23.67 | 20.14 | 21.80 | 23.17 | 23.32 | 24.38 | 24.38 | 25.14 | 25.78 | 26.33 | 27.00 | 25.87 |
| 6.4.3 | Social Security(*s) | 1.57 | 2.99 | 2.22 | 1.70 | 1.74 | 1.67 | 1.95 | 1.86 | 1.86 | 1.63 | 1.61 | 1.61 | 1.65 | 1.68 | 1.76 | 1.50 | 1.73 | 1.59 | 1.49 | 1.54 | 1.61 | 1.55 | 1.55 | 1.54 | 1.33 | 1.25 |
| 6.4.4 | Econ.Affairs(*s) | 58.68 | 57.83 | 58.53 | 64.71 | 60.44 | 59.00 | 56.57 | 58.56 | 61.49 | 62.61 | 61.12 | 52.56 | 50.99 | 50.51 | 45.73 | 37.35 | 36.66 | 38.52 | 36.31 | 38.87 | 39.93 | 39.08 | 38.08 | 37.55 | 37.55 | 35.32 |
| 6.5.1 | Defence (*gdp) | 4.75 | 4.59 | 4.60 | 4.58 | 5.45 | 4.29 | 3.45 | 3.33 | 2.98 | 2.52 | 2.14 | 1.97 | 1.75 | 1.46 | 1.49 | 1.57 | 1.53 | 1.42 | 1.23 | 1.18 | 1.09 | 1.06 | 1.09 | 1.19 | 1.31 | 1.35 |
| 6.5.2 | Edu.& Health(*s) | 3.45 | 4.10 | 1.69 | 4.01 | 4.29 | 4.41 | 4.35 | 4.59 | 4.76 | 4.63 | 4.56 | 4.75 | 4.23 | 3.89 | 3.95 | 3.98 | 3.64 | 3.40 | 3.21 | 3.00 | 3.06 | 3.00 | 3.32 | 3.74 | 4.43 | 4.68 |
| 6.5.3 | Social Security(*s) | 0.43 | 0.82 | 0.58 | 0.52 | 0.54 | 0.45 | 0.45 | 0.40 | 0.41 | 0.35 | 0.35 | 0.35 | 0.31 | 0.28 | 0.29 | 0.30 | 0.31 | 0.25 | 0.22 | 0.20 | 0.20 | 0.19 | 0.19 | 0.22 | 0.22 | 0.23 |
| 6.5.4 | Econ.Affairs(*s) | 16.07 | 15.93 | 15.24 | 19.61 | 18.86 | 15.84 | 12.97 | 12.76 | 13.39 | 13.50 | 12.58 | 11.36 | 9.64 | 8.43 | 7.64 | 7.38 | 6.61 | 6.05 | 5.30 | 5.12 | 4.88 | 4.76 | 4.90 | 5.33 | 6.17 | 6.39 |
| **7** | **COMPETITIVENESS** | | | | | | | | | | | | | | | | | | | | | | | | | | |
| 7.1 | M Wages Manuf (usd) | | | | | | | | | | | | | 31.72 | 30.82 | 31.53 | 34.55 | 34.54 | 38.53 | 38.55 | 39.90 | 44.29 | 36.41 | 35.93 | 41.92 | 48.42 | 41.41 |
| 7.2 | GDP per Wker (id.cs) | 1,705 | 1,671 | 1,734 | 1,706 | 1,375 | 1,946 | 2,025 | 2,153 | 2,518 | 2,886 | 2,730 | 3,122 | 2,939 | 3,266 | 3,642 | 4,060 | 4,373 | 4,908 | 4,639 | 5,141 | 5,416 | 5,646 | 6,175 |
| **8** | **POPULATION** | | | | | | | | | | | | | | | | | | | | | | | | | | |
| 8.1 | urban (ac) | 2.83 | 1.41 | 1.97 | 3.69 | 7.47 | 5.38 | 4.30 | 5.80 | 4.27 | 8.02 | 1.42 | 8.21 | 4.88 | 3.64 | 3.09 | 6.05 | -2.40 | 4.27 | 4.16 | 3.97 | 5.33 | 2.36 | 1.35 | 2.46 | 2.43 | 13.99 |

keys: volume: billions; *gdp: as *% of GDP; ac: annual change; cr: current prices; cs: constant prices; id: international dollars; nc: national currency; pc: per capita; usd: US Dollar.

# JAPAN DATASET (1)

| | | 1951 | 1952 | 1953 | 1954 | 1955 | 1956 | 1957 | 1958 | 1959 | 1960 | 1961 | 1962 | 1963 | 1964 | 1965 | 1966 | 1967 | 1968 | 1969 | 1970 | 1971 | 1972 | 1973 | 1974 |
|---|---|---|---|---|---|---|---|---|---|---|---|---|---|---|---|---|---|---|---|---|---|---|---|---|---|
| **1.** | **GROSS DOMESTIC PRODUCT (GDP)** | | | | | | | | | | | | | | | | | | | | | | | | |
| 1.1 | pc. usd, cr | 177 | 200 | 224 | 243 | 258 | 288 | 328 | 348 | 394 | 473 | 565 | 635 | 719 | 837 | 922 | 1,060 | 1,230 | 1,443 | 1,678 | 1,967 | 2,178 | 2,845 | 3,811 | 4,174 |
| 1.2 | pc. id, cr | 2,625 | 2,884 | 3,028 | 3,146 | 3,330 | 3,523 | 3,733 | 3,877 | 4,180 | 4,657 | 5,188 | 5,586 | 6,009 | 6,631 | 6,917 | 7,584 | 8,358 | 9,411 | 10,357 | 11,396 | 11,792 | 12,620 | 13,327 | 12,958 |
| 1.3 | nc, nc, cs | 12.98 | 33.96 | 25.35 | 20.23 | 16.82 | 7.19 | 6.51 | 7.34 | 9.31 | 13.35 | 12.33 | 8.60 | 8.79 | 11.19 | 5.67 | 10.25 | 11.08 | 11.91 | 11.95 | 10.28 | 4.39 | 8.41 | 8.03 | -1.23 |
| 1.4.1 | Agri (*gdp,nc.cr) | 23.90 | 18.50 | 17.50 | 20.60 | 17.30 | 16.40 | 15.70 | 14.30 | 12.60 | 13.12 | 12.33 | 11.69 | 10.99 | 9.81 | 9.82 | 9.41 | 9.24 | 8.12 | 7.15 | 6.12 | 5.30 | 5.47 | 5.93 | 5.59 |
| 1.4.2 | Manuf(*gdp,nc.cr) | 32.40 | 31.80 | 35.20 | 34.90 | 32.80 | 35.00 | 36.40 | 34.10 | 36.40 | 39.00 | 40.40 | 39.10 | 40.10 | 40.30 | 38.70 | 39.00 | 40.20 | 40.50 | 43.10 | 42.70 | 42.00 | 42.00 | 42.50 | 41.30 |
| **2.** | **INTERNATIONAL TRADE** | | | | | | | | | | | | | | | | | | | | | | | | |
| 2.1.1 | Exports (ac. usd,cr) | 63.8 | -6.1 | 0.5 | 27.8 | 23.4 | 24.4 | 14.3 | 0.5 | 20.3 | 17.3 | 4.5 | 16.1 | 10.9 | 22.4 | 26.6 | 15.7 | 6.8 | 24.2 | 23.3 | 20.8 | 24.4 | 21.2 | 27.3 | 49.8 |
| 2.1.2 | Imports (ac.usd,cr) | 106.2 | 1.8 | 19.0 | -0.4 | 3.0 | 30.7 | 32.7 | -29.2 | 18.7 | 24.8 | 29.4 | -3.0 | 19.5 | 17.8 | 2.9 | 16.6 | 22.5 | 11.4 | 15.7 | 25.7 | -4.4 | 21.1 | 60.9 | 61.4 |
| 2.2.1 | Exports(*gdp,nc.cr) | 14.18 | 11.78 | 10.32 | 10.18 | 11.01 | 11.97 | 11.76 | 11.00 | 11.22 | 10.70 | 9.26 | 9.42 | 9.02 | 9.48 | 10.50 | 10.56 | 9.64 | 10.09 | 10.54 | 10.81 | 11.71 | 10.58 | 10.04 | 13.60 |
| 2.2.2 | Imports(*gdp,nc.cr) | 12.15 | 11.43 | 12.12 | 10.97 | 10.47 | 12.44 | 13.85 | 9.60 | 10.14 | 10.25 | 10.86 | 9.26 | 9.84 | 9.65 | 9.10 | 9.00 | 9.41 | 8.98 | 8.95 | 8.95 | 8.99 | 8.27 | 10.01 | 14.34 |
| 2.3 | E1 Ratio (nc. cr) | 0.68 | 0.63 | 0.53 | 0.68 | 0.81 | 0.77 | 0.67 | 0.95 | 0.96 | 0.90 | 0.73 | 0.87 | 0.81 | 0.84 | 1.03 | 1.03 | 0.90 | 1.00 | 1.06 | 1.02 | 1.22 | 1.22 | 0.96 | 0.90 |
| **3.** | **SUPPLY AND DEMAND** | | | | | | | | | | | | | | | | | | | | | | | | |
| 3.1 | GFCF (*gdp, nc. cr) | | 20.56 | 21.75 | 21.75 | 19.42 | 22.82 | 25.76 | 24.86 | 25.59 | 28.97 | 31.89 | 32.20 | 31.57 | 31.69 | 29.76 | 30.29 | 31.94 | 33.16 | 34.45 | 35.51 | 34.25 | 34.12 | 36.39 | 34.78 |
| 3.2 | Invest,ac. nc. cs) | 53.4 | -11.8 | -2.0 | 12.7 | 17.3 | 15.7 | 21.7 | -6.2 | 18.5 | 29.4 | 27.7 | 6.7 | 12.5 | 16.7 | 3.2 | 13.5 | 21.4 | 20.9 | 34.5 | 20.2 | 0.8 | 10.1 | 11.2 | -6.1 |
| 3.3 | Invest,*gdp-id-cr | 23.34 | 19.21 | 17.80 | 18.53 | 19.64 | 21.84 | 24.98 | 21.75 | 23.60 | 26.73 | 30.28 | 28.78 | 29.84 | 30.90 | 29.85 | 30.33 | 33.00 | 34.71 | 35.98 | 38.49 | 36.51 | 36.74 | 38.33 | 37.49 |
| 3.4 | Invest. (pc. id, cr) | 117.9 | 106.0 | 103.4 | 114.2 | 132.2 | 160.5 | 201.7 | 191.5 | 229.7 | 294.8 | 374.4 | 389.7 | 437.2 | 510.4 | 528.5 | 607.8 | 747.9 | 926.7 | 1,113 | 1,378 | 1,421 | 1,581 | 1,810 | 1,850 |
| 3.5 | Consp(*gdp. nc. cr) | | | | | 75.84 | 73.61 | 71.21 | 71.93 | 70.26 | 66.69 | 64.72 | 65.63 | 67.07 | 65.60 | 66.72 | 66.01 | 64.42 | 62.12 | 60.84 | 59.70 | 61.52 | 62.17 | 61.91 | 63.43 |
| 3.6.1 | Consp.Gov.(*gdp) | | | 10.76 | 11.12 | 11.03 | 10.10 | 9.28 | 8.69 | 8.86 | 8.47 | 8.01 | 7.68 | 7.96 | 8.24 | 7.96 | 8.18 | 8.00 | 7.43 | 7.33 | 7.44 | 7.96 | 8.16 | 8.30 | 9.12 |
| 3.6.2 | Consp.Pri.(*gdp) | | | | | 65.74 | 64.33 | 62.52 | 63.07 | 61.79 | 58.69 | 58.01 | 57.67 | 57.05 | 58.82 | 58.54 | 58.01 | 56.80 | 54.69 | 53.51 | 52.26 | 53.57 | 54.01 | 53.61 | 54.31 |
| 3.7 | Consp (ac. nc. cs) | 11.4 | 15.6 | 12.7 | 4.8 | 8.2 | 7.6 | 6.5 | 7.1 | 10.3 | 9.3 | 8.5 | 8.0 | 11.3 | 6.1 | 10.4 | 9.8 | 9.6 | 10.9 | 7.4 | 5.5 | 8.9 | 5.5 | 8.8 | -0.1 |
| 3.8 | Consp (pc. id, cr) | 283.89 | 329.72 | 371.68 | 386.94 | 415.36 | 452.32 | 491.97 | 538.06 | 583.85 | 644.65 | 709.05 | 771 | 830 | 925 | 983 | 1,107 | 1,237 | 1,403 | 1,590 | 1,766 | 1,920 | 2,136 | 2,378 | 2,543 |
| **4.** | **MONEY AND CURRENCY** | | | | | | | | | | | | | | | | | | | | | | | | |
| 4.1 | M1+2 (*gdp. nc. cr) | | | 56.44 | 58.36 | 52.33 | 55.74 | 57.19 | 64.13 | 65.50 | 65.09 | 64.80 | 68.63 | 72.85 | 74.34 | 77.28 | 77.36 | 76.23 | 73.92 | 74.56 | 73.95 | 83.52 | 90.96 | 87.28 | 81.56 |
| 4.2 | For.Exch.Reser.(usd) | 1.0 | 1.1 | 0.9 | 0.9 | 1.0 | 1.2 | 1.1 | 0.9 | 1.1 | 1.6 | 1.6 | 1.5 | 1.5 | 1.5 | 1.6 | 1.5 | 2.3 | 2.3 | 4.56 | 3.2 | 13.8 | 16.5 | 10.2 | 11.3 |
| 4.3 | Savings(*gdp. id, cr) | 25.26 | 19.54 | 16.08 | 17.78 | 20.17 | 23.06 | 24.69 | 28.67 | 28.94 | 30.71 | 29.04 | 22.37 | 23.23 | 24.76 | 31.22 | 31.87 | 33.20 | 35.79 | 37.53 | 39.73 | 39.17 | 39.00 | 40.23 | 36.73 |
| 4.4 | CPI (1995=100) | 14.53 | 15.26 | 16.26 | 17.32 | 17.15 | 17.71 | 17.63 | 17.82 | 18.46 | 19.46 | 20.78 | 22.37 | 23.23 | 24.76 | 25.67 | 26.02 | 27.05 | 28.50 | 30.00 | 32.30 | 34.37 | 36.03 | 40.23 | 49.54 |
| 5.3 | Change in CP (an.%s) | | 6.57 | 4.98 | 6.51 | -0.97 | 0.000 | 3.27 | -0.45 | 1.05 | 3.59 | 5.41 | 6.77 | 7.66 | 3.84 | 6.59 | 5.08 | 5.37 | 3.98 | 5.24 | 7.67 | 6.42 | 4.82 | 11.65 | 23.16 |
| 4.5 | Ex Rate (1usd: nc) | 361.20 | 361.20 | 360.00 | 360.00 | 360.00 | 360.00 | 360.00 | 360.10 | 359.90 | 360.00 | 360.00 | 360.00 | 360.00 | 360.00 | 360.00 | 360.00 | 360.00 | 360.00 | 360.00 | 360.00 | 349.33 | 303.17 | 271.70 | 292.08 |
| **5.** | **BALANCE OF PAYMENTS (usd, cr)** | | | | | | | | | | | | | | | | | | | | | | | | |
| 5.1 | Overall | | | | | | | | | | | | | | | | | | | | | | | | |
| 5.1.1 | Current | | | | | | | | | | | | | | | | | | | | | | | | |
| 5.1.2 | Capital | | | | | | | | | | | | | | | | | | | | | | | | |
| 5.1.3 | Financial | | | | | | | | | | | | | | | | | | | | | | | | |
| **6.** | **PUBLIC FINANCE (nc, cr)** | | | | | | | | | | | | | | | | | | | | | | | | |
| 6.1 | Balance(*gdp. nc. cr) | 7.63 | 3.30 | 2.88 | 1.85 | 1.29 | 1.73 | 1.95 | 1.06 | 0.77 | 1.36 | 2.34 | 1.78 | 0.74 | 0.46 | 0.15 | 0.24 | 0.42 | 0.23 | 0.31 | 0.37 | 0.51 | 0.93 | 1.76 | 0.95 |
| 6.2 | Exp.Rev. Ratio | 0.54 | 0.81 | 0.83 | 0.88 | 0.90 | 0.87 | 0.85 | 0.92 | 0.94 | 0.89 | 0.82 | 0.87 | 0.94 | 0.96 | 0.99 | 0.98 | 0.98 | 0.98 | 0.97 | 0.97 | 0.96 | 0.93 | 0.88 | 0.94 |
| 6.3.1 | Revenue (*gdp) | 16.45 | 17.35 | 17.37 | 15.20 | 13.45 | 13.08 | 12.88 | 12.59 | 12.11 | 12.25 | 13.01 | 13.43 | 12.87 | 11.67 | 11.48 | 11.93 | 11.85 | 11.44 | 11.42 | 11.53 | 12.35 | 13.85 | 14.90 | 15.18 |
| 6.3.2 | Exp/ture (*gdp) | 8.81 | 14.06 | 14.50 | 13.35 | 12.16 | 11.35 | 10.93 | 11.54 | 11.33 | 10.89 | 10.67 | 11.65 | 12.12 | 11.20 | 11.33 | 11.68 | 11.43 | 11.21 | 11.12 | 11.16 | 11.85 | 12.91 | 13.14 | 14.23 |
| 6.4.1 | Defence (*% tol exp) | 9.16 | 11.91 | 15.47 | 14.86 | 13.36 | 12.58 | 12.89 | 11.38 | 10.51 | 9.38 | 8.86 | 8.50 | 8.05 | 8.50 | 8.24 | 7.78 | 7.53 | 7.32 | 7.22 | 7.25 | 7.25 | 6.82 | 6.50 | 6.46 |
| 6.4.2 | Edu. & Health(*a.) | 13.42 | 10.69 | 12.08 | 13.64 | 14.54 | 14.61 | 15.15 | 14.34 | 13.79 | 14.00 | 14.68 | 14.44 | 14.92 | 15.25 | 15.67 | 14.90 | 14.41 | 13.75 | 13.41 | 13.36 | 13.35 | 12.83 | 12.45 | 12.86 |
| 6.4.3 | Social Security(*a.) | 39.62 | 21.73 | 20.39 | 8.18 | 6.65 | 8.18 | 7.12 | 12.22 | 13.12 | 13.26 | 14.66 | 14.45 | 14.91 | 15.62 | 15.67 | 16.43 | 16.54 | 18.26 | 18.76 | 18.27 | 19.66 | 20.81 | 23.86 | 24.16 |
| 6.4.4 | Econ. Affairs(*a.) | | 1.67 | 2.24 | 1.98 | 1.62 | 1.43 | 1.41 | 8.00 | 5.12 | 9.43 | 8.53 | 7.39 | 7.14 | 8.05 | 8.27 | 11.42 | 11.09 | 10.82 | 12.14 | 12.42 | 11.69 | 11.24 | 13.46 | 12.51 |
| 6.5.1 | Defence (*gdp) | 0.81 | 0.37 | 1.81 | 1.82 | 1.77 | 1.66 | 1.31 | 1.65 | 1.49 | 1.02 | 0.95 | 0.99 | 0.95 | 0.95 | 0.93 | 0.91 | 0.90 | 0.82 | 0.81 | 0.81 | 0.80 | 0.88 | 0.85 | 0.92 |
| 6.5.2 | Edu.& Health(*a.) | 1.18 | 1.50 | 1.75 | 1.76 | 1.67 | 1.66 | 1.44 | 1.46 | 1.56 | 1.52 | 1.57 | 1.68 | 1.81 | 1.71 | 1.78 | 1.74 | 1.65 | 1.54 | 1.49 | 1.49 | 1.58 | 1.66 | 1.64 | 1.83 |
| 6.5.3 | Social Security(*a.) | 3.49 | 3.05 | 2.96 | 1.09 | 0.81 | 0.93 | 1.36 | 1.41 | 1.49 | 1.03 | 1.56 | 1.68 | 1.81 | 1.95 | 1.92 | 1.74 | 1.95 | 1.89 | 2.09 | 2.04 | 2.33 | 2.69 | 3.13 | 3.44 |
| 6.5.4 | Econ. Affairs(*a.) | | | | | | | | | | | | | | 0.90 | 0.94 | 1.33 | 1.27 | 1.21 | 1.35 | 1.39 | 1.39 | 1.45 | 1.77 | 1.78 |
| **7.** | **COMPETITIVENESS** | | | | | | | | | | | | | | | | | | | | | | | | |
| 7.1 | M Wages Manuf(usd) | 32 | 37 | 43 | 45 | 46 | 51 | 53 | 53 | 58 | 63 | 69 | 76 | 84 | 92 | 100 | 113 | 127 | 146 | 172 | 198 | 232 | 309 | 428 | 501 |
| 7.2 | GDP per Wker(id,cs) | 4,492 | 4,828 | 5,044 | 5,228 | 5,337 | 5,861 | 6,225 | 6,396 | 6,880 | 7,689 | 8,577 | 9,164 | 9,800 | 10,782 | 11,167 | 12,184 | 13,402 | 15,047 | 16,495 | 18,098 | 18,736 | 20,119 | 21,314 | 20,735 |
| **8.** | **POPULATION** | | | | | | | | | | | | | | | | | | | | | | | | |
| 8.1 | urban(an:ac) | 11.24 | 10.10 | 9.17 | 8.40 | 7.55 | 3.51 | 3.44 | 2.26 | 3.32 | 3.26 | 2.52 | 2.49 | 2.46 | 2.43 | 2.40 | 2.28 | 2.25 | 2.23 | 2.20 | 2.18 | 3.21 | 2.20 | 3.13 | 2.15 |

keys: volume: billions; *agdp: as % of GDP; ac: annual change; cr: current prices; cs: constant prices; id: international dollars; nc: national currency; pc: per capita; usd: US Dollar.

# JAPAN DATASET (2)

| | 1975 | 1976 | 1977 | 1978 | 1979 | 1980 | 1981 | 1982 | 1983 | 1984 | 1985 | 1986 | 1987 | 1988 | 1989 | 1990 | 1991 | 1992 | 1993 | 1994 | 1995 | 1996 | 1997 | 1998 | 1999 | 2000 |
|---|---|---|---|---|---|---|---|---|---|---|---|---|---|---|---|---|---|---|---|---|---|---|---|---|---|---|
| **1. GROSS DOMESTIC PRODUCT (GDP)** | | | | | | | | | | | | | | | | | | | | | | | | | | |
| 1.1 pc. usd. cr | 4,482 | 4,983 | 6,073 | 8,456 | 8,727 | 9,189 | 10,071 | 9,308 | 10,111 | 10,713 | 11,335 | 16,704 | 20,179 | 24,327 | 24,154 | 24,718 | 28,161 | 30,640 | 35,105 | 38,555 | 42,337 | 37,449 | 34,311 | 31,224 | 35,333 | 37,578 |
| 1.2 pc. id. cr | 13,148 | 13,523 | 13,980 | 14,588 | 15,256 | 15,631 | 15,968 | 16,339 | 16,575 | 17,115 | 17,779 | 18,194 | 18,930 | 20,118 | 21,113 | 22,094 | 22,620 | 22,913 | 24,047 | 23,036 | 24,237 | 23,271 | 24,047 | 24,428 | 24,055 | 24,672 |
| 1.3 ac. nc. cs | 3.09 | 3.97 | 4.39 | 5.27 | 5.48 | 9.58 | 2.87 | 3.18 | 2.57 | 3.75 | 4.62 | 2.96 | 4.33 | 6.52 | 5.32 | 5.23 | 3.29 | 0.89 | 0.36 | 1.06 | 1.83 | 3.47 | 1.86 | -1.15 | 0.17 | 2.76 |
| 1.4.1 Agri (*.gdp.nc.cr) | 5.49 | 5.32 | 5.06 | 4.62 | 4.34 | 3.68 | 3.52 | 3.41 | 3.38 | 3.31 | 3.19 | 3.00 | 2.83 | 2.67 | 2.61 | 2.54 | 2.37 | 2.25 | 2.06 | 2.14 | 1.93 | 1.80 | 1.93 | 1.70 | 1.80 | 1.38 |
| 1.4.2 Manuf (*.gdp.nc.cr) | 38.80 | 38.70 | 37.70 | 37.80 | 37.80 | 37.70 | 37.70 | 36.00 | 36.00 | 36.40 | 36.20 | 35.90 | 35.90 | 36.60 | 33.80 | 33.60 | 33.90 | 34.10 | 33.70 | 33.40 | 32.90 | 32.70 | 32.50 | 31.50 | 29.47 | 29.34 |
| **2. INTERNATIONAL TRADE** | | | | | | | | | | | | | | | | | | | | | | | | | | |
| 2.1.1 Exports (ac. usd.cr) | 0.6 | 20.6 | 20.5 | 21.1 | 4.2 | 27.5 | 16.1 | -8.7 | 6.2 | 15.5 | 4.4 | 19.0 | 9.7 | 14.5 | 3.4 | 5.0 | 9.5 | 8.0 | 6.6 | 9.6 | 11.6 | -7.3 | 2.4 | -7.8 | 8.1 | 14.3 |
| 2.1.2 Imports (ac. usd.cr) | -6.6 | 12.2 | 9.9 | 12.0 | 37.4 | 28.6 | 1.1 | -8.0 | -3.8 | 7.7 | -4.2 | -2.2 | 18.4 | 24.1 | 11.9 | 12.2 | 0.7 | -1.6 | 3.6 | 13.9 | 2.0 | 4.0 | -3.0 | -17.2 | 11.0 | 21.9 |
| 2.2.1 Exports (*.gdp.nc.cr) | 12.80 | 13.56 | 13.10 | 11.12 | 11.57 | 13.49 | 14.49 | 14.27 | 13.66 | 14.70 | 14.11 | 11.13 | 10.16 | 11.13 | 10.31 | 10.38 | 9.93 | 9.81 | 9.07 | 8.98 | 8.99 | 9.68 | 10.72 | 10.66 | 10.04 | 0.45 |
| 2.2.2 Imports (*.gdp.nc.cr) | 12.76 | 12.76 | 11.46 | 9.38 | 12.47 | 14.40 | 13.75 | 13.60 | 11.96 | 12.07 | 10.76 | 7.25 | 7.19 | 7.64 | 8.79 | 9.43 | 8.32 | 7.65 | 6.86 | 6.99 | 7.67 | 9.18 | 9.62 | 8.83 | 8.49 | 0.42 |
| 2.3 E/I Ratio (nc. cr) | 0.96 | 1.04 | 1.14 | 1.23 | 0.93 | 0.92 | 1.06 | 1.08 | 1.16 | 1.25 | 1.36 | 1.68 | 1.33 | 1.41 | 1.31 | 1.25 | 1.33 | 1.46 | 1.50 | 1.44 | 1.32 | 1.18 | 1.24 | 1.38 | 1.35 | 1.26 |
| **3. SUPPLY AND DEMAND** | | | | | | | | | | | | | | | | | | | | | | | | | | |
| 3.1 GFCF (*.gdp. nc. cr) | 32.45 | 31.18 | 30.16 | 30.40 | 31.67 | 31.67 | 30.72 | 29.56 | 28.06 | 27.83 | 27.59 | 27.46 | 28.60 | 29.96 | 30.93 | 32.19 | 31.71 | 30.44 | 29.20 | 28.18 | 27.70 | 28.38 | 28.02 | 26.85 | 26.34 | 25.87 |
| 3.2 Invest.(ac. nc. cs) | -5.6 | -4.0 | 3.4 | 7.1 | 6.0 | 0.4 | 2.3 | -0.2 | -2.2 | 5.1 | 6.3 | 4.4 | 8.6 | 13.6 | 8.7 | 8.1 | 2.6 | -3.7 | -3.6 | -2.1 | -3.6 | 7.6 | -6.0 | -6.0 | -2.1 | 3.1 |
| 3.3 Invest(*.gdp-id-cr) | 34.92 | 34.67 | 33.93 | 34.42 | 35.24 | 34.62 | 34.01 | 33.32 | 31.49 | 31.17 | 31.58 | 31.40 | 32.39 | 34.57 | 35.63 | 36.20 | 36.19 | 33.68 | 32.48 | 31.36 | 31.58 | 32.71 | 32.31 | 30.15 | 28.94 | 29.75 |
| 3.4 Invest. (Ps. id. cr) | 1,933 | 2,071 | 2,219 | 2,522 | 2,859 | 3,082 | 3,396 | 3,647 | 3,636 | 3,826 | 4,179 | 4,411 | 4,874 | 5,726 | 6,400 | 7,035 | 7,585 | 7,200 | 7,088 | 6,994 | 7,253 | 7,866 | 7,993 | 7,435 | 7,228 | 7,712 |
| 3.5 Comp(*.gdp. nc. cr) | 67.18 | 67.56 | 67.33 | 67.35 | 68.41 | 68.56 | 68.55 | 68.35 | 69.85 | 68.98 | 68.10 | 69.05 | 67.30 | 67.06 | 66.29 | 65.23 | 66.35 | 67.20 | 67.06 | 69.38 | 70.25 | 70.20 | 70.03 | 71.19 | 2.94 | 2.61 |
| 3.6.1 Comp.Gov.(*.gdp) | 10.04 | 9.86 | 9.83 | 9.66 | 9.70 | 13.33 | 13.55 | 13.77 | 14.02 | 13.92 | 13.70 | 13.87 | 13.90 | 13.55 | 13.41 | 13.31 | 13.29 | 13.69 | 14.19 | 14.48 | 14.98 | 15.11 | 15.14 | 15.63 | 16.26 | 16.69 |
| 3.6.2 Comp.Pri.(*.gdp) | 57.15 | 57.50 | 57.68 | 57.69 | 56.71 | 55.19 | 54.31 | 54.32 | 55.83 | 55.06 | 54.40 | 54.03 | 54.22 | 53.46 | 53.26 | 52.98 | 52.56 | 53.37 | 54.37 | 54.40 | 55.29 | 55.09 | 54.89 | 55.56 | 56.67 | 55.92 |
| 3.7 Comp (ac. nc. cs) | -4.4 | 2.9 | 4.1 | 5.2 | 6.3 | 15.0 | 4.7 | 4.3 | 3.7 | 5.06 | 5.40 | 4.03 | 4.0 | 4.9 | 4.9 | 4.6 | 3.8 | 2.6 | 2.5 | 1.7 | 2.3 | 1.7 | 0.8 | 0.1 | 1.5 | 1.1 |
| 3.8 Comp (pc. id. cr) | 2,889 | 3,087 | 3,359 | 3,732 | 4,274 | 5,345 | 5,881 | 6,527 | 6,971 | 7,340 | 7,791 | 8,230 | 8,831 | 9,524 | 10,261 | 11,131 | 11,945 | 12,555 | 13,035 | 13,571 | 14,005 | 14,637 | 15,007 | 15,249 | 15,705 | 15,975 |
| **4. MONEY AND CURRENCY** | | | | | | | | | | | | | | | | | | | | | | | | | | |
| 4.1 M1+2(*.gdp. nc. cr) | 84.50 | 85.40 | 85.14 | 87.44 | 87.44 | 85.08 | 87.74 | 89.79 | 92.02 | 92.25 | 93.93 | 98.07 | 104.62 | 107.12 | 111.58 | 112.01 | 107.99 | 105.09 | 106.52 | 108.52 | 110.00 | 109.58 | 110.56 | 116.60 | 122.23 | 122.55 |
| 4.2 For.Exch.Reser.(usd) | 10.6 | 13.9 | 20.1 | 28.9 | 16.4 | 21.6 | 24.7 | 19.2 | 20.4 | 22.3 | 23.3 | 37.7 | 75.7 | 90.5 | 78.0 | 69.5 | 61.8 | 61.9 | 88.7 | 115.1 | 172.4 | 207.3 | 207.9 | 203.2 | 277.7 | 347.2 |
| 4.3 Savings(*.gdp. id. cr) | 34.93 | 35.44 | 35.52 | 36.11 | 34.32 | 33.71 | 34.74 | 34.00 | 33.19 | 33.80 | 34.97 | 35.29 | 35.36 | 36.73 | 37.15 | 37.15 | 37.80 | 35.84 | 34.69 | 33.37 | 32.98 | 33.21 | 33.41 | 31.98 | 30.48 | 31.17 |
| 4.4 CPI (1995=100) | 55.38 | 60.55 | 65.49 | 68.25 | 70.80 | 76.31 | 80.05 | 82.24 | 83.79 | 85.70 | 87.17 | 87.97 | 88.67 | 88.67 | 90.17 | 93.47 | 96.50 | 98.16 | 99.43 | 100.13 | 100.00 | 100.14 | 101.87 | 102.54 | 102.19 | 101.51 |
| 4.5 Change in CP (an *.e) | 11.78 | 9.35 | 8.16 | 4.21 | 3.73 | 7.78 | 4.91 | 2.74 | 1.88 | 2.27 | 2.02 | 0.62 | 0.13 | 0.67 | 2.28 | 3.06 | 3.24 | 1.73 | 1.28 | 0.71 | -0.13 | 0.14 | 1.73 | 0.66 | -0.34 | -0.67 |
| 4.5 Ex.Rate (1usd. nc) | 296.79 | 296.55 | 268.51 | 210.44 | 219.14 | 226.74 | 220.54 | 249.08 | 237.51 | 237.52 | 238.54 | 168.52 | 144.64 | 128.15 | 137.96 | 144.79 | 134.71 | 126.65 | 111.20 | 102.21 | 94.06 | 108.78 | 120.99 | 130.91 | 113.91 | 107.77 |
| **5. BALANCE OF PAYMENTS (usd. cr)** | | | | | | | | | | | | | | | | | | | | | | | | | | |
| 5.1 Overall | 6.49 | 0.96 | -13.14 | 5.03 | 3.64 | -4.71 | 1.55 | 1.12 | -0.50 | 15.13 | 13.08 | 17.56 | -13.05 | -9.09 | -8.39 | 0.62 | 27.47 | 25.27 | 58.61 | 35.14 | 6.57 | -6.16 | | 48.96 | | |
| 5.1.1 Current | 10.91 | 16.35 | -8.74 | 4.77 | -7.5 | 2.80 | 20.80 | 35.00 | 31.13 | 85.88 | 84.35 | 79.25 | 63.22 | 41.08 | 68.20 | 112.57 | 131.64 | 130.26 | 111.64 | 65.79 | 96.81 | 118.57 | 114.60 | 119.66 | | |
| 5.1.2 Capital | | | | | | | | | | | | | | | | | | | | | | | | | | |
| 5.1.3 Financial | -4.96 | -6.70 | -6.82 | 18.88 | 0.26 | -1.56 | -16.20 | -21.32 | -36.57 | -55.20 | -0.49 | -0.77 | -1.01 | -1.39 | -1.06 | -1.20 | -1.30 | -1.46 | -1.85 | -2.23 | -3.29 | -4.05 | -14.45 | -16.47 | -9.26 | |
| **6. PUBLIC FINANCE (nc. cr)** | | | | | | | | | | | | | | | | | | | | | | | | | | |
| 6.1 Balance(*.gdp. nc. cr) | 0.41 | 0.37 | 0.20 | 0.40 | 0.45 | 0.26 | 0.20 | 0.28 | 0.36 | 0.23 | 0.30 | 0.34 | 1.03 | 0.82 | 0.34 | 0.55 | 0.52 | 0.20 | 0.54 | 0.55 | 0.93 | 0.58 | 0.32 | 1.04 | 1.05 | 0.79 |
| 6.2 Exp Rev Ratio | 0.97 | 0.98 | 0.99 | 0.98 | 0.98 | 0.99 | 0.99 | 0.98 | 0.98 | 0.99 | 0.98 | 0.95 | 0.94 | 0.95 | 0.98 | 0.97 | 0.97 | 0.99 | 0.96 | 0.96 | 0.94 | 0.96 | 0.98 | 1.04 | 0.94 | 0.96 |
| 6.3.1 Revenue (*.gdp) | 14.48 | 15.05 | 15.86 | 17.08 | 17.96 | 18.10 | 18.16 | 17.48 | 18.03 | 17.08 | 16.55 | 16.55 | 7.53 | 16.91 | 16.40 | 16.52 | 15.53 | 14.82 | 13.98 | 15.51 | 16.15 | 15.9? | 15.00 | 17.38 | 18.52 | 18.17 |
| 6.3.2 Expenditure(*.gdp) | 14.06 | 14.69 | 15.65 | 16.68 | 17.51 | 17.84 | 17.96 | 17.20 | 17.50 | 16.85 | 16.23 | 15.69 | 16.21 | 16.06 | 16.06 | 15.67 | 15.01 | 14.62 | 15.41 | 14.96 | 15.23 | 15.44 | 15.00 | 16.34 | 17.47 | 17.39 |
| 6.4.1 Defence (*.tol exp) | 6.70 | 6.26 | 5.90 | 5.52 | 5.36 | 5.23 | 5.25 | 5.49 | 5.50 | 5.78 | 6.04 | 6.22 | 6.02 | 6.01 | 5.99 | 6.17 | 6.33 | 6.54 | 6.16 | 6.33 | 6.14 | 6.34 | 6.35 | 5.53 | 5.55 | 5.55 |
| 6.4.2 Edu. & Health(*.e) | 14.28 | 13.78 | 13.28 | 13.02 | 12.60 | 12.08 | 11.71 | 11.62 | 10.85 | 9.78 | 10.53 | 10.37 | 9.92 | 9.23 | 8.93 | 8.90 | 9.06 | 9.63 | 10.01 | 9.44 | 10.09 | 9.30 | 9.22 | 9.50 | 8.65 | 7.53 |
| 6.4.3 Econ. Security(*.e) | 26.08 | 26.04 | 26.06 | 24.67 | 23.81 | 23.02 | 22.12 | 21.97 | 20.75 | 21.33 | 20.98 | 21.20 | 19.91 | 21.13 | 21.51 | 18.37 | 19.11 | 20.40 | 20.54 | 21.47 | 22.29 | 21.91 | 22.38 | 21.29 | 21.36 | 22.03 |
| 6.4.4 Social Security(*.e) | 11.3? | 10.80 | 9.7? | 9.71 | 9.34 | 9.19 | 9.19 | 8.62 | 8.36 | 7.6? | 7.58 | 6.71 | 5.88 | 6.08 | 6.79 | 5.90 | 5.84 | 4.51 | 4.75 | 4.47 | 6.65 | 4.20 | 4.13 | 5.82 | 4.51 | 4.60 |
| 6.5.1 Defence (*.gdp) | 0.94 | 0.92 | 0.92 | 0.92 | 0.94 | 0.93 | 0.94 | 0.95 | 0.97 | 0.97 | 0.98 | 0.98 | 0.98 | 0.97 | 0.96 | 0.97 | 0.95 | 0.96 | 0.95 | 0.95 | 0.95 | 0.95 | 0.95 | 0.96 | 0.97 | 0.96 |
| 6.5.2 Edu. & Health(*.e) | 2.01 | 2.02 | 2.08 | 2.17 | 2.21 | 2.16 | 2.10 | 2.00 | 1.92 | 1.84 | 1.71 | 1.63 | 1.61 | 1.48 | 1.43 | 1.40 | 1.36 | 1.41 | 1.55 | 1.41 | 1.54 | 1.41 | 1.38 | 1.57 | 1.51 | 1.31 |
| 6.5.3 Social Security(*.e) | 3.67 | 3.82 | 4.08 | 4.12 | 4.17 | 4.11 | 3.97 | 3.78 | 3.67 | 3.59 | 3.40 | 3.33 | 3.23 | 3.40 | 3.45 | 2.88 | 2.87 | 2.98 | 3.17 | 3.21 | 3.39 | 3.3? | 3.36 | 3.48 | 3.73 | 3.83 |
| 6.5.4 Econ. Affairs(*.e) | 1.66 | 1.59 | 1.53 | 1.62 | 1.64 | 1.64 | 1.55 | 1.47 | 1.36 | 1.23 | 1.09 | 0.99 | 0.99 | 1.16 | 1.16 | 0.93 | 0.88 | 0.66 | 0.73 | 0.67 | 1.01 | 0.65 | 0.62 | 0.95 | 0.79 | 0.80 |
| **7. COMPETITIVENESS** | | | | | | | | | | | | | | | | | | | | | | | | | | |
| 7.1 M.Wages Manuf(usd) | 552 | 619 | 748 | 1,020 | 1,039 | 1,079 | 1,178 | 1,082 | 1,175 | 1,256 | 1,266 | 1,812 | 2,165 | 2,487 | 2,440 | 2,431 | 2,732 | 2,942 | 3,340 | 3,641 | 3,987 | 3,508 | 3,193 | 2,975 | 3,437 | 3,702 |
| 7.2 GDP per Wker(d.cs) | 21,017 | 21,681 | 22,462 | 23,510 | 24,645 | 25,552 | 25,743 | 26,254 | 26,532 | 27,353 | 28,368 | 28,960 | 30,07? | 31,920 | 33,436 | 35,079 | 36,068 | 36,184 | 36,161 | 36,362 | 36,733 | 37,962 | 38,492 | 37,909 | 37,983 | 38,737 |
| **8. POPULATION** | | | | | | | | | | | | | | | | | | | | | | | | | | |
| 8.1 urban(ac) | 3.04 | 1.03 | 1.02 | 1.01 | 1.00 | 0.99 | 0.99 | 0.13 | 0.98 | 0.97 | 0.96 | 0.18 | 0.18 | 1.00 | 0.18 | 0.18 | 0.18 | 0.18 | 0.99 | 0.18 | 0.18 | 0.98 | 0.18 | 0.18 | 0.97 | 0.05 |

keys: volume: billions; *:gdp: as % of GDP; ac: annual change; cr: current prices; cs: constant prices; id: international dollars; nc: national currency; pc: per capita; usd: US Dollar.

# KOREA DATASET (I)

| | 1951 | 1952 | 1953 | 1954 | 1955 | 1956 | 1957 | 1958 | 1959 | 1960 | 1961 | 1962 | 1963 | 1964 | 1965 | 1966 | 1967 | 1968 | 1969 | 1970 | 1971 | 1972 | 1973 | 1974 |
|---|---|---|---|---|---|---|---|---|---|---|---|---|---|---|---|---|---|---|---|---|---|---|---|---|
| **1. GROSS DOMESTIC PRODUCT (GDP)** | | | | | | | | | | | | | | | | | | | | | | 0.11 | | |
| 1.1 pc. usd. cr | | | 127 | 175 | 109 | 138 | 172 | 179 | 182 | 155 | 94 | 105 | 143 | 120 | 108 | 131 | 157 | 192 | 233 | 275 | 298 | 318 | 397 | 543 |
| 1.2 pc. id. cr | | | 1,393 | 1,418 | 1,530 | 1,533 | 1,617 | 1,611 | 1,591 | 1,571 | 1,611 | 1,607 | 1,722 | 1,820 | 1,869 | 2,061 | 2,127 | 2,329 | 2,615 | 2,777 | 2,957 | 3,034 | 3,361 | 3,559 |
| 1.3 ac. nc. cs | | | | 5.86 | 5.44 | 0.47 | 7.71 | 5.24 | 3.87 | 1.98 | 5.05 | 3.03 | 8.82 | 8.64 | 6.02 | 12.04 | 7.27 | 12.76 | 15.16 | 6.96 | 8.49 | 4.82 | 12.80 | 8.07 |
| 1.4.1 Agri (*egdp.nc.cr) | | | 47.30 | 39.80 | 44.50 | 46.90 | 45.20 | 40.70 | 33.80 | 36.80 | 39.10 | 37.00 | 43.40 | 46.80 | 38.00 | 34.80 | 30.60 | 28.70 | 27.90 | 26.80 | 27.31 | 26.88 | 25.10 | 24.90 |
| 1.4.2 Manuf(*egdp.nc.cr) | | | 9.00 | 11.80 | 11.60 | 11.60 | 11.20 | 12.80 | 14.10 | 13.80 | 13.60 | 14.40 | 14.70 | 15.60 | 18.00 | 18.60 | 19.10 | 20.10 | 20.30 | 24.09 | 24.03 | 25.13 | 27.67 | 28.15 |
| **2. INTERNATIONAL TRADE** | | | | | | | | | | | | | | | | | | | | | | | | |
| 2.1.1 Exports (ac. usd.cr) | | | 42.9 | -40.0 | -25.0 | 38.9 | 9.26 | 42.9 | -39.1 | 60.0 | 28.1 | 36.6 | 55.4 | 35.6 | 46.6 | 45.1 | 27.9 | 42.4 | 36.5 | 34.0 | 27.6 | 52.3 | 98.2 | 38.5 |
| 2.1.2 Imports (ac.usd.cr) | | | 61.2 | -29.6 | 40.3 | 13.2 | 14.5 | -14.5 | -19.6 | 13.2 | -8.1 | 33.5 | 32.7 | -27.9 | 14.6 | 54.6 | 39.1 | 46.9 | 24.7 | 8.8 | 20.7 | 5.3 | 68.1 | 61.6 |
| 2.2.1 Exports(*egdp.nc.cr) | | | 1.92 | 1.07 | 1.68 | 1.40 | 1.53 | 2.07 | 2.73 | 3.37 | 5.42 | 5.11 | 4.76 | 5.92 | 8.60 | 10.43 | 11.48 | 12.84 | 13.51 | 13.64 | 14.99 | 19.48 | 28.97 | 27.23 |
| 2.2.2 Imports(*egdp.nc.cr) | | | 9.92 | 7.47 | 10.08 | 13.26 | 12.11 | 10.87 | 10.37 | 12.75 | 15.03 | 16.7 | 15.91 | 13.56 | 16.01 | 20.30 | 22.19 | 25.57 | 25.44 | 23.69 | 25.46 | 24.15 | 32.02 | 38.46 |
| 2.3 E1 Ratio (nc. cr) | | 0.13 | 0.12 | 0.10 | 0.05 | 0.06 | 0.05 | 0.04 | 0.07 | 0.09 | 0.13 | 0.13 | 0.16 | 0.29 | 0.37 | 0.35 | 0.32 | 0.31 | 0.34 | 0.42 | 0.45 | 0.64 | 0.76 | 0.65 |
| **3. SUPPLY AND DEMAND** | | | | | | | | | | | | | | | | | | | | | | | | |
| 3.1 GFCF (*egdp. nc. cr) | | | 7.38 | 9.30 | 10.34 | 10.46 | 10.73 | 10.23 | 11.16 | 10.90 | 11.77 | 13.79 | 13.61 | 11.43 | 14.91 | 20.49 | 21.81 | 25.38 | 26.09 | 25.26 | 22.60 | 20.82 | 24.10 | 27.17 |
| 3.2 Invest.(ac. nc. cs) | | | | -17.0 | 6.1 | -6.8 | 54.2 | -12.0 | -25.5 | 6.1 | 26.6 | -2.1 | 108.4 | -24.8 | 3.2 | 75.1 | 13.8 | 35.6 | 24.7 | -4.8 | -1.8 | 11.9 | -7.4 | 35.0 | 20.1 |
| 3.3 Invest*.egdp-id-cr | | | 15.78 | 12.56 | 12.39 | 11.70 | 16.28 | 13.82 | 10.21 | 10.69 | 12.78 | 12.02 | 22.10 | 15.19 | 14.90 | 23.02 | 24.65 | 29.63 | 29.96 | 24.02 | 24.54 | 20.89 | 24.81 | 29.51 |
| 3.4 Invest. (pc. id. cr.) | | | 42.41 | 34.65 | 36.92 | 34.80 | 54.20 | 47.32 | 34.95 | 36.08 | 44.55 | 63.40 | 85.53 | 63.40 | 64.77 | 113.26 | 128.91 | 175.70 | 189.03 | 214.59 | 199.81 | 279.15 | 363.59 |
| 3.5 Consp.(*egdp. nc. cr) | | | 92.19 | 94.36 | 95.93 | 102.93 | 95.20 | 95.82 | 96.44 | 99.92 | 98.11 | 97.59 | 91.91 | 91.93 | 93.51 | 89.30 | 90.16 | 86.12 | 82.12 | 83.16 | 84.30 | 82.81 | 77.02 | 79.41 |
| 3.6.1 Consp.Gov.(*egdp) | | | 8.02 | 10.37 | 8.93 | 9.26 | 10.94 | 12.89 | 14.31 | 14.60 | 13.76 | 14.07 | 10.95 | 8.06 | 10.10 | 10.59 | 10.34 | 10.59 | 11.76 | 9.05 | 9.40 | 9.82 | 8.24 | 9.51 |
| 3.6.2 Consp.Pri.(*egdp) | | | 84.18 | 83.99 | 87.00 | 93.67 | 84.26 | 82.93 | 82.13 | 85.31 | 84.35 | 83.51 | 80.96 | 83.34 | 84.14 | 79.20 | 79.82 | 75.53 | 71.76 | 74.10 | 74.90 | 72.99 | 68.78 | 69.90 |
| 3.7 Consp (ac. nc. cs) | | | | 5.6 | 11.4 | 4.8 | 5.8 | 3.1 | 4.8 | 1.7 | 4.3 | 0.5 | 15.5 | 5.4 | 5.1 | 4.0 | 7.4 | 19.5 | 11.2 | 8.3 | 4.9 | 7.3 | 6.7 | |
| 3.8 Consp (pc. id. cr) | | | 214.80 | 226.26 | 251.32 | 260.36 | 275.53 | 283.98 | 293.02 | 292.74 | 296.85 | 305 | 301 | 343 | 357 | 377 | 394 | 429 | 524 | 596 | 659 | 703 | 775 | 882 |
| **4. MONEY AND CURRENCY** | | | | | | | | | | | | | | | | | | | | | | | | |
| 4.1 M1+2 (*egdp. nc. cr) | | | 7.38 | 9.60 | 9.28 | 9.39 | 8.79 | 10.77 | 12.45 | 11.62 | 14.15 | 14.66 | 11.09 | 8.95 | 12.17 | 15.33 | 20.16 | 26.85 | 33.08 | 32.60 | 31.89 | 34.69 | 36.77 | 32.26 |
| 4.2 For.Exch.Reser.(usd) | 0.04 | | 0.11 | 0.11 | 0.10 | 0.10 | 0.11 | 0.15 | 0.15 | 0.16 | 0.21 | 0.17 | 0.13 | 0.13 | 0.14 | 0.24 | 0.35 | 0.39 | 0.55 | 0.58 | 0.40 | 0.48 | 0.83 | 0.28 |
| 4.3 Savings(*egdp. id. cr) | | | 7.86 | 6.17 | 3.98 | -0.27 | 5.54 | 4.87 | 2.38 | 1.06 | 2.97 | 0.20 | 10.96 | 7.53 | 7.33 | 5.59 | 6.18 | 6.85 | 7.71 | 8.95 | 10.15 | 16.20 | 21.76 | 18.25 |
| 4.4 CPI (1995=100) | | | | | | | | | | | | | | | | 5.59 | 6.18 | 6.85 | 7.71 | 8.95 | 10.15 | 11.34 | 11.70 | 14.54 |
| 4.5 Change in CP (an %.s) | | | | | | | | | | | | | | | | 10.56 | 10.92 | 12.50 | 16.08 | 13.44 | 11.67 | 3.22 | 24.30 | |
| 4.5 Ex Rate (usd. nc) | | | 17.82 | 17.82 | 49.50 | 49.51 | 49.51 | 49.51 | 49.51 | 63.13 | 125 | 130 | 130 | 214 | 266 | 271 | 271 | 277 | 288 | 311 | 347 | 393 | 398 | 404 |
| **5. BALANCE OF PAYMENTS (usd. cr)** | | | | | | | | | | | | | | | | | | | | | | | | |
| 5.1 Overall | | | | | | | | | | | | | | | | | | | | | | | | |
| 5.1.1 Current | | | | | | | | | | | | | | | | | | | | | | | | |
| 5.1.2 Capital | | | | | | | | | | | | | | | | | | | | | | | | |
| 5.1.3 Financial | | | | | | | | | | | | | | | | | | | | | | | | |
| **6. PUBLIC FINANCE (nc. cr)** | | | | | | | | | | | | | | | | | | | | | | | | |
| 6.1 Balance(*egdp. nc. cr) | | | | -7.01 | -3.27 | -6.00 | -4.50 | -0.49 | -0.51 | 0.99 | -0.17 | -2.78 | 0.02 | 0.17 | -0.14 | -0.57 | -0.58 | 0.37 | -2.05 | -0.76 | -0.31 | -3.85 | -0.50 | -2.16 |
| 6.2 Exp.Rev. Ratio | | | | 2.00 | 1.86 | 2.09 | 2.70 | 1.90 | 1.54 | 1.28 | 1.58 | 2.23 | 1.58 | 1.45 | 1.44 | 1.20 | 1.10 | 1.02 | 1.09 | 1.06 | 1.05 | 1.35 | 1.04 | 1.04 |
| 6.3.1 Revenue (*egdp) | | | | 5.79 | 5.22 | 5.06 | 4.60 | 8.46 | 11.20 | 10.89 | 9.64 | 9.11 | 7.59 | 6.29 | 7.74 | 13.05 | 15.06 | 17.33 | 18.00 | 15.22 | 15.11 | 13.34 | 12.60 | 13.47 |
| 6.3.2 Expenture (*egdp) | | | | 11.59 | 9.73 | 10.59 | 12.42 | 16.08 | 17.22 | 13.86 | 16.37 | 20.35 | 11.95 | 9.10 | 11.19 | 25.12 | 23.44 | 21.93 | 19.94 | 22.43 | 27.57 | 25.85 | 13.13 | 13.99 |
| 6.4.1 Defence (* x tol exp) | | | | | | | | | | | | | | | | 25.12 | 23.44 | 21.93 | 19.94 | 22.43 | 27.57 | 25.85 | 28.63 | 30.13 |
| 6.4.2 Edu. & Health(*o.) | | | | | | | | | | | | | | | | | | | | | 19.60 | 17.06 | 18.45 | 15.60 |
| 6.4.3 Social Security(*o.) | | | | | | | | | | | | | | | | | | | | | 4.82 | 4.98 | 5.90 | 5.67 |
| 6.4.4 Econ. Affairs(*o.) | | | | | | | | | | | | | | | | | | | | | 20.10 | 25.60 | 18.83 | 23.68 |
| 6.5.1 Defence (*egdp) | | | | | | | | | | | | | | | | 3.93 | 3.87 | 3.88 | 3.90 | 3.61 | 4.39 | 4.64 | 3.76 | 4.22 |
| 6.5.2 Edu.& Health(*o.) | | | | | | | | | | | | | | | | | | | | | 4.82 | 2.83 | 2.23 | 2.02 |
| 6.5.3 Social Security(*o.) | | | | | | | | | | | | | | | | | | | | | | 0.90 | 0.77 | 0.78 |
| 6.5.4 Econ. Affairs(*o.) | | | | | | | | | | | | | | | | | | | | | | 4.56 | 2.47 | 3.29 |
| **7. COMPETITIVENESS** | | | | | | | | | | | | | | | | | | | | | | | | |
| 7.1 M Wages Manuf(usd) | | | | | | | | | | 36.9 | 20.9 | 21.4 | 24.5 | 18.1 | 17.3 | 20.0 | 24.5 | 30.4 | 39.1 | 46.0 | 47.8 | 48.2 | 56.1 | 74.7 |
| 7.2 GDP per Wkerid.cs) | | | 3,726 | 3,817 | 4,162 | 4,198 | 4,510 | 4,515 | 4,477 | 4,471 | 4,576 | 4,534 | 4,896 | 5,110 | 5,205 | 5,771 | 5,926 | 6,486 | 7,217 | 7,596 | 8,032 | 8,157 | 9,010 | 9,481 |
| **8. POPULATION** | | | | | | | | | | | | | | | | | | | | | | | | |
| 8.1 urban(ac) | | | | | | 6.47 | 6.08 | 5.73 | 5.42 | 5.14 | 2.43 | 7.41 | 7.15 | 6.90 | 2.99 | 8.88 | 8.49 | 8.14 | 7.81 | 4.25 | 6.82 | 6.60 | 3.35 | 6.28 |

keys: volume: billions; *egdp: as * of GDP; ac: annual change; cr: current prices; cs: constant prices; id: international dollars; nc: national currency; pc: per capita; usd: US Dollar.

# KOREA DATA SET (2)

| | 1975 | 1976 | 1977 | 1978 | 1979 | 1980 | 1981 | 1982 | 1983 | 1984 | 1985 | 1986 | 1987 | 1988 | 1989 | 1990 | 1991 | 1992 | 1993 | 1994 | 1995 | 1996 | 1997 | 1998 | 1999 | 2000 |
|---|---|---|---|---|---|---|---|---|---|---|---|---|---|---|---|---|---|---|---|---|---|---|---|---|---|---|
| **1 GROSS DOMESTIC PRODUCT (GDP)** | | | | | | | | | | | | | | | | | | | | | | | | | | |
| 1.1 pc. usd. cr | 590 | 807 | 1,018 | 1,354 | 1,708 | 1,632 | 1,797 | 1,893 | 2,063 | 2,242 | 2,290 | 2,611 | 3,248 | 4,297 | 5,199 | 5,893 | 6,819 | 7,194 | 7,823 | 9,017 | 10,850 | 11,422 | 10,360 | 6,829 | 8,666 | 9,763 |
| 1.2 pc. id. cr | 3,720 | 4,077 | 4,432 | 4,770 | 5,048 | 4,830 | 5,058 | 5,351 | 5,847 | 6,264 | 6,601 | 7,244 | 7,969 | 8,732 | 9,203 | 9,959 | 10,801 | 11,246 | 11,723 | 12,585 | 13,553 | 14,320 | 14,786 | 13,436 | 14,813 | 15,881 |
| 1.3 ac. nc. cs | 6.64 | 11.76 | 10.01 | 9.01 | 7.06 | -2.09 | 6.47 | 7.25 | 10.70 | 8.25 | 6.47 | 10.99 | 10.99 | 10.46 | 6.08 | 8.98 | 9.23 | 5.49 | 6.08 | 8.51 | 8.92 | 6.75 | 5.01 | -6.69 | 10.89 | 9.33 |
| 1.4.1 Agri (*agdp.nc.cr) | 25.03 | 23.63 | 22.40 | 20.51 | 19.21 | 14.84 | 15.54 | 14.47 | 13.25 | 12.58 | 12.59 | 11.18 | 10.08 | 10.10 | 9.50 | 8.51 | 7.64 | 7.44 | 6.70 | 6.52 | 6.19 | 5.84 | 5.35 | 4.95 | 5.07 | 4.70 |
| 1.4.2 Manuf (*agdp.nc.cr) | 28.79 | 30.11 | 29.56 | 30.58 | 31.85 | 31.85 | 31.17 | 31.70 | 33.88 | 33.43 | 35.15 | 35.40 | 35.61 | 33.97 | 33.97 | 31.78 | 31.78 | 31.42 | 31.50 | 31.73 | 31.92 | 31.43 | 33.69 | 33.78 | 33.69 | 34.38 |
| **2 INTERNATIONAL TRADE** | | | | | | | | | | | | | | | | | | | | | | | | | | |
| 2.1.1 Exports (ac.usd.cr) | 10.8 | 56.0 | 30.2 | 26.6 | 18.4 | 16.3 | 21.4 | 2.8 | 11.9 | 19.6 | 3.5 | 14.6 | 36.2 | 28.4 | 2.8 | 4.2 | 10.5 | 6.6 | 7.3 | 16.8 | 30.3 | 3.7 | 5.0 | -2.8 | 8.6 | 19.9 |
| 2.1.2 Imports (ac.usd.cr) | 6.2 | 20.6 | 23.2 | 38.5 | 35.8 | 9.6 | 17.2 | -7.2 | 8.0 | 16.9 | 1.6 | 1.4 | 29.9 | 26.3 | 18.6 | 13.6 | 16.7 | 0.3 | 2.5 | 22.1 | 32.0 | 11.3 | -3.8 | -35.5 | 28.3 | 34.0 |
| 2.2.1 Exports (*agdp.nc.cr) | 27.23 | 30.59 | 30.98 | 28.93 | 37.06 | 112.13 | 35.06 | 33.93 | 33.73 | 34.20 | 32.89 | 36.71 | 39.54 | 30.26 | 32.09 | 29.09 | 27.35 | 27.85 | 27.54 | 27.82 | 30.20 | 29.50 | 34.73 | 49.72 | 42.34 | 44.26 |
| 2.2.2 Imports (*agdp.nc.cr) | 35.70 | 32.41 | 31.66 | 32.58 | 34.09 | 40.58 | 40.48 | 36.48 | 34.82 | 34.43 | 32.14 | 31.36 | 32.13 | 30.26 | 29.89 | 30.26 | 30.36 | 29.14 | 27.49 | 28.96 | 31.68 | 33.61 | 35.75 | 36.26 | 35.48 | 41.62 |
| 2.3 ET Ratio (nc.cr) | 0.68 | 0.88 | 0.93 | 0.85 | 0.94 | 0.79 | 0.81 | 0.90 | 0.93 | 0.95 | 0.93 | 1.10 | 1.15 | 1.11 | 1.01 | 0.93 | 0.88 | 0.94 | 0.98 | 0.94 | 0.93 | 0.86 | 0.94 | 1.42 | 1.20 | 1.07 |
| **3 SUPPLY AND DEMAND** | | | | | | | | | | | | | | | | | | | | | | | | | | |
| 3.1 GFCF (*agdp.nc.cr) | 26.83 | 25.67 | 28.46 | 32.70 | 34.07 | 32.36 | 28.21 | 28.63 | 29.67 | 29.29 | 28.82 | 28.44 | 29.32 | 29.86 | 32.17 | 37.30 | 39.03 | 36.96 | 36.16 | 36.00 | 36.69 | 36.79 | 35.10 | 29.77 | 27.79 | 28.39 |
| 3.2 Invest.(ac.nc.cs) | 1.2 | 20.2 | 26.0 | 20.0 | 15.5 | -17.1 | 5.4 | 10.0 | 15.3 | 12.0 | 3.9 | 11.1 | 16.3 | 15.8 | 14.0 | 15.1 | 17.1 | 1.6 | 2.3 | 14.4 | 9.3 | 8.7 | -7.2 | -38.3 | 27.6 | 6.0 |
| 3.3 Invest.(*agdp.id.cr) | 28.22 | 28.71 | 31.95 | 35.42 | 38.47 | 33.66 | 32.91 | 33.22 | 33.91 | 34.18 | 33.28 | 32.11 | 32.87 | 34.37 | 37.10 | 39.07 | 42.15 | 39.64 | 38.40 | 40.23 | 40.50 | 41.64 | 37.65 | 24.66 | 29.05 | 30.78 |
| 3.4 Invest. (pc.id.cr) | 405.08 | 490.46 | 648.32 | 820.31 | 1,006 | 889 | 1,000 | 1,174 | 1,370 | 1,527 | 1,625 | 1,818 | 2,141 | 2,970 | 3,453 | 4,202 | 4,223 | 4,359 | 4,987 | 5,487 | 5,962 | 5,536 | 3,359 | 4,221 | 4,597 | |
| 3.5 Consp.(*agdp.nc.cr) | 81.75 | 76.81 | 73.44 | 71.47 | 72.49 | 76.78 | 76.43 | 75.15 | 71.83 | 69.63 | 69.37 | 65.90 | 62.98 | 59.76 | 62.57 | 62.76 | 62.78 | 63.71 | 63.97 | 64.57 | 64.35 | 65.98 | 65.63 | 63.63 | 66.54 | 67.36 |
| 3.6.1 Consp.Gov.(*agdp) | 10.89 | 10.84 | 10.75 | 10.45 | 10.09 | 11.72 | 11.78 | 11.67 | 11.68 | 10.13 | 10.31 | 10.21 | 9.89 | 9.75 | 10.52 | 10.46 | 10.48 | 10.79 | 10.54 | 10.21 | 9.66 | 10.07 | 10.07 | 10.38 | 10.38 | 10.05 |
| 3.6.2 Consp.Priv(*agdp) | 70.85 | 65.97 | 62.69 | 61.01 | 62.40 | 65.06 | 64.65 | 63.48 | 60.90 | 59.51 | 59.06 | 55.68 | 53.10 | 50.02 | 52.05 | 52.30 | 52.30 | 52.92 | 53.43 | 54.41 | 54.70 | 55.83 | 56.25 | 54.65 | 56.17 | 57.31 |
| 3.7 Consp.(ac.nc.cs) | 4.7 | 7.3 | 4.9 | 7.5 | 7.2 | -1.1 | 4.5 | 6.7 | 8.5 | 7.5 | 6.6 | 8.2 | 7.5 | 8.4 | 10.0 | 9.7 | 8.1 | 5.5 | 5.5 | 7.8 | 9.1 | 6.8 | 3.4 | -10.4 | 10.4 | 1.1 |
| 3.8 Consp.(pc.id.cr) | 1,001 | 1,110 | 1,212 | 1,366 | 1,564 | 1,690 | 1,898 | 2,135 | 2,378 | 2,608 | 2,848 | 3,132 | 3,456 | 3,832 | 4,320 | 4,884 | 5,471 | 5,874 | 6,264 | 6,806 | 7,494 | 8,096 | 8,452 | 7,593 | 8,448 | 8,531 |
| **4 MONEY AND CURRENCY** | | | | | | | | | | | | | | | | | | | | | | | | | | |
| 4.1 M1=2 (*agdp.nc.cr) | 30.79 | 30.04 | 32.73 | 32.72 | 31.83 | 33.17 | 33.07 | 36.57 | 35.92 | 33.84 | 35.13 | 35.67 | 36.22 | 37.04 | 39.57 | 38.43 | 38.68 | 39.18 | 40.44 | 41.18 | 40.80 | 42.61 | 44.90 | 58.18 | 68.22 | 79.13 |
| 4.2 For.Exch.Reser.(usd) | 0.78 | 1.96 | 2.96 | 2.74 | 2.91 | 2.91 | 2.62 | 2.74 | 2.23 | 2.72 | 2.83 | 3.30 | 3.57 | 12.34 | 14.98 | 14.46 | 13.31 | 16.64 | 19.70 | 25.03 | 31.93 | 33.24 | 19.71 | 51.96 | 73.70 | 95.86 |
| 4.3 Savings* (agdp.id.cr) | 19.74 | 26.89 | 30.88 | 31.78 | 31.34 | 35.82 | 32.74 | 30.67 | 32.83 | 33.96 | 33.28 | 37.46 | 40.28 | 41.85 | 39.30 | 37.91 | 39.14 | 38.46 | 38.48 | 38.15 | 39.03 | 37.53 | 36.63 | 38.12 | 35.91 | 33.36 |
| 4.4 CPI (1995=100) | 18.22 | 21.01 | 23.15 | 26.50 | 31.34 | 40.33 | 48.94 | 52.45 | 54.25 | 55.50 | 56.86 | 58.43 | 60.21 | 64.51 | 68.19 | 74.04 | 80.92 | 86.03 | 90.16 | 95.75 | 100.00 | 104.98 | 109.60 | 117.86 | 118.83 | 121.51 |
| 4.5 Change in CP (an %) | 25.31 | 15.30 | 10.67 | 14.46 | 18.27 | 28.70 | 21.34 | 7.19 | 3.42 | 2.31 | 2.46 | 2.75 | 3.05 | 7.15 | 5.70 | 8.58 | 9.30 | 6.31 | 4.80 | 6.20 | 4.44 | 4.98 | 4.40 | 7.54 | 0.83 | 2.25 |
| 4.5 Ex Rate (1usd.nc) | 484 | 484 | 484 | 484 | 484 | 607 | 681 | 731 | 776 | 806 | 870 | 881 | 823 | 731 | 671 | 708 | 733 | 781 | 803 | 803 | 771 | 804 | 951 | 1,401 | 1,189 | 1,131 |
| **5 BALANCE OF PAYMENTS (usd. cr)** | | | | | | | | | | | | | | | | | | | | | | | | | | |
| 5.1 Overall | | -1.31 | 1.37 | 1.35 | 0.73 | 0.87 | 0.18 | -0.25 | 0.01 | -0.12 | 0.39 | 0.21 | 0.03 | 2.10 | 9.33 | 3.64 | -1.21 | -1.15 | 3.72 | 3.01 | 4.61 | 7.04 | 1.42 | -22.98 | 25.93 | 33.26 | 23.79 |
| 5.1.1 Current | | -0.31 | 0.01 | -1.09 | -1.15 | -5.31 | -4.61 | -2.55 | 0.01 | -0.12 | -1.29 | -0.80 | -4.71 | 10.06 | 14.51 | 5.36 | -2.00 | -8.32 | -3.94 | 0.99 | -3.87 | -23.01 | -8.17 | 40.37 | 24.48 | 12.24 | -0.62 |
| 5.1.2 Capital | | | | | | 0.004 | -0.04 | -0.10 | 3.95 | | | | | | | | | -0.33 | -0.41 | -0.48 | -0.44 | -0.49 | -0.60 | -0.61 | 0.17 | -0.39 | -0.62 |
| 5.1.3 Financial | | 1.87 | 1.39 | 2.13 | 5.35 | 5.93 | 4.72 | 3.95 | 2.31 | 3.82 | 2.82 | 1.96 | -3.90 | -8.94 | | -2.57 | 2.90 | 6.74 | 6.99 | 3.22 | 10.73 | 17.27 | 23.92 | -9.20 | -8.38 | 12.71 | 12.73 |
| **6 PUBLIC FINANCE (nc.cr)** | | | | | | | | | | | | | | | | | | | | | | | | | | |
| 6.1 Balance(*agdp.nc.cr) | -1.97 | -1.37 | -1.76 | -1.24 | -1.76 | -2.25 | -3.35 | -3.04 | -1.04 | -1.15 | -1.16 | -0.09 | 0.43 | 0.91 | 0.19 | -0.68 | -1.61 | -0.48 | 0.61 | 0.30 | 0.27 | 0.16 | -1.27 | -3.82 | -4.64 | -1.15 |
| 6.2 Exp.Rev Ratio | 1.03 | 0.99 | 0.95 | 0.92 | 0.96 | 0.96 | 0.93 | 1.01 | 0.93 | 0.94 | 0.94 | 0.91 | 0.85 | 0.92 | 0.91 | 0.89 | 0.97 | 0.93 | 0.93 | 0.88 | 0.88 | 0.86 | 0.86 | 0.92 | 0.95 | 1.05 |
| 6.3.1 Revenue (*agdp) | 15.14 | 16.61 | 16.49 | 16.95 | 17.55 | 18.08 | 18.16 | 18.34 | 18.07 | 17.26 | 17.12 | 16.70 | 16.78 | 17.33 | 17.52 | 17.95 | 17.01 | 17.83 | 18.29 | 18.90 | 19.10 | 20.14 | 20.29 | 21.49 | 21.84 | 21.11 |
| 6.3.2 Expense (*agdp) | 15.65 | 16.39 | 15.63 | 15.60 | 16.84 | 17.37 | 16.98 | 18.58 | 16.73 | 16.27 | 16.40 | 15.76 | 15.24 | 14.73 | 16.04 | 16.60 | 16.45 | 16.60 | 17.00 | 18.66 | 16.52 | 17.35 | 17.43 | 19.80 | 20.68 | 22.25 |
| 6.4.1 Defence (*o tol exp) | 29.06 | 33.50 | 35.96 | 38.03 | 30.57 | 34.31 | 35.19 | 31.28 | 31.89 | 30.09 | 29.67 | 29.25 | 27.31 | 27.08 | 24.90 | 22.98 | 22.16 | 21.36 | 20.08 | 18.66 | 17.83 | 17.27 | 16.66 | 16.09 | 14.36 | 12.98 |
| 6.4.2 Edu.& Health (*o) | 15.06 | 16.34 | 18.47 | 17.61 | 17.60 | 18.33 | 19.27 | 20.90 | 22.11 | 20.46 | 19.88 | 19.63 | 20.69 | 21.23 | 20.55 | 21.49 | 17.77 | 17.00 | 22.40 | 21.05 | 21.13 | 20.58 | 21.29 | 13.79 | 11.49 | 10.89 |
| 6.4.3 Social Security(*o) | 5.22 | 4.60 | 5.02 | 4.92 | 5.40 | 6.35 | 5.97 | 9.63 | 5.16 | 5.49 | 5.65 | 6.36 | 6.44 | 7.43 | 8.34 | 9.02 | 9.49 | 10.01 | 9.99 | 10.11 | 8.70 | 9.21 | 10.79 | 8.19 | 9.26 | 9.08 |
| 6.4.4 Econ. Affairs(*o) | 24.39 | 22.46 | 15.79 | 15.07 | 23.34 | 15.57 | 14.37 | 13.34 | 13.60 | 16.40 | 17.49 | 16.23 | 16.60 | 17.14 | 19.72 | 19.07 | 19.18 | 17.01 | 18.81 | 21.06 | 17.06 | 22.71 | 23.68 | 19.93 | 20.68 | 22.55 |
| 6.5.1 Defence (*agdp) | 4.55 | 5.50 | 5.62 | 5.93 | 5.15 | 5.96 | 5.97 | 5.81 | 5.33 | 4.89 | 4.87 | 4.61 | 4.16 | 3.90 | 4.00 | 3.73 | 3.65 | 3.54 | 3.26 | 3.11 | 2.95 | 3.00 | 2.90 | 3.19 | 2.97 | 2.89 |
| 6.5.2 Edu.& Health(*o) | 2.18 | 2.48 | 2.60 | 2.48 | 2.75 | 2.94 | 3.03 | 3.61 | 3.41 | 3.07 | 3.00 | 2.83 | 2.77 | 2.78 | 2.96 | 3.15 | 2.60 | 2.70 | 3.61 | 3.59 | 3.62 | 3.70 | 3.85 | 3.19 | 3.85 | 3.85 |
| 6.5.3 Social Security(*o) | 0.83 | 0.75 | 0.78 | 0.76 | 0.90 | 1.09 | 1.01 | 1.78 | 0.86 | 0.89 | 0.92 | 0.99 | 0.97 | 1.09 | 1.33 | 1.46 | 1.57 | 1.70 | 1.68 | 1.78 | 1.54 | 1.72 | 2.03 | 2.03 | 2.03 | 2.03 |
| 6.5.4 Econ. Affairs(*o) | 3.80 | 3.66 | 2.45 | 2.34 | 3.88 | 2.68 | 2.43 | 2.47 | 2.26 | 2.65 | 2.84 | 2.53 | 2.51 | 2.50 | 3.14 | 3.08 | 3.17 | 2.88 | 3.17 | 3.71 | 3.99 | 4.23 | 4.44 | 4.44 | 4.44 | 4.44 |
| **7 COMPETITIVENESS** | | | | | | | | | | | | | | | | | | | | | | | | | | |
| 7.1 M Wages Manuf(usd) | 70.3 | 106.8 | 142.9 | 192.0 | 246.9 | 241.5 | 258.7 | 276.5 | 292.3 | 304.3 | 309.9 | 334.1 | 399.6 | 537.4 | 732.2 | 834.7 | 941.3 | 1,023 | 1,103 | 1,273 | 1,457 | 1,568 | 1,394 | 917 | 1,241 | 1,417 |
| 7.2 GDP per Wkent(d,ss) | 9,330 | 10,730 | 11,636 | 12,463 | 13,127 | 12,395 | 12,848 | 13,340 | 14,558 | 15,482 | 16,759 | 17,639 | 19,243 | 21,113 | 22,167 | 23,896 | 25,041 | 26,994 | 28,134 | 30,174 | 32,538 | 34,382 | 35,145 | 31,701 | 34,647 | 36,850 |
| **8 POPULATION** | | | | | | | | | | | | | | | | | | | | | | | | | | |
| 8.1 urban(ac) | 3.14 | 6.67 | 3.58 | 6.33 | 6.13 | 3.23 | 5.22 | 2.74 | 5.29 | 2.59 | 5.09 | 2.74 | 5.17 | 2.60 | 2.53 | 4.91 | 1.19 | 3.53 | 1.16 | 3.45 | 1.14 | 3.19 | 0.94 | 0.93 | 3.11 | 0.91 |

keys: volume: billions; *agdp: as % of GDP; ac: annual change; cr: current prices; cs: constant prices; id: international dollars; nc: national currency; pc: per capita; usd: US Dollar.

# SINGAPORE DATASET (I)

| | 1951 | 1952 | 1953 | 1954 | 1955 | 1956 | 1957 | 1958 | 1959 | 1960 | 1961 | 1962 | 1963 | 1964 | 1965 | 1966 | 1967 | 1968 | 1969 | 1970 | 1971 | 1972 | 1973 | 1974 |
|---|---|---|---|---|---|---|---|---|---|---|---|---|---|---|---|---|---|---|---|---|---|---|---|---|
| **1. GROSS DOMESTIC PRODUCT (GDP)** | | | | | | | | | | | | | | | | | | | | | | | | |
| 1.1 pc. usd. cr | | | | | | | | | | 395 | 438 | 430 | 472 | 464 | 512 | 561 | 619 | 701 | 803 | 896 | 1,010 | 1,247 | 1,367 | 2,408 |
| 1.2 pc. id. cr | | | | | | | | | | 2,280 | 2,318 | 3,257 | 3,606 | 4,273 | 3,151 | 3,409 | 3,761 | 4,251 | 4,773 | 5,319 | 5,870 | 6,555 | 7,255 | 7,602 |
| 1.3 ac. nc. cs | | | | | | | | | | 8.36 | 8.36 | 7.00 | 9.96 | -3.47 | 7.51 | 28.17 | -3.04 | 13.88 | 13.69 | 13.70 | 12.50 | 13.40 | 11.50 | 6.30 |
| 1.4.1 Agri (*sgdp.nc.cr) | | | | | | | | | | | | | | 2.86 | 2.86 | 3.05 | 2.84 | 2.81 | 2.56 | 2.32 | 2.32 | 1.96 | 2.09 | 1.82 |
| 1.4.2 Manuf(*sgdp.nc.cr) | | | | | | | | | | | | | | 15.12 | 15.67 | 15.67 | 16.87 | 17.84 | 19.04 | 21.53 | 23.16 | 25.32 | 24.84 | 23.66 |
| **2. INTERNATIONAL TRADE** | | | | | | | | | | | | | | | | | | | | | | | | |
| 2.1.1 Exports (ac. usd.cr) | 56.8 | -31.3 | -19.9 | 1.2 | 25.5 | 1.7 | 1.4 | -0.7 | 9.6 | 1.1 | -4.8 | 3.2 | 1.7 | -20.2 | 8.3 | 12.3 | 3.4 | 11.5 | 21.9 | 21.9 | 13.3 | 24.3 | 66.9 | 59.0 |
| 2.1.2 Imports (ac.usd.cr) | 53.5 | -25.4 | -19.4 | 0.1 | 27.7 | 1.5 | 4.1 | -11.0 | 7.4 | 4.4 | -2.9 | 1.9 | 6.0 | -18.7 | 9.3 | 6.8 | 8.4 | 15.4 | 22.8 | 20.7 | 15.3 | 19.6 | 51.0 | 63.4 |
| 2.2.1 Exports(*sgdp.nc.cr) | | | | | | | | | | 178 | 141 | 139 | 149 | 125 | 129 | 128 | 118 | 114 | 119 | 111 | 110 | 125 | 130 | 155 |
| 2.2.2 Imports(*sgdp.nc.cr) | | | | | | | | | | 193 | 147 | 141 | 137 | 125 | 141 | 136 | 126 | 120 | 119 | 133 | 133 | 144 | 140 | 171 |
| 2.3 EI Ratio (nc. cr) | | | | | | | | | | 0.85 | 0.83 | 0.85 | 0.81 | 0.80 | 0.79 | 0.83 | 0.79 | 0.77 | 0.76 | 0.63 | 0.62 | 0.64 | 0.71 | 0.69 |
| **3. SUPPLY AND DEMAND** | | | | | | | | | | | | | | | | | | | | | | | | |
| 3.1 GFCF (*sgdp. nc. cr) | | | | | | | | | | 6.57 | 9.48 | 14.32 | 15.99 | 20.15 | 21.14 | 19.66 | 19.70 | 23.11 | 26.41 | 34.27 | 39.21 | 41.74 | 36.51 | 36.97 |
| 3.2 Invest.(nc. nc. cs) | | | | | | | | | | | 63.6 | 10.7 | 20.5 | 28.0 | 12.1 | 6.4 | 13.0 | 21.9 | 23.4 | 41.4 | 16.3 | 16.3 | 8.8 | 19.8 |
| 3.3 Invest*sgdp-id-cr | | | | | | | | | | 24.3 | 32.3 | 23.8 | 26.1 | 28.1 | 43.4 | 41.2 | 41.0 | 42.7 | 46.7 | 57.6 | 58.9 | 55.6 | 53.1 | 60.1 |
| 3.4 Invest. (pc. id. cr.) | | | | | | | | | | 117.28 | 186.29 | 197.57 | 233.93 | 294.98 | 327.30 | 347.68 | 393.07 | 484.15 | 617.26 | 895.46 | 1,057 | 1,157 | 1,280 | 1,664 |
| 3.5 Consp.(*sgdp. nc. cr) | | | | | | | | | | 93.41 | 90.50 | 96.74 | 93.30 | 92.78 | 89.61 | 87.27 | 86.36 | 84.10 | 79.68 | 83.69 | 85.51 | 82.83 | 76.4 | 70.51 |
| 3.6.1 Consp.Gov.(*sgdp) | | | | | | | | | | 9.16 | 8.71 | 9.43 | 9.89 | 10.35 | 10.42 | 10.54 | 10.22 | 10.41 | 11.16 | 12.57 | 13.65 | 13.53 | 11.46 | 10.22 |
| 3.6.2 Consp.Pri.(*sgdp) | | | | | | | | | | 84.26 | 81.78 | 87.31 | 83.41 | 82.43 | 79.19 | 76.73 | 76.13 | 73.70 | 68.53 | 71.12 | 71.86 | 69.30 | 65.01 | 60.29 |
| 3.7 Consp.(ac. nc. cs) | | | | | | | | | | | -3.9 | 56.1 | 8.9 | 21.9 | -39.6 | 7.9 | 14.1 | 8.2 | 12.3 | 9.8 | 12.0 | 10.5 | 4.4 | 7.0 |
| 3.8 Consp.(pc. id. cr) | | | | | | | | | | 418.42 | 392.52 | 603 | 645 | 775 | 463 | 502 | 575 | 636 | 734 | 829 | 950 | 1,067 | 1,145 | 1,307 |
| **4. MONEY AND CURRENCY** | | | | | | | | | | | | | | | | | | | | | | | | |
| 4.1 M1+2 (*sgdp. nc. cr) | | | | | | | | | | | | | 53.19 | 57.38 | 55.78 | 56.80 | 59.05 | 63.92 | 66.37 | 69.81 | 66.67 | 72.19 | 62.57 | 54.52 |
| 4.2 For.Exch.Reser.(usd) | 0.08 | 0.07 | 0.08 | 0.07 | 0.11 | 0.09 | 0.08 | 0.10 | 0.12 | 0.12 | 0.12 | 0.17 | 0.17 | 0.43 | 0.43 | 0.39 | 0.49 | 0.71 | 0.82 | 1.01 | 1.44 | 1.74 | 2.28 | 2.80 |
| 4.3 Savings(*sgdp.id. cr) | | | | | | | | | | 5.69 | 25.06 | 22.06 | 22.73 | 21.47 | 31.31 | 32.93 | 32.56 | 36.18 | 36.07 | 37.33 | 37.20 | 38.76 | 43.00 | 43.86 |
| 4.4 CPI (1995=100) | | | | | | | | | | 33.77 | 33.91 | 34.05 | 34.80 | 35.40 | 35.47 | 36.18 | 37.39 | 37.63 | 37.53 | 37.70 | 38.37 | 39.16 | 46.85 | 57.34 |
| 5.3 Change in CP (an %) | | | | | | | | | | 0.40 | 0.40 | 0.42 | 2.21 | 1.73 | 0.18 | 2.01 | 3.34 | 0.66 | -0.27 | 0.46 | 1.76 | 2.08 | 19.64 | 22.37 |
| 4.5 Ex Rate (1usd. nc) | | | | | | | | | | 3.06 | 3.06 | 3.06 | 3.06 | 3.06 | 3.06 | 3.06 | 3.06 | 3.06 | 3.06 | 3.06 | 3.05 | 2.81 | 2.46 | 2.44 |
| **5. BALANCE OF PAYMENTS (usd. cr)** | | | | | | | | | | | | | | | | | | | | | | | | |
| 5.1 Overall | | | | | | | | | | | | | | | | | | | | | | 0.34 | 0.41 | 0.30 |
| 5.1.1 Current | | | | | | | | | | | | | | | | | | | | | | -0.50 | -0.52 | -1.02 |
| 5.1.2 Capital | | | | | | | | | | | | | | | | | | | | | | | | |
| 5.1.3 Financial | | | | | | | | | | | | | | | | | | | | | | 0.40 | 0.72 | 0.50 |
| **6. PUBLIC FINANCE (nc. cr)** | | | | | | | | | | | | | | | | | | | | | | | | |
| 6.1 Balance* sgdp. nc. cr) | | | | | | | | | | | | | -0.39 | -4.49 | -2.71 | -1.68 | -0.53 | 1.62 | 1.53 | 3.65 | 0.71 | 2.91 | 1.36 | 0.86 |
| 6.2 Exp.Rev Ratio | | | | | | | | | | | | | 0.96 | 1.05 | 0.95 | 0.95 | 0.84 | 0.84 | 0.83 | 0.76 | 0.81 | 0.71 | 0.70 | 0.68 |
| 6.3.1 Revenue (*sgdp) | | | | | | | | | | | | | 17.31 | 16.80 | 18.20 | 18.70 | 18.95 | 19.86 | 18.92 | 24.09 | 24.10 | 25.58 | 22.13 | 21.19 |
| 6.3.2 Expture (*sgdp) | | | | | | | | | | | | | 16.59 | 17.64 | 17.25 | 17.83 | 18.05 | 16.69 | 15.62 | 18.40 | 19.61 | 18.04 | 15.58 | 14.48 |
| 6.4.1 Defence (*a tol exp) | | | | | | | | | | | | | | | | | | | | | | 36.50 | 33.55 | 30.67 |
| 6.4.2 Edu. & Health(*a) | | | | | | | | | | | | | | | | | | | | | | 24.39 | 23.95 | 29.91 |
| 6.4.3 Social Security(*a.) | | | | | | | | | | | | | | | | | | | | | | 4.09 | 9.67 | 7.88 |
| 6.4.4 Econ. Affaurs(*a.) | | | | | | | | | | | | | | | | | | | | | | 10.30 | 10.46 | 9.46 |
| 6.5.1 Defence (*sgdp) | | | | | | | | | | | | | | | | | | | | | | 5.89 | 4.97 | 4.47 |
| 6.5.2 Edu.& Health(*a.) | | | | | | | | | | | | | | | | | | | | | | 2.62 | 2.34 | 2.93 |
| 6.5.3 Social Security(*a.) | | | | | | | | | | | | | | | | | | | | | | 0.09 | 0.44 | 0.26 |
| 6.5.4 Econ. Affaurs(*a.) | | | | | | | | | | | | | | | | | | | | | | 1.66 | 1.55 | 1.38 |
| **7. COMPETITIVENESS** | | | | | | | | | | | | | | | | | | | | | | | | |
| 7.1 M Wages Manuf(usd) | | | | | | | | | | | | | | | | | | | | 67 | 69 | 80 | 102 | 124 |
| 7.2 GDP per Wker(id.cs) | | | | | | | | | | 6,527 | 6,715 | 9,315 | 10,297 | 12,776 | 9,067 | 9,741 | 10,699 | 12,068 | 13,499 | 15,085 | 16,140 | 17,474 | 18,784 | 19,203 |
| **8. POPULATION** | | | | | | | | | | | | | | | | | | | | | | | | |
| 8.1 urban(ac) | | | | | | | | | | 3.40 | 3.49 | 2.82 | 2.57 | 2.62 | 2.44 | 2.49 | 2.28 | 1.72 | 1.54 | 1.57 | 1.83 | 1.85 | 1.91 | 1.69 |

keys: volume: billions; *sgdp: as % of GDP; ac: annual change; cr: current prices; id: international dollars; nc: national currency; pc: per capita; usd: US Dollar.

| SINGAPORE DATASET (2) | 1975 | 1976 | 1977 | 1978 | 1979 | 1980 | 1981 | 1982 | 1983 | 1984 | 1985 | 1986 | 1987 | 1988 | 1989 | 1990 | 1991 | 1992 | 1993 | 1994 | 1995 | 1996 | 1997 | 1998 | 1999 | 2000 |
|---|---|---|---|---|---|---|---|---|---|---|---|---|---|---|---|---|---|---|---|---|---|---|---|---|---|---|
| **1. GROSS DOMESTIC PRODUCT (GDP)** | | | | | | | | | | | | | | | | | | | | | | | | | | |
| 1.1 pc, usd, cr | 2,609 | 2,627 | 2,908 | 3,438 | 4,086 | 4,854 | 5,483 | 5,768 | 6,484 | 6,872 | 6,466 | 6,533 | 7,354 | 8,854 | 10,180 | 12,157 | 13,653 | 15,446 | 17,678 | 20,764 | 23,960 | 25,269 | 25,778 | 22,000 | 21,684 | 23,620 |
| 1.2 pc, id, cr | 7,934 | 8,387 | 8,847 | 9,551 | 10,460 | 11,460 | 11,944 | 12,290 | 13,146 | 14,011 | 13,501 | 13,748 | 14,829 | 16,086 | 16,949 | 17,953 | 18,279 | 18,842 | 20,769 | 21,263 | 22,650 | 24,939 | 26,166 | 25,066 | 26,479 | 28,071 |
| 1.3 ac, nc, cs | 4.10 | 8.40 | 7.80 | 8.60 | 7.00 | 9.60 | 8.20 | 8.30 | 9.00 | 7.30 | -1.60 | 2.30 | 9.70 | 11.66 | 9.00 | 9.70 | 7.30 | 6.50 | 12.70 | 11.40 | 8.50 | 7.30 | 8.50 | -0.90 | 6.40 | 9.40 |
| 1.4.1 Agri(*,gdp,nc,cr) | 1.89 | 1.75 | 1.77 | 1.54 | 1.44 | 1.28 | 1.21 | 1.07 | 0.90 | 0.85 | 0.75 | 0.62 | 0.51 | 0.39 | 0.32 | 0.26 | 0.22 | 0.20 | 0.17 | 0.16 | 0.17 | 0.17 | 0.14 | 0.16 | 0.15 | 0.14 |
| 1.4.2 Manuf(*gdp,nc,cr) | 23.78 | 25.03 | 25.07 | 25.92 | 28.10 | 27.92 | 29.08 | 25.53 | 24.31 | 22.30 | 22.85 | 23.75 | 28.13 | 29.50 | 28.67 | 28.22 | 27.34 | 26.14 | 26.48 | 25.89 | 25.77 | 25.77 | 24.77 | 25.13 | 25.13 | 30.56 |
| **2. INTERNATIONAL TRADE** | | | | | | | | | | | | | | | | | | | | | | | | | | |
| 2.1.1 Exports (ac, usd,cr) | -7.5 | 22.5 | 25.1 | 23.0 | 40.4 | 36.1 | 8.2 | -0.9 | 5.0 | 10.2 | -5.2 | -1.4 | 27.5 | 37.0 | 13.6 | 18.1 | 11.8 | 7.6 | 16.6 | 30.8 | 22.1 | 5.7 | 0.0 | -12.1 | 4.4 | 20.2 |
| 2.1.2 Imports (ac,usd,cr) | -2.9 | 11.5 | 15.4 | 24.7 | 35.1 | 36.1 | 14.8 | 2.2 | 0.0 | 1.8 | -8.3 | -2.9 | 27.6 | 34.7 | 13.2 | 22.4 | 8.8 | 9.2 | 18.1 | 20.5 | 21.3 | 5.5 | 0.8 | -20.9 | 6.1 | 21.1 |
| 2.2.1 Exports(*gdp,nc,cr) | 145 | 161 | 171 | 176 | 198 | 215 | 211 | 199 | 178 | 170 | 168 | 167 | 185 | 207 | 201 | 202 | 193 | 185 | 182 | 173 | 178 | 171 | 165 | 152 | 166 | 141 |
| 2.2.2 Imports(*gdp,nc,cr) | 155 | 169 | 173 | 181 | 205 | 224 | 216 | 203 | 180 | 172 | 170 | 166 | 185 | 199 | 192 | 196 | 183 | 175 | 175 | 158 | 163 | 157 | 152 | 133 | 146 | 133 |
| 2.3 ET Ratio (nc, cr) | 0.66 | 0.73 | 0.74 | 0.78 | 0.81 | 0.81 | 0.76 | 0.74 | 0.78 | 0.84 | 0.87 | 0.88 | 0.88 | 0.90 | 0.90 | 0.87 | 0.89 | 0.88 | 0.87 | 0.84 | 0.95 | 0.94 | 0.84 | 1.05 | 1.05 | 1.02 |
| **3. SUPPLY AND DEMAND** | | | | | | | | | | | | | | | | | | | | | | | | | | |
| 3.1 GFCF (*gdp, nc, cr) | 34.63 | 36.65 | 34.03 | 35.70 | 36.64 | 40.66 | 43.58 | 47.46 | 47.54 | 47.75 | 42.20 | 36.35 | 33.52 | 30.89 | 32.49 | 32.47 | 33.94 | 36.03 | 35.18 | 33.94 | 33.95 | 38.35 | 38.74 | 36.13 | 32.97 | 28.78 |
| 3.2 Invest (ac, nc, cs) | -7.7 | 6.0 | -3.8 | 15.9 | 18.5 | 16.1 | 6.8 | 14.6 | 11.1 | 9.4 | -12.5 | -9.0 | -7.8 | -2.6 | 13.1 | 18.0 | 3.0 | 9.9 | 7.2 | 13.1 | 13 | 14.9 | 17.3 | 13.8 | -9.9 | -4.0 |
| 3.3 Invest* sgdb-id-cr | 53.9 | 52.9 | 46.9 | 50.3 | 54.6 | 57.5 | 55.0 | 57.0 | 57.1 | 57.7 | 52.7 | 47.5 | 47.3 | 40.9 | 41.5 | 44.3 | 42.1 | 42.6 | 44.3 | 39.9 | 41.3 | 43.9 | 45.6 | 40.1 | 37.7 | 37.3 |
| 3.4 Invest, (ps, id, cr) | 1,695 | 1,848 | 1,835 | 2,748 | 2,836 | 3,520 | 3,885 | 4,616 | 5,198 | 5,621 | 5,076 | 4,704 | 5,103 | 5,031 | 5,793 | 6,602 | 6,964 | 7,347 | 8,602 | 8,528 | 9,630 | 10,956 | 12,189 | 10,543 | 9,991 | 10,804 |
| 3.5 Consp.(*gdp, nc, cr) | 70.34 | 70.34 | 68.49 | 67.94 | 64.70 | 61.21 | 58.35 | 57.71 | 54.98 | 54.69 | 59.35 | 60.89 | 60.53 | 58.62 | 57.87 | 56.61 | 55.29 | 54.87 | 54.73 | 52.67 | 50.07 | 50.62 | 49.52 | 47.60 | 50.07 | 49.51 |
| 3.6.1 Comp.Gov. (*gdp) | 10.49 | 10.69 | 10.70 | 11.02 | 9.91 | 9.75 | 9.51 | 10.93 | 10.82 | 10.82 | 14.26 | 13.55 | 12.37 | 10.52 | 10.33 | 10.20 | 9.94 | 9.37 | 9.57 | 8.44 | 8.60 | 9.49 | 9.40 | 9.77 | 9.85 | 10.29 |
| 3.6.2 Comp.Pri.(*gdp) | 59.85 | 59.65 | 57.79 | 56.92 | 54.79 | 51.46 | 48.84 | 46.78 | 44.11 | 43.87 | 45.10 | 47.34 | 48.16 | 48.09 | 47.54 | 46.41 | 45.35 | 45.54 | 45.36 | 44.23 | 41.47 | 41.13 | 40.12 | 37.83 | 40.22 | 39.22 |
| 3.7 Comp (ac, nc, cs) | 5.8 | 4.8 | 7.6 | 5.8 | 2.0 | 4.5 | 9.9 | 3.5 | 2.0 | 8.0 | 4.8 | 7.4 | 14.6 | 6.6 | 4.2 | 6.6 | 4.2 | 5.5 | 5.4 | 8.1 | 5.1 | 3.16 | 6.2 | -3.1 | 5.3 | 9.4 |
| 3.8 Comp (ps, id, cr) | 1,501 | 1,631 | 1,828 | 2,035 | 2,389 | 2,590 | 2,961 | 3,141 | 3,295 | 3,540 | 3,728 | 4,117 | 4,606 | 5,314 | 5,768 | 6,160 | 6,531 | 6,883 | 7,684 | 8,191 | 8,510 | 8,663 | 9,075 | 8,653 | 9,195 | 9,966 |
| **4. MONEY AND CURRENCY** | | | | | | | | | | | | | | | | | | | | | | | | | | |
| 4.1 M1=2(*gdp, nc, cr) | 60.17 | 63.78 | 61.14 | 60.92 | 62.85 | 64.03 | 67.05 | 69.80 | 69.49 | 67.72 | 72.32 | 70.62 | 86.31 | 82.99 | 88.58 | 93.05 | 94.04 | 94.71 | 88.22 | 88.10 | 86.59 | 86.99 | 88.02 | 112.97 | 121.92 | 104.46 |
| 4.2 For.Exch.Reser(usd) | 3.00 | 3.35 | 3.85 | 5.29 | 5.77 | 6.49 | 7.44 | 8.35 | 9.13 | 10.29 | 12.69 | 12.75 | 15.00 | 16.86 | 20.14 | 27.54 | 33.93 | 39.66 | 48.07 | 57.89 | 68.35 | 76.40 | 70.88 | 74.42 | 76.30 | 79.69 |
| 4.3 Savings(*gdp, id, cr) | 43.40 | 44.69 | 44.28 | 45.28 | 47.57 | 49.22 | 50.00 | 53.11 | 55.71 | 55.52 | 50.75 | 48.69 | 81.99 | 83.24 | 50.11 | 50.38 | 52.63 | 52.87 | 52.87 | 54.95 | 56.5 | 57.84 | 58.31 | 59.35 | 56.98 | 55.96 |
| 4.4 CPI (1995=100) | 58.79 | 57.71 | 59.53 | 62.43 | 64.98 | 70.52 | 76.29 | 79.28 | 80.23 | 82.31 | 82.71 | 81.56 | 81.99 | 83.24 | 85.19 | 88.14 | 91.16 | 93.22 | 95.35 | 98.31 | 100.00 | 101.38 | 103.41 | 103.14 | 103.16 | 104.56 |
| 4.5 Change in CPI (m,*a) | 2.54 | 2.47 | 3.16 | 4.87 | 4.08 | 8.53 | 8.18 | 3.92 | 1.20 | 2.60 | 0.48 | -1.39 | 0.52 | 1.52 | 2.35 | 3.46 | 3.43 | 2.26 | 2.29 | 3.10 | 1.72 | 1.38 | 2.00 | -0.27 | 0.02 | 1.36 |
| 4.5 Ex Rate (Jusd, nc) | 2.37 | 2.47 | 2.44 | 2.27 | 2.17 | 2.14 | 2.11 | 2.14 | 2.11 | 2.13 | 2.20 | 2.18 | 2.11 | 2.01 | 1.95 | 1.81 | 1.73 | 1.63 | 1.62 | 1.53 | 1.42 | 1.41 | 1.48 | 1.67 | 1.69 | 1.72 |
| **5. BALANCE OF PAYMENTS (usd, cr)** | | | | | | | | | | | | | | | | | | | | | | | | | | |
| 5.1 Overall | 0.41 | 0.30 | 0.31 | 0.67 | 0.52 | 0.66 | 0.91 | 1.18 | 1.06 | 1.52 | 1.34 | 0.54 | 1.10 | 1.66 | 2.74 | 5.43 | 4.20 | 6.10 | 7.58 | 4.74 | 8.60 | 7.40 | 7.94 | 3.97 | -4.19 | 6.81 |
| 5.1.1 Current | -0.58 | -0.57 | -0.30 | -0.45 | -0.74 | -1.56 | -1.47 | -1.30 | -0.61 | -0.39 | 0.00 | 0.32 | -0.11 | 1.94 | 2.96 | 3.12 | 4.88 | 5.92 | 4.21 | 11.40 | 14.90 | 12.57 | 18.12 | 19.71 | 16.53 | 15.92 |
| 5.1.2 Capital | | | | | | | | | | | | | | | | -0.02 | -0.03 | -0.04 | -0.07 | -0.08 | -0.07 | -0.14 | -0.17 | -0.23 | -0.19 | -0.16 |
| 5.1.3 Financial | 0.58 | 0.85 | 0.61 | 1.01 | 1.00 | 1.58 | 2.17 | 2.31 | 2.46 | 1.58 | 0.70 | -0.45 | 0.47 | 0.99 | 1.25 | 3.95 | 2.35 | 1.79 | -1.21 | -8.84 | -0.88 | -8.7 | -13.64 | -21.01 | -11.36 | -10.84 |
| **6. PUBLIC FINANCE (nc, cr)** | | | | | | | | | | | | | | | | | | | | | | | | | | |
| 6.1 Balance *gdp, nc, cr) | 2.09 | 0.37 | 0.64 | 0.24 | 0.38 | 0.39 | 2.57 | 3.10 | 2.51 | 5.21 | 1.53 | 1.82 | -4.75 | 6.19 | 1.18 | 0.77 | 10.27 | 11.93 | 13.96 | 12.7 | 13.48 | 14.66 | 9.71 | 16.27 | 10.19 | 11.06 |
| 6.2 Exp/Rev Ratio | 0.68 | 0.77 | 0.84 | 0.87 | 0.83 | 0.80 | 0.75 | 0.68 | 0.68 | 0.73 | 0.98 | 0.58 | 1.23 | 0.84 | 0.66 | 0.70 | 0.63 | 0.58 | 0.49 | 0.47 | 0.44 | 0.43 | 0.51 | 0.43 | 0.51 | 0.58 |
| 6.3.1 Revenue (*gdp) | 24.84 | 23.91 | 23.08 | 23.14 | 22.95 | 24.51 | 26.12 | 30.32 | 31.20 | 28.64 | 27.89 | 44.40 | 28.10 | 27.84 | 27.35 | 28.62 | 29.75 | 31.71 | 31.67 | 31.02 | 33.99 | 37.00 | 40.68 | 41.96 | 34.90 | 31.94 |
| 6.3.2 Exp/ture (*gdp) | 16.86 | 18.53 | 19.28 | 20.08 | 19.70 | 19.70 | 19.47 | 20.58 | 21.27 | 20.96 | 27.22 | 25.99 | 33.86 | 23.49 | 18.12 | 19.94 | 18.79 | 18.51 | 15.40 | 14.69 | 14.79 | 16.07 | 20.84 | 17.98 | 18.63 | 18.38 |
| 6.4.1 Defence (* tot exp) | 28.99 | 29.48 | 31.52 | 26.39 | 25.42 | 25.63 | 26.19 | 23.91 | 19.57 | 25.05 | 22.44 | 21.83 | 20.32 | 26.80 | 25.72 | 25.72 | 25.36 | 26.38 | 28.24 | 28.77 | 31.53 | 28.42 | 23.49 | 30.01 | 28.48 | 26.97 |
| 6.4.2 Edu. & Health(*o) | 30.17 | 28.43 | 23.31 | 22.56 | 22.84 | 21.95 | 31.62 | 26.77 | 29.61 | 32.90 | 28.01 | 25.53 | 18.91 | 23.83 | 28.28 | 26.25 | 33.46 | 30.37 | 35.05 | 28.7 | 29.2 | 27.09 | 26.7 | 27.23 | 26.26 | 25.32 |
| 6.4.3 Social Security(*,a) | 9.40 | 9.35 | 10.51 | 9.52 | 9.57 | 7.73 | 10.08 | 8.58 | 5.90 | 8.16 | 5.73 | 18.29 | 11.54 | 14.52 | 14.52 | 8.83 | 8.29 | 9.7 | 12.34 | 15.48 | 14.47 | 23.98 | 8.80 | 13.78 | 14.81 | 15.72 |
| 6.4.4 Econ. Affairs(*,a) | 12.54 | 12.68 | 13.71 | 12.06 | 13.86 | 18.02 | 18.79 | 14.89 | 15.09 | 18.76 | 17.65 | 22.84 | 16.38 | 24.82 | 24.82 | 17.27 | 12.34 | 12.36 | 13.11 | 8.58 | 11.35 | 19.24 | 13.96 | 20.73 | 12.71 | 11.87 |
| 6.5.1 Defence (*gdp) | 4.93 | 5.38 | 6.08 | 5.30 | 4.85 | 5.05 | 5.10 | 4.92 | 4.16 | 5.25 | 6.11 | 5.53 | 5.12 | 4.83 | 4.78 | 5.02 | 4.60 | 4.81 | 4.29 | 4.55 | 4.02 | 4.49 | 4.80 | 4.80 | 4.80 | 4.80 |
| 6.5.2 Edu.& Health(*o) | 3.62 | 3.66 | 2.98 | 2.85 | 2.97 | 2.93 | 4.47 | 4.14 | 4.83 | 5.28 | 5.87 | 5.29 | 5.06 | 4.32 | 3.99 | 4.17 | 4.36 | 4.36 | 4.29 | 3.15 | 3.01 | 3.12 | 3.12 | 3.13 | 3.13 | 3.13 |
| 6.5.3 Social Security(*,a) | 0.33 | 0.29 | 0.27 | 0.25 | 0.30 | 0.27 | 0.32 | 0.30 | 0.23 | 0.24 | 0.35 | 0.46 | 0.45 | 0.46 | 0.44 | 0.44 | 0.46 | 0.45 | 0.66 | 0.40 | 0.76 | 2.21 | 0.30 | 0.30 | 0.30 | 0.30 |
| 6.5.4 Econ. Affairs(*,a) | 2.08 | 2.72 | 2.64 | 2.42 | 2.65 | 3.55 | 3.56 | 3.06 | 3.21 | 3.93 | 4.81 | 5.79 | 5.47 | 3.64 | 4.41 | 3.52 | 2.27 | 2.26 | 1.99 | 1.24 | 1.64 | 3.04 | 2.85 | 2.85 | 2.85 | 2.85 |
| **7. COMPETIVENESS** | | | | | | | | | | | | | | | | | | | | | | | | | | |
| 7.1 M.Wages Manuf(usd) | 151 | 153 | 162 | 187 | 218 | 254 | 311 | 338 | 382 | 422 | 427 | 448 | 479 | 555 | 637 | 770 | 898 | 1,035 | 1,125 | 1,306 | 1,522 | 1,645 | 1,675 | 1,623 | 1,654 | 1,761 |
| 7.2 GDP per W.ker(usd) | 19,395 | 19,964 | 20,426 | 21,648 | 23,108 | 24,739 | 25,930 | 26,258 | 27,956 | 29,614 | 28,239 | 28,648 | 30,875 | 33,410 | 35,200 | 37,319 | 36,164 | 35,587 | 37,510 | 36,776 | 39,186 | 43,161 | | | | |
| **8. POPULATION** | | | | | | | | | | | | | | | | | | | | | | | | | | |
| 8.1 urban(ac) | 1.48 | 1.33 | 1.40 | 1.25 | 1.27 | 1.26 | 4.93 | 4.58 | 2.58 | 1.99 | 1.59 | -0.11 | 1.54 | 2.56 | 2.99 | 3.96 | 2.92 | 3.06 | 2.57 | 3.20 | 3.07 | 4.08 | 3.38 | 3.40 | 0.74 | 1.66 |

keys: volume: billions; *gdp: as % o of GDP; ac: annual change; cr: current prices; cs: constant prices; id: international dollars; nc: national currency; pc: per capita; usd: US Dollar.

# TAIWAN DATASET (1)

| | | 1951 | 1952 | 1953 | 1954 | 1955 | 1956 | 1957 | 1958 | 1959 | 1960 | 1961 | 1962 | 1963 | 1964 | 1965 | 1966 | 1967 | 1968 | 1969 | 1970 | 1971 | 1972 | 1973 | 1974 |
|---|---|---|---|---|---|---|---|---|---|---|---|---|---|---|---|---|---|---|---|---|---|---|---|---|---|
| **1.** | **GROSS DOMESTIC PRODUCT (GDP)** | | | | | | | | | | | | | | | | | | | | | | | | |
| 1.1 | pc. usd, cr | 145 | 196 | 167 | 177 | 203 | 141 | 160 | 173 | 132 | 142 | 151 | 162 | 178 | 202 | 218 | 237 | 268 | 305 | 345 | 426 | 483 | 551 | 691 | 912 |
| 1.2 | pc. id, cr | 997 | 1,078 | 1,141 | 1,209 | 1,260 | 1,279 | 1,330 | 1,374 | 1,430 | 1,468 | 1,525 | 1,597 | 1,697 | 1,849 | 1,998 | 2,117 | 2,278 | 2,421 | 2,581 | 2,899 | 3,112 | 3,461 | 3,828 | 3,791 |
| 1.3 | ac. nc, cs | | 11.98 | 9.33 | 9.54 | 8.11 | 5.50 | 7.36 | 6.71 | 7.65 | 6.31 | 6.88 | 5.90 | 9.35 | 12.20 | 11.13 | 8.91 | 10.71 | 9.17 | 8.95 | 11.52 | 12.77 | 13.25 | 12.87 | 1.16 |
| 1.4.1 | Agri (°egdp,nc,cr) | 32.28 | 31.42 | 30.57 | 29.71 | 28.86 | 28.00 | 27.00 | 27.00 | 29.00 | 28.34 | 27.45 | 25.00 | 23.48 | 24.78 | 23.62 | 22.54 | 20.57 | 19.01 | 15.90 | 15.48 | 13.07 | 12.51 | 12.11 | 12.43 |
| 1.4.2 | Manuf(°egdp,nc,cr) | 21.33 | 21.85 | 22.90 | 22.90 | 23.43 | 23.95 | 24.47 | 25.00 | 25.52 | 26.05 | 26.57 | 27.81 | 29.04 | 30.28 | 31.52 | 32.76 | 33.99 | 35.23 | 36.47 | 37.70 | 38.9 | 39.59 | 40.25 | 40.90 |
| **2.** | **INTERNATIONAL TRADE** | | | | | | | | | | | | | | | | | | | | | | | | |
| 2.1.1 | Exports (ac, usd,cr) | 35.5 | 18.4 | 9.6 | -26.9 | 32.3 | -4.0 | 25.2 | 5.1 | 0.6 | 4.6 | 22.6 | 9.7 | 50.5 | 30.7 | 3.5 | 19.4 | 19.3 | 25.3 | 30.8 | 36.1 | 39.9 | 45.8 | 50.4 | 25.9 |
| 2.1.2 | Imports (ac,usd,cr) | 21.8 | 39.6 | 2.7 | 9.9 | -4.7 | -3.5 | 9.3 | 6.6 | 2.7 | 28.0 | 8.4 | -7.8 | 22.2 | 18.5 | 29.5 | 11.7 | 29.9 | 12.1 | 34.2 | 25.7 | 21.0 | 36.2 | 51.0 | 83.7 |
| 2.2.1 | Exports(°egdp,nc,cr) | 10.19 | 8.03 | 8.64 | 6.48 | 8.26 | 9.04 | 9.68 | 10.43 | 12.68 | 11.51 | 14.00 | 13.61 | 17.92 | 19.98 | 19.33 | 21.84 | 22.14 | 24.29 | 26.88 | 27.66 | 32.54 | 39.85 | 47.27 | 43.85 |
| 2.2.2 | Imports(°egdp,nc,cr) | 14.89 | 14.14 | 13.81 | 14.85 | 12.58 | 15.89 | 14.80 | 16.80 | 20.94 | 19.03 | 21.09 | 18.94 | 19.07 | 19.22 | 22.32 | 21.56 | 24.19 | 27.13 | 27.60 | 27.70 | 30.29 | 33.92 | 41.91 | 51.68 |
| 2.3 | E/I Ratio (nc, cr) | 0.73 | 0.62 | 0.67 | 0.44 | 0.61 | 0.61 | 0.70 | 0.69 | 0.68 | 0.55 | 0.63 | 0.74 | 0.92 | 1.01 | 0.81 | 0.86 | 0.79 | 0.89 | 0.86 | 0.93 | 1.08 | 1.16 | 1.15 | 0.79 |
| **3.** | **SUPPLY AND DEMAND** | | | | | | | | | | | | | | | | | | | | | | | | |
| 3.1 | GFCF (°egdp, nc, cr) | 14.43 | 15.32 | 14.04 | 16.04 | 13.34 | 16.05 | 15.82 | 16.58 | 18.78 | 20.19 | 19.96 | 17.80 | 18.28 | 18.72 | 22.68 | 21.22 | 24.61 | 25.09 | 24.50 | 23.29 | 24.00 | 24.12 | 29.08 | 39.18 |
| 3.2 | Invest(ac, nc, cs) | | 28.9 | 17.3 | 10.0 | -15.2 | 13.4 | 24.5 | 10.7 | 27.5 | 28.8 | 4.0 | 2.3 | 19.6 | 11.7 | 27.9 | 7.7 | 31.3 | 17.1 | 9.2 | 19.7 | | 13.3 | 18.7 | 30.0 |
| 3.3 | Invest-(°egdp-id-cr) | 8.94 | 10.25 | 10.88 | 10.97 | 8.56 | 9.61 | 9.01 | 9.30 | 11.20 | 13.27 | 12.69 | 11.54 | 12.18 | 11.87 | 14.03 | 13.53 | 16.02 | 16.96 | 16.75 | 17.78 | 18.41 | 17.87 | 19.13 | 26.63 |
| 3.4 | Invest. (pc, id, cr) | 16.15 | 20.84 | 23.88 | 25.21 | 20.90 | 23.85 | 24.25 | 26.59 | 33.51 | 41.89 | 42.37 | 41.45 | 48.50 | 53.20 | 67.10 | 71.93 | 94.27 | 110.82 | 124.16 | 151.65 | 183.42 | 209.04 | 256.49 | 361.32 |
| 3.5 | Consp.(°egdp, nc, cr) | 90.25 | 90.79 | 91.10 | 92.34 | 90.99 | 90.80 | 89.31 | 89.78 | 89.49 | 87.33 | 87.13 | 87.54 | 82.87 | 80.52 | 80.31 | 78.51 | 77.44 | 77.76 | 76.23 | 68.01 | 65.24 | 64.07 | 65.61 | 68.57 |
| 3.6.1 | Consp.Gov. (°egdp) | 17.84 | 17.00 | 15.52 | 18.28 | 18.86 | 20.37 | 20.77 | 20.73 | 20.25 | 19.25 | 19.25 | 20.01 | 18.75 | 17.44 | 16.87 | 17.36 | 17.50 | 17.85 | 18.38 | 18.66 | 15.78 | 15.19 | 15.19 | 14.10 |
| 3.6.2 | Consp.Prj.(°egdp) | 72.41 | 73.79 | 75.58 | 74.06 | 72.12 | 70.43 | 69.14 | 69.01 | 68.76 | 68.08 | 67.88 | 67.53 | 64.08 | 63.07 | 63.44 | 61.15 | 59.94 | 59.91 | 57.84 | 51.35 | 49.46 | 48.96 | 50.41 | 54.47 |
| 3.7 | Consp (ac, nc, cs) | | 15.8 | 9.4 | 9.9 | 6.0 | 1.1 | 6.7 | 7.3 | 5.4 | 5.1 | 8.8 | 8.5 | 7.8 | 14.5 | 10.9 | 6.5 | 9.7 | 9.1 | 7.5 | 9.5 | 10.7 | 12.3 | 12.1 | 5.3 |
| 3.8 | Consp (pc, id, cr) | 133 | 151 | 162 | 174 | 178 | 178 | 190 | 204 | 211 | 217 | 231 | 246 | 259 | 292 | 319 | 341 | 374 | 414 | 454 | 510 | 576 | 657 | 757 | 850 |
| **4.** | **MONEY AND CURRENCY** | | | | | | | | | | | | | | | | | | | | | | | | |
| 4.1 | M1+2 (°egdp, nc, cr) | | | | | | | | | | | 35.84 | 50.82 | 61.11 | 66.13 | 72.40 | 75.90 | 75.27 | 72.91 | 70.09 | 61.19 | 67.67 | 91.20 | 108.88 | 106.85 |
| 4.2 | For.Exch.Reser.(usd) | | | | | | | | | | | | | | | | | | | | | | | | |
| 4.3 | Savings(°egdp, id, cr) | 4.24 | 4.15 | 5.72 | 2.61 | 4.25 | 2.75 | 3.89 | 2.92 | 2.94 | 5.75 | 5.61 | 6.21 | 11.04 | 12.63 | 11.03 | 13.81 | 13.97 | 14.12 | 16.02 | 17.73 | 20.87 | 24.18 | 24.49 | 18.79 |
| 4.4 | CPI (1995=100) | | | | | | | | | 12.9 | 15.3 | 16.5 | 16.9 | 17.3 | 17.2 | 17.2 | 17.6 | 18.2 | 19.6 | 20.6 | 21.3 | 21.9 | 22.6 | 24.4 | 36.0 |
| 5.3 | Change in CP (an %,s) | | | | | | | | | | 18.51 | 5.78 | 2.06 | 2.37 | -0.17 | -0.06 | 2.03 | 3.36 | 7.88 | 5.06 | 3.66 | 3.01 | 2.77 | 8.16 | 47.50 |
| 4.5 | Ex Rate (1usd: nc) | 10.30 | 10.3 | 15.55 | 15.55 | 15.55 | 24.78 | 24.78 | 24.78 | 36.38 | 36.38 | 40.00 | 40.00 | 40.00 | 40.00 | 40.00 | 40.00 | 40.00 | 40.00 | 40.00 | 40.00 | 40.00 | 40.00 | 38.25 | 38.00 |
| **5.** | **BALANCE OF PAYMENTS (usd, cr)** | | | | | | | | | | | | | | | | | | | | | | | | |
| 5.1 | Overall | | | | | | | | | | | | | | | | | | | | | | | | |
| 5.1.1 | Current | | | | | | | | | | | | | | | | | | | | | | | | -0.60 |
| 5.1.2 | Capital | | | | | | | | | | | | | | | | | | | | | | | | -1.11 |
| 5.1.3 | Financial | | | | | | | | | | | | | | | | | | | | | | | | 0.46 |
| **6.** | **PUBLIC FINANCE (nc, cr)** | | | | | | | | | | | | | | | | | | | | | | | | |
| 6.1 | Balance(°egdp, nc, cr) | | | | | | -0.53 | 0.46 | 0.36 | 0.07 | -0.14 | -0.06 | -0.49 | -0.71 | 0.55 | 0.87 | 1.07 | 0.62 | 1.32 | 1.61 | 0.83 | 0.87 | 0.80 | 2.38 | 4.70 |
| 6.2 | Exp Rev Ratio | | | | | | 1.02 | 0.98 | 0.98 | 1.01 | 1.01 | 1.04 | 1.03 | 1.04 | 0.97 | 0.96 | 0.95 | 0.97 | 0.94 | 0.96 | 0.96 | 0.93 | 0.96 | 0.89 | 0.73 |
| 6.3.1 | Revenue (°egdp) | 19.46 | 19.88 | 19.43 | 21.79 | 21.75 | 21.41 | 22.64 | 24.09 | 22.13 | 19.37 | 20.03 | 19.49 | 18.15 | 18.69 | 20.76 | 19.99 | 21.70 | 20.74 | 22.88 | 20.61 | 19.90 | 19.74 | 21.84 | 21.08 |
| 6.3.2 | Exp'ture (°egdp) | | | | | | 21.94 | 22.18 | 23.73 | 22.06 | 19.52 | 20.09 | 19.98 | 18.87 | 18.13 | 19.89 | 18.92 | 21.07 | 19.42 | 21.27 | 20.77 | 19.03 | 18.94 | 19.46 | 16.37 |
| 6.4.1 | Defence (°+tol exp) | 49.40 | 49.42 | 49.44 | 49.46 | 49.48 | 49.50 | 49.52 | 49.54 | 49.56 | 49.58 | 49.60 | 48.35 | 47.10 | 45.85 | 44.60 | 43.35 | 42.10 | 40.85 | 39.60 | 38.35 | 37.10 | 35.85 | 34.60 | 33.35 |
| 6.4.2 | Edu. & Health(°+) | 13.60 | 13.74 | 13.88 | 14.02 | 14.16 | 14.30 | 14.44 | 14.58 | 14.72 | 14.86 | 15.00 | 15.36 | 15.72 | 16.08 | 16.44 | 16.80 | 17.16 | 17.52 | 17.88 | 18.24 | 18.60 | 18.51 | 18.42 | 18.33 |
| 6.4.3 | Social Security(°+) | 6.90 | 6.87 | 6.84 | 6.81 | 6.78 | 6.75 | 6.72 | 6.69 | 6.66 | 6.63 | 6.60 | 7.03 | 7.46 | 7.89 | 8.32 | 8.75 | 9.18 | 9.61 | 10.04 | 10.47 | 10.90 | 11.01 | 11.12 | 11.23 |
| 6.4.4 | Econ. Affairs(°+) | 14.00 | 13.91 | 13.82 | 13.73 | 13.64 | 13.55 | 13.46 | 13.37 | 13.28 | 13.19 | 13.10 | 13.43 | 13.76 | 14.09 | 14.42 | 14.75 | 15.08 | 15.41 | 15.74 | 16.07 | 16.40 | 18.17 | 19.94 | 21.71 |
| 6.5.1 | Defence (°egdp) | 9.62 | 9.83 | 9.60 | 10.78 | 10.76 | 10.86 | 10.93 | 11.75 | 10.93 | 9.68 | 9.96 | 9.66 | 8.89 | 8.31 | 8.89 | 8.05 | 7.87 | 7.82 | 7.78 | 7.09 | 6.68 | 5.74 | 6.04 | 4.48 |
| 6.5.2 | Edu.& Health(°+) | 2.65 | 2.73 | 2.70 | 3.05 | 3.08 | 3.05 | 3.17 | 3.18 | 3.25 | 2.63 | 3.14 | 2.85 | 2.65 | 2.50 | 2.48 | 2.74 | 2.79 | 2.86 | 3.14 | 3.22 | 3.34 | 3.29 | 3.29 | 2.73 |
| 6.5.3 | Social Security(°+) | 1.34 | 1.37 | 1.33 | 1.48 | 1.47 | 1.54 | 1.35 | 1.62 | 1.47 | 1.34 | 1.34 | 1.45 | 1.64 | 1.47 | 1.47 | 0.89 | 1.51 | 1.52 | 1.89 | 1.90 | 1.97 | 2.41 | 2.11 | 1.77 |
| 6.5.4 | Econ. Affairs(°+) | 2.73 | 2.77 | 2.68 | 2.99 | 2.97 | 2.67 | 2.38 | 2.50 | 2.93 | 2.70 | 2.83 | 2.57 | 2.64 | 2.51 | 3.78 | 2.69 | 4.65 | 3.20 | 3.66 | 3.54 | 2.95 | 3.47 | 4.44 | 4.13 |
| **7.** | **COMPETITIVENESS** | | | | | | | | | | | | | | | | | | | | | | | | |
| 7.1 | M Wages Manuf(usd) | 2,363 | 2,597 | 2,786 | 2,976 | 3,113 | 3,172 | 3,332 | 3,485 | 3,673 | 3,842 | 3,980 | 4,154 | 4,416 | 4,815 | 5,211 | 5,509 | 5,933 | 6,296 | 6,693 | 7,282 | 8,026 | 8,874 | 9,755 | 9,642 |
| 7.2 | GDP per W,krrid,cs) | | | | | | | | | | | 3.90 | 3.72 | 3.68 | 3.65 | 3.54 | 3.43 | 3.20 | 3.09 | 2.96 | 2.78 | 3.35 | 3.14 | 3.14 | 3.07 |
| **8.** | **POPULATION** | | | | | | | | | | | | | | | | | | | | | | | | |
| 8.1 | urban(as) | | | | | | | | | | | | | | | | | | | | | | | | |

keys: volume: billions; °egdp: as % of GDP; ac: annual change; cr: constant prices; cs: current prices; id: international dollars; nc: national currency; pc: per capita; usd: US Dollar.

# TAIWAN DATA SET (2)

| | 1975 | 1976 | 1977 | 1978 | 1979 | 1980 | 1981 | 1982 | 1983 | 1984 | 1985 | 1986 | 1987 | 1988 | 1989 | 1990 | 1991 | 1992 | 1993 | 1994 | 1995 | 1996 | 1997 | 1998 | 1999 | 2000 |
|---|---|---|---|---|---|---|---|---|---|---|---|---|---|---|---|---|---|---|---|---|---|---|---|---|---|---|
| **1. GROSS DOMESTIC PRODUCT (GDP)** | | | | | | | | | | | | | | | | | | | | | | | | | | |
| 1.1 pe, usd, cr | 961 | 1,128 | 1,298 | 1,562 | 1,899 | 2,326 | 2,655 | 2,631 | 2,798 | 3,112 | 3,224 | 3,870 | 5,167 | 6,192 | 7,418 | 7,881 | 8,727 | 10,224 | 10,709 | 11,565 | 12,438 | 13,024 | 13,382 | 12,217 | 13,066 | 13,888 |
| 1.2 pe, id, cr | 3,920 | 4,364 | 4,711 | 5,265 | 5,573 | 5,850 | 6,107 | 6,232 | 6,672 | 7,257 | 7,530 | 8,325 | 9,260 | 9,850 | 10,570 | 10,995 | 11,710 | 12,433 | 13,211 | 14,035 | 14,784 | 15,589 | 16,434 | 17,056 | 17,827 | 18,665 |
| 1.3 ac, nc, cs | 4.93 | 13.86 | 10.19 | 13.59 | 8.17 | 7.30 | 6.16 | 3.55 | 8.45 | 10.60 | 4.95 | 11.64 | 12.74 | 7.84 | 8.23 | 5.39 | 7.55 | 7.01 | 7.11 | 6.42 | 6.10 | 6.68 | 4.57 | 5.42 | 5.86 | 2.09 |
| 1.4.1 Agri (*ygdp,nc,cr) | 12.70 | 11.37 | 10.60 | 9.38 | 8.55 | 7.69 | 7.30 | 7.74 | 7.30 | 6.33 | 5.78 | 5.55 | 5.31 | 5.04 | 4.90 | 4.18 | 3.79 | 3.60 | 3.64 | 3.51 | 3.48 | 3.19 | 2.55 | 2.47 | 2.56 | 2.09 |
| 1.4.2 Manuf(*ygdp,nc,cr) | 41.55 | 42.21 | 42.86 | 43.51 | 44.16 | 44.82 | 45.47 | 45.67 | 46.08 | 46.08 | 46.68 | 47.11 | 45.31 | 44.84 | 44.23 | 41.23 | 41.07 | 40.08 | 39.35 | 37.71 | 36.38 | 35.71 | 35.32 | 34.57 | 33.18 | 32.38 |
| **2. INTERNATIONAL TRADE** | | | | | | | | | | | | | | | | | | | | | | | | | | |
| 2.1.1 Exports (ac, usd,cr) | -3.9 | 53.8 | 14.6 | 35.7 | 26.8 | 23.0 | 13.7 | -1.9 | 13.6 | 21.3 | 0.8 | 29.5 | 35.4 | 12.4 | 9.4 | 1.3 | 13.5 | 6.9 | 6.8 | 9.7 | 20.1 | 3.7 | 4.6 | -8.7 | 9.9 | 21.6 |
| 2.1.2 Imports (ac,usd,cr) | -14.7 | 27.7 | 12.0 | 29.7 | 33.9 | 33.6 | 7.0 | -11.0 | 7.9 | 8.3 | -8.5 | 20.4 | 43.6 | 43.0 | 5.5 | 4.4 | 15.0 | 14.4 | 6.8 | 10.9 | 21.3 | -2.3 | 12.5 | -7.9 | 5.7 | 26.1 |
| 2.2.1 Exports(*ygdp,ac,cr) | 39.68 | 47.48 | 48.97 | 52.34 | 53.35 | 52.51 | 51.92 | 50.11 | 52.86 | 56.34 | 54.17 | 58.14 | 57.46 | 54.21 | 46.67 | 46.79 | 47.39 | 43.45 | 42.41 | 43.63 | 48.02 | 47.41 | 48.27 | 47.77 | 47.34 | 45.53 |
| 2.2.2 Imports(*ygdp,nc,cr) | 42.91 | 45.36 | 44.03 | 45.89 | 52.18 | 53.72 | 49.89 | 45.00 | 44.43 | 45.24 | 40.42 | 38.18 | 39.85 | 43.71 | 42.14 | 41.79 | 42.82 | 41.77 | 41.10 | 41.93 | 46.31 | 44.02 | 46.11 | 46.76 | 45.53 | 22.48 |
| 2.3 ET Ratio (nc, cr) | 0.89 | 1.07 | 1.10 | 1.13 | 1.09 | 1.00 | 1.06 | 1.11 | 1.24 | 1.38 | 1.33 | 1.64 | 1.38 | 1.23 | 1.21 | 1.13 | 1.21 | 1.13 | 1.10 | 1.09 | 1.08 | 1.14 | 1.05 | 1.05 | 1.09 | 1.06 |
| **3. SUPPLY AND DEMAND** | | | | | | | | | | | | | | | | | | | | | | | | | | |
| 3.1 GFCF (*ygdp, nc, cr) | 30.36 | 30.55 | 28.10 | 28.20 | 32.90 | 33.80 | 29.87 | 25.22 | 23.47 | 22.17 | 19.05 | 17.54 | 19.23 | 20.82 | 22.08 | 22.42 | 22.17 | 24.14 | 25.17 | 24.58 | 24.95 | 22.50 | 22.76 | 23.54 | 22.87 | 23.46 |
| 3.2 Invest (ac, nc, cs) | -9.3 | 15.2 | 5.4 | 15.1 | 19.8 | 8.5 | 1.2 | -7.1 | 2.5 | 6.0 | -7.4 | 6.3 | 30.1 | 21.3 | 7.6 | 5.0 | 11.4 | 18.8 | 10.8 | 6.5 | 4.9 | 3.5 | 14.0 | 7.9 | 10.0 | 7.5 |
| 3.3 Invest(*ygdp-id-cr) | 22.71 | 22.28 | 20.95 | 21.47 | 24.11 | 24.92 | 23.42 | 20.77 | 19.18 | 17.81 | 15.48 | 14.22 | 16.54 | 19.18 | 19.12 | 18.71 | 19.64 | 21.20 | 21.89 | 21.77 | 21.63 | 20.63 | 21.83 | 21.96 | 22.80 | 23.17 |
| 3.4 Invest_(pc, id, cr,) | 360.41 | 424.08 | 458.29 | 554.35 | 702 | 809 | 862 | 892 | 939 | 887 | 949 | 1,248 | 1,554 | 1,810 | 1,903 | 2,103 | 2,447 | 2,750 | 2,933 | 3,102 | 3,216 | 3,673 | 3,896 | 4,303 | 4,602 |  |
| 3.5 Consp (*ygdp, nc, cr) | 72.91 | 67.29 | 67.02 | 65.35 | 65.97 | 67.40 | 68.09 | 69.63 | 67.89 | 66.63 | 67.14 | 62.67 | 62.05 | 65.60 | 69.06 | 71.94 | 72.18 | 72.70 | 72.19 | 72.95 | 73.01 | 73.42 | 73.64 | 73.99 | 74.11 | 74.80 |
| 3.6.1 Consp.Gov.(*ygdp) | 15.78 | 15.19 | 15.54 | 15.16 | 15.43 | 15.91 | 16.11 | 16.88 | 16.26 | 15.87 | 16.14 | 14.81 | 14.40 | 15.05 | 15.65 | 17.17 | 17.39 | 16.73 | 15.65 | 14.57 | 14.24 | 14.30 | 14.32 | 14.32 | 13.15 | 12.90 |
| 3.6.2 Consp.Pri.(*ygdp) | 57.13 | 52.10 | 51.48 | 50.19 | 50.55 | 51.49 | 51.98 | 52.75 | 51.69 | 50.76 | 51.00 | 47.86 | 47.65 | 50.56 | 53.41 | 54.76 | 54.78 | 55.96 | 56.57 | 58.38 | 58.77 | 59.13 | 59.27 | 59.67 | 60.95 | 61.90 |
| 3.7 Consp (ac, nc, cs) | 5.2 | 9.5 | 7.3 | 11.0 | 10.8 | 4.9 | 5.2 | 5.9 | 7.5 | 8.1 | 8.3 | 8.3 | 7.5 | 8.9 | 6.0 | 6.3 | 5.8 | | | | | | | | | |
| 3.8 Consp (pc, id, cr) | 967 | 1,090 | 1,211 | 1,405 | 1,655 | 1,867 | 2,094 | 2,317 | 2,558 | 2,858 | 3,091 | 3,385 | 3,869 | 4,468 | 5,160 | 5,721 | 6,367 | 7,059 | 7,721 | 8,438 | 9,014 | 9,741 | 10,560 | 11,343 | 12,174 | 13,004 |
| **4. MONEY AND CURRENCY** | | | | | | | | | | | | | | | | | | | | | | | | | | |
| 4.1 M1=2 (*ygdp, nc, cr) | 123.39 | 122.64 | 121.62 | 115.83 | 107.78 | 95.86 | 88.48 | 105.88 | 116.84 | 123.59 | 134.93 | 151.52 | 169.56 | 189.25 | 194.22 | 188.70 | 198.75 | 210.52 | 219.10 | 229.63 | 227.54 | 226.62 | 225.84 | 226.44 | 239.53 | 242.05 |
| 4.2 For.Exch.Reser.(usd) | 19.49 | 24.40 | 25.89 | 27.92 | 25.28 | 23.72 | 7.24 | 11.07 | 14.90 | 18.73 | 23 | 46 | 77 | 74 | 72 | 72 | 82 | 82 | 84 | 92 | 90 | 88 | 84 | 90 | 106 | 107 |
| 4.3 Savings(*ygdp, id, cr) | 37.9 | 38.8 | 41.6 | 43.9 | 48.2 | 57.4 | 25.45 | 25.89 | 27.61 | 28.92 | 29.24 | 34.12 | 34.12 | 29.71 | 26.51 | 23.59 | 24.21 | 22.89 | 23.58 | 23.47 | 23.34 | 24.01 | 27.46 | 23.98 | 26.29 | 25.80 |
| 4.4 CPI (1995=100) | 37.9 | 38.8 | 41.6 | 43.9 | 48.2 | 57.4 | 66.8 | 68.8 | 69.7 | 69.6 | 70.0 | 71.3 | 74.5 | 75.5 | 77.5 | 80.3 | 83.9 | 86.4 | 89.9 | 93.2 | 96.1 | 97.0 | 98.6 | 98.8 | 98.8 | 100.0 |
| 4.5 Change in CP (an *,a) | 5.22 | 5.25 | 7.06 | 5.75 | 9.76 | 19.01 | 16.32 | 2.97 | 1.35 | -0.03 | 0.70 | 0.51 | 1.28 | 4.42 | 4.12 | 3.62 | 4.47 | 2.94 | 4.10 | 3.67 | 3.08 | 0.89 | 1.69 | 0.17 | 1.26 |  |
| 4.5 Ex Rate (usd, nc) | 38.00 | 38.00 | 38.00 | 36.95 | 36.00 | 36.00 | 36.79 | 39.12 | 40.06 | 39.62 | 39.86 | 37.85 | 31.87 | 28.61 | 26.41 | 26.89 | 26.82 | 25.16 | 26.39 | 26.46 | 26.49 | 27.46 | 28.70 | 33.46 | 31.40 | 32.99 |
| **5. BALANCE OF PAYMENTS (usd, cr)** | | | | | | | | | | | | | | | | | | | | | | | | | | |
| 5.1 Overall | -0.44 | -0.28 | -0.12 | 0.04 | 1.70 | 0.36 | 0.52 | 2.69 | 4.86 | 7.03 | 9.20 | 16.29 | 18.00 | 10.20 | 11.42 | 10.92 | 9.66 | 1.37 | -1.54 | -4.62 | -3.93 | -1.10 | -0.73 | -4.83 | 18.59 | 2.48 |
| 5.1.1 Current | -0.95 | 1.63 | 2.22 | 2.80 | 0.20 | -0.161 | 3.97 | 8.55 | 12.47 | 8.55 | 12.47 | 10.92 | -0.44 | -0.39 | -0.03 | -0.16 | -0.44 | -0.39 | -0.04 | -0.34 | -0.65 | 10.92 | -0.31 | 3.44 | 8.38 | 8.91 |
| 5.1.2 Capital | 1.05 | 1.63 | 2.22 | 2.80 | 3.39 | 3.97 | 4.56 | 2.62 | 0.69 | -1.24 | -3.17 | 6.94 | 10.46 | 11.45 | -0.03 | -0.16 | -0.44 | -0.39 | -0.33 | -0.34 | -0.65 | -0.65 | -0.31 | -0.18 | -0.17 | -0.29 |
| 5.1.3 Financial | 1.05 | 1.63 | 2.22 | 2.80 | 3.39 | 3.97 | 4.56 | 2.62 | 0.69 | -1.24 | -3.17 | 6.94 | 10.46 | -12.13 | -15.15 | -2.23 | -6.91 | -0.44 | -1.63 | -1.40 | -8.19 | -8.63 | -7.29 | 2.50 | 9.22 | -3.02 |
| **6. PUBLIC FINANCE (nc, cr)** | | | | | | | | | | | | | | | | | | | | | | | | | | |
| 6.1 Balance *ygdp, nc, cr) | 1.29 | 2.30 | 1.49 | 0.64 | 1.81 | 1.63 | 0.98 | 0.18 | 0.54 | 1.19 | -0.15 | -1.12 | 0.26 | 1.10 | -0.78 | -3.92 | -4.69 | -5.70 | -5.74 | -5.01 | -5.00 | -3.12 | -2.09 | 0.68 | -0.49 | -3.68 |
| 6.2 Exp Rev Ratio | 0.94 | 0.94 | 0.97 | 0.92 | 0.92 | 0.93 | 0.95 | 0.99 | 0.98 | 0.95 | 1.01 | 1.05 | 0.99 | 0.95 | 1.31 | 1.00 | 1.21 | 1.22 | 1.24 | 1.22 | 1.22 | 1.15 | 1.10 | 0.97 | 1.02 | 1.13 |
| 6.3.1 Revenue (*ygdp) | 22.73 | 23.47 | 23.38 | 23.56 | 24.04 | 24.74 | 24.67 | 25.83 | 23.86 | 22.80 | 21.93 | 20.48 | 20.09 | 21.72 | 23.40 | 25.36 | 21.82 | 23.56 | 23.93 | 23.25 | 22.22 | 24.01 | 20.47 | 22.97 | 21.58 | 28.82 |
| 6.3.2 Exp.Fianc (*gdp) | 21.44 | 21.17 | 21.89 | 22.93 | 22.12 | 23.11 | 24.00 | 25.65 | 24.70 | 24.75 | 22.08 | 21.60 | 19.83 | 20.62 | 30.65 | 25.48 | 26.52 | 29.25 | 29.68 | 27.22 | 22.90 | 24.01 | 22.56 | 22.07 | 22.07 | 32.50 |
| 6.4.1 Defence (* tot exp) | 32.10 | 30.85 | 29.60 | 28.35 | 27.10 | 25.85 | 24.60 | 24.65 | 24.70 | 24.75 | 24.80 | 24.90 | 23.20 | 22.10 | 15.60 | 19.20 | 17.80 | 15.30 | 14.40 | 17.60 | 14.10 | 15.50 | 15.70 | 15.70 | 14.00 | 11.40 |
| 6.4.2 Edu. & Health(*,) | 18.24 | 18.15 | 18.06 | 17.97 | 17.88 | 17.79 | 17.70 | 18.38 | 19.05 | 19.73 | 20.40 | 20.90 | 20.80 | 20.30 | 17.00 | 20.70 | 22.60 | 20.80 | 19.90 | 20.90 | 18.70 | 20.30 | 20.00 | 20.70 | 20.90 | 20.90 |
| 6.4.3 Social Security(*,) | 11.34 | 11.45 | 11.56 | 11.67 | 11.78 | 11.89 | 12.00 | 13.05 | 14.10 | 15.15 | 16.20 | 16.10 | 16.10 | 18.20 | 12.70 | 18.60 | 18.80 | 18.80 | 18.20 | 19.20 | 21.70 | 26.90 | 28.90 | 27.40 | 26.90 | 28.70 |
| 6.4.4 Econ. Affairs(*,) | 23.48 | 25.25 | 27.02 | 28.79 | 30.56 | 32.33 | 34.10 | 31.90 | 29.70 | 27.50 | 25.30 | 25.10 | 26.70 | 26.50 | 44.80 | 27.50 | 29.60 | 29.60 | 31.10 | 25.60 | 22.90 | 17.90 | 15.70 | 16.80 | 17.10 | 15.10 |
| 6.5.1 Defence (*ygdp) | 5.13 | 5.23 | 5.67 | 5.89 | 6.30 | 6.92 | 5.90 | 6.30 | 6.39 | 5.27 | 5.47 | 5.38 | 4.66 | 4.56 | 4.78 | 4.89 | 4.72 | 4.48 | 4.27 | 4.97 | 3.84 | 3.72 | 3.50 | 3.50 | 3.09 | 3.71 |
| 6.5.2 Edu.& Health(*,) | 3.52 | 3.36 | 3.41 | 3.93 | 3.85 | 5.21 | 4.25 | 3.32 | 3.37 | 3.12 | 4.51 | 4.51 | 4.12 | 4.19 | 5.21 | 5.27 | 5.90 | 6.08 | 5.91 | 5.91 | 5.91 | 4.87 | 4.51 | 4.61 | 4.61 | 6.79 |
| 6.5.3 Social Security(*,) | 2.15 | 2.39 | 2.46 | 2.43 | 2.56 | 2.89 | 3.78 | 3.48 | 3.50 | 3.48 | 3.51 | 4.51 | 4.12 | 3.19 | 3.89 | 5.27 | 4.98 | 5.50 | 5.40 | 5.43 | 5.91 | 6.46 | 6.52 | 6.11 | 5.94 | 9.33 |
| 6.5.4 Econ. Affairs(*,) | 6.36 | 6.73 | 8.05 | 7.19 | 6.48 | 7.30 | 8.19 | 7.76 | 5.77 | 5.92 | 5.59 | 5.42 | 5.29 | 5.46 | 13.73 | 7.01 | 8.66 | 8.66 | 9.23 | 7.23 | 6.23 | 4.30 | 3.54 | 3.74 | 3.77 | 4.91 |
| **7. COMPETITIVENESS** | | | | | | | | | | | | | | | | | | | | | | | | | | |
| 7.1 M Wages Manuf(usd) | 90 | 106 | 128 | 147 | 182 | 223 | 260 | 268 | 278 | 307 | 319 | 369 | 482 | 595 | 737 | 820 | 912 | 1,073 | 1,094 | 1,164 | 1,229 | 1,235 | 1,235 | 1,089 | 1,200 | 1,146 |
| 7.2 GDP per W.tent(d,es) | 9,860 | 10,913 | 11,691 | 13,670 | 14,751 | 14,897 | 15,800 | 17,033 | 17,507 | 19,275 | 21,377 | 22,660 | 24,206 | 25,076 | 28,383 | 30,163 | 32,045 | 35,592 | 37,521 | 38,941 | 40,700 | 42,234 | | | | |
| **8. POPULATION** | | | | | | | | | | | | | | | | | | | | | | | | | | |
| 8.1 urban(ac) | 3.08 | 2.17 | 2.16 | 2.00 | 2.09 | 2.05 | 2.20 | 2.16 | 1.97 | 1.82 | 1.73 | 1.52 | 1.43 | 1.50 | 1.46 | 1.48 | 2.95 | 2.78 | 2.71 | 2.64 | 2.57 | 2.50 | 2.54 | 2.55 | 3.06 | 2.41 |

keys: volume: billions; *ygdp: as % of GDP: ac: annual change: cr: current prices: cs: constant prices: nd: international dollars: nc: national currency: pc: per capita: usd: US Dollar.

# Appendix B
EAE and OECDE comparative data

| EAE/OECDE DATA(I) | 1951 | 1952 | 1953 | 1954 | 1955 | 1956 | 1957 | 1958 | 1959 | 1960 | 1961 | 1962 | 1963 | 1964 | 1965 | 1966 | 1967 | 1968 | 1969 | 1970 | 1971 | 1972 | 1973 | 1974 |
|---|---|---|---|---|---|---|---|---|---|---|---|---|---|---|---|---|---|---|---|---|---|---|---|---|
| **1 Gross Domestic Product Annual Change 1951-2000 (pc, nc, cs)** | | | | | | | | | | | | | | | | | | | | | | | | |
| EAEs | | 22.97 | 16.76 | 9.97 | 9.29 | 7.06 | 6.66 | 10.13 | 7.42 | 5.32 | 0.96 | 4.19 | 9.42 | 9.36 | 9.48 | 14.02 | 4.07 | 8.72 | 13.33 | 11.73 | 9.01 | 8.90 | 11.60 | 3.66 |
| OECDEs | | 3.98 | 5.60 | 4.04 | 6.09 | 4.57 | 3.78 | 1.58 | 4.67 | 6.13 | 5.42 | 4.81 | 5.20 | 6.52 | 4.90 | 4.14 | 3.72 | 4.74 | 6.21 | 5.15 | 4.41 | 5.26 | 5.91 | 2.52 |
| **2 Gross Domestic Product Per capita Annual Change 1962-2000 (pc, nc, cs)** | | | | | | | | | | | | | | | | | | | | | | | | |
| EAEs | | | | | | | | | | | | 1.56 | 6.60 | 6.78 | 7.49 | 11.23 | 1.69 | 6.36 | 10.92 | -0.74 | 6.71 | 6.82 | 9.50 | 1.86 |
| OECDEs | | | | | | | | | | | | 4.42 | 3.80 | 4.19 | 5.33 | 3.79 | 3.36 | 3.07 | 3.82 | 5.01 | 3.69 | 4.25 | 4.96 | 2.28 |
| **3 Savings as Percent of GDP 1951-2000 (pc, cr, usd)** | | | | | | | | | | | | | | | | | | | | | | | | |
| EAEs | 14.75 | 10.27 | 9.66 | 9.29 | 9.34 | 8.71 | 11.03 | 11.73 | 13.28 | 12.00 | 14.62 | 12.97 | 16.73 | 16.74 | 18.75 | 21.16 | 20.86 | 22.76 | 23.20 | 24.83 | 25.53 | 26.64 | 28.70 | 26.63 |
| OECDEs | 22.30 | 22.68 | 22.93 | 22.81 | 24.05 | 24.92 | 25.64 | 24.87 | 25.48 | 26.74 | 27.22 | 26.19 | 25.81 | 27.49 | 27.80 | 27.55 | 27.44 | 26.80 | 27.84 | 28.43 | 27.54 | 27.82 | 28.83 | 27.09 |
| **4 Exports Annual Change 1951-2000 (pc, usd)** | | | | | | | | | | | | | | | | | | | | | | | | |
| EAEs | 48.25 | -2.52 | 11.44 | -5.14 | 15.77 | 15.75 | 13.25 | -3.95 | 17.94 | 12.78 | 5.17 | 12.87 | 24.87 | 15.87 | 19.83 | 19.41 | 9.32 | 20.24 | 23.26 | 17.24 | 25.14 | 35.27 | 60.38 | 38.86 |
| OECDEs | 35.76 | 0.59 | 1.99 | 7.77 | 8.85 | 9.94 | 9.09 | -0.58 | 5.12 | 14.67 | 6.65 | 5.99 | 9.55 | 13.77 | 10.07 | 11.45 | 6.10 | 8.36 | 16.69 | 17.83 | 9.87 | 22.48 | 39.87 | 31.19 |
| WORLD | 27.48 | -6.38 | -0.54 | 4.37 | 18.06 | 11.04 | 8.71 | -3.97 | 6.91 | 10.98 | 3.96 | 4.70 | 9.39 | 11.70 | 8.88 | 9.39 | 4.96 | 11.30 | 14.40 | 14.77 | 12.13 | 18.34 | 38.86 | 47.04 |
| **5 Exports Share of World Total 1951-2000 (pc, usd)** | | | | | | | | | | | | | | | | | | | | | | | | |
| EAEs | 4.82 | 4.51 | 4.55 | 4.94 | 5.17 | 5.41 | 5.86 | 6.50 | 7.09 | 6.42 | 5.82 | 6.09 | 6.10 | 6.28 | 7.01 | 7.28 | 7.22 | 7.55 | 8.22 | 8.42 | 9.33 | 9.85 | 9.73 | 9.57 |
| OECDEs | 50.22 | 53.00 | 51.89 | 51.99 | 55.45 | 49.16 | 57.52 | 56.74 | 56.31 | 58.59 | 59.43 | 59.32 | 58.75 | 59.62 | 59.13 | 59.61 | 60.13 | 60.79 | 60.53 | 61.03 | 60.22 | 60.19 | 59.47 | 53.90 |
| **6 Export/GDP ratio 1951-2000 (pc, cr, usd, EAEs-NS: EAEs without Singapore)** | | | | | | | | | | | | | | | | | | | | | | | | |
| EAEs | | | | | | | | | | | 39.85 | 34.91 | 32.58 | 27.57 | 27.16 | 27.50 | 25.91 | 25.78 | 27.28 | 26.19 | 27.47 | 29.44 | 34.00 | 38.08 |
| EAEs-NS | 10.71 | 6.98 | 5.46 | 4.57 | 6.64 | 6.25 | 6.85 | 6.66 | 6.81 | 6.12 | 6.26 | 6.44 | 7.34 | 8.13 | 8.66 | 9.10 | 9.03 | 9.70 | 10.49 | 11.17 | 13.04 | 15.77 | 19.49 | 19.74 |
| OECDEs | 18.82 | 17.35 | 16.73 | 16.23 | 16.03 | 16.24 | 16.48 | 15.82 | 15.77 | 20.71 | 17.06 | 16.56 | 16.68 | 19.55 | 16.66 | 16.67 | 16.26 | 19.90 | 21.21 | 20.98 | 19.53 | 19.83 | 21.72 | 24.81 |
| **7 Adjusted Net Saving as Percent of GDP 1970-2000 (pc, cr, usd)** | | | | | | | | | | | | | | | | | | | | | | | | |
| EAEs | | | | | | | | | | | | | | | | | | | | 13.53 | 13.80 | 17.30 | 19.92 | 16.78 |
| OECDEs | | | | | | | | | | | | | | | | | | | | 10.06 | 9.24 | 12.58 | 13.63 | 14.48 |
| **8 Real Investment as Percent of GDP 1950-2000 (pc, cr, id, KOST: Korea, Singapore, Taiwan)** | | | | | | | | | | | | | | | | | | | | | | | | |
| KOST | | 8.94 | 10.25 | 13.33 | 11.76 | 10.48 | 10.66 | 12.65 | 11.56 | 10.70 | 16.09 | 19.26 | 15.78 | 20.11 | 18.37 | 24.10 | 25.91 | 27.22 | 29.78 | 30.13 | 33.15 | 33.95 | 31.44 | 32.36 |
| EAEs | 17.26 | 16.14 | 12.54 | 13.59 | 13.24 | 12.61 | 13.44 | 15.36 | 15.12 | 16.90 | 19.07 | 19.69 | 16.52 | 19.82 | 19.32 | 22.91 | 24.42 | 25.03 | 26.95 | 27.48 | 30.67 | 30.84 | 29.10 | 30.17 |
| OECDEs | 24.53 | 24.12 | 22.40 | 23.78 | 23.93 | 25.14 | 25.86 | 26.53 | 25.50 | 26.47 | 27.53 | 28.43 | 27.64 | 27.77 | 29.53 | 29.61 | 29.13 | 28.55 | 27.79 | 28.17 | 28.81 | 28.69 | 28.03 | 29.45 |
| **9 Total physical cap. stock as Percent of GDP 1951-1990 (pc, cs, nc)** | | | | | | | | | | | | | | | | | | | | | | | | |
| EAEs | 0.88 | 0.71 | 0.72 | 0.71 | 0.74 | 0.76 | 0.79 | 0.83 | 0.86 | 0.89 | 1.16 | 1.40 | 1.49 | 1.43 | 1.41 | 1.39 | 1.37 | 1.46 | 1.56 | 1.52 | 1.52 | 1.61 | 1.69 | 1.73 |
| OECDEs | 2.11 | 2.13 | 2.15 | 2.14 | 2.16 | 2.17 | 2.20 | 2.25 | 2.32 | 2.35 | 2.35 | 2.37 | 2.40 | 2.42 | 2.43 | 2.47 | 2.52 | 2.58 | 2.61 | 2.60 | 2.63 | 2.67 | 2.68 | 2.69 |
| **10 Gross Fixed Capital Formation as Percent of GDP (pc, cr, nc)** | | | | | | | | | | | | | | | | | | | | | | | | |
| EAEs | 14.43 | 15.92 | 15.62 | 16.94 | 15.75 | 19.15 | 18.85 | 21.25 | 23.61 | 24.66 | 21.43 | 20.91 | 21.66 | 22.81 | 23.25 | 24.17 | 24.08 | 25.04 | 27.04 | 29.99 | 30.10 | 29.94 | 30.47 | 32.06 |
| OECDEs | 16.99 | 18.50 | 18.72 | 19.22 | 19.81 | 20.27 | 20.76 | 20.70 | 21.01 | 21.53 | 21.98 | 22.37 | 22.93 | 23.69 | 23.31 | 23.65 | 23.54 | 23.20 | 23.02 | 23.63 | 24.59 | 24.70 | 25.01 | 24.73 |
| **11 Real Consumption as Percent of GDP 1951-2000 (pc, id)** | | | | | | | | | | | | | | | | | | | | | | | | |
| KOST | 73.36 | 74.45 | 76.97 | 78.77 | 78.77 | 79.62 | 76.66 | 77.06 | 77.98 | 80.70 | 74.13 | 76.27 | 71.59 | 73.68 | 70.03 | 66.69 | 66.30 | 64.00 | 63.84 | 62.95 | 62.03 | 60.28 | 57.64 | 60.49 |
| EAEs | 67.12 | 69.88 | 72.29 | 73.27 | 73.04 | 73.18 | 71.54 | 71.29 | 70.21 | 72.46 | 70.08 | 72.03 | 68.60 | 69.35 | 66.79 | 64.43 | 65.06 | 63.44 | 62.82 | 61.52 | 60.54 | 59.70 | 58.09 | 59.71 |
| OECDEs | 65.91 | 64.95 | 64.76 | 65.00 | 64.11 | 63.29 | 62.51 | 63.12 | 62.66 | 61.50 | 60.70 | 61.41 | 61.60 | 60.15 | 59.63 | 59.58 | 59.27 | 59.73 | 58.81 | 57.77 | 58.27 | 57.84 | 57.05 | 58.05 |
| **12 Labor Productivity GDP per worker (id)** | | | | | | | | | | | | | | | | | | | | | | | | |
| KOST | 2,363 | 2,597 | 3,175 | 3,256 | 3,397 | 3,638 | 3,685 | 3,921 | 4,000 | 4,075 | 4,946 | 5,091 | 6,001 | 6,536 | 7,367 | 6,495 | 7,007 | 7,519 | 8,284 | 9,137 | 9,988 | 10,732 | 11,501 | 12,516 |
| EAEs | 4,041 | 3,427 | 2,845 | 3,175 | 3,287 | 3,498 | 3,624 | 3,938 | 3,938 | 4,080 | 4,764 | 5,097 | 5,677 | 6,134 | 6,851 | 6,425 | 6,947 | 7,491 | 8,262 | 9,085 | 9,929 | 10,506 | 11,248 | 12,107 |
| OECDEs | 15,060 | 15,086 | 15,293 | 15,981 | 16,582 | 17,489 | 18,157 | 18,630 | 18,648 | 19,450 | 20,487 | 21,287 | 22,049 | 22,847 | 24,185 | 25,005 | 25,786 | 26,424 | 27,339 | 28,249 | 29,765 | 30,557 | 31,647 | 33,155 |

keys: cr: current prices; cs: constant prices; id: international dollars; nc: national currency; usd: US Dollar.

**EAE/OECDE DATA(2)**

| | 1975 | 1976 | 1977 | 1978 | 1979 | 1980 | 1981 | 1982 | 1983 | 1984 | 1985 | 1986 | 1987 | 1988 | 1989 | 1990 | 1991 | 1992 | 1993 | 1994 | 1995 | 1996 | 1997 | 1998 | 1999 | 2000 |
|---|---|---|---|---|---|---|---|---|---|---|---|---|---|---|---|---|---|---|---|---|---|---|---|---|---|---|
| **1 Gross Domestic Product Annual Change 1951-2000 (pc, nc, cs)** | | | | | | | | | | | | | | | | | | | | | | | | | | |
| EAEs | 5.11 | 7.06 | 8.08 | 8.83 | 7.40 | 5.94 | 6.06 | 6.00 | 8.12 | 9.22 | 5.59 | 7.33 | 9.87 | 9.54 | 6.67 | 6.48 | 7.31 | 6.90 | 7.81 | 8.08 | 7.14 | 6.80 | 6.17 | 0.73 | 6.00 | 7.07 |
| OECDEs | -0.47 | 4.61 | 3.33 | 3.09 | 3.96 | 2.35 | 1.56 | 0.48 | 1.55 | 3.19 | 3.07 | 3.09 | 2.97 | 3.75 | 3.67 | 2.85 | 1.51 | 1.34 | 0.86 | 3.40 | 2.89 | 2.72 | 3.87 | 3.89 | 3.79 | 4.27 |
| **2 Gross Domestic Product Per capita Annual Change 1962-2000 (pc, nc, cs)** | | | | | | | | | | | | | | | | | | | | | | | | | | |
| EAEs | 3.44 | 5.39 | 6.46 | 7.41 | 5.72 | 3.77 | 3.88 | 3.90 | 6.76 | 7.79 | 4.63 | 6.46 | 8.61 | 8.09 | 5.22 | 5.03 | 6.02 | 5.57 | 6.53 | 6.70 | 5.80 | 5.26 | 4.77 | -0.54 | 5.27 | 5.77 |
| OECDEs | -1.24 | 3.88 | 2.85 | 2.57 | 5.00 | 1.66 | 0.87 | 0.05 | 1.28 | 2.92 | 2.74 | 2.52 | 2.52 | 3.12 | 3.18 | 2.22 | -0.22 | 0.66 | 0.29 | 2.82 | 2.38 | 2.24 | 3.38 | 3.39 | 3.25 | 3.63 |
| **3 Savings as Percent of GDP 1951-2000 (pc, cr, usd)** | | | | | | | | | | | | | | | | | | | | | | | | | | |
| EAEs | 26.94 | 30.69 | 30.69 | 32.16 | 31.36 | 30.01 | 30.82 | 32.30 | 33.37 | 33.87 | 33.10 | 34.49 | 35.36 | 35.27 | 34.41 | 34.03 | 35.14 | 34.00 | 34.20 | 34.91 | 35.19 | 35.34 | 35.67 | 35.56 | 34.54 | 33.81 |
| OECDEs | 24.71 | 24.80 | 23.91 | 24.36 | 24.12 | 23.50 | 22.52 | 22.58 | 22.70 | 23.73 | 23.77 | 23.96 | 23.49 | 24.54 | 25.41 | 24.87 | 24.46 | 23.45 | 23.60 | 24.36 | 25.06 | 25.03 | 25.89 | 25.75 | 25.44 | 26.57 |
| **4 Exports Annual Change 1951-2000 (pc, usd)** | | | | | | | | | | | | | | | | | | | | | | | | | | |
| EAEs | 1.65 | 28.64 | 19.76 | 27.75 | 25.30 | 27.19 | 16.22 | -1.45 | 7.26 | 16.86 | 1.64 | 14.97 | 27.26 | 22.56 | 7.96 | 9.36 | 12.24 | 9.44 | 8.50 | 19.76 | 21.42 | 1.48 | 6.61 | -6.19 | 7.42 | 20.76 |
| OECDEs | 6.26 | 9.87 | 14.13 | 21.81 | 25.96 | 17.82 | -6.23 | -4.18 | 0.84 | 6.70 | 5.18 | 19.47 | 19.96 | 11.42 | 8.83 | 18.93 | 0.66 | 6.47 | -5.74 | 12.88 | 22.04 | 3.81 | 0.77 | 3.15 | 1.79 | 4.02 |
| WORLD | 4.22 | 12.88 | 13.31 | 15.83 | 29.17 | 19.39 | 0.21 | -7.66 | -2.43 | 6.11 | 1.26 | 8.92 | 18.18 | 14.33 | 8.80 | 13.76 | 2.62 | 6.52 | 0.11 | 13.76 | 19.65 | 4.32 | 3.49 | -1.59 | 3.68 | 12.58 |
| **5 Exports Share of World Total 1951-2000 (pc, usd)** | | | | | | | | | | | | | | | | | | | | | | | | | | |
| EAEs | 9.27 | 10.04 | 10.65 | 11.37 | | 10.53 | 12.20 | 12.50 | 13.67 | 14.97 | 15.25 | 16.44 | 16.46 | 16.99 | 16.51 | 15.52 | 16.80 | 17.17 | 18.44 | 18.75 | 18.46 | 17.43 | 17.80 | 16.96 | 17.59 | 18.65 |
| OECDEs | 55.73 | 54.27 | 53.92 | 55.81 | 54.12 | 52.92 | 51.09 | 52.60 | 52.73 | 52.45 | 53.52 | 56.38 | 56.45 | 56.55 | 55.83 | 57.46 | 56.62 | 56.24 | 57.27 | 56.52 | 56.94 | 56.87 | 56.08 | 58.20 | 56.87 | 53.34 |
| **6 Export GDP ratio 1951-2000 (pc, cr, usd. EAEs-NS: EAEs without Singapore)** | | | | | | | | | | | | | | | | | | | | | | | | | | |
| EAEs | 33.49 | 39.97 | 42.27 | 43.34 | 47.61 | 51.88 | 49.76 | 46.30 | 44.55 | 46.72 | 46.54 | 46.38 | 50.03 | 51.88 | 48.65 | 47.36 | 46.26 | 43.71 | 42.70 | 46.21 | 47.92 | 46.10 | 46.54 | 48.31 | 48.49 | 52.69 |
| EAEs-NS | 18.38 | 21.76 | 21.50 | 21.87 | 21.81 | 23.52 | 24.45 | 23.83 | 24.29 | 26.34 | 25.94 | 26.48 | 27.40 | 25.86 | 23.39 | 23.25 | 23.38 | 22.30 | 21.27 | 23.10 | 24.32 | 23.39 | 25.10 | 28.08 | 26.66 | 29.56 |
| OECDEs | 22.16 | 22.65 | 22.56 | 22.62 | 24.01 | 24.59 | 24.72 | 24.78 | 25.69 | 28.11 | 28.83 | 25.63 | 25.09 | 25.30 | 26.58 | 25.73 | 24.62 | 24.08 | 26.23 | 27.72 | 29.17 | 29.19 | 30.63 | 30.93 | 30.87 | 33.79 |
| **7 Adjusted Net Saving as Percent of GDP 1970-2000 (pc, cr, usd)** | | | | | | | | | | | | | | | | | | | | | | | | | | |
| EAEs | 15.26 | 17.00 | 18.45 | 19.66 | 18.72 | 17.33 | 16.81 | 18.81 | 20.84 | 22.06 | 20.96 | 21.69 | 21.31 | 21.85 | 20.91 | 21.96 | 23.73 | 23.61 | 22.69 | 25.64 | 25.68 | 25.40 | 27.08 | 26.27 | 25.42 | 26.96 |
| OECDEs | 13.04 | 13.75 | 13.20 | 12.39 | 12.39 | 10.85 | 9.42 | 9.14 | 9.09 | 10.14 | 10.60 | 11.46 | 11.12 | 12.19 | 12.37 | 12.29 | 12.17 | 11.72 | 11.64 | 12.58 | 13.30 | 13.22 | 13.98 | 13.71 | 11.99 | 12.98 |
| **8 Real Investment as Percent of GDP 1950-2000 (pc, cr, id. KOST; Korea, Singapore, Taiwan)** | | | | | | | | | | | | | | | | | | | | | | | | | | |
| KOST | 38.73 | 34.95 | 34.62 | 33.27 | 35.74 | 39.06 | 38.69 | 37.11 | 36.99 | 36.72 | 36.57 | 33.81 | 31.27 | 32.24 | 31.47 | 32.59 | 34.03 | 34.62 | 34.48 | 34.87 | 33.97 | 34.48 | 35.40 | 35.01 | 28.89 | 29.87 |
| EAEs | 33.89 | 31.38 | 30.88 | 29.99 | 32.33 | 34.21 | 33.72 | 32.32 | 32.13 | 31.68 | 31.60 | 30.67 | 29.06 | 29.69 | 29.87 | 30.69 | 31.36 | 31.81 | 31.32 | 32.06 | 31.12 | 31.50 | 32.19 | 31.83 | 27.68 | 27.91 |
| OECDEs | 29.36 | 26.52 | 26.78 | 26.11 | 25.54 | 25.98 | 25.82 | 24.61 | 24.24 | 23.00 | 23.57 | 23.18 | 23.49 | 23.69 | 24.74 | 24.98 | 24.31 | 24.13 | 22.19 | 21.50 | 21.71 | 22.31 | 22.23 | 23.08 | 23.84 | 23.44 |
| **9 Total physical cap. stock as Percent of GDP 1951-1990 (pc, cs, nc)** | | | | | | | | | | | | | | | | | | | | | | | | | | |
| EAEs | 1.88 | 1.99 | 2.08 | 2.12 | 2.15 | 2.21 | 2.31 | 2.37 | 2.45 | 2.47 | 2.48 | 2.57 | 2.61 | 2.58 | 2.57 | 2.61 | 2.66 | | | | | | | | | |
| OECDEs | 2.75 | 2.89 | 2.88 | 2.90 | 2.92 | 2.92 | 2.97 | 3.04 | 3.11 | 3.14 | 3.11 | 3.10 | 3.09 | 3.09 | 3.08 | 3.09 | 3.11 | | | | | | | | | |
| **10 Gross Fixed Capital Formation as Percent of GDP (pc, cr, nc)** | | | | | | | | | | | | | | | | | | | | | | | | | | |
| EAEs | 30.81 | 30.57 | 29.49 | 30.63 | 31.47 | 32.15 | 30.13 | 30.51 | 30.14 | 30.18 | 29.02 | 28.42 | 29.08 | 29.38 | 28.50 | 29.48 | 30.30 | 31.35 | 32.95 | 31.91 | 31.42 | 31.77 | 31.33 | 30.64 | 30.04 | 29.75 |
| OECDEs | 23.92 | 23.13 | 23.23 | 22.81 | 22.97 | 23.37 | 22.62 | 21.81 | 20.89 | 20.17 | 19.89 | 20.26 | 20.75 | 21.57 | 21.84 | 21.84 | 21.12 | 20.00 | 19.06 | 18.94 | 19.17 | 19.43 | 19.85 | 20.72 | 19.67 | 19.74 |
| **11 Real Consumption as Percent of GDP 1951-2000 (pc, cr, id)** | | | | | | | | | | | | | | | | | | | | | | | | | | |
| KOST | 59.49 | 55.92 | 53.93 | 52.98 | 53.58 | 54.61 | 53.54 | 51.67 | 50.00 | 49.64 | 50.31 | 49.19 | 49.01 | 50.01 | 51.25 | 51.91 | 51.17 | 52.16 | 52.08 | 51.96 | 51.56 | 51.25 | 51.38 | 50.85 | 52.46 | 52.46 |
| EAEs | 59.33 | 57.26 | 55.78 | 54.45 | 55.12 | 56.79 | 56.10 | 55.44 | 54.79 | 54.35 | 54.79 | 54.15 | 54.04 | 54.63 | 55.07 | 55.17 | 54.70 | 55.56 | 55.47 | 55.26 | 55.29 | 55.12 | 54.80 | 54.68 | 56.02 | 55.48 |
| OECDEs | 59.54 | 59.59 | 60.07 | 60.16 | 60.38 | 60.55 | 60.99 | 60.88 | 60.68 | 59.90 | 59.86 | 59.99 | 61.42 | 62.62 | 61.79 | 63.00 | 64.30 | 65.19 | 66.04 | 65.38 | 66.31 | 66.33 | 65.73 | 66.07 | 65.70 | 62.86 |
| **12 Labor Productivity GDP per worker (id)** | | | | | | | | | | | | | | | | | | | | | | | | | | |
| KOST | 12,775 | 13,029 | 13,869 | 14,584 | 15,664 | 16,635 | 17,149 | 17,743 | 18,205 | 19,448 | 20,710 | 20,628 | 21,854 | 23,865 | 25,728 | 27,193 | 28,762 | 29,603 | 30,322 | 31,935 | 33,012 | 35,160 | 37,712 | 36,333 | 35,321 | 37,673 |
| EAEs | 12,143 | 12,362 | 12,992 | 13,590 | 14,441 | 15,285 | 15,729 | 16,200 | 16,604 | 17,428 | 18,400 | 18,557 | 19,450 | 20,912 | 22,408 | 23,559 | 24,864 | 25,629 | 26,158 | 27,205 | 27,954 | 29,374 | 31,201 | 29,075 | 28,492 | 29,744 |
| OECDEs | 33,508 | 32,595 | 33,585 | 34,143 | 34,749 | 35,581 | 35,969 | 35,730 | 35,458 | 35,671 | 36,743 | 37,523 | 38,459 | 39,384 | 40,895 | 42,178 | 42,536 | 42,704 | 42,675 | 42,577 | 43,804 | 45,171 | 45,983 | 47,625 | 49,179 | 50,648 |

keys: cr: current prices; cs: constant prices; id: international dollars; nc: national currency; usd: US Dollar.

# Appendix C

## East Asian Growth timelines
## (1951–2000)

Please refer to "Notes on data and appendices" on pp. 224–5 for sources and keys in this Appendix.

# 1. General growth orientations

**1951–1960**

| | 1951 | 1952 | 1953 | 1954 | 1955 | 1956 | 1957 | 1958 | 1959 | 1960 |
|---|---|---|---|---|---|---|---|---|---|---|
| China | post-war recovery | | nationalization and collectivization, Soviet model | | | | Great Leap Forward | | | |
| Japan | import substitution | | export-led growth | | | | heavy & chemical Industry drive | | | |
| Korea | | war time economy | | | primary import substitution | | | | | |
| Taiwan | KMT arrival boom | | | primary import substitution | | | | | | |
| Singapore | | | | | | | | | | |

**1961–1970**

| | 1961 | 1962 | 1963 | 1964 | 1965 | 1966 | 1967 | 1968 | 1969 | 1970 |
|---|---|---|---|---|---|---|---|---|---|---|
| China | aftermath | | Soviet model | | radical Chinese model of socialist economy | | | | | |
| Japan | | | | | export-led growth expansion | | | | | |
| Korea | | | | | | labor-intensive export-led growth | | | | |
| Taiwan | | | | | | labor intensive export-led growth | | | | |
| Singapore | labor intensive import substitution | | | | | | labor-intensive export-led growth | | | |

**1971–1980**

| | 1971 | 1972 | 1973 | 1974 | 1975 | 1976 | 1977 | 1978 | 1979 | 1980 |
|---|---|---|---|---|---|---|---|---|---|---|
| China | radical Chinese model of socialist economy | | | | | | Great Leap Forward II | | | |
| Japan | export-led growth | | | | | Adjustment to oil shocks | | | | |
| Korea | export-led growth | | | | Heavy and Chemical Industrial Drive | | | | | |
| Taiwan | | | | | infrastructure drive | | | | | |
| Singapore | | | | | Labor-intensive export-led growth | | | | | |

**1981–1990**

| | 1981 | 1982 | 1983 | 1984 | 1985 | 1986 | 1987 | 1988 | 1989 | 1990 |
|---|---|---|---|---|---|---|---|---|---|---|
| China | | | | | export-led growth | | | | | |
| Japan | restructuring, upgrading, diversification | | | | | | bubble economy | | | bubble busts |
| Korea | technology-intensive growth | | | | | | | | | |
| Taiwan | high technology drive | | | | | | | | | |
| Singapore | industrial restructuring & expansion to services sector | | | | adjustment, diversification, internationalization | | | | | |

**1991–2000**

| | 1991 | 1992 | 1993 | 1994 | 1995 | 1996 | 1997 | 1998 | 1999 | 2000 |
|---|---|---|---|---|---|---|---|---|---|---|
| China | export-led growth | | | | | | | | adjustment to crisis | |
| Japan | low growth stagnation | | | | | | | | | |
| Korea | restructuring, upgrading, diversification | | | | | | | crisis and adjustment | | |
| Taiwan | restructuring, upgrading, diversification | | | | | | | | adjustment to crisis | |
| Singapore | regionalization, globalization, services-oriented | | | | | | | | adjustment to crisis | |

## 2. Macro economic conditions

| | 1951 | 1952 | 1953 | 1954 | 1955 | 1956 | 1957 | 1958 | 1959 | 1960 |
|---|---|---|---|---|---|---|---|---|---|---|
| China | | | | | | | | | | economic crisis |
| Japan | Korean War boom | | Investment boom | | Jimmu Boom | | recession | | Iwato Boom | |
| Korea | US aid | 1st macroeconomic cycle | | | | | 2nd macroeconomic cycle | | | |
| Taiwan | | | | | | | | | | |
| Singapore | | | | | | | | | | |

| | 1961 | 1962 | 1963 | 1964 | 1965 | 1966 | 1967 | 1968 | 1969 | 1970 |
|---|---|---|---|---|---|---|---|---|---|---|
| China | crisis | | adjustment | | | | austerity economy | | | |
| Japan | 3K deficit | | expansion | recession | national bond | | | Izanagi boom | | |
| Korea | | 3rd macroeconomic cycle | | | | 4th macroeconomic cycle | | | | |
| Taiwan | | budget deficits under control, unitary exchange rate | | | US aid ends | | | | | |
| Singapore | | entrepôt economy, reliance on UK military base | | | economic difficulties with Malaysia, Indonesia and UK | | | | | |

| | 1971 | 1972 | 1973 | 1974 | 1975 | 1976 | 1977 | 1978 | 1979 | 1980 |
|---|---|---|---|---|---|---|---|---|---|---|
| China | | | austerity economy | | | | | | | 1st macroeconomic |
| Japan | | Yen floats, price revolution | | | tight monetary & fiscal policies | | | Yen 180 USD | | tight mon policy |
| Korea | | | 5th macroeconomic cycle | | | | | 6th macroeconomic cycle | | |
| Taiwan | | | High inflation, high interest rate, NT$ appreciates 73 | | | | | NT appreciates | | labor shortage |
| Singapore | | | full employment | | Gov surplus | | | | | 3% unemployment rate |

| | 1981 | 1982 | 1983 | 1984 | 1985 | 1986 | 1987 | 1988 | 1989 | 1990 |
|---|---|---|---|---|---|---|---|---|---|---|
| China | cycle | | | 2nd macroeconomic cycle | | | 3rd macroeconomic cycle | | | |
| Japan | restructuring | US Farm Trade Agm't | | Plaza Accords | easy money | | Neikei at 38,915, massive US acquisitions | | | Neikei at 28,000 |
| Korea | structural difficulties | | | | 3 low boom | | | | | trade deficits |
| Taiwan | | | export surpluses, budget deficit | NT$ appreciates | | | | | | |
| Singapore | tight labor market, pressure on wages | | | | recession | | more regional competition, low technological base | | | |

| | 1991 | 1992 | 1993 | 1994 | 1995 | 1996 | 1997 | 1998 | 1999 | 2000 |
|---|---|---|---|---|---|---|---|---|---|---|
| China | | 4th macroeconomic cycle | | | | | | | | |
| Japan | | | | | 80 Yen USD, revitalizing measures | | international market challenges | expansionary fiscal policy | | |
| Korea | fiscal deficit 2 trn, structural difficulties | | | | | OECD member | economic crisis, IMF package | | | |
| Taiwan | | | | | | | | | | |
| Singapore | | | | | more regional competition, low technological base, higher costs | | | | | |

## 3. Industrial promotion, restructuring, and adjustment

| | 1951 | 1952 | 1953 | 1954 | 1955 | 1956 | 1957 | 1958 | 1959 | 1960 |
|---|---|---|---|---|---|---|---|---|---|---|
| China | land reforms, socialist transformation | | | | | | | mass movement of industrialization | | |
| Japan | Dodge Plan | Export promotion | | CIRL, COBIRL | 5YP on petrochemicals, 2nd SIRP, 1st 5YP for JNR, shipbuilding | | | | | |
| Korea | land reforms | land reforms | | | | | | | | |
| Taiwan | | | ITA, import controls | | | | export promotion | | | SFI |
| Singapore | | | | | | early industrial drive | | 5Y Tax Holiday | | |

| | 1961 | 1962 | 1963 | 1964 | 1965 | 1966 | 1967 | 1968 | 1969 | 1970 |
|---|---|---|---|---|---|---|---|---|---|---|
| China | | | | | | | | | | |
| Japan | ICPL | TME,SDI | BSBL | | | | EIPSML | | | |
| Korea | | export promotion | | | | foreign investment push | | | farm reforms, IPL | |
| Taiwan | | | | | | EPZs | | ELIA,EPC | | |
| Singapore | | Jurong Industrial Estate | | | PCP, export promotion | | | JTC, ADM | | |

| | 1971 | 1972 | 1973 | 1974 | 1975 | 1976 | 1977 | 1978 | 1979 | 1980 |
|---|---|---|---|---|---|---|---|---|---|---|
| China | | | | | | | | | | HRS, SEZs |
| Japan | industrial expansion | | | responses to land problems | | | expansionary policies | | | Nakasone |
| Korea | | | targeting on heavy & chemical Industries, TDPA | | | | Big Push | | | |
| Taiwan | | | | 10 major infrastructure projects | | | 12 new infrastructure projects | | | interest rate freed |
| Singapore | ADBM | SDC, NPB | | | Move to high skill, high value added activity | SIFS | | | SDF, 2nd industrial structuring program 79 | |

| | 1981 | 1982 | 1983 | 1984 | 1985 | 1986 | 1987 | 1988 | 1989 | 1990 |
|---|---|---|---|---|---|---|---|---|---|---|
| China | export subsidies, negotiated tax rates | | | tax-for-profit | dual pricing, ECRS | SFCIC / LDI | | | | |
| Japan | reforms | market opening measures | | financial deregulations | | | | | US aimed import promotion | |
| Korea | drive to upgrade to high tech industries | | | tariff reduction plan | | | | service sector liberalization | | |
| Taiwan | 2nd land reform | | | liberalization & internationalization | | | | further trade & financial liberalization, SIU | | |
| Singapore | Foreign com 100% ownership | | | SIMEX | privatization program, SEOC | | | foreign exchange call market | | |

| | 1991 | 1992 | 1993 | 1994 | 1995 | 1996 | 1997 | 1998 | 1999 | 2000 |
|---|---|---|---|---|---|---|---|---|---|---|
| China | | | | deepening of SEO reforms | | | stimulation packages | | WRDS | |
| Japan | | land value tax | | | | | | | | |
| Korea | stimulation package, NIP | | | | | | FSC | ELSFF / CRA | | |
| Taiwan | 10 new Strategic Industrial Priority Projects | | | | Asia-Pacific Operation Center proposal | | | | Industry 21, AIA | |
| Singapore | deepening technology base; cluster development; promoting manf and Services; global hub, | | | | | | | | | |

# 4. Control and competition

## 1951–1960

| | 1951 | 1952 | 1953 | 1954 | 1955 | 1956 | 1957 | 1958 | 1959 | 1960 |
|---|---|---|---|---|---|---|---|---|---|---|
| China | | | | | | | | | | |
| Japan | FCL, 307 Yen/USD, FRPL | | | consolidated income tax | | | decentralization | free trade and exchange policy | | |
| Korea | | multiple exchange rate | | | | | | | | |
| Taiwan | | | | major efforts to promote industrial competitiveness | | | | liberalizing reforms | | SEC |
| Singapore | | | | | | | | | | |

## 1961–1970

| | 1961 | 1962 | 1963 | 1964 | 1965 | 1966 | 1967 | 1968 | 1969 | 1970 |
|---|---|---|---|---|---|---|---|---|---|---|
| China | | | | | | | | | | |
| Japan | relaxing trade & For Ex | | GATT Art. 11 accepted | | IMF Article 8 accepted | | | capital liberalization | | |
| Korea | | | | Won depreciates | interest rate reform, UER | | | | | stock market |
| Taiwan | TSE, UER | | | | | | | ADM | | adjustment in |
| Singapore | | | | | | Nationalizing major national companies | | | | |

## 1971–1980

| | 1971 | 1972 | 1973 | 1974 | 1975 | 1976 | 1977 | 1978 | 1979 | 1980 |
|---|---|---|---|---|---|---|---|---|---|---|
| China | | | | | | | | | | opening, decollect n |
| Japan | FFER | | | | | | | | | |
| Korea | | | | | | | | | | trade & HSP, HDP |
| Taiwan | import controls | | | rice price guaranteed | all tariff barriers lifted | Op Mon Market | FFER | For Exc Market / all exchange controls lifted | | |
| Singapore | MAS | | SSE, MFER, GATT | | | | | | | SSP |

## 1981–1990

| | 1981 | 1982 | 1983 | 1984 | 1985 | 1986 | 1987 | 1988 | 1989 | 1990 |
|---|---|---|---|---|---|---|---|---|---|---|
| China | reorientation | | | Industrial, bank reforms | | export promotion, GPFDIC | | CAEDS | | priority industries |
| Japan | | | | | US frictions | | Land Law revised | | | bubble control |
| Korea | | financial liberalization, FTA | | | CIPMP | | rates liberalized | IDA | | land trans controls |
| Taiwan | | | | 14 major infrastructure projects | | | | Land Tax Law amended, new bank law | | |
| Singapore | NPC | | STDB | | wage correction policy | | | SEC | | |

## 1991–2000

| | 1991 | 1992 | 1993 | 1994 | 1995 | 1996 | 1997 | 1998 | 1999 | 2000 |
|---|---|---|---|---|---|---|---|---|---|---|
| China | stock markets | UER, export planning & subsidies end | | | FTL / CBL | Big Band | | Securities Law, ISRC | | |
| Japan | | | rice market opens under GATT | | | | | | emergency & reform measures | |
| Korea | import liberalization | | TSRP | reforms for open foreign investment | | | PCTR | | privatization, chaebol reform | |
| Taiwan | Fin reforms, FTL | | Financial Sector Reform Plan | | Big Bang, GST | | ACL reform | | | |
| Singapore | | AFTA | | | CPF in stock markets | | | | | |

## 5. Economic decision-making and planning

| | 1951 | 1952 | 1953 | 1954 | 1955 | 1956 | 1957 | 1958 | 1959 | 1960 |
|---|---|---|---|---|---|---|---|---|---|---|
| China | | adopting the Soviet model | | | 1st 5YP | SEC | | 2nd 5YP | | |
| Japan | MITI, IDA, ESB, JDB, JIEB | | JIEB | EPA, SEC | | | Long Range Eco Plan | | 2nd 5YP | IDP |
| Korea | BOK | | | KDB, Nathan Report | | | | | | |
| Taiwan | CUSA, IDC | | 1st 4YP, ESB | | | | 2nd 4YP | ESB ends, CUSA | | |
| Singapore | | | | | CPF | | SIPB | | 1st Dev Plan | HDP |

| | 1961 | 1962 | 1963 | 1964 | 1965 | 1966 | 1967 | 1968 | 1969 | 1970 |
|---|---|---|---|---|---|---|---|---|---|---|
| China | | 3rd 5YP | | | | | | 4th 5YP | | |
| Japan | | CNDP | | ISC | Medium-term Economic Plan | | 1st ESDP | | 2nd CNDP | 2nd ESDP |
| Korea | BPB | 1st 5YP, KTPC, PMEPC | | | | | KFEB, 2nd 5YP | | | Manufac. |
| Taiwan | 3rd 4YP | | CIECD | | 4th 4Y Plan | | | | NSC | 5th 5YP |
| Singapore | EDB | | | STPBS | | | POSBank | | DBS | HDB |

| | 1971 | 1972 | 1973 | 1974 | 1975 | 1976 | 1977 | 1978 | 1979 | 1980 |
|---|---|---|---|---|---|---|---|---|---|---|
| China | | 5th 5YP | | | | | | 6th 5YP | | revised 10YP |
| Japan | | | 3rd ESDP | | | | 3rd CNDP | | 7YP, MITI Vision | |
| Korea | expansion | | 3rd 5YP on heavy industrial expan. | | | 6YP | | 4th 5YP on ind. expan. | | CSP |
| Taiwan | IDB, CETRA | | | 6th 4TP, EPC | | | | CEPD | | MTI |
| Singapore | key economic agencies reforms II | | | | | | | | | |

| | 1981 | 1982 | 1983 | 1984 | 1985 | 1986 | 1987 | 1988 | 1989 | 1990 |
|---|---|---|---|---|---|---|---|---|---|---|
| China | DRC | | PBC as central bank | | new reform momentum | | central & commercial banking separate | | | |
| Japan | | Plan for 80s | | | | | | | | |
| Korea | | | 2nd NLDP, 5th 5YP on liberalization | | | | 6th 5YP on regional balance | | | 10th MITEDP |
| Taiwan | | 8th 4YP | | | | 9th MTEDP | | | | Strategic |
| Singapore | | SITAS | | EC | | OHQ, NITP, LIUP | | SME | | |

| | 1991 | 1992 | 1993 | 1994 | 1995 | 1996 | 1997 | 1998 | 1999 | 2000 |
|---|---|---|---|---|---|---|---|---|---|---|
| China | | 9th 5YP | | CFETS, SDB | new banking system | | | SETC, 10th 5YP, PBC reforms, FWC | | |
| Japan | | | Hashimoto Reforms | | | | FSA | | | |
| Korea | | | 7th 5YP | EPB ends | | | KEACO | FSC, CRCC | | |
| Taiwan | | | | | | | | | | |
| Singapore | Economic Plan, NSTB | | CPOE | CDF | IDS | SPSB | | | | |

# 6. Major political, social, and international developments

|  | 1951 | 1952 | 1953 | 1954 | 1955 | 1956 | 1957 | 1958 | 1959 | 1960 |
|---|---|---|---|---|---|---|---|---|---|---|
| China |  |  |  |  |  |  |  |  |  |  |
| Japan | SPP, union reforms | US Sec Pact., Occup ends, IMF |  |  | GATT |  | Spring Wage Offensive |  |  |  |
| Korea | Civil conflict |  |  |  |  |  |  |  |  | Rhee resigns |
| Taiwan | KMT rules |  |  | US Security Treaty |  |  | Jinmen & Mazhu Crisis |  |  | Labor regulations |
| Singapore |  |  |  |  | CPF |  |  | Internal self-rule; PAP won elections 59 |  |  |
| World | Korean War, San Francisco Treaty |  | Korean War ends |  |  |  |  |  |  |  |

|  | 1961 | 1962 | 1963 | 1964 | 1965 | 1966 | 1967 | 1968 | 1969 | 1970 |
|---|---|---|---|---|---|---|---|---|---|---|
| China |  |  |  |  |  | Cultural Revolution |  |  |  |  |
| Japan | US Treaty renewed |  |  | OECD |  |  |  |  |  |  |
| Korea | military coup, Park President |  | 3rd Republic |  | normalizing ties w Japan |  | GATT |  | Park seeks reelc | US textile talks |
| Taiwan |  |  |  |  |  |  |  |  |  |  |
| Singapore | 5YP on education |  |  | joins Malaysia | independence |  |  | EA, SDF, Britain to withdraw |  |  |
| World |  |  |  | Vietnam War | PBEC |  | ASEAN |  |  |  |

|  | 1971 | 1972 | 1973 | 1974 | 1975 | 1976 | 1977 | 1978 | 1979 | 1980 |
|---|---|---|---|---|---|---|---|---|---|---|
| China | joins UN | US Rapprochement |  |  |  | Mao dies |  |  | CCP reform Plenum |  |
| Japan |  |  |  |  |  | Lockheed scandal |  |  |  |  |
| Korea | New Village Movement, Martial Law, N-S dialogue, US grant ends |  |  |  |  | Labor shortage | GATT |  | Park assas'ed | Kwangju |
| Taiwan | leaves UN |  |  |  | KS Chiang dies |  |  |  | US ties end, leaves IMF, WB |  |
| Singapore | NWC, NTUC |  |  |  |  |  |  |  | SDF, CPTE |  |
| World | Nixon Shock | Nixon Shock II | 1st oil crisis USD devalues 10% |  | 2nd oil crisis |  |  |  | Iran-US hostage crisis |  |

|  | 1981 | 1982 | 1983 | 1984 | 1985 | 1986 | 1987 | 1988 | 1989 | 1990 |
|---|---|---|---|---|---|---|---|---|---|---|
| China | HRS |  |  |  |  |  |  |  | Tiananmen |  |
| Japan |  |  |  |  |  |  | Recruit Scandal |  | Uno resigns |  |
| Korea | Chun President |  |  |  | Pension reform from EPS to NPS | new labor laws | direct president election | Roh President, LMCA |  |  |
| Taiwan | labor shortage |  |  | labor disputes, LSL | opposition parties, CLA | new labor laws | marshal law ends | CK Chiang dies |  | Lee steps down |
| Singapore |  |  |  |  | WTP |  |  | OWTI |  |  |
| World | Reagan and Thatcher Conservatism |  |  |  | Thatcher's Big Bang |  | Black Monday |  | APEC | Gulf War |

|  | 1991 | 1992 | 1993 | 1994 | 1995 | 1996 | 1997 | 1998 | 1999 | 2000 |
|---|---|---|---|---|---|---|---|---|---|---|
| China |  | Deng's Southern Tour |  |  |  |  | Hong Kong handover |  |  |  |
| Japan |  | Sagawa Scandal | LDP rule ends |  | Product Liability Act |  | AMF proposal |  |  |  |
| Korea | Join ILO |  | wage agreement |  | Industrial Peace | PCIRR | New Labor Law | Tripartite Commision |  |  |
| Taiwan | martial law lifted, new labor & welfare standards |  |  |  |  | direct presidential election |  |  |  |  |
| Singapore |  |  |  |  |  |  |  |  |  |  |
| World | US New World Order |  |  |  |  |  | Asian Economic Crisis |  |  |  |

# Notes

## Introduction

1 Throughout this book, I will refer to them as East Asian countries, or EACs; their economies as East Asian economies, or EAEs; and their economic growth during their rapid growth period as East Asian Growth. While a main aim of this book is to generalize the growth experiences of East Asia, and thus the book itself will explain why it focuses on these five economies, a few words are needed here on Hong Kong. Hong Kong had been on the list of the EAEs in the early stage of the research. While there are different views as to whether Hong Kong bore the same EAE institutional burden as the rest of the EAEs (Chau 1993), one would naturally consider Hong Kong as one of the EAEs, due to the fact that there was a similar growth, it is part of the growth in the greater China area, and, indeed, as in the case of Singapore, Hong Kong was one of the four original "dragons" (Vogel 1991).

   Nevertheless, the deeper the research delved, and the more data that was collected, the more the unique form of growth in Hong Kong became obvious. This unique form is well researched, as shown in the study done by Stephen W. K. Chiu *et al.* in comparison with Singapore 1997). The important fact is that there has been little of the "institutional enhancement" as has been seen in the other EAEs. Hong Kong did not have a "state" found to be a critical component of the growth system in East Asian Growth. There was little in terms of industrial policy to separate the domestic market from the international one. There was no growth alliance or corporate grouping of the kind found in the other EAEs. Hong Kong was eventually dropped from the list.

2 The growth system here refers to a coherent set of dynamic and effective relationships among significant growth participants, such as individuals (as consumers or investors), corporations, labor unions, government, international capitals, etc.; the rules that affect and regulate the behaviors of the growth participants; and the cultural conditions, social structure, and external environment, under which the rules and growth participants operate and interact. See more discussion of the growth system in Chapter 5.

## 1 Making sense of the 50-year growth: theories and evidence

1 Representative works would be suggested in discussions of each theory for those interested in pursuing further.

2 Woo-Cummings summarizes Johnson's original argument to include key aspects such as nationalism, war, and goal culture; state control of finance; bureaucracy; state–business relations; authoritarianism; being internationally closed off – almost all the things later attributed to the success of the East Asian economies.

For her, the developmental state is "a shorthand for the seamless web of political, bureaucratic, and moneyed influences that structured economic life in capitalist Northeast Asia" (Woo-Cummings 1999: 2, 7–22).

3   These OECD countries will be referred to in this study as OECDCs and their economies OECDEs.

4   The original OECD members are selected because subsequent additions to the OECD have tended to lack the original sense of what it is to be an "industrialized country," and hence complicate the rationale for the comparison. In addition, because of the bad quality of data for Turkey for many years in the period examined, it is also excluded from the OECD list. Judged by Turkey's economic performance, and for the purpose of the comparison at hand, this is perhaps appropriate.

5   PWT6.1 was produced by Alan Heston, Robert Summers, and Bettina Aten at the University of Pennsylvania as the latest product of the project on international comparisons. PWT allows a realistic comparison of key economic indicators across national boundaries in constant and current international prices over a historical period. Version 6.1 provides annual data on 179 countries from 1950 to 2000, with 25 variables that include – for our purposes here – current savings as share of GDP in international dollars.

6   For discussions of the validity of these two as indicators of the industrial level and their "quantitative criterion," see Chowdhury and Islam (1993: 3–4).

7   Because of the five-year moving average of the data line, the box border may not match the threshold line exactly.

8   This data is well recognized, sanctioned by the Economic Freedom Network of national research centers on economic freedom around the world, and authored by James Gwartney and Robert Lawson, with Walter Park, Smita Wagh, Chris Edwards, and Veronique de Rugy (Gwartney and Lawson 2002) under the auspices of the Fraser Institute. It covers the period of 1970 to 2000 and employs a number of variables that can be validly used as our indicators. All data are presented on a scale of 0 to 10, with 10 indicating the maximum freedom.

## 2   Initial conditions: growth imperatives and alternative scenarios

1   The dataset was compiled by Vikram Nehru and Ashok Dhareshwar at the World Bank, in the paper, "A New Database on Physical Capital Stock: Sources, Methodology and Results" (1993). The data is annual, covers the period 1950 to 1990 for 95 countries, and has 11 variables, including data on total physical capital, human capital stock, and gross domestic fixed investment.

2   These measure respectively the value of capital goods acquired over the time and the value of produced assets at the time.

3   For example, in current international dollars, Japan's GDP was only 12.7 percent of US GDP in 1951.

4   The unemployment population is arrived at via the total population minus the populations below 9 years, and above 65 years and over, and the economically active population. A group total (e.g. EAEs) is the sum of the populations of the group's members. For the justification for the formula, see ILO (1997).

5   Based on PWT6.1 data, CGDP (real GDP per capita in current international prices), and POP (population).

6   The original "cc" in PWT6.1 allows us to measure total real consumption as percentage of GDP in current international prices, while the "CGDP" measures real GDP per capita in current international prices. Several steps of conversion are involved to arrive at the CPC with the aid of POP: (1) total real GDP (rGDP) is calculated from CGDP; (2) then, real consumption (rC) is calculated from cc with rGDP; and (3) CPC is calculated from rC with POP.

7 Data are calculated with the same procedures as (1) and (2) in note 6.
8 For example, it is used in a larger study by Robert Barro and Xavier Sala-i-Martin on economic growth (1995), in Nehru and Dhareshwar's study on physical and human capital (1993), as well as the World Bank's Global Development Network Data: *Global Development Finance and World Development Indicators* (WB-GDN).
9 This may have to do with the original assertion by Chalmers Johnson about MITI's unique role in shaping Japan's industrial policy, see also Johnson (1982). Since then, many of his fellow East Asian Growth watchers, not to mention the mass media, would simply take that view for granted.
10 The three reparation proposals between 1946 and 1948 – the Pauley Report, the Strike Report, and the Johnstone Report – planned ¥2,466, 1,648, and 662 million respectively as reparations, totaling ¥4.8 billion (Nakamura 1981). These figures later proved to be a false alarm, as the USA soon changed its mind with regard to its relationship with Japan in its overall strategic thinking in the region, and the issue of reparations has never been pursued to an extent anywhere close to the level proposed in any one of these reports.
11 Ishibashi Tanzan was the first Finance Minister of the Yoshida cabinet. In his view, post-war Japanese inflation was not really inflation, and, therefore, the problem should be countered with a more expansionist fiscal policy, even through the government deficit budget (Kosai and Kaminski 1986; Nakamura 1981, 1995).
12 A term coined by Akamatsu Kaname in depicting the pattern of a, perhaps, "causal" sequence of economic takeoffs in the EAEs, in a shape of a group of flying geese with Japan as the leader (Akamatsu 1962).

## 4   Cultural and social setting

1 We don't not have enough space here to elaborate on the variations in cultural and social setting among the EACs. This is specially an issue for Japan, where modern institutions have started to rise from the Meiji Restoration. But our discussion here follows the assumption that, with the historical events over the first half of the twentieth century in Japan, and to the extent we are discussing the aspects of the cultural and social conditions in terms of the pattern of individual behavior and overall social structure, we can generally treat Japan in the same category as the rest of the EACs at the start of their rapid growth periods.
2 The notion of "Western" here carries both Christian and modern connotations.
3 For the notion of dependency, see Ebrey (1991), Pye (1985), and Doi (1986).

## 5   Crafting the national growth system

1 The Yoshida Doctrine is named after Yoshida Shigeru, the first prime minister of post-World War II Japan, and his policy of post-war recovery, which "consisted of focusing the country's resources on economic production supported by well-trained workers while adopting the US' stance on issues of security and international politics" (*Columbia Encyclopedia* 2001: "Yoshida Doctrine").
2 Though views of the Japanese political system range from those seeing Japan as "a fully functioning liberal democracy" (McCargo 2000) to those believing "soft authoritarianism" is a more accurate term for Japan (Simone and Feraru 1995).
3 Cases have been made concerning military developers in Korea, along with Indonesia and Thailand (Simone and Feraru 1995).
4 In fact, on the single variable of years in school, the Barro–Lee data does not give the EACs any edge over OECDEs.

5 While Singapore is often cited as an example of high pay for high performance, where "Entry-level bureaucrats earn anywhere from 10% to 50% more than similar positions in the private sector" (Mutsuko and McCawley 1999), there is a lack of evidence that the other EACs offered comparable high salary levels to their civil servants.

6 And, of course, you have the other side of the debate: see Emmott (1989) and Woronoff (1991).

7 For more detailed discussions of Korea's *chaebol*, and its definition, historical roots, evolution, structure, and operation, and role in Korea's rapid growth, in comparison with Japan's kereitsu, see Ungson *et al.* (1997) and Kang (1996).

8 For detailed statistical data, see Chapter 2, "Labor Movement and Asian Industrialization," in Deyo (1989).

9 For more coverage on this, see Deyo (1989) and White *et al.* (1998).

10 The mission statement reads: "To promote active citizenship and multiracial harmony; To connect the citizens for community bonding and volunteer work; To provide affordable access to lifestyle activities; To bring the people closer to one another and to the government" (People's Association 2000).

11 This concept differs from what Takafusa Nakamura called "dual structure" in the case of Japan, or the Lewis–Fei–Ranis model in general. The dual structure means "politicized, market-defying policies in the primary sector and nonpoliti-cized, market conforming policies in most manufacturing sectors" (Okimoto 1989: 177; also Nakamura 1995). In our discussion, market bifurcation is principally between the domestic and the international.

12 See Li Haijian, "Challenge and response in economic security during the 10th five year period," *People's Daily* ("shiwu shiqi baozhang woguo jinji snquan de silu he duice," *renmin wang*), April 27, 2001; and Leijia Mashu and Zhu Jianzhe, "The problem of international economic relations affecting our national economic security," *China's Economic Outlook,* ("yingxian woguo guojia jingji anquan de guoji jingji guanxi wenti," *zhongquo jingji zhanwang wang*), August 28, 2001.

13 In the economic sense, this term connotes the complete separation and lack of interaction between the socialist and capitalist economic systems during the Cold War.

## 6   The dynamism and consequences of East Asian Growth

1 A great deal of discussion on rent-seeking activities concerns this issue, from a different perspective.

2 There is a classical debate among observers of East Asian Growth, concerning the link between economic growth and political liberalization in the EACs (Bell *et al.* 1995; Clague *et al.* 1997; Diamond 1992; Kohli 1986; Lipset 1959; Olson 1993). More solid research, however, is needed to provide a definitive answer. Perhaps we will never get a satisfactory answer, as the relations between the two are more complex than simply whether there is a direct link, and how this link operates. For our purposes, we can leave the issue as it is.

3 To borrow the phrase, "growing out of the plan" from Barry Naughton (1996).

## 7   Conclusion: institutional competitiveness and East Asian Growth

1 "Generally" here is used to indicate that there were some temporary destruc-tions of their above-the-threshold performances during their rapid growth period. See related discussions in Chapter 1's reality check.

2 Named after Joseph Dodge, who came to Japan in 1949 as financial adviser to the Supreme Commander of the Allied Powers (SCAP).

# Bibliography

Please note: some data sources are listed in "Notes on data and appendices" on pp. 224–5.

Abe, Hitoshi (1994) *The Government and Politics of Japan*, Tokyo: University of Tokyo Press.

Agenor, Pireer-Richard, Marcus Miller, David Vines, and Axel Weber (1999) *The Asian Financial Crisis: Causes, Contagion, and Consequences*, New York: Cambridge University Press.

Akamatsu, Kaname (1962) "A historical pattern of economic growth in developing countries," *Developing Economies*, 1(1): 3–25.

Amsden, Alice H. (1989) *Asia's Next Giant: South Korea and Late Industrialization*, New York: Oxford University Press.

Amsden, Alice H. (1994) "Why isn't the whole world experimenting with the East Asian model to develop? A review of the East Asian miracle," *World Development*, 22(4): 627–33.

Aoki, Masahiko and Ronald P. Dore (eds) (1994) *The Japanese Firm: Sources of Competitive Strength*, Oxford: Oxford University Press.

Bachman, David M. (1991) *Bureaucracy, Economy, and Leadership in China: The Institutional Origins of the Great Leap Forward*, Cambridge: Cambridge University Press.

Barrel, Richard and Martin K. Whyte (1982) "Dependency theory and Taiwan: analysis of a deviant case," *American Journal of Sociology* 87(5): 1064–89.

Barro, Robert J. and Xavier Sala-i-Martin (1995) *Economic Growth*, New York: McGraw-Hill.

Barro, Robert J. and Jong-Wha Lee (1993) *International Comparisons of Educational Attainment*, NBER Working Papers, Cambridge, MA: National Bureau of Economic Research.

Beasley, William G. (1963) *The Modern History of Japan*, London: Weidenfeld & Nicolson.

Bell, Daniel A., David Brown, Kanishka Jayasuriya, and David Martin Jones (eds) (1995) *Towards Illiberal Democracy in Pacific Asia*, New York: St Martin's Press.

Bello, Walden and Stephanie Rosenfeld (1992) *Dragons in Distress: Asia's Miracle Economies in Crisis*, London: Penguin.

Berger, Brigitte (ed.) (1991) *The Culture of Entrepreneurship*, San Francisco, CA: Institute for Contemporary Studies.

Berger, Peter L. and Hsin-huang Michael Hsiao (eds) (1988) *In Search of an East Asian Development Model*, New Brunswick, NJ: Transaction Books.

Bienefeld, Manfred (1980) "The international context for national development strategies: constraints and opportunities in a changing world," in M. Bienefeld and M. Godfrey (eds) *The Struggle for Development: National Strategies in an International Context*, Chichester: John Wiley, pp. 25–64.

Bienefeld, Manfred (1989) "The significance of the newly industrializing countries for the development debate," *Studies in Political Economy*, 25(1): 7–39.

Biersteker, Thomas J. (1978) *Distortion or Development: Contending Perspectives on the Multinational Corporation*, Cambridge, MA: MIT Press.

Biersteker, Thomas J. (1980) "The illusion of state power: translation corporations and the neutralization of host country legislation," *Journal of Peace Research*, 17(3): 207–21.

Biersteker, Thomas J. (1987) *Multinationals, the State, and Control of the Nigerian Economy*, Princeton, NJ: Princeton University Press.

Biggart, Nicole W. (1997) "Explaining Asian economic organization: toward a Weberian institutional perspective," in Nicole Woolsey Biggart, Marco Orru, and Gary G. Hamilton, *The Economic Organization of East Asian Capitalism*, Beverly Hills, CA: Sage, pp. 3–32.

Biggart, Nicole W., Marco Orru, and Gary G. Hamilton (1997) *The Economic Organization of East Asian Capitalism*, Beverly Hills, CA: Sage.

Birdsall, Nancy and Frederick Jasperson (1997) *Pathways to Growth: Comparing East Asia and Latin America*, Baltimore, MD: Johns Hopkins University Press.

Birdsall, Nancy and Richard Sabot (1993) *Virtuous Circles: Human Capital, Growth and Equity in East Asia*, Washington, DC: World Bank.

Blau, Francine, Marianne Ferber, and Anne Winkler (1998) *Economics of Women, Men and Work*, New York: Prentice Hall.

Bo, Yang (1992) *The Ugly Chinaman and the Crisis of Chinese Culture*, North Sydney: Allen & Unwin.

Bond, Michael H. and Geert Hofstede (1990) "The cash value of Confucian values," in Steward R. Clegg, S. Gordon Redding, and Monica Cartner (eds) *Capitalism in Contrasting Cultures*, Berlin: Walter de Gruyter, pp. 383–91.

Bowie, Alasdair (1991) *Crossing the Industrial Divide: State, Society and the Politics of Economic Transformation in Malaysia*, New York: Columbia University Press.

Bradford, Colin I. (1986) "East Asian 'Model': myths and lessons," in John P. Lewis and Valeriana Kallab (eds) *Development Strategies Reconsidered*, New Brunswick, NJ: Transaction Books.

Brander, James A. and Barbara J. Spencer (1985) "Export subsidies and market-share rivalry," *Journal of International Economics*, 18: 83–100.

Burkett, Paul and Martin Hart-Landsberg (2000) *Development, Crisis and Class Struggle: Learning from Japan and East Asia*, Basingstoke: Macmillan.

Burnell, Peter J. (1986) *Economic Nationalism in the Third World*, Brighton: Wheatsheaf Books.

Calder, Kent E. (1993) *Strategic Capitalism: Private Business and Public Purpose in Japanese Industrial Finance*, Princeton, NJ: Princeton University Press.

Campos, Ed (1993) *The Institutional Foundations of High-speed Growth in the High-performing Asian Economies: Part I, Insulation Mechanisms and Public Sector–Private Sector Relations*, Washington, DC: World Bank.

Cardoso, Fernando H. and Enzo Faletto (1979) *Dependency and Development in Latin American*, Berkeley, CA: University of California Press.

Chan, Steven, Cal Clark, and Danny Lam (eds) (1998) *Beyond the Developmental State: East Asia's Political Economies Reconsidered*, New York: St Martin's Press.

Chang, Ha-Joon (1994) *The Political Economy of Industrial Policy*, New York: St Martin's Press.

Chang, Ha-Joon (1999) "The economic theory of the developmental state," in Woo-Meredith Cumings (ed.) *The Developmental State*, Ithaca, NY: Cornell University Press, pp. 182–99.

Chau, Leung Chuen (1993) *Lessons of East Asia: Hong Kong: A Unique Case of Development*, Washington, DC: World Bank.

Cheng, Chu-yuan (1982) *China's Economic Development: Growth and Structural Change*, Boulder, CA: Westview Press.

Cheng, Tun-jen (1990) "Political regimes and development strategies: South Korea and Taiwan," in Gary Gereffi and Donald L. Wyman (eds) *Manufacturing Miracles: Paths of Industrialization in Latin America and East Asia*, Princeton, NJ: Princeton University Press, pp. 139–78.

Cheng, Tun-jen (1998) "Institutions and growth in Korea and Taiwan: the bureaucracy," *Journal of Development Studies*, 34(6): 87–112.

Cheng, Tun-jen (1989) "Democratizing the quasi-Leninist regime in Taiwan," *World Politics*, 41(4): 471–99.

Cheng, Tun-jen, Stephan Haggard, and David Kang *et al.* (1998) "Institutions and growth in Korea and Taiwan: the bureaucracy," *Journal of Development Studies*, 34(6): 87–112.

Cheng, Yuk-shing, Siow Yue Chia, and Christopher Findlay (1998) "Hong Kong and Singapore," in Ross H. McLeod and Ross Garnaut (eds) *East Asia in Crisis: From Being A Miracle to Needing One?* London: Routledge, pp. 162–78.

Cheng, Yuk-shing, Siow Yue Chia, and Christopher Findlay (2000) "Governance in the city-states: Hong Kong and Singapore," in Peter Drydale (ed.) *Reform and Recovery in East Asia: The Role of the State and Economic Enterprise*, London: Routledge, pp. 229–54.

Chiew, Seen-kong (1983) "Ethnicity and national integration: the evolution of a multi-ethnic society," in Peter S. J. Chen (ed.) *Singapore: Development Policies and Trends*, Singapore: Oxford University Press, pp. 29–64.

Chiu, Stephen W. K., Kong-Chong Ho, and Tai-lok Lui (1997) *City-states in the Global Economy: Industrial Restructuring in Hong Kong and Singapore*, Boulder, CO: Westview Press.

Chow, Peter C. Y. and Bates Gill (2000) *Weathering the Storm: Taiwan, Its Neighbors and the Asian Financial Crisis*, Washington, DC: The Brookings Institute.

Chow, Peter C. Y. and Mitchell H. Kellman (1993) *Trade: The Engine of Growth in East Asia*, New York: Oxford University Press.

Chowdhury, Anis and Iyanatul Islam (1993) *The Newly Industrializing Economies of East Asia*, London: Routledge.

Chu, Wan-wen (1989) "Import substitution and export-led growth: a study of Taiwan's petrochemical industry," *World Development* 22(5): 781–94.

Chu, Yun-han (1989) "State structure and economic adjustment of the East Asian newly industrializing countries," *International Organization*, 43(3): 647–72.

Chua, Beng Huat and Eddie C. Y. Kuo (1995) "The making of a new nation: cultural construction and national identity," in Beng Huat Chua (ed.) *Communitarian Ideology and Democracy in Singapore*, London: Routledge, pp. 101–23.

Clague, Christopher (ed.) (1997) *Institutions and Economic Development*, Washington, DC: Johns Hopkins University Press.

Clague, Christopher, Philip Keefer, Stephen Knack, and Mancur Olson (1997) "Democracy, autocracy, and the institutions supportive of economic growth," in Christopher Clague (ed.) *Institutions and Economic Development*, Washington, DC: Johns Hopkins University Press, pp. 91–120.

Clammer, John R. (1998) *Race and State in Independent Singapore, 1965–1990: The Cultural Politics of Pluralism in a Multiethnic Society*, Brookfield, VT: Ashgate.

Clark, Rodney (1979) *The Japanese Company*, New Haven, CT: Yale University Press.

Clegg, Stewart R. and S. Gordon Redding (1990) *Capitalism in Contrasting Cultures*, Berlin: Walter de Gruyter.

Clifford, Mark (1994) *Troubled Tiger: Business, Bureaucrats and Generals in South Korea*, Armonk, NY: Sharpe.

Clifford, Mark L. and Pete Engardio (1999) *Meltdown: Asia's Boom, Bust, and Beyond*, Paramus: Prentice Hall Press.

Cline, William (1982) "Can the East Asian model of development be generalized?," *World Development*, 10: 81–90.

Cole, David C. (1980) "Foreign assistance and Korea development," in Yongil Lim, David C. Cole, and Paul W. Kuznets (eds) *The Korean Economy: Issues of Development*, Berkeley, CA: University of California Press.

Coleman, James S. (1988) "Social capital in the creation of human capital," *American Journal of Sociology*, 94(2): 95–120.

Collcutt, Martin (1991) "The legacy of Confucianism in Japan," in Gilbert Rozman (ed.) *The East Asian Region: Confucian Heritage and Its Modern Adaptation*, Princeton, NJ: Princeton University Press, 111–56.

Corbo, Vittorio and Sang-Mok Suh (eds) (1992) *Structural Adjustment in a Newly Industrialized Country*, Baltimore, MD: Johns Hopkins University Press.

Cutts, Robert L. (1992) "Capitalism in Japan: cartels and keiretsu," *Harvard Business Review*, 70: 48–55.

de Bary, Wm Theodore (1981) *Neo-Confucian Orthodoxy and the Learning of Mind-and Heart*, New York: Columbia University Press.

de Bary, Wm Theodore (1988) *East Asian Civilizations: A Dialogue in Five Stages*, Cambridge, MA: Harvard University Press.

Deyo, Frederic C. (ed.) (1987) *The Political Economy of the New Asian Industrialism*, Ithaca, NY: Cornell University Press.

Deyo, Frederic C. (1989) *Beneath the Miracle: Labor Subordination in the New Asian Industrialism*, Berkeley, CA: University of California Press.

Diamond, Larry (1992) "Economic development and democracy revisited," *American Behavioral Scientist*, 15: 450–99.

Dick, William G. (1974) "Authoritarian versus nonauthoritarian approaches to economic development," *Journal of Political Economy*, 82(4): 817–27.

Doi, Takeo (1986) *The Anatomy of Self: The Individual vs Society*, Tokyo and New York: Kodansha International.

Doner, Richard (1992) "Limits of state strength: toward an institutionalist view of economic development," *World Politics*, 44(4): 398–431.

Ebrey, Patricia (1991) "The Chinese family and the spread of Confucian values," in Gillbert Rozman (ed.) *The East Asian Region: Confucian Heritage and Its Modern Adaptation*, Princeton, NJ: Princeton University Press.

Eli, Max (1990) *Japan Inc.: Global Strategies of Japanese Trading Corporations*, New York: McGraw-Hill.

Elvin, Mark (1984) "Why China failed to create an endogenous industrial capitalism: a critique of Max Weber's explanation," *Theory and Society*, 13: 379–91.

Emmott, Bill (1989) *The Sun Also Sets: Why Japan Will Not Be Number One*, London: Simon & Schuster.

Evans, David and Parvin Alizadeh (1984) "Trade, industrialization, and the visible hand," *Journal of Development Studies*, 21(1): 22–44.

Evans, Peter (1978) *Dependent Development: The Alliance of Multinational, State, and Local Capital in Brazil*, Princeton, NJ: Princeton University Press.

Evans, Peter (1995) *Embedded Autonomy: States and Industrial Transformation*, Princeton, NJ: Princeton University Press.

Evans, Peter (1998) "Transferable lessons? Re-examining the institutional prerequisites of East Asian economic policies," *Journal of Development Studies* 34(6): 66–81.

Evans, Peter and John Stephens (1988) "Studying development since the Sixties: the emergence of a new comparative political economy," *Theory and Society*, 17: 713–45.

Fallows, James (1994) *Looking at the Sun: The Rise of the New East Asian Economic and Political System*, New York: Pantheon.

Fei, John and Gustav Ranis (1961) "A theory of economic development," *American Economic Review*, 51: 283–313.

Felix, David (1989) "Import substitution and late industrialization: Latin America and Asia compared," *World Development*, 17(9): 1455–70.

Fields, Karl J. (1995) *Enterprises and the State in Korea and Taiwan*, Ithaca, NY: Cornell University Press.

Frank, Andre G. (1967) *Capitalism and Underdevelopment in Latin America*, New York: Monthly Review Press.

Friedman, David (1988) *The Misunderstood Miracle*, Ithaca, NY: Cornell University Press.

Fruin, W. Mark (1992) *The Japanese Enterprise System: Competitive Strategies and Cooperative Structure*, Oxford: Clarendon Press.

Fukuyama, Francis (1995) *Trust: The Social Virtues and The Creation of Prosperity*, New York: Free Press.

Gardels, Nathan (1995) "The culture of prosperity," *New Perspectives Quarterly*, 12(1): 4–10.

Geertz, Clifford (1973) *The Interpretation of Cultures*, New York: Basic Books.

Gellner, Ernest (1994) *Conditions of Liberty: Civil Society and Its Rivals*, London: Hamish Hamilton.

Gereffi, Gary and Donald L. Wyman (1990) *Manufacturing Miracles: Paths of Industrialization in Latin America and East Asia*, Princeton, NJ: Princeton University Press.

Gerlach, Michael L. (1992) *Alliance Capitalism: The Social Organization of Japanese Business*, Berkeley, CA: University of California Press.

Gerschenkron, Alexander (1962) *Economic Backwardness in Historical Perspective*, Cambridge, MA: Harvard University Press.

Golay, Frank H. (1969) *Underdevelopment and Economic Nationalism in Southeast Asia*, Ithaca, NY: Cornell University Press.

Goldsmith, Maurice M. (1966) *Hobbes's Science of Politics*, New York: Columbia University Press.

Gubbings, John H. (1973) *The Making of Modern Japan*, Wilmington, DE: Scholarly Resources.

Gwartney, James and Robert Lawson, with Walter Mark, Smita Wagh, Chris Edwards, and Veronique de Rugy (2002) *Economic Freedom of The World 2000, Annual Report*, Vancouver, BC: The Fraser Institute.

Haboush, JaHyun Kim (1991) "The Confucianization of Korean society," in Gilbert Rozman (ed.) *The East Asian Region: Confucian Heritage and Its Modern Adaptation*, Princeton, NJ: Princeton University Press, pp. 84–110.

Haggard, Stephan (1990) *Pathways from the Periphery: The Politics of Growth in the Newly Industrializing Countries*, Ithaca, NY: Cornell University Press.

Haggard, Stephan (1997) "Democratic institutions, economic policy, and development," in Christopher Clague (ed.) *Institutions and Economic Development*, Washington, DC: Johns Hopkins University Press.

Haggard, Stephan and Chung-in Moon (1990) "Institutions and economic growth: theory and a Korean case study," *World Politics*, 42: 210–37.

Haggard, Stephan and Chien-kuo Pang (1994) "The transition to export-led growth," in David Dollar, Kenneth L. Sokoloff, and Joel D. Aberbach (eds) *The Role of the State in Taiwan's Development*, Armonk, NY: Sharpe.

Haley, George T., Chin Tiong Tan, and Usha C. V. Haley (1998) "The overseas Chinese today: not the family business, but the family as a business," in George T. Haley, Chin Tiong Tan, and Usha C. V. Haley (eds) *New Asian Emperors: The Overseas Chinese, Their Strategies and Competitive Advantages*, Boston, MA and Oxford: Butterworth-Heinemann.

Hamilton, Gary G. (1984) "Patriachalism in Imperial China and Western Europe: a revision of Weber's sociology of domination," *Theory and Society*, 13: 393–425.

Hamilton, Gary and Nicole W. Biggart (1988) "Market, culture and authority: a comparative analysis of management and organization in the Far East," *American Journal of Sociology* 94 (Supplement): S52–S94.

Hamilton, Gary G. and Cheng-shu Gao (1990) "The institutional foundations of Chinese business: the family firm in Taiwan," *Comparative Social Research*, 12: 135–51.

Han, Sung-Joo (1999) *Changing Values in Asia: Their Impact on Governance and Development*, Tokyo: Japan Center for International Exchange.

Harrison, Lawrence E. (1992) *Who Prospers: How Cultural Values Shape Economic and Political Success*, New York: Basic Books.

Heilperin, Michael (1960) *Studies in Economic Nationalism*, Geneva: Libraire E. Droz.

Henke, Holger and Ian Boxill (eds) (2000) *The End of the "Asian Model"?*, Amsterdam and Philadelphia, PA: John Benjamin's.

Heston, Alan, Robert Summers, and Daniel A. Nuxoll (2002) *Penn World Tables 6.1*, Philadelphia, PA: Center for International Comparisons, University of Pennsylvania.

Hicks, George L. and S. Gordon Redding (1982) *Industrial East Asia and the Post-Confucianism Hypothesis: A Challenge to Economics*, Hong Kong: University of Hong Kong.

Hill, Michael and Lian Kwen Fee (1995) *The Politics of Nation-Building and Citizenship in Singapore*, London: Routledge.

Hirschmeier, Johannes (1964) *The Origins of Entrepreneurship in Meiji Japan*, Cambridge, MA: Harvard University Press.

Ho, Samuel P. (1978) *Economic Development of Taiwan, 1860–1970*, New Haven, CT: Yale University Press.

Hobbes, Thomas (1651) *Leviathan*, New York: Prometheus Books, 1988.

Hofheinz, Roy and Kent Calder (1982) *The East Asia Edge*, New York: Basic Books.

Huang, Xiaoming (2000) *The Political Economic Transition in East Asia: Strong Market and Weakening State*, Washington, DC: Georgetown University Press; London: Curzon.

Huff, W. G. (1994) *Economic Growth of Singapore: Trade and Development in the Twentieth Century*, Cambridge: Cambridge University Press.

Hunter, W. Curt, George G. Kaufman, and Thomas H. Krueger (1999) *The Asian Financial Crisis: Origins, Implications, and Solutions*, Boston, MA: Kluwer Academic Publishers.

Hutchcroft, Paul (1991) "Oligarchs and cronies in the Philippine state: the politics of patrimonial plunder," *World Politics*, 43(2): 414–50.

Ichimura, Shinichi (1998) *Political Economy of Japanese and Asian Development*, Tokyo: Springer.

Imai, Ken'ichi (1986) "The corporate network in Japan," *Japanese Economic Studies*, 16: 3–37.

International Labor Organization (ILO) (1997) *Economically Active Population 1950–2010*, Geneva: ILO.

Ishinomori, Shotaro (1988) *Japan Inc.: An Introduction to Japanese Economics*, Berkeley, CA: University of California Press.

Islam, Iyanatul and Anis Chowdhury (1997) *Asian-Pacific Economies*, London: Routledge.

Itoh, Motoshige (2000) "Competition in the Japanese distribution market and market access from abroad," in Takatoshi Ito and Anne O. Krueger (eds) *Deregulation and Interdependence in the Asia-Pacific Region*, Chicago, IL: University of Chicago Press, pp. 139–56.

Jacoby, Neil (1966) *US Aid to Taiwan: A Study of Foreign Aid, Self-help and Development*, New York: Praeger.

Jepperson, Ronald L. (1991) "Institutions, institutional effects, and institutionalism," in Walter Powell and Paul Dimaggio (eds) *The New Institutionalism in Organizational Analysis*, Chicago, IL: University of Chicago Press, pp. 143–63.

Johnson, Chalmers (1982). *MITI and the Japanese Miracle*, Stanford, CA: Stanford University Press.

Johnson, Chalmers (1987) "Political institutions and economic performance: the government–business relationship in Japan, South Korea, and Taiwan," in Frederic C. Deyo (ed.) *The Political Economy of the New Asian Industrialism*, Ithaca, NY: Cornell University Press.

Johnson, Harry G. (1968) "A theoretical model of economic nationalism in new and developing states," in Harry Johnson (ed.) *Economic Nationalism in Old and New States*, London: Allen & Unwin.

Johnson, Paul M. (2000) *A Glossary of Political Economy Terms*. Online version, www.auburn.edu/~johnspm/gloss (accessed April 2, 2002).

Jones, David M. (1997) *Political Development in Pacific Asia*, London: Polity Press.

Jung, Woo S. and Peyton J. Marshall (1985) "Exports, growth and causality in developing countries," *Journal of Development Economics*, 18(1): 1–12.

Junnosuke, Masumi (1995) *Contemporary Politics in Japan*, Berkeley, CA: University of California Press.

Kahn, Herman (1979) *World Economic Development: 1979 and Beyond*, London: Croom Helm.

Kang, Myung Hun (1996) *The Korean Business Conglomerates: Chaebol Then and Now*, Berkeley, CA: Center for Korean Studies, Institute of East Asian Studies.

Keefer, Philip and Stephen Knack (1993) *Why Don't Poor Countries Catch Up? A Cross National Test of an Institutional Explanation*, College Park, MD: University of Maryland.

Keeing, Donald B. (1988) *Institutional Support for Export Marketing: The Experiences of Singapore, Hong Kong, Taiwan and Korea*, Washington, DC: Country Economics Department, World Bank.

Kim, Eun Mee (1987) *From Dominance to Symbiosis: State and the Chaebol in the Korean Economy*, PhD dissertation, Brown University, Providence, RI.

Kim, Samuel S. (2002) *East Asia and Globalization*, Lanham, MD: Rowman & Littlefield.

Kim, Won Bae (1998) "Family, social relations, and Asian capitalism," *Journal of International and Area Studies*, 5(1): 65–79.

Knight, Jack (1992) *Institutions and Social Conflict*, Cambridge: Cambridge University Press.

Kohli, Atul (1986) "Democracy and development," in John P. Lewis and Valeriana Kallab (eds) *Development Strategies Reconsidered*, Washington, DC: Overseas Development Council, pp. 152–82.

Kornai, Janos (1971) *Anti-Equilibrium*, Amsterdam: North-Holland.

Kornai, Janos (1980) *Economics of Shortage*, Amsterdam: North-Holland.

Kosai, Yutaka and Jacqueline Kaminski (1986) *The Era of High Speed Growth: Notes on The Postwar Japanese Economy*, Tokyo: University of Tokyo Press.

Krueger, Anne O. (1974) "The political economy of the rent-seeking society," *American Economic Review*, June: 291–303.

Krueger, Anne O. (1981) "Export-led industrial growth reconsidered," in Wontack Hong and Lawrence B. Krause (eds) *Trade and Growth of the Advanced Developing Countries in the Pacific Rim*, Seoul: Korea Development Institute, 3–34.

Krugman, Paul (1994) "The myth of Asia's miracle," *Foreign Affairs*, 73(6): 62–79.

Kuhn, Thomas S. (1970) *The Structure of Scientific Revolution*, Chicago, IL: Chicago University Press.

Kuo, Shirley W. Y. and John C. H. Fei (1985) "Causes and roles of export expansion in the Republic of China," in Walter Galenson (ed.) *Foreign Trade and Investment: Economic Development in the Newly Industrializing Countries*, Madison, WI: University of Wisconsin Press.

Lakatos, Imre (ed.) (1978) *The Methodology of Scientific Research Programs*, London: Cambridge University Press.

Lakatos, Imre and Alan Musgrave (eds) (1970) *Criticism and the Growth of Knowledge*, Cambridge: Cambridge University Press.

Lal, Deepak (1999) "Culture, democracy and development: the impact of formal and informal institutions on development," paper presented at the IMF Conference on Second Generation Reforms, IMF Headquarters, Washington, DC, November 8–9, 1999.

Lam, Danny and Cal Clark (1994) "Beyond the developmental state: the cultural roots of 'guerrilla capitalism' in Taiwan," *Governance*, 7(4): 412–30.

Lawrence, Robert Z. (1993) *The Global Environment for the East Asian Model*, Washington, DC: World Bank.

Lee, Chung H. and David H. Bohm (2002) *Financial Liberalization and the Economic Crisis in Asia*, London, Curzon Press.

Lee, Hyung-koo (1996) *The Korean Economy: Perspectives for the Twenty-First Century*, Albany, NY: State University of New York Press.

Lee, Kyung Tae (2002) *Globalization and the Asia Pacific Economy*, London: Routledge.

Lee, Lai-To (2000) "Singapore's globalization strategy," *East Asia: An International Quarterly*, 18(2): 36–42.

Le Heron, Richard and Sam Ock Park (1995) *The Asian-Pacific Rim and Globalization: Enterprises, Governance and Territoriality*, Avebury: Atheneum Press.

Lele, Jayant and Wisdom Tettey (1996) *Asia–Who Pays for Growth?: Women, Environment, and Popular Movements*, Aldershot/Brookfield: Dartmouth.

Leudde-Neurath, Richard (1988) "State intervention and export-oriented development: neo-classical theory and Taiwan practice," in Gordon White (ed.) *Developmental States in East Asia*, London: Macmillan, pp. 68–112.

Lewis, W. Arthur (1954) "Economic development with unlimited supplies of labour," *Manchester School Economic Papers*, 22: 139–91.

Li, Kuo-ting (1995) *The Evolution of Policy Behind Taiwan's Development Success*, New Haven, CT: Yale University Press.

Lim, Chong Yah and Chwee Huay Ow (1971) "The economic development of Singapore in the 1960s and beyond," in Poh Seng You and Chong Yah Lim (eds) *The Singapore Economy*, Singapore: Eastern Universities Press, pp. 1–42.

Lim, Linda Y. C. (1983) "Singapore's success: the myth of the free market economy," *Asian Survey*, 23(6): 752–65.

Lincoln, James R., Michael L. Gerlach, and Peggy Takahashi (1992) "Keiretsu networks in the Japanese economy: a dyad analysis of intercorporate ties," *American Sociological Review*, 57: 561–85.

Lingle, Christopher (1996) *Singapore's Authoritarian Capitalism*, Fairfax: Locke Institute.

Lingle, Christopher (1998) *The Rise and Decline of the Asian Century: False Starts on the Path to the Global Millennium*, Hong Kong: Asia 2000.

Lipset, Seymour Martin (1959) "Some social requisites of democracy: economic development and political legitimacy," *American Political Science Review*, 53: 69–105.

List, Friedrich (1841) *The National System of Political Economy*, London: Frank Cass, 1983.

Liu, Wu-chi (1955) *Confucius: His Life and Time*, New York: Philosophical Library.

Low, Linda, Thoh Mun Heng, Soon Teck Wong, Tan Kong Yam, and Helen Hughes (1993) *Challenges and Response: Thirty Years of the Economic Development Board*, Singapore: Times Academic Press.

Lukauskas, Arvid John and Francisco L. Rivera-Batiz (2001) *The Political Economy of the East Asian Crisis and Its Aftermath: Tigers in Distress*, Cheltenham: Edward Elgar.

McCargo, Duncan (2000) *Contemporary Japan*, London: Macmillan.

McCloud, Donald G. (1995) *Southeast Asia: Tradition and Modernity in the Contemporary World*, Boulder, CO: Westview.

McCraw, Thomas K. (1992) "The trouble with Adam Smith," *The American Scholar*, 61(3): 353–74.

Machiavelli, Niccolo (1950) *The Prince and the Discourses*, New York: The Modern Library.

MacIntyre, Andrew (ed.) (1994) *Business and Government in Industrializing Asia*, Sydney: Allen & Unwin.

Marsh, Robert (1979) "Does democracy hinder economic development in the late-comer developing nations?," *Comparative Social Research*, 2: 215–49.

Mathews, Trevor and John Ravenhill (1994) "Strategic trade policy: the Northeast Asian experience," in Andrew Macintyre (ed.) *Business and Government in Industrializing Asia*, St Leonard's: Allen & Unwin, pp. 29–90.

Mauro, Paolo (1995) "Corruption and growth," *Quarterly Journal of Economics*, 110: 681–712.

Mettzger, Thomas A. (1977) *Escape from Predicament: Neo-Confucianism and China's Evolving Political Culture*, New York: Columbia University Press.

Milne, R. S. and Diane K. Mauzy (1990) *Singapore: The Legacy of Lee Kuan Yew*, Boulder, CO: Westview.

Minami, Ryoshin (1986) *The Economic Development of Japan: A Quantitative Study*, New York: St Martin's Press.

Moon, Chung-in and Rashemi Prasad (1994) "Beyond the developmental state: networks, politics and institutions," *Governance*, 7(4): 360–86.

Morishima, Michio (1982) *Why Has Japan Succeeded?: Western Technology and the Japanese Ethos*, Cambridge: Cambridge University Press.

Morishima, Michio (1987) "Confucius and capitalism," *UNESCO Courier*, December: 34–7.

Mutsuko, Murakami and Tom McCawley (1999) "An image problem: government jobs remain unpopular," *Asiaweek*, March 5.

Myrdal, Gunnar (1957) *Economic Nationalism and Internationalism*, Melbourne: Australian Institute of International Affairs.

Nakamura, Takafusa (1981, 1995) *The Postwar Japanese Economy: Its Development and Structure*, Tokyo: University of Tokyo Press.

Naughton, Barry (1996) *Growing Out of the Plan*, London: Cambridge University Press.

Nehru, Vikram and Ashok Dhareshwar (1993) "A new database on physical capital stock: sources, methodology and results," *Revista de Analisis Economico*, 8(1): 37–59.

Noble, Gregory W. and John Ravenhill (2000) *The Asian Financial Crisis and the Architecture of Global Finance*, Cambridge, Cambridge University Press.

Noguchi, Yukio (1994) "The 'bubble' and economic policies in the 1980s," *Journal of Japanese Studies*, 20(2): 291–329.

Noland, Marcus and Howard Pack (2003) *Industrial Policy in an Era of Globalization: Lessons from Asia*, Washington, DC: Institute for International Economics.

North, Douglas C. (1990) *Institutions, Institutional Change, and Economic Perform-ance*, Cambridge: Cambridge University Press.

Oh, John Kie-chiang (1999) *Korean Politics*, Ithaca, NY: Cornell University Press.

Okimoto, Daniel I. (1989) *Between MITI and the Market: Japanese Industrial Policy for the High Technology*, Stanford, CA: Stanford University Press.

Okimoto, Daniel I. and Thomas P. Rohlen (1988) *Inside the Japanese System: Readings on Contemporary Society and Political Economy*, Stanford, CA: Stanford University Press.

Okochi, Akio and Shigeaki Yasuoka (eds) (1984) *Family Business in the Era of Industrial Growth: Its Ownership and Management*, Tokyo: University of Tokyo Press.

Olson, Mancur (1965) *The Logic of Collective Action: Public Goods and the Theory of Groups*, Cambridge, MA: Harvard University Press.

Olson, Mancur (1993) "Dictatorship, democracy and development," *American Political Science Review*, 87(3): 567–77

Palma, Gabriel (1978) "Dependency: a formal theory of underdevelopment or a methodology for the analysis of concrete situations of underdevelopment?," *World Development*, 6: 881–924.

Park, Yung Chul (2001) *The East Asian Dilemma: Restructuring Out or Growing Out?* Princeton, NJ: International Economics Section, Department of Economics, Princeton University.

Peebles, Gavin and Peter Wilson (1996) *The Singapore Economy*, Cheltenham: Edward Elgar.

Pempel, T. J. (1998) *Regime Shift: Comparative Dynamics of the Japanese Political Economy*, Ithaca, NY: Cornell University Press.

Pempel, T. J. and Keiichi Teunekawa (1979) "Corporatism without labor," in Philippe C. Schmitter and Gerald Lembruch (eds) *Trends Towards Corporatist Intermediation*, London: Sage.

Peterson, Peter G. (1984) *Economic Nationalism and International Interdependence: The Global Costs of National Choices*, Washington, DC: Per Jacobson Foundation.

Putnam, Robert D. (1993) *Making Democracy Work: Civic Traditions in Modern Italy*, Princeton, NJ: Princeton University Press.

Pye, Lucian W. (1985) *Asian Power and Politics: The Cultural Dimensions of Authority*, Cambridge, MA: Harvard University Press.

Pye, Lucian W. (1999) "Civility, social capital, and civil society: three powerful concepts for explaining Asia," *The Journal of Interdisciplinary History*, 29(4): 763–5.

Quah, Jon S. T. (1990) "National values and nation-building: defining the problem," in Jon S. T. Quah (ed.) *In Search of Singapore's National Values*, Singapore: Time Academic Press.

Ramseyer, J. Mark and Frances M. Rosenbluth (1993) *Japan's Political Marketplace*, Cambridge, MA: Harvard University Press.

Redding, S. Gordon (1988) "The role of the entrepreneur in the new Asian capitalism," in Peter L. Berger and Hsin-Hung Michael Hsiao (eds) *In Search of an East Asian Development Model*, New Brunswick, NJ: Transaction Books, pp. 99–111.

Redding, S. Gordon (1993) *The Spirit of Chinese Capitalism*, Berlin: Walter de Gruyter.

Richter, Frank-Jurgen (2000) *The East Asian Development Model: Economic Growth, Institutional Failure and the Aftermath of the Crisis*, London: Palgrave.

Riedel, James (1984) "Trade as the engine of growth in developing countries revisited," *Economic Journal*, 94(1): 56–73.

Rosenau, James N. (1971) *The Scientific Study of Foreign Policy*, New York: Free Press.

Rowen, Henry S. (ed.) (1998) *Behind East Asian Growth: The Political and Social Foundations of Prosperity*, London: Routledge.

Roy, Denny (1994) "Singapore, China and the 'soft-authoritarian' challenge," *Asian Survey*, 34(3): 231–42.

Rozman, Gilbert (ed.) (1991) *The East Asian Region: Confucian Heritage and Its Modern Adaptation*, Princeton, NJ: Princeton University Press.

Ruttan, Vernon W. (1998) "The new growth theory and development economics: a survey," *Journal of Development Studies* 35(2): 1–3.

Saptari, Ratna (1999) *CLARA Workshop Report: Subcontract Labor in Asia*, Bangkok: CLARA.

Sarel, Michael (1997) *Growth in East Asia: What We Can and Cannot Infer*, Economic Issues, Washington, DC: IMF.

Schive, Chi (1990) "The next stage of industrialization in Taiwan and South Korea," in Gary Gereffi and Donald L. Wyman (eds) *Manufacturing Miracles: Paths of Industrialization in Latin America and East Asia*, Princeton, NJ: Princeton University Press, pp. 267–91.

Schumpeter, Joseph (1943) *Capitalism, Socialism and Democracy*, New York: Harper, 1975.

Scott, David L. (1997) *Wall Street Words: An Essential A to Z Guide for Today's Investor*, Boston, MA: Houghton Mifflin.

Sharma, Shalendra (2003) *The Asian Financial Crisis: New International Financial Architecture: Crisis, Reform and Recovery*, New York: Manchester University Press.

Shinoda, Toru (1997) "Rengo and policy participation: Japanese-style neo-corporatism?," in Mari Sako and Hiroki Sato (eds) *Japanese Labor and Management in Transition: Diversity, Flexibility and Participation*, London: Routledge, pp. 187–214.

Shiraishi, Takashi (1998) "The currency crisis and the end of Asia's old politico-economic setup," *Japan Echo*, 25(4): 31–5.

Simone, Vera and Anne Thompson Feraru (1995) *The Asian Pacific Political and Economic Development in a Global Context*, New York: Longman.

Smith, Heather (1998) "Korea," in Ross H. McLeod and Ross Garnaut (eds) *East Asia in Crisis: From Being A Miracle to Needing One?* London: Routledge.

Smith, Robert J. (1992) "The cultural context of the Japanese political economy," in Shumpei Kumon and Henry Rosovsky (eds) *The Political Economy of Japan, Vol 3: Cultural and Social Dynamics*, Stanford, CA: Stanford University Press, pp. 13–31.

Smith, Thomas C. (1959) *The Agrarian Origins of Modern Japan*, Stanford, CA: Stanford University Press.

Smith, Warren W. Jr (1959) *Confucianism in Modern Japan*, Tokyo: The Hokuseido Press.

SMTI (Singapore Ministry of Trade and Industry) (2001) *Economic Development: Economic Milestones*, Singapore: Singapore Government.

Song, Byung-nak (1990) *The Rise of the Korean Economy*, Hong Kong: Oxford University Press.

Steers, Richard, Keun-shin Yoo, and Geraldo Ungson (1989) *The Chaebol: Korea's New Industrial Might*, New York: Harper & Row.

Stiglitz, Joseph E. and Shahid Yusuf (2001) *Rethinking the East Asian Miracle*, Washington, DC: World Bank.

Suh, Sang-Mok (1992) "The economy in historical perspective," in Vittorio Corbo and Sang-Mok Suh (eds), *Structural Adjustment in a Newly Industrialized Country*, Baltimore, MD: Johns Hopkins University Press.

Sun, Chung-hsing (1986) "From the Protestant ethnic to the Confucian ethnic," *The Chinese Intellectual*, 2(2): 46–57.

Tai, Hung-chao (1989) *Confucianism and Economic Development: An Oriental Alternative*, Washington, DC: Washington Institute Press.

Tanzi, Vito (1998) "Corruption around the world: causes, consequences, scope and curses," *International Monetary Fund Staff Papers*, 45(4): 559–77.

Tanzi, Vito and Hamid Davoodi (1997) *Corruption, Public Investment and Growth*, IMF Working Papers, Washington, DC: IMF.

Teranishi, Juro (1994) "Japan: development and structural change of the financial system," in Hugh T. Patrick and Yung Chul Park (eds) *The Financial Development of Japan, Korea, and Taiwan*, New York: Oxford University Press, pp. 27–80.

Terry, Edith (1996) "An East Asian paradigm?," *Atlantic Economic Journal*, 23(3): 183–99.

Tsuru, Shigeto (1993) *Japan's Capitalism: Creative Defeat and Beyond*, New York: Cambridge University Press.

Tu, Wei-ming (1991a) "Cultural China: the periphery as the center," *Daedalus*, 120(2): 1–32.

Tu, Wei-ming (1991b) *The Triadic Chord: Confucian Ethnics, Industrial East Asia and Max Weber*, Singapore: Institute of East Asian Philosophies.

Tu, Wei-ming (ed.) (1994) *The Living Tree: The Changing Meaning of Being Chinese Today*, Stanford, CA: Stanford University Press.

Tu, Wei-ming (1996) *Confucian Traditions in East Asian Modernity*, Cambridge, MA: Harvard University Press.

Unger, Jonathan and Anita Chan (1995) "China, corporatism, and the East Asian model," *The Australian Journal of Chinese Affairs*, 33(1): 29–54.

Ungson, Gerardo R., Richard M. Steers, and Seung-Ho Park (1997) *Korean Enterprise: The Quest for Globalization*, Cambridge, MA: Harvard Business School Press.

Viroli, Maurizio (1998) *Machiavelli*, Oxford: Oxford University Press.

Vogel, Ezra F. (1979) *Japan as Number One: Lessons for America*, Cambridge, MA: Harvard University Press.

Vogel, Ezra F. (1991) *The Four Little Dragons: The Spread of Industrialization in East Asia*, Cambridge, MA: Harvard University Press.

Wade, Robert (1990) *Governing the Market: Economic Theory and the Role of Government in East Asian Industrialization*, Princeton, NJ: Princeton University Press.

Wade, Robert (1992) "East Asia's economic success: conflicting perspectives, partial insights and shaky evidence," *World Politics*, 44(1): 270–320.

Weber, Max (1930) *The Protestant Ethic and the Spirit of Capitalism*, London: Allen & Unwin.

Weber, Max (1951) *The Religion of China: Confucianism and Taoism*, Glencoe: Free Press.

Weiss, Linda and John M. Hobson (1995) *States and Economic Development: A Comparative Historical Analysis*, Cambridge, MA: Polity Press.

Weiss, Roger W. (1967) "Economic nationalism in Britain in the nineteenth-century," in Harry G. Johnson (ed.) *Economic Nationalism in Old and New States*, Chicago, IL: University of Chicago Press, pp. 31–47.

White, Gordon (ed.) (1988) *Developmental States in East Asia*, London: Macmillan.

White, Gordon, Roger Goodman, and Huckj-ju Kwon (1998) "The politics of welfare in East Asia," in Richard Maidment, David Goldblatt, and Jeremy Mitchell (eds) *Governance in the Asia-Pacific*, London: Routledge, pp. 195–220.

Whitley, Richard D. (1991) "The social construction of business systems in East Asia," *Organizational Studies*, 12(1): 1–28.

Wiarda, Howard J. (1997) *Corporatism and Comparative Politics: The Other Great "ism,"* Armonk, NY: Sharpe.

Williamson, Oliver E. (1985) *The Economic Institutions of Capitalism: Firms, Markets, Relational Contracting*, New York: Free Press.

Winckler, Edwin A. (1984) "Institutionalization and participation on Taiwan: from hard to soft authoritarianism," *The China Quarterly*, 99(3): 481–99.

Woo, Wing Thye, Jeffrey D. Sachs, and Klaus Schwab (2000) *The Asian Financial Crisis: Lessons for a Resilient Asia*, Cambridge, MA: MIT Press.

Woo-Cumings, Meredith (1999) *The Developmental State*, Ithaca, NY: Cornell University Press.

Wood, Christopher (1994) *The End of Japan Inc.: And How the New Japan Will Look*, New York: Simon & Schuster.

World Bank (1993) *The East Asian Miracle: Economic Growth and Public Policy*, Oxford: Oxford University Press.

World Bank (1994) *East Asia's Trade and Investment: Regional and Global Gains From Liberalization*, Washington, DC: World Bank.

World Bank (2000) *East Asia: Recovery and Beyond*, Washington, DC: World Bank.

World Bank (2001) *Social Capital for Development*, Washington, DC: World Bank.

World Bank (2002) *Adjusted Net Saving*, Washington, DC: World Bank.

Woronoff, Jon (1982) *Inside Japan, Inc.*, Tokyo: Lotus Press.

Woronoff, Jon (1991) *Japan As – Anything But – Number One*, Armonk, NY: Sharpe.

Yakabe, Katsumi (1974) *Labor Relations in Japan: Fundamental Characteristics*, Tokyo: International Society for Education Information.

Yamauchi, Hirotaka (2000) "Toward a more liberal sky in Japan: an evolution of policy change," in Takatoshi Ito and Anne O. Krueger (eds) *Deregulation and Interdependence in the Asia-Pacific Region*, Chicago, IL: University of Chicago Press, pp. 195–226.

Yoda, Yoshiie (1996) *The Foundations of Japan's Modernization: A Comparison with China's Path Towards Modernization*, Leiden: Brill.

Yoffie, David B. (1981) "The newly industrializing countries and the political economy of protectionism," *International Studies Quarterly*, 24(4): 569–99.

Youngson, Alexander J. (1982) *Hong Kong: Economic Growth and Policy*, Oxford: Oxford University Press.

Yu, Ying-shih (1985) "Confucian thought and economic development: early modern Chinese religious ethics and the spirit of the merchant class," *The Chinese Intellectual*, 2: 3–55.

Zweig, David (1999) "Undemocratic capitalism: China and the limits of economism," *The National Interest*, 56: 63–72.

# Index

Country-specific entries are listed under the country.

# eBooks

eBooks – at www.eBookstore.tandf.co.uk

## A library at your fingertips!

eBooks are electronic versions of printed books. You can store them on your PC/laptop or browse them online.

They have advantages for anyone needing rapid access to a wide variety of published, copyright information.

eBooks can help your research by enabling you to bookmark chapters, annotate text and use instant searches to find specific words or phrases. Several eBook files would fit on even a small laptop or PDA.

**NEW:** Save money by eSubscribing: cheap, online access to any eBook for as long as you need it.

## Annual subscription packages

We now offer special low-cost bulk subscriptions to packages of eBooks in certain subject areas. These are available to libraries or to individuals.

For more information please contact webmaster.ebooks@tandf.co.uk

We're continually developing the eBook concept, so keep up to date by visiting the website.

## www.eBookstore.tandf.co.uk